Intermediate Statistics
Using SPSS®

Dedicated to my best math teachers:

Mr. Lamm, Mrs. Milner, Mrs. Whitaker,
Mr. Reed, Mrs. Jarvis, Mr. McHugh, Mr. Prince,
Mr. Davis, Dr. Davison, Ms. Siderow, Dr. Baum, Dr. Shaw,
Dr. Torcivia, Dr. Wilsoncroft, Dr. Seltzer, Dr. Webb, Dr. Lindsey, and Dr. Franke.

Intermediate Statistics
Using SPSS®

Herschel Knapp

University of Southern California

Los Angeles | London | New Delhi
Singapore | Washington DC | Melbourne

FOR INFORMATION:

SAGE Publications, Inc.
2455 Teller Road
Thousand Oaks, California 91320
E-mail: order@sagepub.com

SAGE Publications Ltd.
1 Oliver's Yard
55 City Road
London EC1Y 1SP
United Kingdom

SAGE Publications India Pvt. Ltd.
B 1/I 1 Mohan Cooperative Industrial Area
Mathura Road, New Delhi 110 044
India

SAGE Publications Asia-Pacific Pte. Ltd.
3 Church Street
#10-04 Samsung Hub
Singapore 049483

Printed in the United States of America

ISBN 978-1-5063-7743-8

Acquisitions Editor: Helen Salmon
Editorial Assistant: Chelsea Neve
e-Learning Editor: Katie Ancheta
Production Editor: Kelly DeRosa
Copy Editor: Gretchen Treadwell
Typesetter: C&M Digitals (P) Ltd.
Proofreader: Wendy Jo Dymond
Indexer: Will Ragsdale
Cover Designer: Anupama Krishnan
Marketing Manager: Shari Countryman

This book is printed on acid-free paper.

18 19 20 21 10 9 8 7 6 5 4 3 2

Brief Contents

Detailed Contents

PART III: MEASURING DIFFERENCES BETWEEN GROUPS

4. *t* Test and Mann-Whitney *U* Test

7. MANOVA   166

11. Correlation and Regression: Pearson and Spearman 276

Preface

Somewhere, something incredible is waiting to be known.

—Dr. Carl Sagan

DOWNLOADABLE DIGITAL LEARNING RESOURCES

Download (and unzip) the digital learning resources for this book from the website **study.sagepub.com/intermediatestats**. This website contains tutorial videos, prepared data sets, and the solutions to all of the odd-numbered exercises. These resources will be discussed in further detail toward the end of the Preface.

OVERVIEW OF BOOK

This book covers the statistical functions most frequently used in evidence-based research publications; this should not be considered a complete compendium of useful statistics, however, because in other technological fields that you are likely already familiar with (e.g., word processing, spreadsheet, presentation software, etc.), you have probably discovered that the "90/10 rule" applies: You can get 90% of your work done using only 10% of the functions. For example, if you were to thoroughly explore each submenu of your word processor, you would likely discover more than 100 functions and options; however, in terms of actual productivity, 90% of the time, you are probably using only about 10% of them to get your work done (e.g., load, save, copy, delete, paste, font, tab, center, print, spell check). Back to statistics: If you can master the statistical processes contained in this text, it is expected that this will arm you with what you need to effectively analyze the majority of your own data and confidently interpret the statistical publications of others.

This book is not about abstract statistical theory or the derivation or memorization of statistical formulas; rather, it is about *applied* statistics. This book is designed to provide you with practical answers to the following questions: (1) *What statistical test should I use for this kind of data?* (2) *How do I set up the data?* (3) *What parameters should I specify when ordering the test?* and (4) *How do I interpret the results?*

In terms of performing the actual statistical calculations, we will be using IBM® SPSS® Statistics*, an efficient statistical processing software package. This facilitates speed and accuracy when it comes to producing quality statistical results in the form of tables and graphs, but SPSS is not an automatic program. In the same way that your word processor does not write your papers for you, SPSS does not know what you want done with your data until you tell it. Fortunately, those instructions are issued through clear menus. Your job will be to learn what statistical procedure suits which circumstance, to configure the data properly, to order the appropriate tests, and to mindfully interpret the output reports.

The abstracts, providing a summary of the study and statistical findings, are composed using the American Psychological Association (APA) writing guidelines. Detailed APA composition protocols are available in the latest versions of the *Publication Manual of the American Psychological Association* (American Psychological Association) and *An EasyGuide to APA Style* by Schwartz, Landrum, and Gurung (SAGE Publishing).

The 14 chapters are grouped into six parts.

BRIEF TABLE OF CONTENTS

Part I: Statistical Fundamentals

This set of chapters provides the basis for working in statistics.

Chapter 1: Research Principles focuses on foundational statistical concepts, delineating what statistics are, what they do, and what they do not do.

Chapter 2: Working in SPSS orients you to the SPSS (also known as PASW—Predictive Analytics Software) environment so that you can competently load existing data sets or configure it to contain a new data set.

Part II: Summarizing Variables

This chapter explains how to explore variables on an individual basis.

Chapter 3: Descriptive Statistics provides guidance on comprehending the values contained in continuous and categorical variables.

Part III: Measuring Differences Between Groups

These chapters provide tests for detecting differences between groups that involve continuous variables.

Chapter 4: *t* Test and Mann-Whitney *U* Test shows how the *t* test is used in two-group designs (e.g., control vs. treatment) to detect if one group significantly

*SPSS is a registered trademark of International Business Machines Corporation.

outperformed the other. In the event that the data are not fully suitable to run a *t* test, the Mann-Whitney *U* test provides an alternative.

Chapter 5: ANOVA and Kruskal-Wallis Test illustrates how the ANOVA is similar to the *t* test, but it is capable of processing *more than two groups*. In the event that the data are not fully suitable to run an ANOVA, the Kruskal-Wallis test provides an alternative.

Chapter 6: ANCOVA is similar to ANOVA, but it is capable of including a *covariate*, which adjusts the results to account for the influence of a potentially identified confounding variable.

Chapter 7: MANOVA is similar to ANOVA, but it is capable of processing *more than one* outcome (dependent) variable.

Part IV: Measuring Differences Over Time

These chapters provide statistics for detecting change(s) in a continuous variable over time using a single group.

Chapter 8: Paired *t* Test and Wilcoxon Test illustrates how the paired *t* test is generally used to gather data on a variable before and after an intervention to determine if the performance on the posttest is significantly better than the pretest. In the event that the data are not fully suitable to run a paired *t* test, the Wilcoxon test provides an alternative.

Chapter 9: ANOVA Repeated Measures is similar to the paired *t* test, but it is capable of assessing a variable over *more than two time points*.

Part V: Measuring Relationship Between Variables

These chapters compute statistics that describe the nature of the relationship(s) between the variables.

Chapter 10: Chi-Square assesses the relationship between categorical variables.

Chapter 11: Correlation and Regression: Pearson and Spearman demonstrates how to use the Pearson statistic to assess the relationship between two continuous variables. Similarly, the Spearman statistic is generally used to assess the relationship between two ordered lists.

Chapter 12: Multiple Regression indicates the relative weight that each variable has in terms of predicting the value of a continuous outcome variable.

Chapter 13: Logistic Regression predicts the odds of a dichotomous outcome occurring (or not) based on data from continuous and/or categorical predictors.

Part VI: Data Handling

This chapter demonstrates supplemental techniques in SPSS to enhance your capabilities, versatility, and data processing efficiency.

Chapter 14: Supplemental SPSS Operations explains how to generate random numbers, sort and select cases, recode variables, import non-SPSS data, and practice appropriate data storage protocols.

After you have completed Chapters 3 through 13, the following table will help you navigate this book to efficiently select the statistical test(s) best suited to your (data) situation. For now, it is advised that you skip this table, as it contains statistical terminology that will be covered thoroughly in the chapters that follow.

Overview of Statistical Functions

Chapter	Statistic	When to Use	Results
3	Descriptive statistics	Any continuous or categorical variable	Generates a summary of a variable using figures and graphs
4	t Test and Mann-Whitney U test	Two groups with continuous variables	Indicates if there is a statistically significant difference between the two groups $(G_1 : G_2)$
5	ANOVA and Kruskal-Wallis test	Similar to the t test except it is used when there are more than two groups	Similar to the t test except it compares all pairs of groups $(G_1 : G_2, G_1 : G_3, G_2 : G_3)$
6	ANCOVA	Similar to ANOVA but adjusts results per known confounding continuous variable	Similar to ANOVA except results are adjusted per the identified confounding variable
7	MANOVA	Similar to ANOVA but processes two or more dependent (outcome) variables	Similar to ANOVA except instead of results revealing between-group differences for one (outcome) variable, the results reflect differences between groups for two or more outcome variables
8	Paired t test and Wilcoxon test	Compares pretest to posttest (continuous variables within one group)	Indicates if there is a statistically significant difference between the pretest and posttest $(T_1 : T_2)$
9	ANOVA repeated measures	Similar to the paired t test except it is used when there are more than two time points	Similar to the paired t test except it compares scores from all pairs of time points $(T_1 : T_2, T_2 : T_3, T_1 : T_3)$

(Continued)

(Continued)

Chapter	Statistic	When to Use	Results
10	Chi-square	Two categorical variables	Indicates if there is a statistically significant association between two categorical variables
11	Correlation and regression	Two continuous variables for each subject/record or two ranked lists	Indicates the strength and direction of the relationship between two variables
12	Multiple regression	More than one predictor variable and one continuous outcome variable	Indicates the weight that each predictor variable has in influencing a continuous outcome
13	Logistic regression	More than one predictor variable and one dichotomous outcome variable	Indicates how each predictor variable is associated with the dichotomous outcome

Considering that the names of some of these statistics are fairly abstract (e.g., chi-square, logistic regression, Mann-Whitney U test), Chapters 3 through 13 begin with the When to Use This Statistic dialogue box. This provides succinct guidance in selecting the statistic most suitable to address your analytic needs based on your research question, design, and variables. The Results sections provide concisely worded explanations to facilitate concrete recall of each statistic and are not intended as comprehensive documentation suitable for publication.

LAYERED LEARNING

This book has six parts. Parts III and IV use *layered learning* to explain similar concepts in a cumulative fashion. For example, **Part III: Measuring Differences Between Groups** contains four conceptually connected chapters: **Chapter 4: *t* Test and Mann-Whitney *U* Test** shows how to determine if one group outperformed the other (e.g., Control : Treatment). **Chapter 5: ANOVA and Kruskal-Wallis Test** builds on the concept of the *t* Test, but instead of comparing just two groups to each other (e.g., Control : Treatment), ANOVA can compare three or more groups to each other (e.g., Control : Treatment₁ : Treatment₂). Essentially, ANOVA is just one step up from what you will already understand from having mastered the *t* test, so the learning curve is not as steep. **Chapter 6: ANCOVA** is essentially the same as an ANOVA test, but it adjusts the results based on the values of an identified confounding variable. **Chapter 7: MANOVA** is the last chapter in Part III, which is just one more variation in this set. The point is you will not be starting from square one in each of these chapters—as you enter Chapters 5, 6, and 7, you will see that you are already more than halfway there to understanding the new statistic, based on your comprehension of the prior chapter(s). This form of layered learning is akin to simply adding one more layer to an *already existing* cake (hence, the layer cake icon).

Similarly, **Part IV: Measuring Differences Over Time** contains two chapters: **Chapter 8: Paired *t* Test and Wilcoxon Test** are used to compare the scores from two time points (e.g., pretest : posttest); **Chapter 9 ANOVA Repeated Measures** builds on this concept, but instead of assessing scores from (only) two time points, ANOVA repeated measures can compare scores spanning more than two time points (e.g., score at Day 1, score at Day 30, score at Day 60, etc.).

DIGITAL LEARNING RESOURCES

The exercises in **Chapter 2: Working in SPSS** include the data definitions (codebooks) and corresponding concise data sets printed in the text for manual entry; this will enable you to learn how to set up SPSS from the ground up. This is an essential skill for conducting original research.

Chapters 3 through 13 teach each statistical process using an appropriate example and corresponding data set. The practice exercises at the end of these chapters provide you with the opportunity to master each statistical process by analyzing actual data sets. For convenience and accuracy, these prepared SPSS data sets are available for download.

The website for this book is **study.sagepub.com/intermediatestats**, which contains the following resources.

VIDEOS

The (.mp4) videos provide an overview of each statistical process, directions for processing the pretest checklist criteria, ordering the statistical test, and interpreting the results.

DATA SETS

The downloadable file also contains prepared data sets for each example and exercise to facilitate prompt and accurate processing. Additionally, it contains the documented solutions to odd-numbered exercises to check the quality of your learning.

The examples and exercises in this text were processed using Version 18 of the software and should be compatible with most other versions.

RESOURCES FOR INSTRUCTORS

Password-protected instructor resources are available on the website for this book at **study.sagepub.com/intermediatestats** and include the following:

- All student resources (listed previously)
- Editable PowerPoint presentations for each chapter
- Solutions to all Practice Exercises

MARGIN ICONS

The following icons provide navigation in each chapter (in this order):

 When to Use This Statistic—Selection criteria for using this statistic and the results it produces

 Video*—Tutorial video demonstrating the **Pretest Checklist** and **Test Run**

 Layered Learning—Identifies chapters that are conceptually connected

 Overview—Summary of what statistics does and when it should be used

 Data Set*—Specifies which prepared example/exercise data set to load

 Pretest Checklist—Instructions to check that the data meet the criteria necessary to run a statistical test

 Test Run—Procedures and parameters for running a statistical test

 Results—Interpretation of the output from the **Test Run**

 Hypothesis Resolution—Accept/reject hypotheses based on the **Results**

 Abstract—Summary of implementation and findings based on the **Hypothesis Resolution**

The following four icons are used on an as-needed basis:

 Reference Point—This point is referenced elsewhere in the text (think of this as a bookmark)

 Key Point—Important fact

 Technical Tip—Helpful data processing technique

 Formula—Useful formula that SPSS does not perform but can be easily processed on any calculator

*Go to **study.sagepub.com/intermediatestats** and download the tutorial videos, prepared data sets, and solutions to all of the odd-numbered exercises.

Acknowledgments

SAGE and the author acknowledge and thank the following reviewers whose feedback contributed to the development of this text:

Todd Franke, University of California, Los Angeles

Mary Martinasek, University of Tampa

Robyn Cooper, Drake University

Zhigang Wang, Carleton University

John Hazy, Youngstown State University

Joshua C. Watson, Texas A&M University-Corpus Christi

Kay Davis, Pepperdine University

Benjamin C. Ngwudike, Jackson State University

Maxwell Hsu, University of Wisconsin-Whitewater

David Okech, University of Georgia

Myung H. Jin, Virginia Commonwealth University

Yukiko Maeda, Purdue University

Elaine Trudelle-Jackson, Texas Woman's University

We extend special thanks to Ann D. Bagchi for her skillful technical proofreading to better ensure the precision of this text.

We also gratefully acknowledge the contribution of Dean Cameron, whose cartoons enliven this book.

About the Author

Herschel Knapp, PhD, MSSW, has more than 25 years of experience as a health care professional in a variety of domains. In addition to his clinical work as a psychotherapist, primarily in hospital settings, he has provided project management for innovative implementations designed to improve the quality of patient care via multisite, health science implementations. He teaches master's-level courses at the University of Southern California; he has also taught at the University of California, Los Angeles and California State University, Los Angeles. Dr. Knapp has served as the lead statistician on a longitudinal cancer research project and managed the program evaluation metrics for a multisite, nonprofit children's center. His clinical work includes emergency/trauma therapy in hospital settings. Dr. Knapp has developed and implemented innovative telehealth systems, using videoconferencing technology to facilitate optimal health care service delivery to remote patients and to coordinate specialty consultations among health care providers, including interventions to diagnose and treat people with HIV and hepatitis, with special outreach to the homeless. He is currently leading a nurse research mentorship program and providing research and analytic services to promote excellence within a health care system. The author of numerous articles in peer-reviewed health science journals, he is also the author of other textbooks, including *Introductory Statistics Using SPSS* (2nd ed., 2017), *Practical Statistics for Nursing Using SPSS* (2017), *Therapeutic Communication: Developing Professional Skills* (2nd ed., 2014), and *Introduction to Social Work Practice: A Practical Workbook* (2010).

PART I

Statistical Fundamentals

This set of chapters provides the basis for working in statistics.

Chapter 1: Research Principles focuses on foundational statistical concepts, delineating what statistics are, what they do, and what they do not do.

Chapter 2: Working in SPSS orients you to the SPSS (also known as PASW—Predictive Analytics Software) environment so that you can competently load existing data sets or configure it to contain a new data set.

C H A P T E R 1

Research Principles

These fundamentals will get things started.

- Rationale for Statistics
- Research Questions
- Treatment and Control Groups
- Rationale for Random Assignment
- Hypothesis Formulation
- Reading Statistical Outcomes
- Accept/Reject Hypothesis
- Levels of Measure
- Types of Variables

*The scientific mind does not so much
provide the right answers as ask the right questions.*

—Claude Levi-Strauss

Learning Objectives

Upon completing this chapter, you will be able to do the following:

- Discuss the rationale for using statistics.
- Identify various forms of research questions.
- Differentiate between *control* and *treatment* groups.
- Comprehend the rationale for random assignment.
- Understand the basis for hypothesis formulation.
- Understand the fundamentals of reading statistical outcomes.
- Appropriately accept/reject hypotheses based on statistical outcomes.
- Understand the four levels of measure.
- Determine the variable type: *categorical* or *continuous*.

OVERVIEW—RESEARCH PRINCIPLES

This chapter introduces statistical concepts that will be used throughout this book. Applying statistics involves more than just processing tables of numbers; it involves being curious and assembling mindful questions in an attempt to better understand what is going on in a setting. As you will see, statistics extends far beyond simple averages and headcounts. Just as a toolbox contains a variety of tools to accomplish a variety of diverse tasks (e.g., screwdriver to place or remove screws, saw to cut materials, etc.), there are a variety of statistical tests, each suited to address a different type of research question.

RATIONALE FOR STATISTICS

While statistics can be used to track the status of an *individual*, answering questions such as *What is my academic score over the course of the term?* or *What is my weight from week to week?* this book focuses on using statistics to understand the characteristics of *groups* of people.

Chapter 3 explains how descriptive statistics are used to comprehend one variable at a time answering questions such as *What is the average age of people in this group?* or *How many females and males are there in this group?* Chapters 4 through 13 include *inferential* statistics, which enable us to make determinations such as *Which patrolling method is best for reducing crime in this neighborhood? Which teaching method produces the highest test scores? Is Treatment A better than Treatment B for a particular disorder? Is there a relationship between salary and happiness? and Are females or males more likely to graduate?*

Statistics enable professionals to implement *evidence based practice* (EBP), meaning that instead of simply taking one's best guess at the optimal choice, one can use statistical results to help inform such decisions. Statistical analyses can aide in (more) objectively determining the most effective patrolling method, the best available teaching method, or the optimal treatment for a specific disease or disorder.

Evidence based practice involves researching the (published) statistical findings of others who have explored a field that you are interested in pursuing; the statistical results in such reports provide evidence as to the effectiveness of such implementations. For example, suppose a researcher has studied 100 people in a sleep lab and now has statistical evidence showing that people who listened to soothing music at bedtime fall asleep faster than those who took a sleeping pill. Such evidence based findings have the potential to inform professionals regarding best practices—in this case, how to best advise someone who is having problems falling asleep.

Evidence based practice, which is supported by statistical findings, helps to reduce the guesswork and paves the way to more successful outcomes with respect to assembling more plausible requests for proposals (RFP's); independent proposals for new implementations; plans for quality improvement, which could involve modifying or enhancing existing implementations; creating or amending policies; or assembling best-practices guidelines for a variety of professional domains.

Even with good intentions, without evidence-based practice, we risk adopting implementations which may have a neutral or even negative impact, hence, failing to serve, or possibly harming the targeted population.

Additionally, statistics can be used to evaluate the performance of an existing program, which people may be simply assuming is effective, or statistics can be built into a proposal for a new implementation as a way of monitoring the performance of the program on a progressive basis. For example, instead of simply launching a new program designed to provide academic assistance to students with learning disabilities, one could use evidence-based practice methods to design the program, wherein the program that would be launched would be composed of elements that have demonstrated efficacy. Furthermore, instead of just launching the program and hoping for the best, the design could include periodic grade audits, wherein one would gather and statistically review the grades of the participants at the conclusion of each term to determine if the learning assistance program is making the intended impact. Such findings could suggest which part(s) of the program are working as expected and which require further development.

Consider another concise example wherein a school has implemented an evidence based strategy aimed at reducing absenteeism. Without a statistical evaluation, we would have no way of knowing if it worked or not. Alternatively, statistical analysis may reveal that the intervention has reduced absences except on Fridays—in which case, a supplemental attendance strategy could be considered overall, or the staff may work in a focused manner to develop a strategy to include some special Friday incentives.

RESEARCH QUESTIONS

A statistician colleague of mine once said, "I want the numbers to tell me a story." Those nine words elegantly describe the mission of statistics. Naturally, the story depends on the nature of the statistical question. Some (statistical) **research questions** render descriptive (summary) statistics, such as the following: *How many people visit a public park on weekends? How many cars cross this bridge per day? What is the average age of students at a school? How many accidents have occurred at this intersection? What percentage of people in a geographical region has a particular disease? What is the average income per household in a community? What percentage of students graduates from high school?* Attempting to comprehend such figures simply by inspecting them visually may work for a few dozen numbers, but visual inspection of these figures would not be feasible if there were hundreds or even thousands of numbers to consider. To get a reasonable idea of the nature of these numbers, we can mathematically and graphically summarize them and thereby better understand any amount of figures using a concise set of **descriptive statistics**, as detailed in Chapter 3.

Another form of research question involves comparisons; often this takes the form of an experimental outcome. Some questions may involve comparisons of scores between two groups, such as the following: *In a fourth-grade class, do girls or boys do better on math tests? Do smokers sleep more than nonsmokers? Do students whose parents are teachers have better test scores than students whose parents are not teachers? In a two-group clinical trial, one group was given a new drug to lower blood pressure, and the other group was given an existing drug; does the new drug outperform the old drug in lowering blood pressure?* These sorts of questions, involving the scores from two groups, are answered using the *t* test or the Mann-Whitney *U* test, which are covered in Chapter 4.

Research questions and their corresponding designs may involve several groups. For example, in a district with four elementary schools, each uses a different method for teaching spelling: *Is there a statistically significant difference between spelling scores from one school to another?* Another example would be a clinical trial aimed at discovering the optimal dosage of a new sleeping pill; Group 1 gets a placebo, Group 2 gets the drug at a 10-mg dose, and Group 3 gets the drug at a 15-mg dose; *is there a statistically significant difference between the groups in terms of number of hours of sleep per night?* Questions involving analyzing the scores from more than two groups are processed using ANOVA (analysis of variance) or the Kruskal-Wallis test, which are covered in Chapter 5.

Occasionally, an identifiable extraneous factor may influence the outcome of a study. Suppose we want to determine which of two different relaxation techniques is best; as such, we would gather the pulse rate of each of the participants at the end of the treatment; however, we know that some of the participants in this study smoke. Because we know that smoking can raise the pulse rate, we can tell the analysis of covariance (ANCOVA) processor how many cigarettes each participant smokes per day. This will enable the results to be adjusted accordingly. ANCOVA is covered in Chapter 7.

There may be times when a single intervention may affect more than one thing. For example, consider a three-group study designed to increase academic performance. Group 1 gets no treatment, Group 2 gets 1 hour of private tutoring per week, and Group 3 gets 1 hour of private tutoring per school day. Naturally, we would want to measure the grades of the students; we would expect that the tutored groups would have higher grades, but we also may be interested in the impact that this program might have on depression—we may expect to see depression go down among those in the tutored groups. To determine how an intervention impacts more than one outcome, we would use multivariate analysis of variance (MANOVA), as detailed in Chapter 8.

Some research questions involve assessing the effectiveness of a treatment by administering a pretest, then the treatment, and then a posttest to determine if the group's scores improved after the treatment. For example, suppose it is expected that brighter lighting may enhance mood. To test for this, the researcher administers a mood survey under normal lighting to a group, which renders a score (e.g., 0 = *very depressed*, 10 = *very happy*). Next, the lighting is brightened, after which that group is asked to reanswer the mood test. The question is, *According to the pretest and posttest scores, did the group's mood (score) increase significantly after the lighting was changed?* Consider another example: Suppose it is expected that physical exercise enhances math scores. To test this, a fourth-grade teacher administers a multiplication test to each student. Next, the students are taken out to the playground to run to the far fence and back three times, after which the students immediately return to the classroom to take another multiplication test. The question is, *Is there a statistically significant difference between the test scores before and after the physical activity?* Questions involving before-and-after scores within a group are processed with the paired *t* test or the Wilcoxon test, which are covered in Chapter 8.

As useful as the pretest/posttest design is, there are occasions when we want to track an outcome over more than just two time points (pretest and posttest); for example, a pretest/posttest design for a smoking cessation intervention may gather pretest data (number of cigarettes smoked daily), then implement the smoking cessation intervention, and gather posttest data 30 days later. Suppose the findings indicate that participants were able to reduce their smoking by 60%. Instead of stopping there, we could continue to follow these participants and gather smoking data on a monthly basis to see what happens to smoking rates over time. Whereas the paired *t* test enables us to determine the change spanning (only) two time points (pretest : posttest), we may want to (statistically) measure the participant's progress several times over a longer time (e.g., Day 1, Day 30, Day 60, Day 90, etc.). This would reveal if smoking rates go back up, level off, or continue to reduce over time. The statistic for assessing progress within individuals over time is the ANOVA repeated measures, which is covered in Chapter 9.

Research questions may also involve comparisons between categories. For example, *Is there a difference in ice cream preferences (chocolate, strawberry, vanilla) based on gender (male, female)*—in other words, *Does gender have any bearing on ice cream flavor selection?* We could also investigate questions such as *Does the marital status of the parents (divorced, not divorced) have any bearing on the child's graduation from high school (graduated, not graduated)?* Questions involving comparisons among categories are processed using **chi-square** (chi is pronounced *kai*; rhymes with *eye*). which is covered in Chapter 10.

Another kind of research question may seek to understand the (co)relation between two variables. For example, *What is the relationship between the number of homework hours per week and grade?* We might expect that as homework hours go up, the grade would go up as well. Similarly, we might ask, *What is the relationship between exercise and weight (if exercise goes up, does weight go down)? What is the relationship between mood and hours of sleep per night (when mood is low, do people sleep less)?* Alternatively, we may want to assess the sequence (ranking) of two lists to determine how similarly (or dissimilarly) they are to each other. Questions involving the correlation between two scores are processed using correlation and regression with the Spearman or Pearson tests, which are covered in Chapter 11.

On occasion, you may have several variables that you expect may be associated with an outcome, and you want to determine which of those variables actually predict that outcome. For example, suppose you are running a weight loss program, and you have data pertaining to the characteristics of each participant: age, gender, ethnicity, hours of exercise per week, daily caloric intake, daily pedometer data (number of steps taken), standing or sitting job, and marital status. **Multiple regression** could assess these (predictor) variables and determine their statistical association (if any) with respect to the outcome variable—weight loss; this procedure is covered in Chapter 12.

Some research focuses on comprehending the odds of an outcome occurring (or not). For example, it would be useful to know who is most likely to contract a particular disease, who is likely to drop out of school, or who is vulnerable to using recreational drugs. Such findings may reveal that the odds of dropping out of high school are four times higher among students who drink alcohol regularly, compared to those who do not drink. Such results are derived using **logistic regression**, which is covered in Chapter 13.

As you can see, a variety of statistical questions can be asked and answered. An important part of knowing which statistical test to reach for involves understanding the nature of the question and the type of data at hand.

TREATMENT AND CONTROL GROUPS

Even if you are new to statistics, you have probably heard of *treatment* and *control groups*. To understand the rationale for using this two-group design, we will explore the results of four examples aimed at answering the research question, *Does classical music enhance plant growth?*

Example 1 (Figure 1.1) is a one-group design consisting of a **treatment group** only, with no **control group**, wherein a good seed is planted using quality soil in an appropriate planter. The plant is given proper watering, sunlight, and 8 hours of classical music per day for 6 months.

Figure 1.1 One group: treatment group only (positive treatment effect presumed).

At 6 months, the researcher will measure the plant's growth by counting the number of leaves. In this case, the plant produced 20 full-sized healthy leaves, leading the researchers to reason that *classical music facilitates quality plant growth.*

Anyone who is reasonably skeptical may ponder: *The plant had a lot of things going for it—a quality seed, rich soil, the right planter, regular watering and sunlight, and classical music. So, how do we really know that it was the classical music that made the plant grow successfully? Maybe it would have done fine without it?* Example 2 (Figure 1.2) uses a two-group design, consisting of a treatment group and a control group to address that reasonable question.

Figure 1.2	Two groups: treatment group performs the same as control group (neutral treatment effect).

Treatment Group   Control Group

Notice that in Example 2 (Figure 1.2), the treatment group is precisely the same as in Example 1, which involves a plant grown with a quality seed, rich soil, the right planter, regular watering and sunlight, and classical music. The exact same protocol is given to the other plant, which is placed in the control group except for one thing: The control plant will receive *no music.* In other words, everything is the same in these two groups except that one plant gets the music and the other does not—this will help us to isolate the effect of the music.

At 6 months, the researcher would then assess the plant growth for each group: In this case, the treatment plant produced 20 leaves, and the control plant also produced 20 leaves. Now we are better positioned to answer the question, *How do we really know that it was the classical music that made the plant grow successfully?* The control group is the key to answering that question. Both groups were handled identically except for one thing: The treatment group got classical music, and the control group did not. Because the control plant received no music but did just as well as the plant that did get the music, we can reasonably conclude that the classical music had a *neutral* effect on the plant growth. Without the control group, we may have mistakenly concluded that classical music had a *positive* effect on plant growth, because the (single) plant did so well in producing 20 leaves.

Next, consider Example 3, which is set up the same as Example 2: A treatment group, where the plant gets music, and a control group, where the plant gets no music (Figure 1.3).

Figure 1.3 Two groups: treatment group outperforms control group (positive treatment effect).

Treatment Group   Control Group

In Example 3, we see that the plant in the treatment group produced 20 leaves, whereas the plant in the control group produced only 8 leaves. The only difference between these two groups is that the treatment group got the music and the control group did not, so the results of this experiment therefore suggest that the music had a *positive* effect on plant growth.

Finally, Example 4 (Figure 1.4) shows that the plant in the treatment group produced only 8 leaves; however, the control plant produced 20 healthy leaves. These results suggest that the classical music had a *negative* effect on plant growth.

Figure 1.4 Two groups: control group outperforms treatment group (negative treatment effect).

Treatment Group   Control Group

Clearly, having the control group provides a comparative basis for more realistically evaluating the outcome of the treatment group. As in this set of examples, in the best circumstances, the treatment group and the control group should begin as identically as possible in every respect, except that the treatment group will get the specified treatment and the control group proceeds without the treatment or treatment as usual (TAU). Intuitively, to determine the effectiveness of an intervention, we are looking for substantial differences in the performance between the two groups—is there a significant difference between the results of those in the treatment group compared with the control group?

The statistical tests covered in this text focus on different types of procedures for evaluating the difference(s) between groups (control : treatment) to help determine the effect of the intervention—whether the treatment group significantly outperformed the control group.

To simplify the foregoing examples, the illustrations were drawn with a single plant in each group. If this had been an actual experiment, the design would have been more robust if each group contained multiple plants (e.g., about 30 plants per group), and instead of counting the leaves on a single plant, we would compute an average (mean) number of leaves in each group. This would help protect against possible anomalies; for example, the results of a design involving only one plant per group could be compromised if, unknowingly, a good seed was used in one group and a bad seed was used in the other group. Such adverse effects such as this would be minimized if more plants were involved in each group.

RATIONALE FOR RANDOM ASSIGNMENT

Understanding the utility of randomly assigning subjects to control/treatment groups is best explained by example: Dr. Zinn and Dr. Zorders have come up with *Q-math*, a revolutionary system for teaching multiplication. The Q-math package is shipped out to schools in a local district to determine if it is more effective than the current teaching method (treatment as usual). The instructions specify that each fourth-grade class should be divided in half and routed to separate rooms, with students in one room receiving the Q-math teaching and students in the other room getting their regular math lesson. At the end, both groups are administered a multiplication test, with the results of both groups compared. The question is, *How should the class be divided into two groups?* This is not such a simple question. If the classroom is divided into boys and girls, this may influence the outcome; gender may be a relevant factor in math skills—if by chance we send the gender with stronger math skills to receive the Q-math intervention, this may serve to inflate those scores. Alternatively, suppose we decided to slice the class in half by seating—this introduces a different potential confound; what if the half who sits near the front of the classroom are naturally more attentive than those who sit in the back half of the classroom? Again, this grouping method may confound the findings of the study. Finally, suppose the teacher splits the class by age; this presents yet another potential confound—maybe older students are able to perform math better than younger students. In addition, it is unwise to allow subjects to self-select which group they want to be in; it may be that more proficient math students, or students who take their studies more seriously, may systemically opt for the Q-math group, thereby potentially influencing the outcome.

Through this simple example, it should be clear that the act of selectively assigning subjects to (control/treatment) groups can unintentionally affect the outcome of a study; it is for this reason that we often opt for **random assignment** to assemble more balanced groups. In this example, the Q-math instructions may specify that a coin flip be used to assign students to each of the two groups: Heads assigns a student to Q-math, and tails assigns a student to the usual math teaching method (treatment as usual). This random assignment method ultimately means that regardless of factors such as gender, seating position, age, math proficiency, and academic motivation, each student will have an equal (50/50) chance of being assigned to either group. The process of random assignment will generally result in roughly the same proportion of math-smart students, the same proportion of front- and back-of-the-room students, and the same proportion of older and younger students being assigned to each group. If done properly, random assignment helps to cancel out the exceptional factor(s) endemic in subjects that may have otherwise biased the findings one way or another.

HYPOTHESIS FORMULATION

Everyone has heard of the word *hypothesis*; hypotheses simply spell out each of the anticipated possible outcomes of an experiment. In simplest terms, before we embark on the experiment, we need one hypothesis that states that nothing notable happened, because sometimes experiments fail. This would be the **null hypothesis (H$_0$)**, basically meaning that the treatment had a null effect, and nothing notable happened.

Another possibility is that something notable did happen (the experiment worked), so we would need an **alternate hypothesis (H$_1$)** that accounts for this. In this text, the alternate hypothesis will be consistently referred to as H$_1$, however some other literature denotes the alternate hypothesis as H$_A$.

Continuing with the previous example involving Q-math, we first construct the null hypothesis (H$_0$); as expected, the null hypothesis states that the experiment produced null results; basically, the experimental group (the group that got Q-math) and the control group (the group that got regular math) performed about the same. Essentially, that would mean that Q-math was no more effective than the traditional math lesson—the treatment had a *null* effect. The alternate hypothesis (H$_1$) is phrased indicating that the treatment (Q-math) group outperformed the control (regular math lesson) group. Hypotheses are typically written in this fashion:

H$_0$:   Q-math and regular math teaching methods produced equivalent test results.

H$_1$:   Q-math produced higher test results compared with regular teaching methods.

When the results are in, we would then know which hypothesis to reject and which to accept; from there, we can document and discuss our findings.

Remember: In simplest terms, the statistics that we will be processing are designed to answer the question, *Do the members of the treatment group (that get the innovative treatment) significantly outperform the members of the control group (who get no treatment, a placebo, or treatment as usual)?* As such, the hypotheses need to reflect each possible outcome. In this simple example, we can anticipate two possible outcomes: (1) H$_0$ states that there is *no* significant difference between the treatment group and the control group, suggesting that *the treatment was ineffective.* (2) On the other hand, we need another hypothesis that anticipates that the treatment will significantly outperform the control condition. As such, H$_1$ states that there *is* a significant difference in the outcomes between the treatment and control conditions, suggesting that *the treatment was effective.* The outcome of the statistical test will point us to which hypothesis to accept and which to reject.

READING STATISTICAL OUTCOMES

Statistical tests vary substantially in terms of the types of research questions each are designed to address, the format of the source data, their respective equations, and the content of their results, which can include figures, tables, and graphs. Although there are some similarities in reading statistical outcomes (e.g., means [averages], alpha [α] level, p value), these concepts are best explained in the context of working examples. As such, discussion of how to read statistical outcomes will be thoroughly explained as each emerges in future chapters.

ACCEPT/REJECT HYPOTHESES

As is the case with reading statistical outcomes, the decision to accept or reject a hypothesis depends on the nature of the test and, of course, the results: the alpha (α) level, p value, and, in some cases, the means. Just as with reading statistical outcomes, instructions for accepting or rejecting hypotheses for each test are best discussed in the context of actual working examples; these concepts will be covered in future chapters.

VARIABLE TYPES/LEVELS OF MEASURE

Comprehending the types of variables involved in a **data set** or research design is essential when it comes to properly selecting, running, and documenting the results of statistical tests. There are two types of variables: **continuous** and **categorical**. Each has two levels of measure; continuous variables may be either **interval** or **ratio**, and categorical variables may be either **nominal** or **ordinal**.

Basically, you will need to be able to identify the types of variables that you will be processing (*continuous* or *categorical*), which will help guide you in selecting and running the proper statistical analyses.

Continuous

Continuous variables contain the kinds of numbers that we are accustomed to dealing with in counting and mathematics. A continuous variable may be either interval or ratio.

Interval

Interval variables range from $-\infty$ to $+\infty$, like numbers on a number line. These numbers have equal spacing between them; the distance between 1 and 2 is the same as the distance between 2 and 3, which is the same as the distance between 3 and 4, and so on. Such variables include bank account balance (which could be negative) and temperature (e.g., $-40°\ldots 85°$), as measured in either Fahrenheit or Celsius. Interval variables are considered continuous variables.

Ratio

Ratio variables are similar to interval variables, except that interval variables can have negative values, whereas ratio variables cannot be less than zero. Examples of ratio variables include weight, distance, income, calories, academic grades (0% ... 100%), number of pets, number of pencils in a pencil cup, number of siblings, or number of members in a group. Ratio variables are considered continuous variables.

> **Learning tip:** Notice that the word *ratio* ends in *o*, which looks like a *zero*.

Categorical

Categorical variables (also known as discrete variables) involve assigning a number to an item in a category. A categorical variable may be either nominal or ordinal.

Nominal

Nominal variables are used to represent categories that defy ordering. For example, suppose you wish to code eye color and there are six choices: amber, blue, brown, gray, green, and hazel. There is really no way to put these in any order; for coding and computing purposes, we could assign 1 = amber, 2 = blue, 3 = brown, 4 = gray, 5 = green, and 6 = hazel. Because order does not matter among nominal variables, these eye colors could have just as well been numbered differently: 1 = blue, 2 = green, 3 = hazel, 4 = gray, 5 = amber, and 6 = brown. Nominal variables may be used to represent categorical variables such as gender (1 = female, 2 = male), agreement (1 = yes, 2 = no), religion (1 = atheist, 2 = Buddhist, 3 = Catholic, 4 = Hindu, 5 = Jewish, 6 = Taoist, etc.), or marital status (1 = single, 2 = married, 3 = separated, 4 = divorced, 5 = widow/widower).

Because the numbers are arbitrarily assigned to labels within a category, it would be inappropriate to perform traditional arithmetic calculations on such numbers. For example, it would be foolish to compute the average marital status (e.g., would 1.5 indicate a *single married* person?). The same principle applies to other nominal variables such as gender or religion. There are, however, appropriate statistical operations for processing nominal variables that will be discussed in **Chapter 3: Descriptive Statistics**. In terms of statistical tests, nominal variables are considered categorical variables.

> **Learning tip:** There is no order among the categories in a nominal variable; notice that the word *nominal* starts with *no*, as in *no order*.

Ordinal

Ordinal variables are similar to nominal variables in that numbers are assigned to represent items within a category. Whereas nominal variables have no real rank order to them (e.g., amber, blue, brown, gray, green, hazel), the values in an ordinal variable can be placed in a ranked order. For example, there is an inherent order to educational degrees (1 = high school diploma, 2 = associate's degree, 3 = bachelor's degree, 4 = master's degree, 5 = doctorate degree). Other examples of ordinal variables include military rank (1 = private, 2 = corporal, 3 = sergeant, etc.) and meals (1 = breakfast, 2 = brunch, 3 = lunch, 4 = dinner, 5 = late-night snack). In terms of statistical tests, ordinal variables are considered categorical variables.

Learning tip: Notice that the root of the word *ordinal* is *order,* suggesting that the categories have a meaningful *order* to them.

Summary of Variable Types

Continuous	{ Interval	$(\dots -3, -2, -1, 0, 1, 2, 3 \dots)$
	Ratio	$(0, 1, 2, 3)$
Categorical	{ Nominal	(Red, Blue, Green)
	Ordinal	(Breakfast, Lunch, Dinner)

GOOD COMMON SENSE

As we explore the results of multiple statistics throughout this text, keep in mind that no matter how precisely we proceed, the process of statistics is not perfect. Our findings do not *prove* or *disprove* anything; rather, statistics helps us to reduce uncertainty—to help us better comprehend the nature of those that we study.

Additionally, what we learn from statistical findings speaks to the *group* that we studied on an overall basis, not any one *individual.* For instance, suppose we find that the average age within a group is 25; this does not mean that we can point to any one person in that group and confidently proclaim, "You are 25 years old."

Key Concepts

- Rationale for statistics
- Research question
- Treatment group
- Control group
- Random assignment
- Hypotheses (null, alternate)
- Statistical outcomes
- Accepting/rejecting hypotheses
- Types of data (continuous, categorical)
- Level of data (continuous: interval, ratio; categorical: nominal, ordinal)

Practice Exercises

Each of the following exercises describes the basis for an experiment that would render data that could be processed statistically.

Exercise 1.1

It is expected that aerobic square dancing during the 30-minute recess at an elementary school will help fight childhood obesity.

    a. State the research question.

    b. Identify the control and experimental group(s).

    c. Explain how you would randomly assign participants to groups.

    d. State the hypotheses (H_0 and H_1).

    e. Discuss the criteria for accepting or rejecting the hypotheses.

Exercise 1.2

Recent findings suggest that residents at a senior living facility may experience fewer depressive symptoms when they participate in pet therapy with certified dogs for 30 minutes per day.

    a. State the research question.

    b. Identify the control and experimental group(s).

    c. Explain how you would randomly assign participants to groups.

    d. State the hypotheses (H_0 and H_1).

    e. Discuss the criteria for accepting or rejecting the hypotheses.

Exercise 1.3

A chain of retail stores has been experiencing substantial cash shortages in cashier balances across 10 of their stores. The company is considering installing cashier security cameras.

    a. State the research question.

    b. Identify the control and experimental group(s).

    c. Explain how you would randomly assign participants to groups.

    d. State the hypotheses (H_0 and H_1).

    e. Discuss the criteria for accepting or rejecting the hypotheses.

Exercise 1.4

Anytown Community wants to determine if implementing a neighborhood watch program will reduce vandalism incidents.

    a. State the research question.

    b. Identify the control and experimental group(s).

    c. Explain how you would randomly assign participants to groups.

    d. State the hypotheses (H_0 and H_1).

    e. Discuss the criteria for accepting or rejecting the hypotheses.

Exercise 1.5

Employees at Acme Industries, consisting of four separate buildings, are chronically late. An executive is considering implementing a *get out of Friday free* lottery; each day an employee is on time, he or she gets one token entered into the weekly lottery.

    a. State the research question.

    b. Identify the control and experimental group(s).

    c. Explain how you would randomly assign participants to groups.

    d. State the hypotheses (H_0 and H_1).

    e. Discuss the criteria for accepting or rejecting the hypotheses.

Exercise 1.6

The Acme Herbal Tea Company advertises that its product is *". . . the tea that relaxes."*

    a. State the research question.

    b. Identify the control and experimental group(s).

    c. Explain how you would randomly assign participants to groups.

    d. State the hypotheses (H_0 and H_1).

    e. Discuss the criteria for accepting or rejecting the hypotheses.

Exercise 1.7

Professor Madrigal has a theory that singing improves memory.

    a. State the research question.

    b. Identify the control and experimental group(s).

c. Explain how you would randomly assign participants to groups.

d. State the hypotheses (H_0 and H_1).

e. Discuss the criteria for accepting or rejecting the hypotheses.

Exercise 1.8

Mr. Reed believes that providing assorted colored pens will prompt his students to write longer essays.

a. State the research question.

b. Identify the control and experimental group(s).

c. Explain how you would randomly assign participants to groups.

d. State the hypotheses (H_0 and H_1).

e. Discuss the criteria for accepting or rejecting the hypotheses.

Exercise 1.9

Ms. Fractal wants to determine if working with flashcards helps students learn the multiplication table.

a. State the research question.

b. Identify the control and experimental group(s).

c. Explain how you would randomly assign participants to groups.

d. State the hypotheses (H_0 and H_1).

e. Discuss the criteria for accepting or rejecting the hypotheses.

Exercise 1.10

A manager at the Acme Company Call Center wants to see if running a classic movie on a big screen (with the sound off) will increase the number of calls processed per hour.

a. State the research question.

b. Identify the control and experimental group(s).

c. Explain how you would randomly assign participants to groups.

d. State the hypotheses (H_0 and H_1).

e. Discuss the criteria for accepting or rejecting the hypotheses.

Working in SPSS

We can get **SPSS** to do all the hard work for us.

- Data View
- Variable View
- Codebook
- Saving Data Files

Computers are useless. They can only give you answers.

—Pablo Picasso

Learning Objectives

Upon completing this chapter, you will be able to do the following:

- Operate in the two primary views in SPSS: Variable View and Data View.
- Establish or modify variable definitions on the *Variable View* screen: name, type, width, decimals, label, values, missing, columns, align, measure, and role.
- Use the *Value Label* icon to alternate between numeric and label (text) displays.
- Interpret and use a codebook to configure variables in SPSS.
- Enter data into SPSS.
- Save and identify SPSS data files.

VIDEO

The video for this chapter is **Ch 02 – Working in SPSS.mp4**. This video provides guidance on setting up an SPSS database, entering data, and saving SPSS files.

OVERVIEW—SPSS

Based on what you have read thus far, you have probably figured out that when it comes to statistics, larger sample sizes facilitate more robust statistical findings. Appropriately large sample sizes are also important when it comes to gathering a *representative sample*, which helps when it comes to generalizing the findings from your sample to the overall population from which it was drawn (*external validity*). Processing large samples can involve hundreds or even thousands of calculations. For most statistical formulas, the mathematical complexity does not go beyond simple algebra, however; such formulas typically involve multiple mathematical operations on each record. Attempting to process such data by hand would be inefficient in two ways: (1) It would be very time-consuming, and (2) accuracy would be compromised. Performing multiple calculations on a lengthy data set is bound to produce some errors along the way. Even if each mathematical operation was correct, the data would be vulnerable to cumulative rounding error. With the advent of affordable, powerful computers and menu-driven statistical programs, it is now possible to accurately perform a variety of statistical analyses in a matter of seconds with relative ease. This chapter will provide you with what you need to know to get started using SPSS. SPSS, which originally stood for Statistical Program for the Social Sciences, has gone through some substantial evolution over time; some versions are referred to as PASW, Predictive Analytics Software. For the remainder of the text, the term *SPSS* will be used. Regardless of the name, the SPSS functionality of the statistics covered in this text has remained relatively stable across the evolution of the software.

TWO VIEWS: VARIABLE VIEW AND DATA VIEW

SPSS is laid out as two main screens: The **Variable View**, which is used for establishing or modifying the characteristics of each variable, and the **Data View**, which contains the gathered data. We will begin with the Variable View.

Variable View

The Variable View provides a screen for you to systematically set up the variables that will contain your data. This is where you will assign the name and characteristics of each variable that you will be including in the data set. To access the *Variable View* screen, click on the tab at the bottom of the screen that says *Variable View*, as shown in Figure 2.1.

Figure 2.1   SPSS *Variable View* screen.

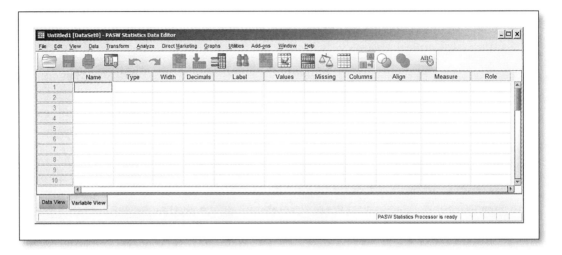

Basically, for each variable, you are telling SPSS the name of the variable and the kind of data it will contain (e.g., regular numbers, dates, text, etc.), along with some other properties (parameters). Once you have established each variable in the *Variable View* screen, you can proceed to enter the data that you have gathered on the *Data View* screen, which resembles a traditional spreadsheet. The *Variable View* screen has 11 properties that you can set for each variable. Some versions of SPSS may have a different amount of properties; you should be able to proceed nonetheless. Naturally, you will use care when establishing variables on the *Variable View* screen, but there is no need to be nervous; even after you have entered data on the *Data View* screen, you can always return to the *Variable View* screen and make changes (e.g., include more variables, delete variables, rename variables, and modify the properties of existing variables).

The cursor is initially positioned in the *Name* column for the first variable; this is where the data definition process begins.

Name

Each variable needs a unique name. Variable names can contain upper- and lowercase letters, but variable names are not case sensitive, meaning that you cannot have a variable named *AGE* and another variable (in the same database) named *age, Age* or *aGe*. The name can contain up to 64 letters and numbers, and the first character must be a letter. Some older versions of SPSS allow only eight characters for variable names, so you may need to be imaginative when it comes to assigning briefer variable names. Spaces are not allowed in the variable name, but you can use the underscore (_) character instead. For your own convenience, try to assign meaningful names (e.g., *Age, Date_of_Birth*,

First_Name, Last_Name, Gender, Test01, Question01, Question02, Question03, etc.). It is okay if you are unable to assign a perfect variable name; this will be discussed in more detail when we look at the *Label* property.

Initially, the cursor is positioned in the first cell for the first variable. We will build a database containing two variables: *Gender* (a categorical variable) and *Age* (a continuous variable). Begin by entering *Gender* (in row 1 under *Name*). When you press *Enter*, notice that SPSS automatically enters default values for all of the remaining properties except for label. Each of these properties can be changed, but we will accept the automatic defaults for some.

Type

The system needs to know what *Type* of data the variable will contain. The system assigns the default type as a numeric variable with a width of eight integer digits and two decimal digits (which you can change), meaning that this variable will accommodate a number such as 12345678.12 (Figure 2.2).

To access the menu shown in Figure 2.2, click on the *Type* cell for that variable. The options for variable type are fairly self-explanatory except for *String*; a *string* variable contains alphanumeric (letters and numbers) data (e.g., name, note, comment, memo, etc.).

Figure 2.2 SPSS *Variable Type* window.

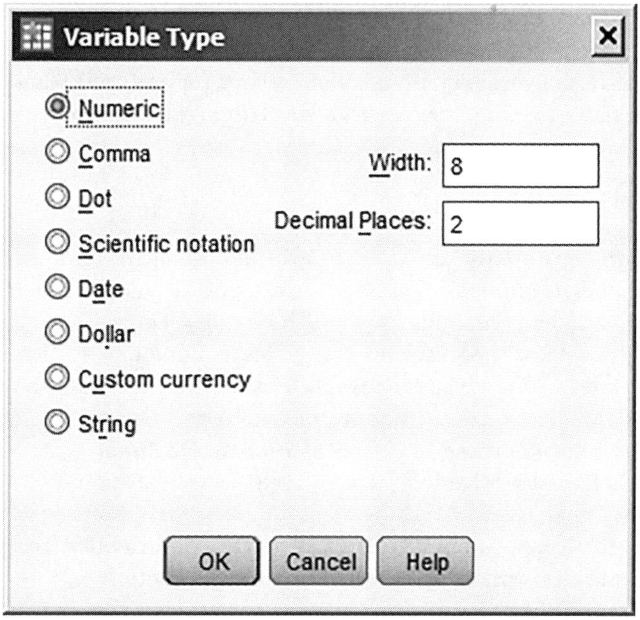

A string variable is useful for data that contain information that will not be processed mathematically consisting of letters, numbers, punctuation, or a mixture of letters and numbers, such as an ID code, an address, or a name (e.g., APB-373, 852 S. Bedford Street, Dusty Jones, etc.); if your data are not a date or a numeric value, then consider it alphanumeric and select *String* type. While string variables may contain valuable information, it is not possible to perform statistical operations on such variables.

Width

The *Width* refers to the number of characters SPSS will allow you to enter for the variable. If it is a numerical value with decimals, the total *Width* has to include the decimal point and each digit (Figure 2.2). For example, if you were entering data for income (including dollars and cents) and the largest value expected was 123456.78, you would want to be sure to set the *Width* to at least 9 (8 digits for the numbers plus 1 for the decimal point).

Decimals

The *Decimals* property refers to the number of digits that will appear to the right of the decimal point (Figure 2.2). The default is two decimal places. For example, a cash amount should have two decimal places (for the cents), whereas for categorical variables (e.g., Gender: Female = 1, Male = 2), a decimal is not needed, so the value should be set to 0.

Label

If the *Label* property is left blank, SPSS will use the variable *Name* in all output reports; otherwise, it will use whatever you specify as the label. For example, suppose the name of the variable is *DOB*, but in your reports, you want it to display as *Date of Birth*; in that case, simply enter *Date of Birth* in the *Label* property. Notice that the *Label* can contain spaces, but the *Name* cannot.

Values

The *Values* property provides a powerful instrument for assigning meaningful names to the values (numbers) contained in categorical variables. For example, *Gender* is a nominal variable containing two categories (1 = Female, 2 = Male). When it comes to nominal variables, SPSS handles categories as numbers (1, 2) as opposed to the textual names (*Female, Male*). The *Values* property allows you to assign the textual name to each category number, so even though you will code *Gender* using 1s and 2s, the output reports will exhibit these 1s and 2s as *Female* and *Male*.

Here is how it works:

1. In the *Name* column, create a variable called *Gender*; accept all the default values, except change the *Decimals* property to *0*.

2. Click on the *Values* cell for *Gender*; this will bring up the *Value Labels* menu (Figure 2.3).

3. Assign the values one at a time; begin by entering *1* in *Value* and *Female* in *Label*; then click *Add*.

4. Do the same for the second category: Enter *2* in *Value* and *Male* in *Label*; then click *Add*.

5. To finalize these designations, click *OK*.

You will see the utility of this labeling system when you enter data on the *Data View* screen and when you run your first report.

Figure 2.3 SPSS *Variable Labels* window.

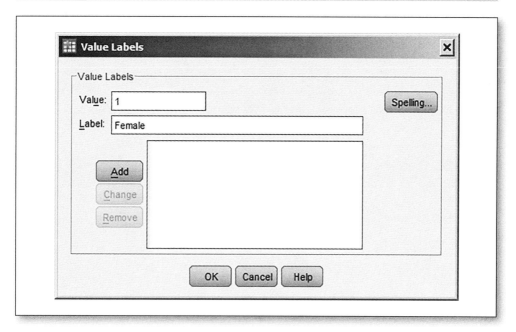

Missing

Sometimes, when the source data are either erroneous or missing, the cell is simply left blank, in which case, the *Missing* property can remain blank as well. Other times, special numeric codes represent the erroneous or missing data; a common convention is to code erroneous data as 888, and missing data are represented as 999—this conveys that a blank cell is not an oversight. Consider the variable *Age*; if the data contained an erroneous entry (e.g., "I'm a kid"), or if the entry was left blank, the corresponding 888 or 999 codes would radically throw off the statistical (Age) calculations. The *Missing* property enables us to specify such codes (888 and 999) that we want SPSS to ignore so that they will not be processed in the statistical calculations.

Here is how it works:

1. Create a variable with the name *Age*; accept all the default values, except change the *Decimals* property to *0*.

2. Click on *Discrete missing values* and enter *888* and *999* (Figure 2.4).

3. If you need to indicate more than three such values, you may opt for the *Range* plus one optional discrete missing value function, which would enable you to specify a range of values (e.g., *Low: 888, High: 999*, meaning that all values from 888 through 999 inclusive will be omitted from all statistical analysis for that variable). In addition, you can specify one additional value (e.g., Discrete value: −1).

4. To finalize these designations, click *OK*.

The numbers 888 and 999 have been generally adopted as special values because they are visually easy to recognize in a data set. Also, if these special values are not properly designated as erroneous or missing values, statistical clues will begin to emerge, such as a report indicating an average age of 347 or a maximum height of 999 inches or centimeters. Such extreme results alert you to check that the missing or erroneous designations have been properly specified for a variable.

Figure 2.4   SPSS *Missing Values* window.

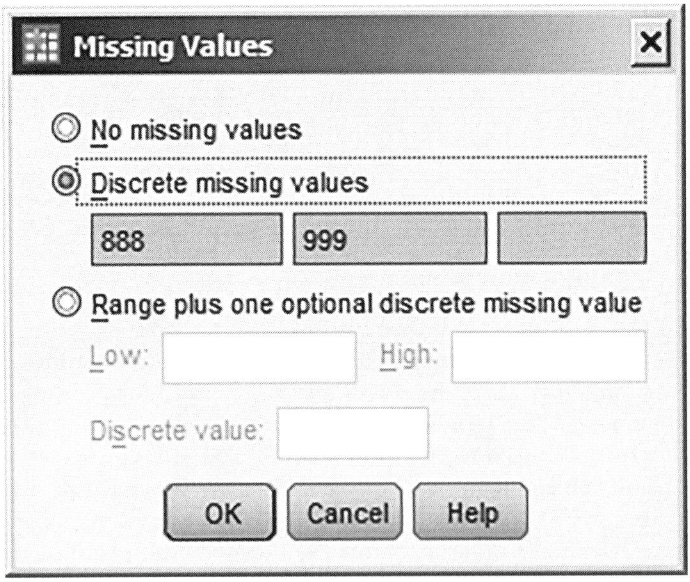

Columns

The *Columns* property allows you to change the column width on the Data View screen and in the reports; you can specify how many characters wide you want that column to be.

Align

The *Align* property lets you specify how you want the variable to be presented on the *Data View* screen and in the output reports. Typically, *Right* alignment (justification) is used for numeric data, and *Left* alignment is used for text such as string data or categorical variables with data labels assigned to them. *Center* is also an option.

Measure

The *Measure* property pertains to the four levels of measures (*nominal, ordinal, interval,* and *ratio*) covered in the Variable Types/Levels of Measure section in Chapter 1. For variables that contain *continuous* (interval or ratio) variables, select *Scale*. For *categorical* (*nominal* or *ordinal*) variables, which may contain value labels, select either *Nominal* or *Ordinal*, depending on the variable type.

Role

Some versions of SPSS have the *Role* property; do not panic if the version that you are using does not include this property—it will not be used in this text. Role enables you to define how the variable will be used in the statistical processes. If your version of the software includes the *Role* property, just use the default setting: *Input*.

Use SPSS to set up the *Variable View* screen to establish the *Gender* and *Age* variables as shown in Figure 2.5.

Figure 2.5   SPSS *Variable View* screen.

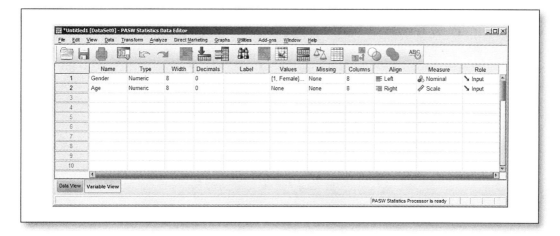

Data View

Now that the properties for each variable have been established on the *Variable View* screen, the next step is to enter the actual data. To switch to the data entry mode, click on the *Data View* tab at the bottom of the screen. As you enter the data in Table 2.1 into the *Data View* screen, notice that for the *Gender* variable, you can access the pull-down menu in each cell to select *Female* or *Male*. Alternatively, you can enter the corresponding numbers that you defined: *1* for *Female* or *2* for *Male*. Notice that SPSS will not allow you to type the words *Female* or *Male* directly into the *Gender* field; you will need to enter a number (in this case, 1 or 2) or use the pull-down menu feature to select *Female* or *Male* for this variable. The Data View screen should resemble Figure 2.6.

Table 2.1 *Gender* and *Age* source data.

	Gender	Age
1	Male	24
2	Female	25
3	Male	31
4	Male	19
5	Female	27

NOTE: You do not need to enter the numbers in the shaded leftmost column (1, 2, 3, 4, 5); this column pertains to the row (record) numbers that SPSS provides automatically.

Figure 2.6 *Data View* screen with data entered.

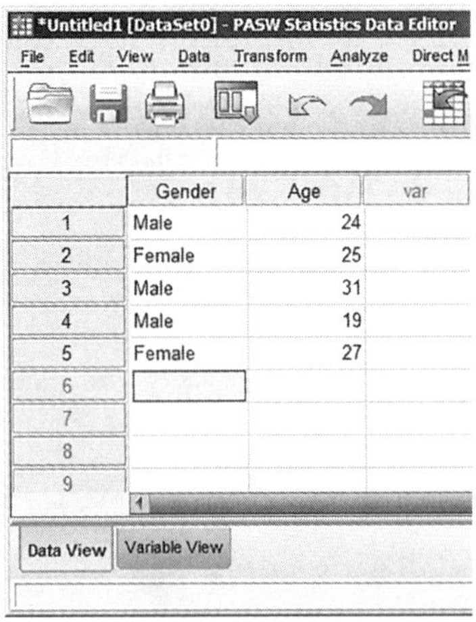

Value Labels Icon

When it comes to viewing your data, there will be times when you will want to see the value labels (e.g., *Female, Male*) and other times when you will want to see the source numbers (e.g., 1, 2). To toggle this display back and forth, from numbers to text (and back), click on the *Value Labels* icon (with the *1 A* on it), as shown in Figure 2.7.

Figure 2.7	The *Value Labels* icon alternates the display of categorical variables from text to numeric display (and back).

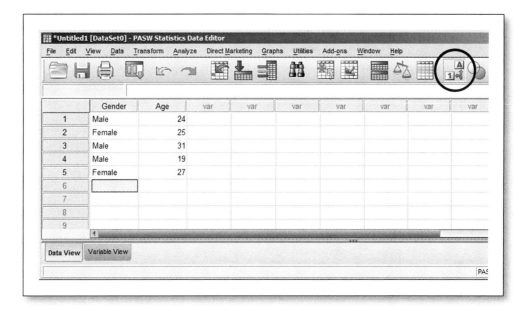

Codebook

For learning purposes, the two-variable data set used in this chapter is admittedly simple. Even so, without being told that for the variable *Gender, 1* stands for *Female* and *2* stands for *Male*, this coding scheme would lead to confusion. Designations such as *1 = Female* and *2 = Male* and other characteristics of each variable in a data set are traditionally contained in the *codebook*, which is the companion to the data set. The codebook is written by the person who develops the experiment or survey; it provides a list description of each variable contained in a data set. This is particularly valuable in data sets that contain numerous variables with arcane names. For example, suppose you came across a variable named *Q105* (*Question 105*), and it appeared to contain dates. Without the codebook, we would have no idea what any of this means; we would not know how this variable was gathered, nor would we be able to assign any meaning to these dates (e.g., birth date, death date, graduation date, anniversaries, date of arrest, date admitted to a hospital, etc.). If you do not know the story of a variable, these data are virtually useless, hence the codebook is as valuable as the actual data set. Although there is no standard form for codebooks, a quality codebook should indicate the information essential to understanding each variable in the data set. Continuing with the *Q105* example, a reasonable codebook entry for this variable might look like this:

Codebook

Variable: Q105

Definition: High school graduation date (Question #105)

Type: Date (MM/DD/YYYY)

The codebook for our simple two-variable database detailed in Table 2.1 looks like this (this concise codebook format will be used throughout this book):

Codebook

Variable: Gender

Definition: Gender of respondent

Type: Categorical (1 = Female, 2 = Male)

Variable: Age

Definition: Age of respondent

Type: Continuous

SAVING DATA FILES

To save the file, click on the *Save this document* icon as shown in Figure 2.8. Use the file name *First Data Set*; SPSS automatically appends the **.sav file extension** (suffix) to the *File name*. The file on your system will be listed as *First Data Set.sav*.

GOOD COMMON SENSE

The acronym **GIGO** (pronounced *gig-oh*) comes from the early days of computing; it stands for *garbage in, garbage out*, and it is just as valid today. Basically, it means that if you input inaccurate data into a program, the output will be inaccurate too. Inaccurate data can consist of missing or erroneous responses, responses to

Figure 2.8 The *Save this document* icon.

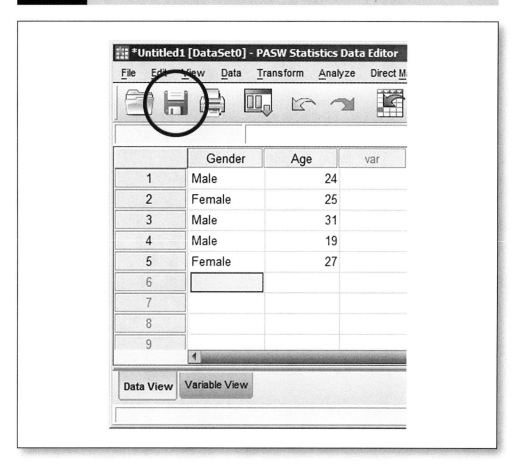

misconstrued questions, data entry errors (typos), omitted data, double or multiple entries of data, or other anomalies that may have allowed imprecise data to be entered into the database. Skillful statisticians will inspect and assess the data for such errors prior to embarking on analyses; this process is referred to as *cleaning the data*.

For example, a survey question may ask for the participant's age; however, the respondent enters a date (e.g., 9/18/1980). Clearly, data in date format will not fit into a variable that is configured to accept a three-digit numeric (*Age*) value. The statistician would then need to make a judgment call: The data could be omitted or coded as 888 (error); alternatively, one might presume that the date provided is the participant's birthdate, in which case, one might opt to use that date to calculate the *Age*, and if the age seemed reasonable, it could be entered into the specified (*Age*) field.

The accuracy of the statistical tests that you run will depend on the accuracy of the data definitions (on the *Variable View* screen) and the data entered (on the *Data View* screen). Considering that this book focuses on learning specific statistics, opposed to coping with erroneous or missing data, the data sets that are provided contain *clean* data with no missing values, which is ready for processing.

Key Concepts

- Variable View

  - Name
  - Type
  - Width
  - Decimals
  - Label
  - Values
  - Missing
  - Columns
  - Align
  - Measure
  - Role

- Data View

  - *Value Labels* icon
  - Codebook
  - Saving data files

    - *Save this document* icon
    - .sav files

Practice Exercises

Use the provided codebook in each exercise to establish the variables on the *Variable View* screen, and then enter the data on the *Data View* screen.

To check your work, produce a variable list; click on *Analyze, Reports, Codebook*, as shown in Figure 2.9.

Next, select all the variables that you want to include in the codebook report; move the variables from the left *Variables* window to the right *Codebook Variables* window (using double-click, drag and drop, or the arrow button); then click *OK*, as shown in Figure 2.10. This will generate a *Variable Information* report showing the properties of all variables, as shown in Table 2.2.

Figure 2.9 Ordering a list of all variables; click on *Analyze, Reports, Codebook.*

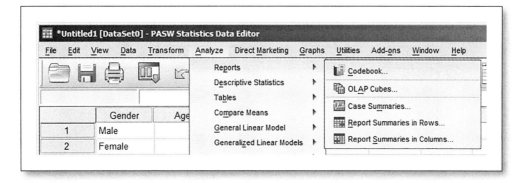

Figure 2.10 Codebook report order screen; move variables of interest to right (*Codebook Variables*) window.

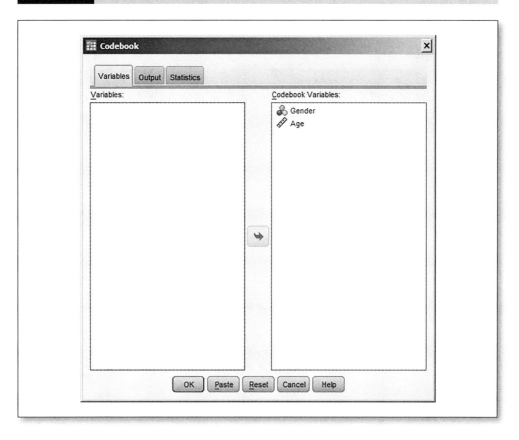

Table 2.2 Codebook report displaying the variable properties.

Gender

		Value	Count	Percent
Standard Attributes	Position	1		
	Label	<none>		
	Type	Numeric		
	Format	F8		
	Measurement	Nominal		
	Role	Input		
Valid Values	1	Female	2	40.0%
	2	Male	3	60.0%

Age

		Value
Standard Attributes	Position	2
	Label	<none>
	Type	Numeric
	Format	F8
	Measurement	Scale
	Role	Input
N	Valid	5
	Missing	0
Central Tendency and Dispersion	Mean	25.20
	Standard Deviation	4.382
	Percentile 25	24.00
	Percentile 50	25.00
	Percentile 75	27.00

After each exercise, clear out the data; click on *File, New, Data*, as shown in Figure 2.11.

Figure 2.11 Clearing the data; click on *File, New, Data*.

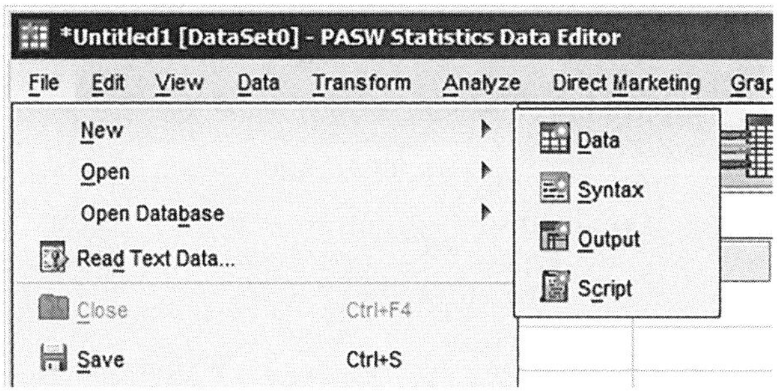

Exercise 2.1

Codebook

Variable:	Enrolled
Definition:	Currently enrolled in school
Type:	Categorical (1 = Yes, 2 = No)

Variable:	Units
Definition:	Number of units the student is enrolled in
Type:	Continuous

Variable:	Grade
Definition:	Overall grade
Type:	Continuous

Data:

	Enrolled	Units	Grade
1	Yes	12	70
2	Yes	12	93
3	No	0	81
4	Yes	6	72
5	Yes	16	91

NOTE: Do not enter the numbers in the first shaded column (1, 2, 3, 4, 5); this column corresponds to the leftmost column in SPSS, indicating the record (row) number.

Exercise 2.2

Codebook

Variable: ID

Definition: ID number

Type: String

Variable: Volunteer_Hours

Definition: Volunteer hours worked per week

Type: Continuous

Data:

	ID	Volunteer_Hours
1	QF732	2.00
2	AL331	1.50
3	JW105	3.00
4	RK122	.50
5	DD987	4.00

Exercise 2.3

Codebook

Variable: Degree

Definition: Highest degree completed

Type: Categorical (1 = Associate's, 2 = Bachelor's, 3 = Master's, 4 = Doctorate)

Variable: Pretest

Definition: Pretest score

Type: Continuous

Variable: Posttest

Definition: Posttest score

Type: Continuous

Data:

	Degree	Pretest	Posttest
1	Associate's	22	29
2	Master's	31	48
3	Bachelor's	28	38
4	Bachelor's	25	34
5	Master's	30	46

Exercise 2.4

Codebook

Variable:	Employ
Definition:	Employment status
Type:	Categorical (1 = Unemployed, 2 = Temporary, 3 = Part-time, 4 = Full-time)
Variable:	Work_Hours
Definition:	Average hours worked per week
Type:	Continuous
Variable:	Sleep_Hours
Question:	Average sleep hours per day
Type:	Continuous (0 . . . 24)

Data:

	Employ	Work_Hours	Sleep_Hours
1	Unemployed	0	10.00
2	Temporary	16	9.00
3	Full-time	40	7.50
4	Full-time	45	8.00
5	Part-time	20	7.00

Exercise 2.5

Codebook

Variable:	First_Initial
Definition:	First letter of first name
Type:	String

Variable:	Last_Name
Definition:	Last name
Type:	String

Variable:	Siblings
Definition:	Number of brothers and sisters
Type:	Continuous

Variable:	Adopted
Definition:	Are you adopted?
Type:	Categorical (1 = Yes, 2 = No)

Data:

	First_Initial	Last_Name	Siblings	Adopted
1	J	Gower	0	No
2	D	Freeman	2	No
3	T	Rexx	3	No
4	P	Smith	2	Yes
5	V	Jones	1	No

Exercise 2.6

Codebook

Variable:	Patient_ID
Definition:	Patient ID number
Type:	Continuous

Variable: Age

Definition: Patient's age

Type: Continuous

Variable: Temp

Definition: Body temperature (°F)

Type: Continuous

Variable: Flu_Shot

Definition: Has the patient had a flu shot this season?

Type: Categorical (1 = Yes; 2 = No, and I don't want one; 3 = Not yet, but I'd like one)

Variable: Rx

Definition: Current medications

Type: String

Data:

	Patient_ID	Age	Temp	Flu_Shot	Rx
1	2136578099	22	98.6	Yes	
2	8189873094	24	99.0	No, and I don't want one	Multivitamin
3	2144538086	53	101.5	Not yet, but I want one	
4	8046628739	81	98.8	Yes	
5	5832986812	38	100.9	Yes	Xamine, Tutsocol

NOTE: Drug names are fictitious.

Exercise 2.7

Codebook

Variable: Passport

Definition: Do you have a valid passport?

Type: Categorical (1 = Yes, 2 = No, 3 = Decline to answer)

Variable:	Fired
Definition:	Have you ever been fired from a job?
Type:	Categorical (1 = Yes, 2 = No, 3 = Decline to answer)

Variable:	ER
Definition:	Have you ever been treated in an emergency room?
Type:	Categorical (1 = Yes, 2 = No, 3 = Decline to answer)

Variable:	DOB
Definition:	Date of birth
Type:	Date

Data:

	Passport	Fired	ER	DOB
1	No	Decline to answer	No	01/23/1936
2	Yes	No	Yes	08/18/1928
3	Yes	No	No	03/01/1987
4	No	Yes	No	06/07/1974
5	No	No	Yes	11/30/2001

Exercise 2.8

Codebook

Variable:	Dogs
Definition:	I like dogs.
Type:	Categorical (1 = Strongly disagree, 2 = Disagree, 3 = Neutral, 4 = Agree, 5 = Strongly agree)

Variable:	Cats
Definition:	I like cats.
Type:	Categorical (1 = Strongly disagree, 2 = Disagree, 3 = Neutral, 4 = Agree, 5 = Strongly agree)

Variable:	Pets
Definition:	How many pets do you currently have?
Type:	Continuous

Data:

	Dogs	Cats	Pets
1	Strongly agree	Disagree	1
2	Agree	Strongly agree	0
3	Strongly agree	Neutral	0
4	Strongly agree	Strongly agree	2
5	Neutral	Strongly disagree	3

Exercise 2.9

Codebook

Variable:	Blood_Type
Definition:	What is your blood type (respond "?" if you don't know)?
Type:	Categorical (1 = A−, 2 = A+, 3 = B−, 4 = B+, 5 = AB−, 6 = AB+, 7 = O−, 8 = O+, 9 = Don't know)

Variable:	Gender
Definition:	Gender
Type:	Categorical (1 = Female, 2 = Male)

Variable:	Prior_Donor
Definition:	Have you ever donated blood before?
Type:	Categorical (1 = Yes, 2 = No)

Data:

	Blood_Type	Gender	Prior_Donor
1	B+	Female	Yes
2	Don't know	Female	No
3	A−	Male	No
4	AB+	Male	No
5	O−	Male	Yes

Exercise 2.10

Codebook

Variable:	Entree_Food
Definition:	Entrée food
Type:	Categorical (1 = Fish, 2 = Chicken, 3 = Beef, 4 = Vegetarian)

Variable:	Entree_Quality
Definition:	Entrée quality
Type:	Continuous (1 = Poor . . . 10 = Excellent)

Variable:	Dessert_Quality
Definition:	Dessert quality
Type:	Continuous (1 = Poor . . . 10 = Excellent)

Data:

	Entree_Food	Entree_Quality	Dessert_Quality
1	Fish	9	7
2	Fish	8	9
3	Fish	9	10
4	Beef	10	8
5	Fish	7	10

PART II

Summarizing Variables

This chapter explains how to explore variables on an individual basis.

Chapter 3: Descriptive Statistics provides guidance on comprehending the values contained in continuous and categorical variables.

C H A P T E R   3

Descriptive Statistics

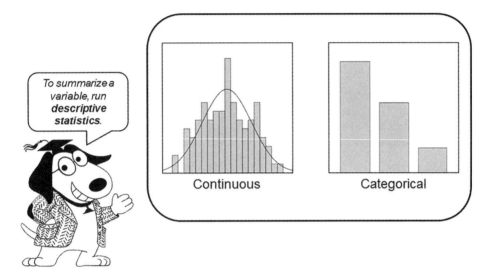

To summarize a variable, run **descriptive statistics.**

Continuous

Categorical

Whenever you can, count.

—Sir Francis Galton

Learning Objectives

Upon completing this chapter, you will be able to do the following:

- Comprehend the meaning of each descriptive statistic: number (*n*), mean (M), median, mode, standard deviation (SD), variance, minimum, maximum, and range.
- Understand central tendency.
- Load an SPSS data file.
- Order and interpret descriptive statistics for continuous variables: Frequency Statistics table, histogram with normal curve, and skewed distribution.
- Order and interpret descriptive statistics for categorical variables: Frequency Statistics table, bar chart, and pie chart.
- Select records to process/rule out.
- Select all records to process.

WHEN TO USE THIS STATISTIC

Guidelines for Selecting Descriptive Statistics

Overview: These statistics summarizes the numbers contained within a variable.

Variables: These statistics processes any (continuous or categorical) individual variable.

Results: We surveyed 27 women and 23 men between 18 and 31 years old with a mean age of 24 (SD = 2.86).

 VIDEOS

The videos for this chapter are **Ch 03 – Descriptive Statistics**, **Continuous.mp4** and **Ch 03 – Descriptive Statistics**, **Categorical.mp4**. These videos provide guidance on setting up, processing and interpreting descriptive (summary) statistics for continuous and categorical variables using the data set: **Ch 03 – Example 01 – Descriptive Statistics.sav**.

 OVERVIEW—DESCRIPTIVE STATISTICS

Statistics is about understanding data, which could consist of one or many groups and involve data sets of virtually any size. Take a look at the data set in Table 3.1; if someone were to ask you to describe this data set, you might say, "It looks like a list of about half women and half men, mostly in their 20s," which would be right, but we can be more precise than that. This list consists of 50 records and 100 data items, but how would you make a viable summary statement if the list consisted of 100, 1,000, or even 100,000 records? Such data would span multiple pages and defy cursory visual inspection.

To better comprehend and communicate the nature of a data set, we use **descriptive statistics**, sometimes referred to as *summary statistics*. Descriptive statistics enable us to concisely understand a data set of any size using a handful of figures and simple graphs that serve to summarize the contents of a variable.

Continuous variables can be summarized using the nine descriptive statistics: number (*n*), mean, median, mode, standard deviation, variance, minimum, maximum, and range. Graphically, continuous variables can be depicted using a histogram (a kind of bar chart) with a normal curve.

Categorical variables can be summarized using number (*n*) and percent. Graphically, categorical variables are depicted using a simple **bar chart** or **pie chart**. You can see examples of a histogram with a normal curve for a continuous variable and a bar chart for a categorical variable on the first page of this chapter.

Table 3.1	Data set containing 50 records with two variables per record: *Gender* and *Age*.

Male	24	Male	30	Female	22	Male	26	Female	25
Male	25	Male	25	Male	25	Male	25	Female	25
Male	31	Female	26	Male	25	Female	24	Female	22
Female	19	Male	27	Female	24	Male	29	Male	22
Female	27	Male	24	Female	23	Male	23	Female	20
Male	20	Female	25	Male	25	Female	21	Female	22
Male	28	Male	24	Female	19	Female	22	Male	18
Female	23	Female	26	Female	23	Female	21	Female	18
Male	26	Female	23	Female	28	Female	24	Female	23
Male	24	Male	22	Female	24	Male	26	Female	27

We will begin with an explanation of the nine summary statistics used to analyze continuous variables. For simplicity, we will work with a small data set, the first 10 ages drawn from the second column of Table 3.1: 24, 25, 31, 19, 27, 20, 28, 23, 26, and 24.

DESCRIPTIVE STATISTICS

Number (*n*)

The most basic descriptive statistic is the **number**, represented by the letter *n*. To compute the *n*, simply count the number of elements (numbers) in the sample; in this case, there are 10 elements: 24 is the first, 25 is the second, 31 is the third, . . . 24 (at the end) is the tenth, so *n* = 10.

The lowercase *n* is the number of elements in a sample, whereas the uppercase *N* is the number of elements in the (whole) population. SPSS output reports always use the capital *N*. Because it is rare to be processing a data set consisting of an entire population, it is considered good practice to use the lowercase *n* in your documentation, as such: *n(Age) = 10*.

Mean (M)

In statistical language, the *average* is referred to as the **mean**. The calculation for the mean is the same as the average: Add up all the numbers and then divide that amount by the total amount of numbers involved (*n* = 10):

Mean(Age) = (24 + 25 + 31 + 19 + 27 + 20 + 28 + 23 + 26 + 24) ÷ 10

Mean(Age) = 247 ÷ 10

Mean(Age) = 24.7

M(Age) = 24.7

The abbreviation for the mean of a sample is **M**. Occasionally, the mean for a population is represented with lowercase Greek letter μ (pronounced *myoo*) or as the variable with a horizontal bar over it; hence, the mean may be documented as such:

M(Age) = 24.7

μ(Age) = 24.7

$\overline{\text{Age}}$ = 24.7

For consistency throughout the rest of this text, the mean will be documented using the more common *M(Age) = 24.7* or *Age (M = 24.7)* style.

Median

The **median** is the middle value of a variable. Think of the term *median* in terms of a street—the median is in the middle; it splits the street in half. To find the median, arrange the data in the variable from lowest to highest and then select the middle value(s). In smaller data sets, the mean can be altered substantially by outlier scores—scores that are unexpectedly high or low. In such instances, the median can provide a more stable indicator of the central value than the mean.

When the *n* is even, as in the data set below (*n* = 10), there are two middle numbers: 24 and 25. The median is the mean of these two middle numbers:

19, 20, 23, 24, 24, 25, 26, 27, 28, 31

Median(Age) = (24 + 25) ÷ 2

Median(Age) = (49) ÷ 2

Median(Age) = 24.5

When the *n* is odd, as in this small data set below (*n* = 5), there is (only) one middle number. Hence, the median is simply the (one) middle number: 86.

6, 24, 86, 91, 99

Because the median is the center value in a variable, it splits the data set in half; half of the values are below the median, and the other half of the values are above the median.

Mode

The **mode** is the most common number in the data set. Notice that *mode* and *most* share the first two letters. In this case, we see that each number in this data set is present only once, except for 24, which occurs twice, and hence, the mode is 24.

19, 20, 23, (24, 24) 25, 26, 27, 28, 31

It is possible for a data set to have more than one mode. The example below has two modes: 24 and 31 because both have the most (there are two 24s and two 31s; all the other numbers appear just once). Such a variable would be referred to as *bimodal,* meaning two modes.

19, 20, 23, (24, 24) 25, 26, 27, 28, (31, 31)

Although it is relatively rare, a variable may have more than two modes, which would be referred to as **multimodal**.

When SPSS detects more than one mode within a variable, it only reports the lowest one and provides a footnote indicating that there is more than one mode.

The mean, the median, and the mode are referred to as *measures of central tendency,* as they suggest the *center point* of the variable, where most of the data typically resides. Usually, the mean is exhibited as the best representation of the central values within a variable. In cases where the *n* is relatively low, the mean can be unstable, in that one or several outliers (extremely low or high values) can radically influence the mean. In these cases, the median is typically considered more stable as it is less vulnerable to the presence of such outliers. The mode is generally of interest, as it indicates the most frequent value (score) within a variable.

Standard Deviation (SD)

The **standard deviation (SD)** indicates the dispersion of the numbers within a variable. If a variable contains numbers that are fairly similar to each other, this produces a low(er) standard deviation; conversely, if there is more variety in the numbers, this renders a high(er) standard deviation.

Take a look at Figure 3.1. First, notice that the three people in Group A are all around the same height (67", 68", and 67"); their heights are just slightly above or below the mean (M = 67.33). Statistically speaking, their heights do not *deviate* much from the mean; hence, this group produces a low(er) standard deviation (SD = .577).

Now, focus on the three people in Group B; notice that they have very diverse heights (86", 45", and 71"); their heights are fairly far apart from each other—substantially above or below the mean (M = 67.33). Statistically speaking, their heights deviate much more from the mean, producing a high(er) standard deviation (SD = 20.744)—more than 35 times the standard deviation for Group A (SD = .577).

Figure 3.1   Standard deviation (SD) illustrated: Low(er) diversity (Group A) renders lower standard deviation; higher diversity (Group B) renders high(er) standard deviation.

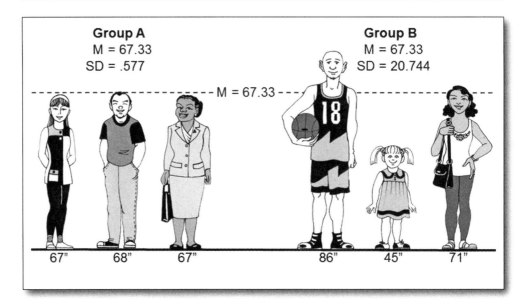

For clarity, the heights for Groups A and B have been set to produce the same means (M = 67.33). The point is, if all we had was the mean for each group, we might get the (wrong) impression that the heights in Group A are just like the heights in Group B. The standard deviation statistic tells us if the numbers contained within a variable deviate a little from the mean, as in Group A, wherein the heights are fairly similar to the mean (and each other), or if the numbers deviate more from the mean (and each other), as in Group B, wherein the heights are more different from each other.

In statistical reporting, the standard deviation is often presented with the mean as such: *M = 67.33, SD = .577,* or *M = 67.33 (.577).*

Variance

The **variance** is simply the standard deviation squared. For example, we will calculate the variance of the heights for Group B, where SD = 20.774:

$$\text{Variance(Height)} = (\text{Standard deviation[Height]})^2$$

$$\text{Variance(Height)} = 20.774^2$$

$$\text{Variance(Height)} = 20.774 \times 20.774$$

$$\text{Variance(Height)} = 431.559$$

The variance is seldom included in statistical reports. It is primarily used as a term within other statistical formulas.

Minimum

The **minimum** is the smallest number in a variable. In the data set below, the minimum is 19.

$$\textcircled{19}\ 20, 23, 24, 24, 25, 26, 27, 28, 31$$

Maximum

The **maximum** is the largest number in a variable. In the data set below, the maximum is 31.

$$19, 20, 23, 24, 24, 25, 26, 27, 28, \textcircled{31}$$

Identifying the minimum and maximum values has some utility, but try not to bring inappropriate suppositions to your interpretation of such figures—bigger is not necessarily better. The meaning of the minimum and maximum values depends on the nature of the variable. For example, high bowling scores are good, while low golf scores are good, and high (or low) phone numbers are neither good nor bad.

Range

The **range** is the span of the data set; the formula for the range is *maximum – minimum*. In the data set below, we would calculate: 31 – 19 = 12; the range is 12 (years).

$$\textcircled{19}\ 20, 23, 24, 24, 25, 26, 27, 28, \textcircled{31}$$

SPSS—LOADING AN SPSS DATA FILE

For clarity, the examples used thus far have involved only 10 data items ($n = 10$). Now it is time to use SPSS to process descriptive statistics using the entire data set consisting of 50 records and both variables (*Gender* and *Age*).
   Run SPSS.

DATA SET

Use the *Open Data Document* icon (Figure 3.2) to load the SPSS data file: **Ch 03 – Example 01 – Descriptive Statistics.sav**.

Codebook

Variable:	Gender
Definition:	Gender of participant
Type:	Categorical (1 = Female, 2 = Male)

Variable:	Age
Definition:	Age of participant
Type:	Continuous

Figure 3.2 *Open Data Document icon.*

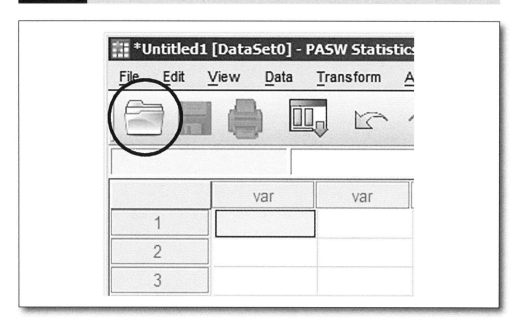

 TEST RUN

 SPSS—DESCRIPTIVE STATISTICS: CONTINUOUS VARIABLES (AGE)

There are two types of variables in this SPSS file: *Age* is a continuous variable, and *Gender* is a categorical variable. In this section, we will process descriptive statistics for the continuous variable (*Age*). Later in this chapter, we will process the categorical variable (*Gender*).

1. After loading the data, click on *Analyze, Descriptive Statistics, Frequencies* (Figure 3.3).

Figure 3.3 Running descriptive statistics report; click on *Analyze, Descriptive Statistics, Frequencies.*

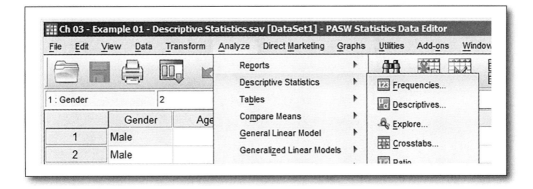

2. SPSS will then prompt you to select the variable(s) that you would like to process. Move the *Age* variable to the *Variable(s)* window (Figure 3.4).

Figure 3.4 Move the variable(s) to be analyzed (*Age*) from the left window to the right *Variable(s)* window.

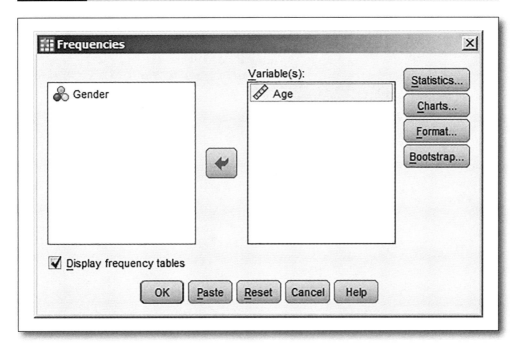

3. Click on the *Statistics* button.

Figure 3.5   *Frequencies: Statistics* menu.

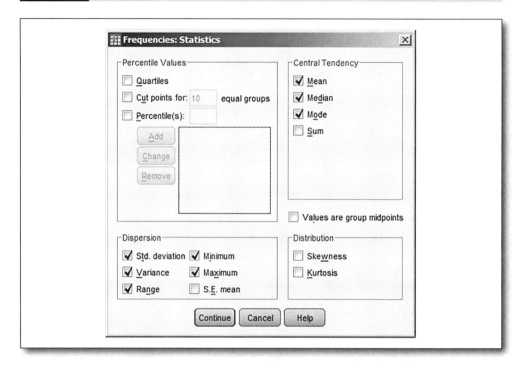

4. Select the descriptive statistics indicated by the checkboxes (Figure 3.5): *Mean, Median, Mode, Std. deviation, Variance, Range, Minimum*, and *Maximum*.

5. Click on the *Continue* button. This will take you back to the *Frequencies* menu (Figure 3.4).

6. On the *Frequencies* menu (Figure 3.4), click on the *Charts* button.

7. Select *Histograms* and *Show normal curve on histogram* (Figure 3.6).

8. Click on the *Continue* button. This will take you back to the *Frequencies* menu (Figure 3.4).

9. Click on the *OK* button on the *Frequencies* menu; this tells SPSS to process the Frequencies report based on the parameters that you just specified. SPSS should produce this report in under a minute.

Statistics Tables

The *Statistics* table (Table 3.2) shows the summary statistical results as discussed earlier.

Figure 3.6   *Frequencies: Charts* menu; select *Histograms* and *Show normal curve on histogram.*

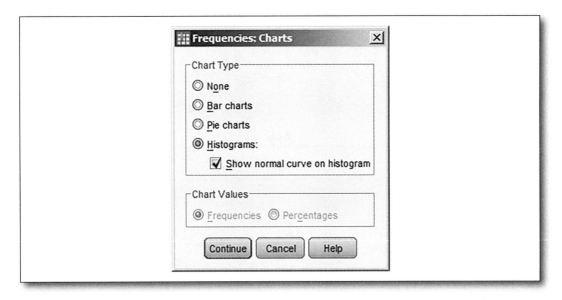

Table 3.2   *Statistics* table showing summary statistics for *Age*.

Statistics

Age

N	Valid	50
	Missing	0
Mean		24.00
Median		24.00
Mode		25
Std. Deviation		2.857
Variance		8.163
Range		13
Minimum		18
Maximum		31
Sum		1200

The report also includes the frequency of each value in the *Age* variable (Table 3.3). Focus on Columns 1 and 2 of this table, which show that the numbers 18, 19, 20, and 21 each occur twice in the data set; 22 and 23 each occur six times; 24 occurs eight times; 25 occurs nine times; and so on.

Table 3.3 *Frequency Statistics* table showing the frequency of each value in the *Age* variable.

Age				
		Frequency	Percent	Valid Percent	Cumulative Percent
Valid	18	2	4.0	4.0	4.0
	19	2	4.0	4.0	8.0
	20	2	4.0	4.0	12.0
	21	2	4.0	4.0	16.0
	22	6	12.0	12.0	28.0
	23	6	12.0	12.0	40.0
	24	8	16.0	16.0	56.0
	25	9	18.0	18.0	74.0
	26	5	10.0	10.0	84.0
	27	3	6.0	6.0	90.0
	28	2	4.0	4.0	94.0
	29	1	2.0	2.0	96.0
	30	1	2.0	2.0	98.0
	31	1	2.0	2.0	100.0
	Total	50	100.0	100.0	

Histogram With Normal Curve

The next part of this report is the histogram of the *Age* variable, using a **histogram with a normal curve**. The histogram is simply a graphical representation of the frequency statistics. Basically, Figure 3.7 is a picture of the data in Table 3.3. Notice that the first four bars are each two units tall; this is because the first four numbers in the table (18, 19, 20, and 21) each occur two times in the data set. Notice that the tallest bar is nine units tall; this is because the number 25 occurs nine times in the data set.

The histogram provides further insight into the (descriptive) characteristics of a continuous variable—a picture is indeed worth a thousand words.

In addition to the bars, which constitute the histogram, it is also traditional to include a **normal curve**, sometimes referred to as a "bell curve" because of its shape. The normal

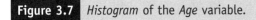

Figure 3.7 *Histogram* of the *Age* variable.

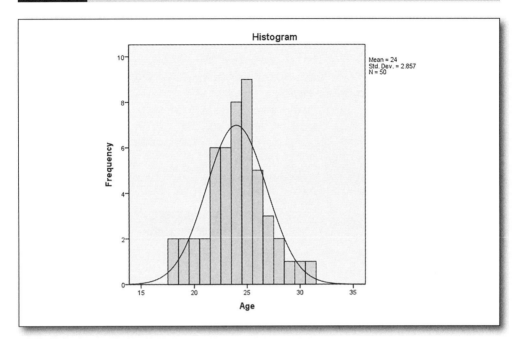

curve is derived from the same source data as the bar chart; you can think of this normal curve as the smoothed-out version of the bar chart. More often than not, we see this sort of symmetrical (bell-shaped) distribution in continuous variables. Most of the values are gathered toward the middle, with the frequencies progressively dropping off as the values depart above or below the mean.

For example, if we were to measure the height of 100 randomly selected people, we would expect to find that most people are moderate height (which would constitute the tallness in the middle of the normal curve). We would also expect to find a few exceptionally short people and about the same amount of exceptionally tall people, which would account for the tapering off seen on the left and right tails of the normal curve. This phenomenon of the bell-shaped distribution is so common that it is referred to as a *normal distribution*, as represented by the normal curve. When inspecting a histogram for normality, it is expected that the bars may have some jagged steps from bar to bar; however, to properly assess a variable for normality, our focus is on the symmetry of the normal curve more so than the bars. If we were to slice a proper normal curve vertically down the middle, the left half of the normal curve should resemble a mirror image of the right half.

Skewed Distribution

As with any rule, there are exceptions; not all histograms produce normally shaped curves. Depending on the distribution of the data within the variable, the histogram may be **skewed**, meaning that the distribution is shifted to one side or the other, as shown in Figures 4.8 and 4.9.

In Figure 3.8, we see that most of the data are on the right, between about 150 and 300, but there is a small scattering of lower values (under 100), forcing the left tail of the curve to be extended out. These few low values that substantially depart from the majority of the data are referred to as *outliers*. Typically, outliers become apparent when graphing the data. We would say that the histogram in Figure 3.8 has outliers to the left. Hence, it is *skewed left*, or *negatively skewed*.

Outliers can also be positive. Figure 3.9, which is a virtual mirror image of Figure 3.8, shows outliers scattered to the right; this distribution would be referred to as being *skewed right*, or *positively skewed*. The notion of normality of the data distribution will be discussed further in future chapters.

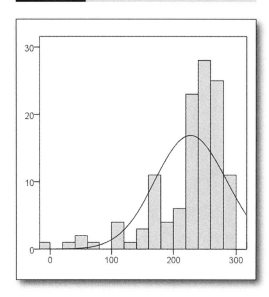

Figure 3.8 Negative (left) skew.

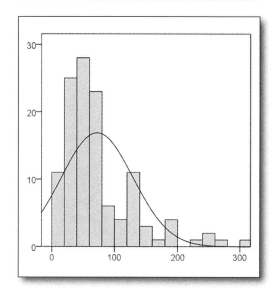

Figure 3.9 Positive (right) skew.

SPSS—DESCRIPTIVE STATISTICS: CATEGORICAL VARIABLES (GENDER)

Descriptive statistics for categorical variables are derived using the same ordering menus as for continuous variables, except you will be specifying different options. Although it is plausible to compute the mode for a categorical variable to determine which is the largest category, it would be inappropriate to compute statistics such as mean, median, maximum, minimum, range, standard deviation, and variance. For example, in this data set, the *Gender* variable is coded as 1 for *Female* and 2 for *Male*; if we ordered the mean for *Gender*, the result would be 1.46, which is essentially meaningless. Furthermore, because the coding designation for this categorical variable is fairly arbitrary, we could have coded the categories for *Gender* as 14 for *Females* and 83 for *Males*, in which case, instead of 1.46, the mean for *Gender* would now be 45.74, which is equally meaningless.

1. Click on *Analyze, Descriptive Statistics, Frequencies* (Figure 3.10).

Figure 3.10 Running descriptive statistics report; click on *Analyze, Descriptive Statistics, Frequencies.*

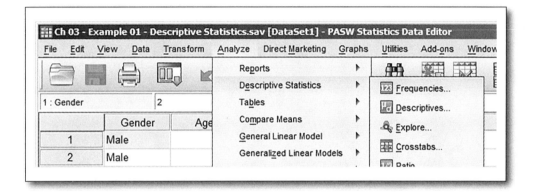

2. First, click on *Reset*; this will clear the parameters on the submenus that you specified when running the summary statistics for *Age*.

3. Next, move the *Gender* variable from the left window to the right *Variable(s)* window (Figure 3.11).

4. Click on the *Charts* button.

5. On the *Frequencies: Charts* menu, there are two viable options for categorical variables: *Bar charts* or *Pie charts* (Figure 3.12). In statistics, bar charts are used more often than pie charts. You can also choose to represent the numbers as *frequencies* (the actual counts) or *percentages*. For this example, select *Frequencies*.

6. Click on the *Continue* button; this will return you to the *Frequencies* menu.

7. Click on the *OK* button on the *Frequencies* menu; this tells SPSS to process the *Frequencies* report based on the parameters that you just specified.

Figure 3.11 Click on the *Reset* button to clear the prior options, and then move the variable(s) to be analyzed (*Gender*) from the left window to the right *Variable(s)* window.

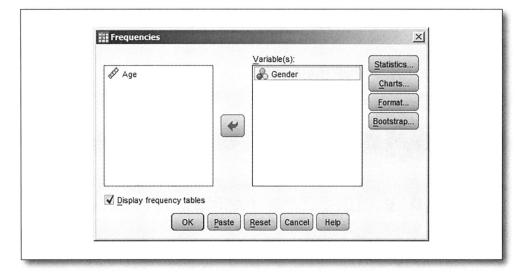

Figure 3.12 *Frequencies: Charts* menu; select *Bar charts* and *Frequencies.* After running this analysis as specified, feel free to return to this menu to rerun this analysis using different settings (e.g., *Bar charts* with *Percentages, Pie charts*).

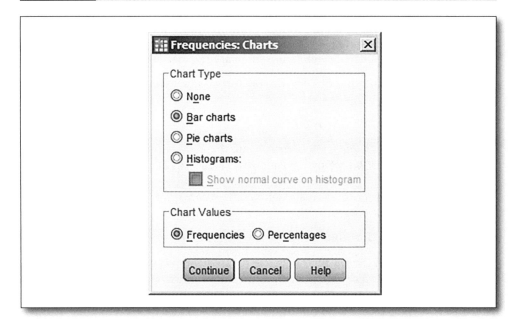

Frequency Statistics Tables

The first part of this frequency report shows the overall n (N) – the total number of entries (records) in the variable: 50 valid records and 0 missing as shown (Table 3.4).

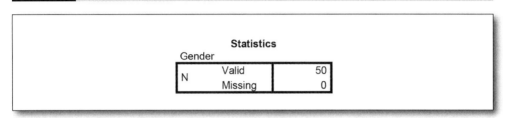

Table 3.4 Descriptive statistics for *Gender*: n, Valid and Missing.

Statistics

Gender

N		
	Valid	50
	Missing	0

The next part of the report provides more detailed information regarding the N, indicating the frequency (actual number) and percent for each category within the *Gender* variable (*Female* and *Male*), as shown in Table 3.5.

Table 3.5 Descriptive statistics for *Gender*: *Frequency* and *Percent*.

Gender

		Frequency	Percent	Valid Percent	Cumulative Percent
Valid	Female	27	54.0	54.0	54.0
	Male	23	46.0	46.0	100.0
	Total	50	100.0	100.0	

Incidentally, to calculate the percent, divide the frequency for the category by the (valid) n and multiply by 100, so for *Female*, it would be $(27 \div 50) \times 100 = 54\%$.

Percentage Formula

(Part ÷ Total) × 100

(27 ÷ 50) × 100

.54 × 100

54%

Bar Chart

Last, the report provides a bar chart representing the two *Gender* categories (*Female* and *Male*) (Figure 3.13).

Figure 3.13   *Bar chart* of the *Gender* variable.

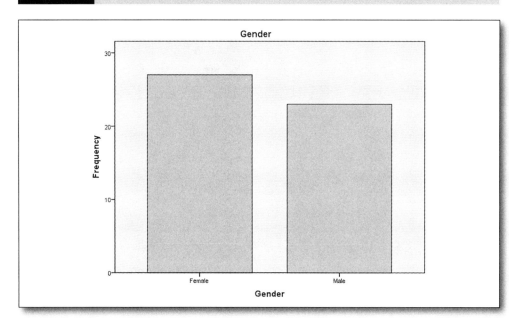

 SPSS—DESCRIPTIVE STATISTICS: CONTINUOUS VARIABLES (AGE) SELECT BY CATEGORICAL VARIABLE (GENDER)—FEMALES ONLY

So far, we have processed the continuous variable, *Age*, with both genders combined, but it is also possible to produce separate reports for *Females* only and *Males* only, showing the summary statistics and histograms for each. This technique not only satisfies curiosity about what is going on in each category, but it will also be essential for running the *pretest checklist* reports that will be covered in future chapters.

We will begin with processing the *Age* summary statistics for *Females* only, and then we will repeat the process selecting data for *Males* only. The *Select Cases* option allows you to efficiently specify which cases (rows of data, also known as *records*) you would like to process; SPSS will temporarily ignore all other cases, and they will not be included in any statistical computations until you choose to reselect them.

The following procedure will select only the cases where *Gender* = 1 (*Female*):

1. Click on the *Select Cases* icon (Figure 3.14).

Figure 3.14 The *Select Cases* icon.

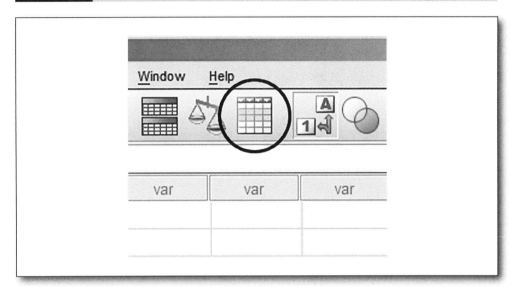

2. On the *Select Cases* menu (Figure 3.15), the default selection is *All cases*. Click on *If condition is satisfied*; then click on the *If* button.

Figure 3.15 The *Select Cases* menu (top only).

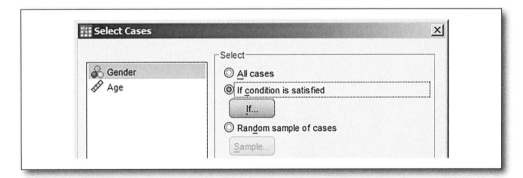

3. This will bring you to the *Select Cases: If* menu (Figure 3.16).

4. Remember: SPSS handles categorical variables as numbers; earlier, we established that for the categorical variable *Gender*, 1 = *Female* and 2 = *Male*. Since we want statistical reports on *Females* only, we enter the inclusion criteria, *Gender = 1*, in the big box at the top of the menu. Then click on the *Continue* button.

Figure 3.16 The *Select Cases: If* menu (top only).

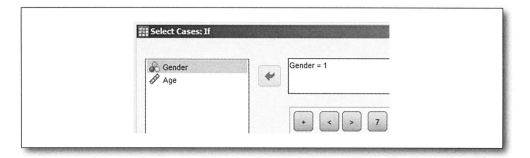

5. This will return you to the *Select Cases* menu. Click on the *OK* button, and the system will process your selection criteria.

6. Switch back to the *Data View* screen. First, notice that the record (row) numbers for each *Male* is slashed out (Figure 3.17). You can think of all the data in the slashed-out rows as being in a sort of penalty box—they are still part of the data set, but they cannot play in any of the rounds of analyses until they are reselected; however, you can still edit such data.

Figure 3.17 The *Data View* screen after *Select Cases (Gender = 1)* has been executed (section only).

	Gender	Age	filter_$	var
1	Male	24	Not Selected	
2	Male	25	Not Selected	
3	Male	31	Not Selected	
4	Female	19	Selected	
5	Female	27	Selected	
6	Male	20	Not Selected	
7	Male	28	Not Selected	
8	Female	23	Selected	
9	Male	26	Not Selected	
10	Male	24	Not Selected	

*Ch 03 - Example 01 - Descriptive Statistics.sav [DataSet1] - PASW Sta

File Edit View Data Transform Analyze Direct Marketing Graphs

1 : Gender   2

Notice that SPSS has created the temporary variable *filter_$* in the last column, which corresponds to the slashes in each row. If you click on the *Value Labels* icon or go to the *Variable View* screen, you will see that the *filter_$* variable contains two categories: *0 = Not Selected* and *1 = Selected*.

Because we selected only cases where *Gender = 1*, this means that if we were to (re)run the descriptive statistics, the summary statistics and histogram would reflect Females only, as opposed to the earlier report that combined Females and Males.

7. Rerun the analysis for the *Age* variable using the procedure (go to the ★ icon on page 52). The resulting statistical report should resemble the data shown in Table 3.6.

Table 3.6 *Frequency Statistics* table showing summary statistics for *Age* for Females only.

Statistics

Age

N	Valid	27
	Missing	0
Mean		23.19
Median		23.00
Mode		23
Std. Deviation		2.543
Variance		6.464
Range		10
Minimum		18
Maximum		28

8. Notice that the *N* has changed from 50, which included both *Females* and *Males*, to 27, which is *Females* only. Compared to the first report, all of the other statistics have changed as well. Continuing our analysis of the *Females* only, observe the frequency statistics (Table 3.7) and corresponding histogram (Figure 3.18).

9. As you can see, there is a lot to be learned by selecting the data and examining statistics pertaining to *Females* only. The next step is to run the same reports for *Males* only.

10. Begin the *Males* only analysis by selecting only the cases that pertain to males only; go to the ★ icon on page 62, except when you get to **Step 4,** instead of specifying *Gender = 1*, change that to *Gender = 2* (remember, we established *Gender* as *1* for *Female* and *2* for *Male*).

Table 3.7   *Frequency Statistics* table showing the frequency of each value in the *Age* variable for *Females* only.

Age

		Frequency	Percent	Valid Percent	Cumulative Percent
Valid	18	1	3.7	3.7	3.7
	19	2	7.4	7.4	11.1
	20	1	3.7	3.7	14.8
	21	2	7.4	7.4	22.2
	22	4	14.8	14.8	37.0
	23	5	18.5	18.5	55.6
	24	4	14.8	14.8	70.4
	25	3	11.1	11.1	81.5
	26	2	7.4	7.4	88.9
	27	2	7.4	7.4	96.3
	28	1	3.7	3.7	100.0
	Total	27	100.0	100.0	

Figure 3.18   Histogram of the *Age* variable for *Females* only.

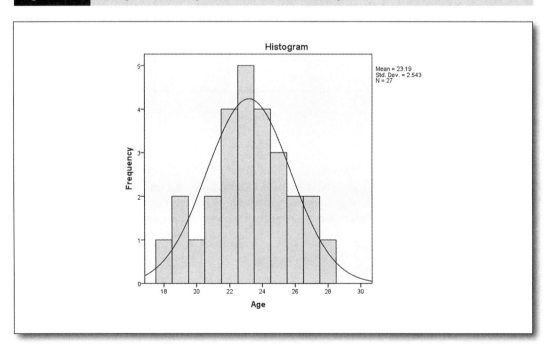

11. Upon rerunning the data for *Males*, notice that the slashes, *filter_$*, and output reports have all changed to reflect *Males* only (see Table 3.8, Table 3.9, and Figure 3.19).

Table 3.8 *Frequency Statistics* table showing summary statistics for *Age* for *Males* only.

Statistics

Age

N	Valid	23
	Missing	0
Mean		24.96
Median		25.00
Mode		25
Std. Deviation		2.962
Variance		8.771
Range		13
Minimum		18
Maximum		31

Table 3.9 *Frequency Statistics* table showing the frequency of each value in the *Age* variable for *Males* only.

Age

		Frequency	Percent	Valid Percent	Cumulative Percent
Valid	18	1	4.3	4.3	4.3
	20	1	4.3	4.3	8.7
	22	2	8.7	8.7	17.4
	23	1	4.3	4.3	21.7
	24	4	17.4	17.4	39.1
	25	6	26.1	26.1	65.2
	26	3	13.0	13.0	78.3
	27	1	4.3	4.3	82.6
	28	1	4.3	4.3	87.0
	29	1	4.3	4.3	91.3
	30	1	4.3	4.3	95.7
	31	1	4.3	4.3	100.0
	Total	23	100.0	100.0	

Figure 3.19 Histogram of the *Age* variable for *Males* only.

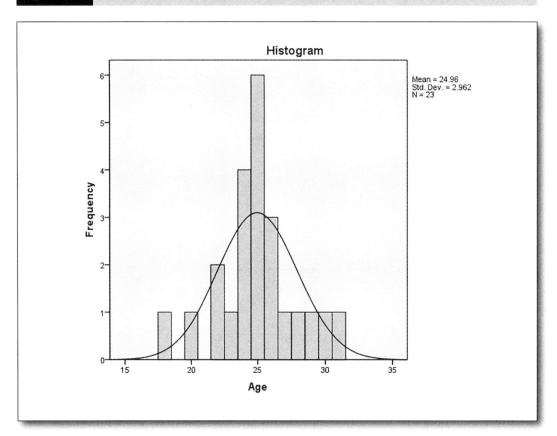

 SPSS—(RE)SELECTING ALL VARIABLES

At this point, we have run three sets of descriptive statistics on *Age*: (1) all records, (2) *Females* only, and (3) *Males* only. Now, suppose we want to perform further analyses using the entire data set again. There are several ways to reactivate all of the slashed-out records:

- On the *Data View* screen, click on the column header *filter_$* (which will highlight the whole column) and press the *Delete* key.
- On the *Variable View* screen, click on the corresponding row number—in this case, Row 3 (which will highlight the whole row)—and press the *Delete* key.
- Click on the *Select Cases* icon; then click on the *All Cases* button. Finally, click on the *OK* button.

GOOD COMMON SENSE

Although SPSS is proficient at processing statistical data, keep in mind that the program has no real intelligence per se—it just pushes the numbers through the behind-the-scenes formulas using the parameters that you specify. As such, it is up to you to enter the data accurately and make intelligent processing selections.

In the examples detailed in this chapter, we ordered a variety of statistical analyses on the *Age* variable, which makes sense, knowing the mean age can be useful. Larger databases are likely to contain other numeric variables such as patient ID numbers, street addresses, phone numbers, serial numbers, license numbers, and so on. Technically, you could order SPSS to compute descriptive statistics on such variables. SPSS is not bright enough to know that computing the mean for a series of phone numbers makes no sense; SPSS, or any other statistical processing software, would mindlessly process the variable and provide you with an average phone number, which would be useless. In summary, it is up to you to proceed mindfully when using any such software.

Key Concepts

- Descriptive statistics

  - Number (n)
  - Mean (M)
  - Median
  - Mode
  - Standard deviation (SD)
  - Variance
  - Minimum
  - Maximum
  - Range

- Central Tendency
- Loading SPSS data files

  - Histogram
  - Normal curve

- Skew

  - Negative (left) skew
  - Positive (right) skew

- Outliers
- Bar chart
- Pie chart
- Select cases
- Good common sense

Practice Exercises

Use the prepared SPSS data sets (download from **study.sagepub.com/intermediatestats**). Load the specified data sets; then process and document your findings for each exercise.

Exercise 3.1

A survey was conducted in Professor Lamm's class and Professor Milner's class. The question that students responded to is, "How many siblings do you have?"

Data set: **Ch 03 – Exercise 01.sav**

Codebook

Variable:	Class
Definition:	Class designation
Type:	Categorical (1 = Prof. Lamm, 2 = Prof. Milner)

Variable:	Siblings
Definition:	Number of siblings
Type:	Continuous

a. Run descriptive statistics and a histogram with a normal curve for Siblings for the whole data set.

b. Run descriptive statistics and a bar chart for Class for the whole data set.

c. Run descriptive statistics and a histogram with a normal curve for Siblings for members of Professor Lamm's class only.

d. Run descriptive statistics and a histogram with a normal curve for Siblings for members of Professor Milner's class only.

Exercise 3.2

While waiting in line to donate blood, donors were asked, "How many times have you donated before?" The researcher recorded their gender and number of prior donations.

Data set: **Ch 03 – Exercise 02.sav**

Codebook

Variable:	Gender
Definition:	Gender
Type:	Categorical (1 = Female, 2 = Male)

Variable:	Donated
Definition:	Total number of blood donations given before today
Type:	Continuous

a. Run descriptive statistics and a histogram with a normal curve for Donated for the whole data set.

b. Run descriptive statistics and a bar chart for Gender for the whole data set.

c. Run descriptive statistics and a histogram with a normal curve for Donated for Females only.

d. Run descriptive statistics and a histogram with a normal curve for Donated for Males only.

Exercise 3.3

You want to know if typing proficiency is associated with better spelling skills. You administer a spelling test consisting of 20 words to the students in a classroom. At the bottom of the sheet, there is a question: Can you type accurately without looking at the keyboard?

Data set: **Ch 03 – Exercise 03.sav**

Codebook

Variable:	Looker
Definition:	Does the student look at the keyboard to type?
Type:	Categorical (1 = Looks at keyboard, 2 = Doesn't look at keyboard)

Variable:	Spelling
Definition:	Score on spelling test
Type	Continuous

a. Run descriptive statistics and a histogram with a normal curve for Spelling for the whole data set.

b. Run descriptive statistics and a bar chart for Looker for the whole data set.

c. Run descriptive statistics and a histogram with a normal curve for Spelling for "Looks at keyboard" only.

d. Run descriptive statistics and a histogram with a normal curve for Spelling for "Doesn't look at keyboard" only.

Exercise 3.4

You are interested in the length of time it takes for individuals to complete their transaction(s) at an ATM. You use a stopwatch to record your unobtrusive observations and gather two pieces of information on each person: gender and the length of his or her ATM session (in seconds).

Data set: **Ch 03 – Exercise 04.sav**

Codebook

Variable:	Gender
Definition:	Gender
Type:	Categorical (1 = Female, 2 = Male)

Variable:	ATMsec
Definition:	Number of seconds spent at ATM
Type:	Continuous

a. Run descriptive statistics and a histogram with a normal curve for ATMsec for the whole data set.

b. Run descriptive statistics and a bar chart for Gender for the whole data set.

c. Run descriptive statistics and a histogram with a normal curve for ATMsec for Female only.

d. Run descriptive statistics and a histogram with a normal curve for ATMsec for Male only.

Exercise 3.5

You are interested in finding out how many units students are enrolled in. You conduct a survey of 40 students and record two pieces of information: the degree (level) the student is working on (bachelor's, master's, doctorate) and total number of units he or she is taking this term.

Data set: **Ch 03 – Exercise 05.sav**

Codebook

Variable:	Degree
Definition:	Highest degree the person has
Type:	Categorical (1 = Bachelor's, 2 = Master's, 3 = Doctorate)

Variable:	Units
Definition:	Current number of enrolled units
Type:	Continuous

a. Run descriptive statistics and a histogram with a normal curve for Units for the whole data set.

b. Run descriptive statistics and a bar chart for Degree for the whole data set.

c. Run descriptive statistics and a histogram with a normal curve for Units for Bachelor's degree only.

 d. Run descriptive statistics and a histogram with a normal curve for Units for Master's degree only.

 e. Run descriptive statistics and a histogram with a normal curve for Units for Doctorate only.

Exercise 3.6

You stand at a register in a hospital cafeteria; for each patron, you gather two pieces of information: professional role (nurse, doctor, other), as indicated on his or her badge, and the amount of his or her bill (as shown on the register).

Data set: **Ch 03 – Exercise 06.sav**

Codebook

Variable:	ProfRole
Definition:	Professional role
Type:	Categorical (1 = Nurse, 2 = Doctor, 3 = Other)

Variable:	Bill
Definition:	Total as shown on the register
Type:	Continuous

 a. Run descriptive statistics and a histogram with a normal curve for Bill for the whole data set.

 b. Run descriptive statistics and a bar chart for ProfRole for the whole data set.

 c. Run descriptive statistics and a histogram with a normal curve for Bill for Nurse only.

 d. Run descriptive statistics and a histogram with a normal curve for Bill for Doctor only.

 e. Run descriptive statistics and a histogram with a normal curve for Bill for Other only.

Exercise 3.7

You recruit a group of people who agree to report their total email counts (sent + received) for 30 days. Each participant also completed a survey regarding his or her employment status (Full-time, Part-time, Unemployed).

Data set: **Ch 03 – Exercise 07.sav**

Codebook

Variable:	Employ
Definition:	Employment status
Type:	Categorical (1 = Full-time, 2 = Part-time, 3 = Unemployed).

Variable: Emails

Definition: Total number of emails sent and received for 30 days

Type: Continuous

a. Run descriptive statistics and a histogram with a normal curve for Emails for the whole data set.

b. Run descriptive statistics and a bar chart for Employ for the whole data set.

c. Run descriptive statistics and a histogram with a normal curve for Emails for Full-time only.

d. Run descriptive statistics and a histogram with a normal curve for Emails for Part-time only.

e. Run descriptive statistics and a histogram with a normal curve for Emails for Unemployed only.

Exercise 3.8

The members of an exercise walking group agree to partake in your study; you randomly give half of the group walking music in a major key, and the others are given walking music in a minor key. Each participant can walk as often and for as long as he or she likes. The participants will record and submit the total number of minutes that they walked in a week.

Data set: **Ch 03 – Exercise 08.sav**

Codebook

Variable: MusicKey

Definition: Music key

Type: Categorical (1 = Major, 2 = Minor)

Variable: MinWalk

Definition: Total number of minutes walked

Type: Continuous

a. Run descriptive statistics and a histogram with a normal curve for MinWalk for the whole data set.

b. Run descriptive statistics and a bar chart for MusicKey for the whole data set.

c. Run descriptive statistics and a histogram with a normal curve for MinWalk for Major only.

d. Run descriptive statistics and a histogram with a normal curve for MinWalk for Minor only.

Exercise 3.9

The administrator of a two-ward hospital randomly selects one ward wherein the nurses will be assigned to tend to two patients each; nurses in the other ward will tend to four patients each. Over the course of a month, upon discharge, each patient will complete a nursing care satisfaction survey, which renders a score ranging from 1 to 100 (1 = Very unsatisfied . . . 100 = Very satisfied).

Data set: **Ch 03 – Exercise 09.sav**

Codebook

Variable:	Ward
Definition:	Ward number
Type:	Categorical variable (1 = 2 patients per nurse, 2 = 4 patients per nurse)
Variable	Nsatisfy
Definition:	Patient's nurse satisfaction score
Type:	Continuous

a. Run descriptive statistics and a histogram with a normal curve for Nsatisfy for the whole data set.

b. Run descriptive statistics and a bar chart for Ward for the whole data set.

c. Run descriptive statistics and a histogram with normal curve for Nsatisfy for the 2 patients per nurse ward only.

d. Run descriptive statistics and a histogram with a normal curve for Nsatisfy for the 4 patients per nurse ward only.

Exercise 3.10

To determine if dancing enhances mood, you recruit 100 voluntary participants. You randomly select 50 and give them seven free dance lessons; the other 50 get no dance lessons. After the seventh class, you administer the Acme Happiness Scale Survey (AHSS) to all 100 individuals; this survey renders a score ranging from 1 to 30 (1 = Extremely unhappy . . . 30 = Extremely happy).

Data set: **Ch 03 – Exercise 10.sav**

Codebook

Variable:	Dance
Definition:	Dance class membership status
Type:	Categorical (1 = Dancer, 2 = Nondancer)

Variable:	AHSS
Definition:	Score on Acme Happiness Scale Survey
Type:	Continuous (1 = Extremely unhappy . . . 30 = Extremely happy)

a. Run descriptive statistics and a histogram with a normal curve for AHSS for the whole data set.

b. Run descriptive statistics and a bar chart for Dance for the whole data set.

c. Run descriptive statistics and a histogram with a normal curve for AHSS for the Dancers only.

d. Run descriptive statistics and a histogram with a normal curve for AHSS for the Nondancers only.

Measuring Differences Between Groups

These chapters provide tests for detecting differences between groups that involve continuous variables.

Chapter 4: *t* Test and Mann-Whitney *U* Test shows how the *t* test is used in two-group designs (e.g., control vs. treatment) to detect if one group significantly outperformed the other. In the event that the data are not fully suitable to run a *t* test, the Mann-Whitney *U* test provides an alternative.

Chapter 5: ANOVA and Kruskal-Wallis Test illustrates how the ANOVA is similar to the *t* test, but it is capable of processing *more than two groups*. In the event that the data are not fully suitable to run an ANOVA, the Kruskal-Wallis test provides an alternative.

Chapter 6: ANCOVA is similar to ANOVA, but it is capable of including a *covariate*, which adjusts the results to account for the influence of a potentially identified confounding variable.

Chapter 7: MANOVA is similar to ANOVA, but it is capable of processing *more than one* outcome (dependent) variable.

C H A P T E R   4

t Test and
Mann-Whitney *U* Test

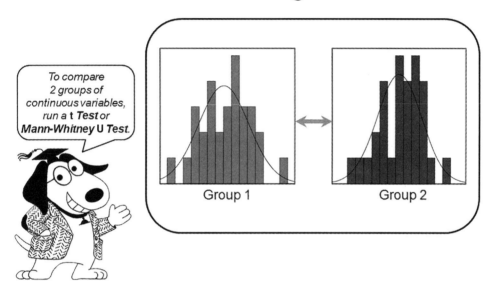

To compare
2 groups of
continuous variables,
run a t **Test** or
Mann-Whitney **U Test**.

Group 1   Group 2

The difference between a violin and a viola is that a viola burns longer.

—Victor Borge

Learning Objectives

Upon completing this chapter, you will be able to do the following:

- Determine when it is appropriate to run a *t* test.
- Verify that the data meet the criteria for *t* test processing: normality, *n*, and homogeneity of variance.
- Order a *t* test.
- Interpret the test results.

(Continued)

(Continued)

- Comprehend the α and p value.
- Resolve the hypotheses.
- Know when and how to run and interpret the Mann-Whitney U test.
- Write an appropriate abstract.
- Understand the implications of Type I and Type II errors.
- Apply techniques for reducing the likelihood of committing Type I and Type II errors.

NOTE: From here forward, the M character will be used to symbolize the mean.

WHEN TO USE THIS STATISTIC

Guidelines for Selecting the *t* Test and Mann-Whitney *U* Test

Overview: This statistic is for a two-group design to determine if one group outperformed another.

Variables: This statistic requires two variables for each record: (1) a categorical variable to designate the group, and (2) a continuous variable to contain the outcome score.

Results: Among those diagnosed with anxiety, we discovered that those who received 30 minutes of pet therapy had a statistically significantly lower mean pulse rate (M = 79.9) than those in the control group (M = 84.1), suggesting that pet therapy was effective ($p = .009$, $\alpha = .05$).

VIDEOS

The videos for this chapter are **Ch 04 – t Test.mp4** and **Ch 04 – Mann-Whitney U Test. mp4**. These videos provide overviews of these tests, instructions for carrying out the pretest checklist, run, and interpreting the results of this test using the data set: **Ch 04 – Example 01 – t Test and Mann-Whitney U Test.sav**.

OVERVIEW—*t* TEST

The *t* **test** is one of the most common and versatile statistical tests in the realm of experimental research and survey methodology. The *t* test is used when there are two groups, wherein each group renders a continuous variable for the outcome (e.g., height, age, weight, number of teeth, bank account balance, IQ score, score on a depression assessment instrument, pulse rate, test score, number of crimes, typing speed, etc.).

In the most basic experimental setting, the design consists of two groups: a control group, which gets nothing, a placebo, or treatment as usual, and a treatment group, which gets the innovative intervention that is the focus of the study.

We can compute the mean for each group, and we would not expect the two means to be identical; they would likely be different. The *t* test answers the question, "Is there a statistically significant difference between M(Control) and M(Treatment)?" In other words, the result of the *t* test helps us to determine if one group *substantially* outperformed the other, or if the differences between the means are essentially *incidental*.

In cases where the three pretest criteria are not satisfied for the *t* test, the Mann-Whitney *U* test, which is conceptually similar to the *t* test, is the better option; this alternate test is explained near the end of this chapter.

Example

A research team has recruited a group of individuals who have been diagnosed with acute stress disorder to determine the effectiveness of supplemental nonpharmaceutical treatments for reducing stress: (1) no supplemental therapy or (2) pet therapy with certified therapy dogs.

Research Question

Is pet therapy effective in reducing stress among those diagnosed with acute stress disorder?

Groups

A researcher recruits a total of 60 participants who meet the diagnostic criteria for acute stress disorder. Participants will be scheduled to come to the research center one at a time. Upon arriving, each participant will be assigned to one of two groups on an alternating basis: Those assigned to Group 1 will constitute the control group and will not partake in the pet therapy. Those in Group 2 will be in the treatment group and will receive pet therapy.

Procedure

Each participant will be guided to a room with a comfortable sofa. Those in the control group will be instructed to just sit and relax, and the researcher will return in 30 minutes to measure their pulse rate and dismiss them. Those in the treatment group will be introduced to the therapy dog by name and instructed that the participant may hold the dog in his or her lap, pet the dog on the sofa, brush the dog, or give the dog the allotted treats in whatever combination they wish. After 30 minutes, the researcher will return to the room, measure the participant's pulse rate, and dismiss them. The lower pulse rate would reflect more relaxation.

Hypotheses

The null hypothesis (H_0) is phrased to anticipate that the treatment (encounter with the therapy dog) fails, indicating that on average, participants who had no treatment (in the control group) will have the same mean pulse rate as those who had the pet therapy; in other words, there is no difference between the pulse rates for these two groups. The alternative hypothesis (H_1) states that on the average, one group significantly outperformed the other in terms of pulse rate:

H_0:   There is no difference in pulse rates across the groups.

H_1:   There is a difference in pulse rates across the groups.

Data Set

Use the following data set: **Ch 04 – Example 01 – t Test and Mann-Whitney U test.sav.**

Codebook

Variable:	Group
Definition:	Group assignment
Type:	Categorical (1 = Control, 2 = Pet therapy)

Variable:	Pulse
Definition:	Heartbeats per minute measured 30 minutes after start.
Type:	Continuous

NOTE: In this data set, records (rows) 1 through 30 are for Group 1 (Control), and records 31 through 60 are for Group 2 (Pet therapy). The data are arranged this way just for visual clarity, and the order of the records has no bearing on the statistical results.

If you go to the *Variable View* and open the *Values* menu for the variable *Group*, you will see that the corresponding categorical labels have been assigned: *1* for *Control* and *2* for *Pet therapy* (Figure 4.1).

Figure 4.1   Value labels for a *t* test analysis.

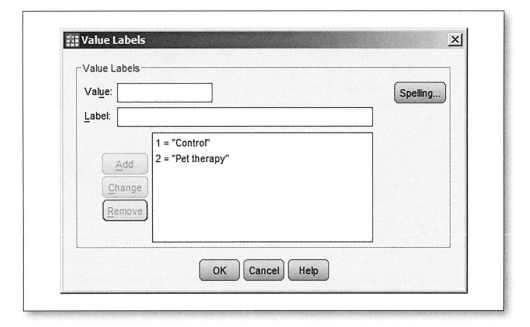

Pretest Checklist

t Test Pretest Checklist

☑ 1. Normality*

☑ 2. *n* quota*

☑ 3. Homogeneity of Variance**

*Run prior to *t* test

**Results produced upon *t* test run

NOTE: If any of the pretest checklist criteria are not satisfied, rerun the analysis using the nonparametric version of this test: the Mann-Whitney *U* test (p. 94).

The statistical **pretest checklist** is akin to looking both ways before you cross the street; certainly you could cross the street without looking, but you would probably wind up in much better shape if you looked first. In terms of statistical tests, certainly you could run the statistical test without tending to the pretest checklist, but you may unknowingly generate misleading findings.

The formulas that compose each statistical test require that the source data meet a unique set of criteria in order for that test to operate properly. These criteria are referred to as *assumptions*—we *assume* that the data meet the criteria specified by the test at hand. Actually, we need to do more than just passively assume that the data are suitable for processing; we need to *actively assess* the source data before proceeding with the test.

When the tests on the pretest checklist (statistical assumptions) are satisfied, we can consider the statistical results to be relatively robust. If there are minor deviations in these criteria, one could still proceed with the analysis, but we would be a bit less confident in the solidity of our findings. In the interest of proper scientific ethics and the principles of full disclosure, it would be appropriate to mention any such (statistical) shortcomings when discussing the results.

In instances where one or more of the specified pretest criteria are substantially not satisfied, the better option is to use the nonparametric version of the test, in this case, the Mann-Whitney *U* test, which was mentioned earlier. This notion pertains to the unique pretest checklists associated with the other tests covered in this text as well.

The pretest criteria for running a *t* test involve checking the data for (1) **normality**, (2) ***n* quota**, and (3) **homogeneity** (pronounced *hoe-moe-juh-nay-it-tee*) **of variance**.

Pretest Checklist Criterion 1—Normality

Checking for normality involves producing a histogram with a normal curve for each of the two groups. In this instance, you would click on the *Select Cases* icon to select the records pertaining to the *Control* group, and the selection criteria would be *Group = 1*. Next, run a histogram (with normal curve) on the variable *Pulse*. Then repeat the process for the *Pet therapy* group (*Group = 2*). For more details on this procedure, please refer to **Chapter 3: Descriptive Statistics**, and the following section: SPSS—Descriptive Statistics: Continuous Variables (Age) Select by Categorical Variable (Gender)—Females Only; see the star (★) icon on page 62.

This will produce two histograms with normal curves—one for *Pulse* in the *Control* group and the other for the *Pulse* in the *Pet therapy* group. The histograms should resemble the graphs shown in Figures 4.2 and 4.3.

As we read these two histograms, set aside the X,Y scales and the possible irregularities among the bars; our attention is instead focused primarily on the shape of the normal curves that are superimposed over the bars. We are looking for normality (symmetry) within each curve. Although the normal curve in Figure 4.2 is shorter and fatter than the normal curve in Figure 4.3, in terms of normality, this is not an issue. The critical thing to observe is that both normal curves are sufficiently symmetrical. In other words, if you

Figure 4.2   Histogram of *Pulse* for Group 1: *Control.*

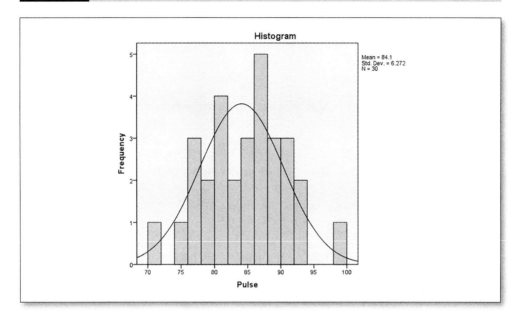

Figure 4.3   Histogram of *Pulse* for Group 2: *Pet therapy.*

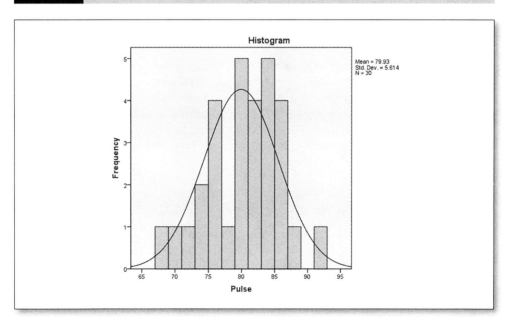

sliced this curve vertically down the middle, the left side would resemble a mirror image of the right side; sometimes this normal curve is aptly referred to by its characteristic shape as a "bell curve." In this example, we see that both curves are symmetrical; there is no notable skew in either curve. Hence, we would say that the criteria of normality are satisfied for both *Control* and *Pet therapy*.

Pretest Checklist Criterion 2—*n* Quota

Technically, you can process a *t* test with an *n* of any size in each group, but when the *n* is at least 30 in each group, the result of the *t* test is considered more robust. With an *n* of at least 30, it is likely that a normal distribution will emerge, however, if you are seeing a normal curve in a smaller data set, then the *n* quota criterion is less of an issue. The histograms with normal curves (Figures 4.2 and 4.3) include the *n*'s associated with each group; in this case *n* = 30 for each group. This principle regarding the *normality* criterion outweighing the n *quota* criterion also applies to the statistical tests covered in Chapters 5, 6, and 7 (ANOVA, ANCOVA, and MANOVA).

Pretest Checklist Criterion 3—Homogeneity of Variance

Homogeneity pertains to sameness. The homogeneity of variance criteria involves checking that the variances of the two groups are similar to each other. As a rule of thumb, homogeneity of variance is likely to be achieved if the variance (standard deviation squared) from one group is not more than twice the variance of the other group. In this case, the variance for *Pulse* in the *Control* group is 39.3 (derived from Figure 4.2: $6.272^2 = 39.338$), and the variance for *Pulse* in the *Pet therapy* group is 31.5 (derived from Figure 4.3: $5.614^2 = 31.517$). Clearly, 39.3 is not more than twice the value of 31.5, so we would expect that the homogeneity of variance test would pass.

In SPSS, the homogeneity of variance test is an option selected during the actual run of the *t* test. If the homogeneity of variance test renders a significance (*p*) value that is greater than .05, then this suggests that there is no statistically significant difference between the variance from one group to the other group. This would mean that the data passes the homogeneity of variance test. The notion of the *p* value will be discussed in detail in the Results section in this chapter, when we examine the findings produced by the *t* test.

Test Run

You may have noticed a variety of *t* test options on the *Analyze, Compare Means* pull-down menu. We will be using the *One-Way ANOVA* menu to process the *t* tests. The reasoning for this option is threefold: (1) This is an easier menu to fill out, (2) it will produce the desired *t* test results, and (3) this will prepare you to efficiently run the ANOVA in the next chapter. NOTE: The *t* test is basically a two-group ANOVA.

1. First, be sure to reactivate all of the records; the easiest way to do this is to delete the *filter_$* variable, or click on the *Select Cases* icon and under *Select*, and click on *All cases*.

2. On the main screen, click on *Analyze, Compare Means, One-Way ANOVA* (Figure 4.4).

Figure 4.4   Running a *t* test. Click on *Analyze, Compare Means, One-Way ANOVA*.

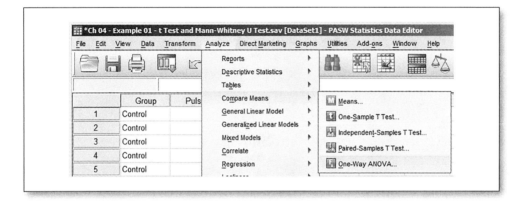

3. On the *One-Way ANOVA* menu, move the continuous variable that you wish to analyze (*Pulse*) into the *Dependent List* window, and move the variable that contains the categorical variable that specifies the groups (*Group*) into the *Factor* window (Figure 4.5).

Figure 4.5   The *One-Way ANOVA* menu.

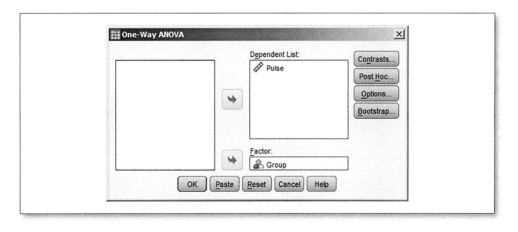

4. Click on the *Options* button. On the *One-Way ANOVA: Options* menu, check ☑ *Descriptive* and ☑ *Homogeneity of variance test*; then click on the *Continue* button (Figure 4.6). This will take you back to the *One-Way ANOVA* menu.

Figure 4.6 The *One-Way ANOVA: Options* menu.

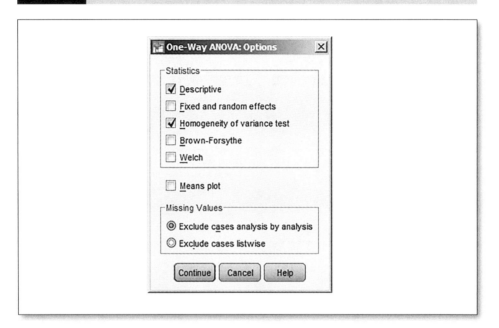

5. On the *One-Way ANOVA* menu (Figure 4.5), click on the *OK* button, and the test will process.

Results

Table 4.1 provides the descriptive statistics for each group: M(*Control*) = 84.10 and M(*Pet therapy*) = 79.93, and n = 30 for each group.

Table 4.1 Descriptive Statistics for each group.

Descriptives

Pulse

	N	Mean	Std. Deviation	Std. Error	95% Confidence Interval for Mean Lower Bound	95% Confidence Interval for Mean Upper Bound	Minimum	Maximum
Control	30	84.10	6.272	1.145	81.76	86.44	71	98
Pet therapy	30	79.93	5.614	1.025	77.84	82.03	68	92
Total	60	82.02	6.264	.809	80.40	83.63	68	98

Table 4.2	*Homogeneity of variance test results.*

Test of Homogeneity of Variances

Pulse

Levene Statistic	df1	df2	Sig.
.745	1	58	.392

Pretest Checklist Criterion 3—Homogeneity of Variance

The last column of the *Test of Homogeneity of Variances* table (Table 4.2) shows a Sig.(nificance) of .392—this is the **p value**. Because this is greater than the α level of .05, this tells us that there is no statistically significant difference between the variances in the *Pulse* variable for the *Control* group compared with the *Pet therapy* group. We would conclude that the criteria of homogeneity of variance have been satisfied. (NOTE: The Sig.[nificance] and α level are clarified in the following section.)

p Value

At this point, you have probably noticed that the means on the two histograms (Figures 4.2 and 4.3), shows that the mean *Pulse* for the *Pet therapy* group (79.93) is lower than the mean of the *Control* group (84.10). On the basis of these means, you may hastily conclude that *Pet therapy* is the best because the participants in that group had a lower pulse rate than those in the control group, but in statistics, the world is not so simple.

Statisticians recognize and actively acknowledge that we do not live in a perfect world; no matter how hard we try to conduct quality investigations, the scientific process can be a messy proposition littered with multiple confounding variables—conditions for which we cannot fully control or account for that can influence the outcome variable(s).

In our simple example, judging by the mean pulse rates of the two groups, it looks like the *Pet therapy* group outperformed the *Control* group, and this may in fact turn out to be the case, but other factors may have contributed to the differences observed between the (mean) pulse rates of these two groups. For example, maybe the random distribution process unexpectedly routed more relaxed people to the *Pet therapy* group; maybe the majority of more anxious people were unintentionally routed to the *Control* group; maybe the members of the *Control* group had more coffee that day, compared to the *Pet therapy* group. Any number of these or other factors that we may not know about may have been occurring over the course of this study.

As you can see, there is virtually no limit to the variety of confounding variables that could potentially influence the outcome of a study. We cannot fully account for or compensate for such confounds and therefore know we do not have a perfect experimental setting. Hence, we do not speak of our statistical findings with *absolute certainty*; rather, we speak of how much *confidence* we have in our findings.

The key question in this case is, *How certain can we be that the 4.17 beats per minute difference that we detected between the group means (M(Control) = 84.10 and M(Pet therapy) = 79.93) is actually due to the genuine superiority of pet therapy and not due to chance alone?* In other words, we want a metric that will tell us how likely we would detect this result (the 4.17 beats per minute difference in the means) if *Pet therapy* was actually no different from doing nothing (as in the *Control* group). This number is known as the *significance level*, represented by the letter p.

Here is how the significance (p) value works: Look at the last column of Table 4.3, showing the Sig.(nificance) score is .009; this is the p value. This tells us that we would expect to see the 4.17 beats per minute difference in the group pulse rates about 1%

Table 4.3   Comparing *Control* : *Pet therapy, t* test results.

ANOVA					
Pulse					
	Sum of Squares	df	Mean Square	F	Sig.
Between Groups	260.417	1	260.417	7.352	.009
Within Groups	2054.567	58	35.424		
Total	2314.983	59			

of the time if it were occurring by (random) chance alone. In other words, based on the data gathered, if the *Control* is exactly as effective as *Pet therapy*, we would see the *Pet therapy* group outperform the *Control* group by 4.17 beats per minute about 1% of the time.

Because the p value tells us how often we would be accepting the intervention as effective, when in fact it really is not, the lower the p value, the more significant the findings.

To exemplify the point further, suppose this experiment produced a p value of .01. This tells us that if pet therapy were in fact equivalent to the control condition, and we ran this experiment 100 times, 1 of those iterations would, through random chance, produce results wherein pet therapy would outperform the control. If the p value was .001, this indicates that we would have to run this (null) experiment 1,000 times to see an instance where pet therapy outperforms the control condition (merely due to random chance). Essentially, the lower the p value, the less likely it is that the findings (differences between the means of the groups) are occurring merely due to random chance, suggesting the stronger likelihood that the observed differences are due to the intervention—in this case, the effectiveness of pet therapy.

In the next section, we will see how we use the p value to determine which hypothesis to reject and which to accept.

H_0 Hypothesis Resolution

We need to have a way of using the p value to guide us in making decisions about our pending hypotheses. This is known as the **hypothesis resolution**:

H_0: There is no difference in pulse rates across the groups.

H_1: There is a difference in pulse rates across the groups.

α Level

To do this, before we embark on our research process, we draw a somewhat arbitrary numerical line in the sand, known as the alpha (α) level. Typically, the α level is set to .05. Think of the α level as a sort of statistical significance threshold—any *p* (Sig.) value that is .05 or less is considered statistically significant—hence, we reject H_0, which states that there is no significant difference between the groups. If the *p* value is greater than .05, then the differences between the means are not considered statistically significant—hence, we do not reject H_0. This will guide us in making our decisions regarding the hypotheses.

---

p Value Summary

- If $p \le \alpha$, then there is a statistically significant difference; reject H_0.
- If $p > \alpha$, then there is no statistically significant difference; do not reject H_0.

NOTE: α = .05 (.05 is the typical value used; some more stringent studies may use .01 or lower.)

Knowing that the *p* is .009, which is less than or equal to α (.05), we would determine that there is a statistically significant difference between the mean pulse rates derived from the two groups—specifically, that 79.93 is statistically significantly fewer beats per minute than 84.10, suggesting that the pet therapy treatment was effective. To finalize the hypotheses, we would reject H_0 and accept H_1:

REJECT H_0:   There is no difference in pulse rates across the groups.

ACCEPT H_1:   There is a difference in pulse rates across the groups.

Abstract

Although it is essential to comprehend the meaning of the key values in the statistical reports, it would be inappropriate to simply present the figures in a results section without providing a concise narrative. While all figures that follow are technically correct, try to avoid documenting your findings as such:

Accurate but Inappropriate Numerical Statistical Abstract

Control: $n = 30$, M = 84.10 (SD = 6.27)

Pet therapy: $n = 30$, M = 79.93 (SD = 5.61)

$p = .009$, α = .05, therefore, provide pet therapy

While the preceding data may be useful in assembling a table, it is important that you become proficient at translating your methodology and numerical findings into a brief textual abstract detailing the story of the study. Your documentation should specify the research question, along with an overview of how you got from the research question to the results.

Appropriate Textual Statistical Abstract

We recruited 60 participants who were diagnosed with acute stress disorder. Half of the participants were assigned to the control group and received no supplemental treatment, while the other half were provided a 30-minute pet therapy session with certified therapy dogs. At the end of the session, the researcher recorded the pulse rate of each participant.

Those in the pet therapy had a mean pulse rate of 79.93 beats per minute (SD = 5.61), whereas those in the control group had a mean pulse rate of 84.10 beats per minute (SD = 6.27).

A t test revealed that this 4.17 difference in pulse rate is statistically significant (p = .009, α = .05), suggesting that the pet therapy was an effective supplemental treatment in reducing anxiety.

In addition to the full manuscript, scientific journals also require authors to submit an abstract that tells the overall story of the study and key findings. Usually the limit for the abstract is about 200 words. While initially it can be a challenge to write technical information so concisely, this is a worthy skill to develop. The above abstract is about 120 words.

NOTE: In the example processed in this chapter, we saw that the *t* test assessed the means of the two groups and revealed that the mean *Pulse* for the treatment group (pet therapy) was statistically significantly lower than the mean for the control group, signifying the success of the pet therapy in reducing anxiety. As you will see in the exercises for this chapter, the *t* test is equally effective in detecting statistically significant differences when the mean of the treatment group is higher than the mean of the control group. For example, instead of the treatment (pet therapy) that is designed to *decrease* the pulse rate, in Exercise 4.3 in the Practice Exercises, the treatment (mentorship) is designed to *increase* probationary compliance for the juvenile offender.

Type I and Type II Errors

The world is imperfect. Despite all best efforts, errors can occur in virtually any realm no matter how careful you are. Consider the two types of errors that can occur in a legal verdict:

Error 1:   The court finds the defendant guilty when, in fact, he or she is actually not guilty.

Error 2:   The court finds the defendant not guilty when, in fact, he or she actually is guilty.

These same two types of errors can happen in statistics. Consider this standard set of hypotheses:

H_0:   There is no significant difference between the groups ($p > .05$; the treatment failed).

H_1:   There is a statistically significant difference between the groups ($p \leq .05$; the treatment worked).

Type I Error

A **Type I error**, also known as an alpha **(α) error**, occurs when the findings indicate that there is a statistically significant difference between two variables (or groups) ($p \leq .05$) when, in fact, on the whole, there actually is not, meaning that you would erroneously reject the null hypothesis. The consequence is that you would conclude that the treatment was effective when, in fact, on the whole, it was not. This is connected with the *p* value. A *p* value of .05 means that there is a 5% chance that you have committed a Type I error. Hence, the lower the *p* value, the less likely that you have committed a Type I error. A Type I error can be thought of as the court finding the defendant guilty when, in fact, he or she is actually not guilty.

Type II Error

A **Type II error**, also known as a beta **(β) error**, occurs when the findings indicate that there is no statistically significant difference between two variables (or groups) ($p > .05$) when, in fact, on the whole, there actually is, meaning that you would erroneously accept the null hypothesis. The consequence is that you would conclude that the treatment was ineffective when, in fact, on the whole, it was. Sample size is inversely related to Type II errors—the higher the sample size, the lower the likelihood of committing a Type II error. A Type II error can be thought of as a court finding the defendant not guilty when, in fact, he or she actually is guilty.

There is no formal metric that you can run that will tell you if you have a Type I or Type II error on hand; they are just characteristics endemic in the realm of statistical testing. The point to keep in mind is that even if a statistical test produces a statistically significant *p* value (e.g., *p* ≤ .05), this does not mean that you have solid evidentiary proof of anything; at best, you have reduced uncertainty. Essentially, a *p* value of .05 means that if the effect of the treatment group were the same as the control group (null intervention), we would see this (anomalous) statistical outcome, where the treatment group outperforms the control group, just by chance, about 5% of the time. Since *p* never goes to zero, there is always some level of uncertainty in statistical findings.

Occasionally, SPSS will produce results wherein the Sig. (*p*) value is .000. In such instances, the *p* value is so low that rounding it to three decimal digits produces the *.000* readout. In documenting such an occurrence, instead of writing p = *.000* or p = *0*, it is customary to document it as p < *.001*.

Remember: Statistics is not about *proving* or *disproving* anything; statistics is about *reducing uncertainty*—there is always some margin of error, no matter how small. The notion of Type I and Type II errors pertains to all other tests covered in the chapters that follow.

OVERVIEW—MANN-WHITNEY *U* TEST

The **Mann-Whitney *U* test** is best thought of as a variation on the *t* test. As mentioned earlier, one of the pretest criteria that must be met prior to running a *t* test states that the data from each group must be normally distributed (Figure 4.7); minor variations in the normal distribution are acceptable. Occasionally, you may encounter data that are substantially skewed (Figure 4.8), **bimodal** (Figure 4.9), flat (Figure 4.10), or may have

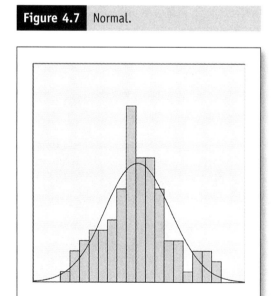

Figure 4.7 Normal.

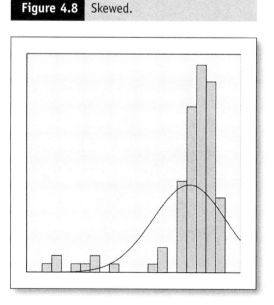

Figure 4.8 Skewed.

Figure 4.9 Bimodal.

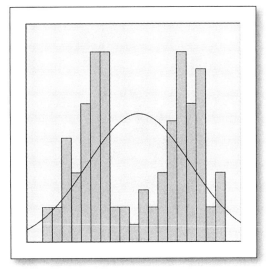

Figure 4.10 Flat.

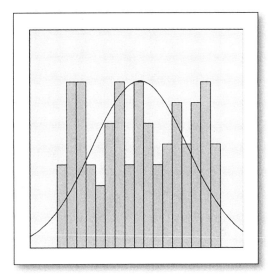

some other atypical distribution. In such instances, the Mann-Whitney *U* statistic is an appropriate alternative to the *t* test.

Test Run

For exemplary purposes, we will run the Mann-Whitney *U* test using the same data set (**Ch 04 – Example 01 – t Test and Mann-Whitney U Test.sav**) even though the data are normally distributed. This will enable us to compare the results of a *t* test to the results produced by the Mann-Whitney *U* test.

1. On the main screen, click on *Analyze, Nonparametric Tests, Legacy Dialogs, 2 Independent Samples* (Figure 4.11).

2. On the *Two-Independent-Samples Tests* menu, move *Pulse* to the *Test Variable List* window.

3. Move *Group* to the *Grouping Variable* box (Figure 4.12).

4. Click on *Group(? ?)*; then click on *Define Groups*.

5. On the *Two Independent Sample* submenu, for *Group 1*, enter *1*; for *Group 2*, enter *2* (this is because we defined *Control* as 1 and *Pet therapy* as 2) (Figure 4.13).

6. Click *Continue*; this will close this submenu.

7. On the *Two-Independent-Samples Tests* menu, click on *OK*.

Figure 4.11 Ordering the Mann-Whitney *U* test: Click on *Analyze, Nonparametric Tests, Legacy Dialogs, 2 Independent Samples.*

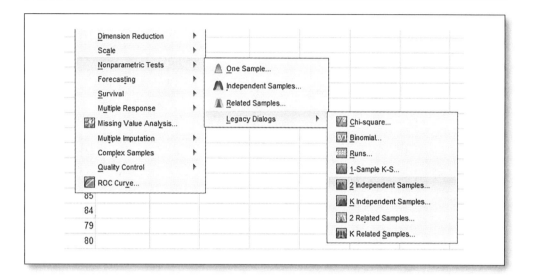

Figure 4.12 On the *Two-Independent-Samples Tests* menu, move *Pulse* to the *Test Variable List*, and move *group* to the *Grouping Variable* box.

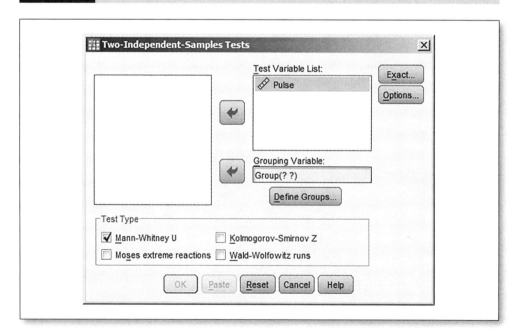

Figure 4.13 On the *Two Independent Samples* submenu, for *Group 1*, enter *1*; for *Group 2*, enter *2*.

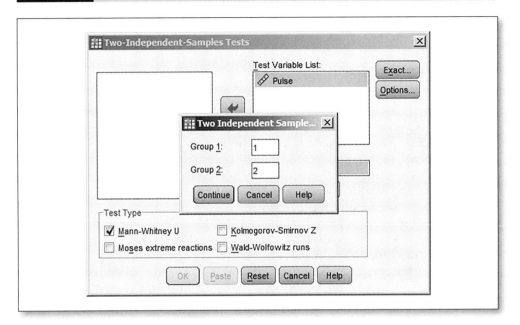

Results

The Mann-Whitney *U* test result is found on the *Test Statistics* table (Table 4.4); the Asymp. Sig. (2-tailed) statistic rendered a *p* value of .012. This is less than α (.05), so we would conclude that there is a statistically significant difference between the performances of the treatments.

Table 4.4 Mann-Whitney *U* test *p* value = .012.

Test Statistics[a]

	Pulse
Mann-Whitney U	281.000
Wilcoxon W	746.000
Z	-2.503
Asymp. Sig. (2-tailed)	.012

a. Grouping Variable: Group

Referring back, remember that the *t* test produced a *p* value of .009. The differences in these *p* values are due to the internal transformations that the Mann-Whitney *U* test conducts on the data. If one or more substantial violations are detected when running the pretest checklist for the *t* test, then the Mann-Whitney *U* test is considered a viable alternative.

GOOD COMMON SENSE

Clearly, it is essential that you comprehend key figures of the statistical reports that you order, but when it comes to using these findings to make decisions in the real world, other considerations should be taken into account.

For example, suppose you measured the results of a new treatment to improve motivation using a 100-point scale (0 = Low motivation . . . 100 = High motivation), wherein Group 1, the control group, received the usual treatment, and Group 2 received the new treatment. Your analysis revealed that M(Group 1) = 88.1, M(Group 2) = 88.3, and *p* = .01. Your first reaction might be to leap to the conclusion that because *p* = .01, and this is less than the α level of .05, Group 2 statistically significantly outperformed Group 1, so we should adopt the treatment that was used for Group 2. Statistically speaking, you would be right, but consider some other real-world factors: Group 2 outperformed Group 1 by (only) .2 points; one might wonder if, in the real world, a .2-point difference is of any *practical* significance. Can anyone really detect the difference between an outcome of 88.1 and 88.3?

Also, scarce resources may be an issue; the intervention used for Group 2 might have been very costly, time-consuming, labor intensive, or complex to carry out. It would be reasonable to consider if the cost, time, labor, and inconvenience involved are really worth the .2-point improvement.

Another concern might be the initial goal of the intervention: If the goal was to raise the score to at least 80, then clearly both groups achieved the desired effect. In this light, the innovative treatment would seem less impressive, especially if it is more complex, time-consuming, or costly to implement.

The lesson at hand is that when interpreting statistical findings, it is important that you not only tend to the numbers but also mindfully comprehend that those numbers are only a part of the picture when it comes to making *practical* decisions in the real world.

Key Concepts

- *t* test
- Pretest checklist
  - Normality
  - *n*
  - Homogeneity of variance

- α
- *p*
- Hypothesis resolution
- Documenting results
- Type I (α) error
- Type II (β) error
- Mann-Whitney *U* test
- Good common sense

Practice Exercises

Use the prepared SPSS data sets (download from **study.sagepub.com/intermediatestats**).

Exercise 4.1

You want to determine the optimal tutor-to-student ratio. Students seeking tutoring will be randomly assigned to one of two groups: Group 1 will involve each tutor working with only one student, and in Group 2, each tutor will work with two students. At the end of the term, students will be asked to complete the Tutor Satisfaction Survey, which renders a score from 0 to 100.

Data set: **Ch 04 – Exercise 01A.sav**

Codebook

Variable:	Group
Definition:	Group number
Type:	Categorical (1 = One-to-one, 2 = Two-to-one)
Variable:	TSS
Definition:	Tutor Satisfaction Survey score
Type:	Continuous (0 = Very unsatisfied . . . 100 = Very satisfied)

a. Write the hypotheses.

b. Run each criterion of the pretest checklist (normality, homogeneity of variance, and *n*) and discuss your findings.

c. Run the *t* test and document your findings (*n*s, means, and Sig. [*p* value]).

d. Write an abstract under 200 words detailing a summary of the study, the *t* test results, hypothesis resolution, and implications of your findings.

Repeat this exercise using data set: **Ch 04 – Exercise 01B.sav**.

Exercise 4.2

Clinicians at a nursing home facility want to see if giving residents a plant to tend to will help lower depression. To test this idea, the residents are randomly assigned to one of two groups: Those assigned to Group 1 will serve as the control group and will not be given a plant. Members of Group 2 will be given a small bamboo plant along with a card detailing care instructions. After 90 days, all participants will complete the Acme Depression Scale, which renders a score between 1 and 100 (1 = Low depression . . . 100 = High depression).

Data set: **Ch 04 – Exercise 02A.sav**

Codebook

Variable:	Group
Definition:	Group number
Type:	Categorical (1 = No plant, 2 = Bamboo)

Variable:	Depress
Definition:	Acme Depression Scale
Type:	Continuous (1 = Low depression . . . 100 = High depression)

a. Write the hypotheses.

b. Run each criterion of the pretest checklist (normality, homogeneity of variance, and *n*) and discuss your findings.

c. Run the *t* test and document your findings (*n*s, means, and Sig. [*p* value]).

d. Write an abstract under 200 words detailing a summary of the study, the *t* test results, hypothesis resolution, and implications of your findings.

Repeat this exercise using data set: **Ch 04 – Exercise 02B.sav**.

Exercise 4.3

A judge mandates that juvenile offenders who have priors be assigned to a trained delinquency prevention mentor. To assess this intervention, offenders will be randomly assigned to one of two groups: No mentor, or a peer mentor who is 3 to 5 years older than the offender. The following data will be gathered on each participant: Probation officer's compliance evaluation (0% . . . 100%).

Data set: **Ch 04 – Exercise 03A.sav**

Codebook

Variable:	Group
Definition:	Mentor group assignment
Type:	Categorical (1 = No mentor, 2 = Peer mentor)

Variable: Probation_compliance

Definition: Probation officer's overall assessment of the youth's probation compliance

Type: Continuous (0 = Completely noncompliant . . . 100 = Completely compliant)

a. Write the hypotheses.

b. Run each criterion of the pretest checklist (normality, homogeneity of variance, and *n*) and discuss your findings.

c. Run the *t* test and document your findings (*n*s, means, and Sig. [*p* value]).

d. Write an abstract under 200 words detailing a summary of the study, the *t* test results, hypothesis resolution, and implications of your findings.

Repeat this exercise using data set: **Ch 04 – Exercise 03B.sav**.

Exercise 4.4

In an effort to determine the effectiveness of light therapy to alleviate depression, you recruit a group of individuals who have been diagnosed with depression. The participants are randomly assigned to one of two groups: Group 1 will be the control group—members of this group will receive no light therapy. Members of Group 2 will get light therapy for 1 hour on even-numbered days over the course of 1 month. After 1 month, all participants will complete the Acme Mood Scale, consisting of 10 questions; this instrument renders a score between 1 and 100 (1 = Extremely bad mood . . . 100 = Extremely good mood).

Data set: **Ch 04 – Exercise 04A.sav**

Codebook

Variable: Group

Definition: Group number

Type: Categorical (1 = No light therapy, 2 = Light therapy: even days)

Variable: Mood

Definition: Acme Mood Scale

Type: Continuous (1 = Extremely bad mood . . . 100 = Extremely good mood)

a. Write the hypotheses.

b. Run each criterion of the pretest checklist (normality, homogeneity of variance, and *n*) and discuss your findings.

c. Run the *t* test and document your findings (*n*s, means, and Sig. [*p* value]).

d. Write an abstract under 200 words detailing a summary of the study, the *t* test results, hypothesis resolution, and implications of your findings.

Repeat this exercise using data set: **Ch 04 – Exercise 04B.sav**.

Exercise 4.5

To assess the workplace benefits of providing paid time off (PTO), the Human Resources (HR) Department implements and evaluates different PTO plans at each of the company's two sites: Site 1 will serve as the control group; employees at this site will continue to receive 2 weeks of PTO per year. Employees at Site 2 will receive 2 weeks of PTO per year plus the fourth Friday of each month off (with pay). The HR Department will use a web-based survey to gather the following data from all employees: Score on the Acme Morale Scale (1 = Extremely low morale . . . 25 = Extremely high morale).

Data set: **Ch 04 – Exercise 05A.sav**

Codebook

Variable:	Site
Definition:	Work site
Type:	Categorical (1 = 2 Weeks PTO, 2 = 2 Weeks PTO + 4th Fridays off)

Variable:	Morale
Definition:	Score on Acme Morale Scale
Type:	Continuous (1 = Extremely low morale . . . 25 = Extremely high morale)

a. Write the hypotheses.

b. Run each criterion of the pretest checklist (normality, homogeneity of variance, and *n*) and discuss your findings.

c. Run the *t* test and document your findings (*n*s, means, and Sig. [*p* value]).

d. Write an abstract under 200 words detailing a summary of the study, the *t* test results, hypothesis resolution, and implications of your findings.

Repeat this exercise using data set: **Ch 04 – Exercise 5B.sav**.

Exercise 4.6

It is thought that exercising early in the morning will provide better energy throughout the day. To test this idea, participants are recruited and randomly assigned to one of two groups: Members of Group 1 will constitute the control group and not be assigned any walking. Members of Group 2 will walk from 7:00 to 7:30 a.m., Monday through Friday, over the course of 30 days. At the conclusion of the study, each participant will answer the 10 questions on the Acme End-of-the-Day Energy Scale. This instrument produces a score between 1 and 100 (1 = Extremely low energy . . . 100 = Extremely high energy).

Data set: **Ch 04 – Exercise 06A.sav**

Codebook

Variable:	Group
Definition:	Walking group assignment
Type:	Categorical (1 = No walking, 2 = Walking: 30 Minutes)

Variable:	Energy
Definition:	Acme End-of-the-Day Energy Scale
Type:	Continuous (1 = Extremely low energy . . . 100 = Extremely high energy)

a. Write the hypotheses.

b. Run each criterion of the pretest checklist (normality, homogeneity of variance, and *n*) and discuss your findings.

c. Run the *t* test and document your findings (*n*s, means, and Sig. [*p* value]).

d. Write an abstract under 200 words detailing a summary of the study, the *t* test results, hypothesis resolution, and implications of your findings.

Repeat this exercise using data set: **Ch 04 – Exercise 06B.sav**.

Exercise 4.7

A political consulting firm wants to determine the characteristics of voters when it comes to issues involving alternative energy. The researchers recruit a group of participants and randomly assign them to one of two groups: Group 1 will be the control group; they will not be exposed to any advertising materials, and Group 2 will be shown a print advertisement that will be used in a postal mailing. Finally, each participant will indicate his or her voting intentions for Proposition 86, which involves tax deductions for hybrid cars on a 1 to 7 scale (1 = Will definitely vote no . . . 7 = Will definitely vote yes).

Data set: **Ch 04 – Exercise 07A.sav**

Codebook

Variable:	Group
Definition:	Advertising media
Type:	Categorical (1 = Control, 2 = Print)

Variable:	Prop_86
Definition:	Likely voting decision on tax deductions for hybrid cars
Type:	Continuous (1 = Will definitely vote no . . . 7 = Will definitely vote yes)

a. Write the hypotheses.

b. Run each criterion of the pretest checklist (normality, homogeneity of variance, and *n*) and discuss your findings.

c. Run the *t* test and document your findings (*n*s, means, and Sig. [*p* value]).

d. Write an abstract under 200 words detailing a summary of the study, the *t* test results, hypothesis resolution, and implications of your findings.

Repeat this exercise using data set: **Ch 04 – Exercise 07B.sav**.

Exercise 4.8

A team of educational researchers want to assess traditional classroom instruction compared to online options. Students who are enrolled in a course will be randomly assigned to one of two sections: Students in Section 1 will take the class in a traditional classroom. Students in Section 2 will take the course online with an interactive video cast of the instructor wherein students can ask the instructor questions during the session. The researchers will gather the course grade of each student (0% . . . 100%).

Data set: **Ch 04 – Exercise 08A.sav**

Codebook

Variable:	Section
Definition:	Learning modality
Type:	Categorical (1 = Classroom, 2 = Online live interactive)

Variable:	Grade
Definition:	Final grade in course
Type:	Continuous (0 . . . 100)

a. Write the hypotheses.

b. Run each criterion of the pretest checklist (normality, homogeneity of variance, and *n*) and discuss your findings.

c. Run the *t* test and document your findings (*n*s, means, and Sig. [*p* value]).

    d. Write an abstract under 200 words detailing a summary of the study, the *t* test results, hypothesis resolution, and implications of your findings.

Repeat this exercise using data set: **Ch 04 – Exercise 08B.sav**.

Exercise 4.9

The Acme Company claims that its new reading lamp increases reading speed; you want to test this. You will record how long (in seconds) it takes for participants to read a 1,000-word essay. Participants will be randomly assigned to one of two groups: Group 1 will be the control group; they will read the essay using regular room lighting. Those in Group 2 will read the essay using the Acme lamp.

Data set: **Ch 04 – Exercise 09A.sav**

Codebook

Variable:	Group
Definition:	Lighting group assignment
Type:	Categorical (1 = Room lighting, 2 = Acme lamp)
Variable:	Seconds
Definition:	The time it takes to read the essay
Type:	Continuous

    a. Write the hypotheses.

    b. Run each criterion of the pretest checklist (normality, homogeneity of variance, and *n*) and discuss your findings.

    c. Run the *t* test and document your findings (*n*s, means, and Sig. [*p* value]).

    d. Write an abstract under 200 words detailing a summary of the study, the *t* test results, hypothesis resolution, and implications of your findings.

Repeat this exercise using data set: **Ch 04 – Exercise 09B.sav**.

Exercise 4.10

Due to numerous complications involving missed medication dosages, you implement a study to determine the best strategy for enhancing medication adherence. Patients who are on a daily medication regime will be recruited, will receive a complimentary 1-month dosage of their regular medication(s), and will be randomly assigned to one of two groups: Group 1 will serve as the control group (no treatment), and Group 2 will participate in a 1-hour in-person pharmacist-administered medication adherence workshop. At the end of 1 month, participants will present their prescription bottle(s); you will count the remaining pills and calculate the dosage adherence percentage (e.g., 0 pills remaining = 100% adherence).

Data set: **Ch 04 – Exercise 10A.sav**

Codebook

Variable:	Group
Definition:	Group number
Type:	Categorical (1 = Control, 2 = Rx workshop)

Variable:	RxAdhere
Definition:	Percentage of medication adherence
Type:	Continuous (0 – 100)

a. Write the hypotheses.

b. Run each criterion of the pretest checklist (normality, homogeneity of variance, and *n*) and discuss your findings.

c. Run the *t* test and document your findings (*n*s, means, and Sig. [*p* value]).

d. Write an abstract under 200 words detailing a summary of the study, the *t* test results, hypothesis resolution, and implications of your findings.

Repeat this exercise using data set: **Ch 04 – Exercise 10B.sav**.

CHAPTER 5

ANOVA and Kruskal-Wallis Test

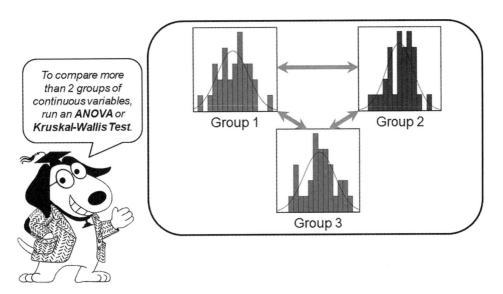

To compare more than 2 groups of continuous variables, run an *ANOVA* or *Kruskal-Wallis Test*.

Group 1

Group 2

Group 3

Three is a magic number.

—Bob Dorough

Learning Objectives

Upon completing this chapter, you will be able to do the following:

- Determine when it is appropriate to run an ANOVA test.
- Verify that the data meet the criteria for ANOVA processing: normality, n, and homogeneity of variance.
- Order an ANOVA test with graphics.
- Select an appropriate ANOVA post hoc test: Tukey or Sidak.
- Derive results from the Descriptives and Multiple Comparisons tables.

(Continued)

107

(Continued)

- Calculate the unique pairs formula.
- Resolve the hypotheses.
- Know when and how to run and interpret the Kruskal-Wallis test.
- Write an appropriate abstract.

WHEN TO USE THIS STATISTIC

Guidelines for ANOVA and Kruskal-Wallis Tests

Overview: This statistic is for designs that involve more than two groups to determine which group(s) (if any) outperformed another.

Variables: This statistic requires two variables for each record: (1) a categorical variable to designate the group, and (2) a continuous variable to contain the outcome score.

Results: Among those diagnosed with anxiety, we separated our participants into three groups and measured their pulse rates after 30 minutes of treatment. The mean pulse rates were 84.1 for the control group, 79.9 for the pet therapy group, and 80.1 for the meditation group. The pulse rate for the pet therapy group is statistically significantly lower than the control group ($p = .025$, $\alpha = .05$).

VIDEOS

The videos for this chapter are **Ch 05 – ANOVA.mp4** and **Ch 05 – Kruskal-Wallis Test .mp4.** These videos provide overviews of these tests, instructions for carrying out the pretest checklist, run, and interpreting the results of each test using the data set: **Ch 05 – Example 01 – ANOVA and Kruskal-Wallis.sav**.

LAYERED LEARNING

The *t* test and ANOVA (analysis of variance) are so similar that this chapter will use the same example and the same 10 exercises used in Chapter 4 (*t* Test); the only difference is that the data sets have been enhanced to include a third or fourth group. If you are proficient with the *t* test, you are already more than halfway there to comprehending ANOVA. The only real differences between the *t* test and ANOVA are in ordering the test run and interpreting the test results; several other minor differences will be pointed out along the way.

That being said, let us go into the expanded example, drawn from Chapter 4, which involved measuring the pulse rate of anxious participants from two groups: Group 1 (Control), Group 2 (Pet therapy), and now a third group: Group 3 (Meditation). The ANOVA test will reveal which (if any) of these three treatments statistically significantly outperforms the others in terms of lowering the resting pulse rate.

OVERVIEW—ANOVA

The **ANOVA** test is similar to the *t* test, except whereas the *t* test compares two groups of continuous variables to each other, the ANOVA test can compare three or more groups to each other.

In cases where the three pretest criteria are not satisfied for the ANOVA, the Kruskal-Wallis test, which is conceptually similar to the ANOVA, is the better option; this alternate test is explained near the end of this chapter.

Example

A research team has recruited a group of individuals who have been diagnosed with acute stress disorder to determine the effectiveness of supplemental nonpharmaceutical treatments for reducing stress: (1) no supplemental therapy, (2) pet therapy with certified therapy dogs, or (3) meditation.

Research Question

Is pet therapy or meditation effective in reducing stress among those diagnosed with acute stress disorder?

Groups

A researcher recruits a total of 90 participants who meet the diagnostic criteria for acute stress disorder. Participants will be scheduled to come to the research center one at a time. Upon arriving, each participant will be assigned to one of three groups on a sequential basis (first assigned to Group 1, second assigned to Group 2, third assigned to Group 3, fourth assigned back to Group 1, etc.). Those assigned to Group 1 will constitute the control group and will be instructed to sit and relax for 30 minutes (with no treatment). Those in Group 2 will receive 30 minutes of pet therapy, and those in Group 3 will meditate for 30 minutes.

Procedure

Each participant will be guided to a room with a comfortable sofa. Those in the control group will be instructed to just sit and relax. Those in the pet therapy group will be introduced to the therapy dog by name and instructed that the participant may hold the dog in his or her lap, pet the dog on the sofa, brush the dog, or give the dog the allotted treats in whatever combination they wish. Those in the meditation group will listen to a recording of gentle music with a narrative taking the participant through a guided meditation. After 30 minutes, the researcher will return to each participant to measure the participant's pulse rate and dismiss him or her. The lower pulse rate would reflect more relaxation.

Hypotheses

The null hypothesis (H_0) is phrased to anticipate that the treatments (pet therapy and meditation) fail to reduce anxiety (as measured by pulse rate), indicating that on average, participants in each of the three groups all have about the same pulse rates; in other words, no group outperforms any other when it comes to lowering the participant's pulse rates. The alternative hypothesis (H_1) states that on the average, at least one group will outperform another group:

H_0:   There is no difference in pulse rates across the groups.

H_1:   There is a difference in pulse rates across the groups.

Admittedly, H_1 is phrased fairly broadly. The *Post Hoc Multiple Comparisons* table, which is covered in the Results section, will identify which treatment(s), if any, outperformed which.

Data Set

Use the following data set: **Ch 05 – Example 01 – ANOVA and Kruskal-Wallis Test.sav**. Notice that this data set has 90 records; the first 60 records (rows) are the same as the *t* test and Mann-Whitney *U* test example data set used in Chapter 4 (records 61 through 90 are new for Group 3):

Codebook

   Variable: Group

   Definition: Group assignment

   Type: Categorical (1 = Control, 2 = Pet therapy, 3 = Meditation)

   Variable: Pulse

   Definition: Heartbeats per minute measured 30 minutes after start

   Type: Continuous

NOTE: In this data set, records (rows) 1 through 30 are for Group 1 (Control), records 31 through 60 are for Group 2 (Pet therapy), and records 61 through 90 are for Group 3 (Meditation). The data are arranged this way just for visual clarity; the order of the records has no bearing on the statistical results.

If you go to the *Variable View* and open the *Values* menu for the variable *Group*, you will see that the label *Meditation* for the third group has been assigned to the value 3 (Figure 5.1).

Figure 5.1 Value labels for a three-group ANOVA analysis.

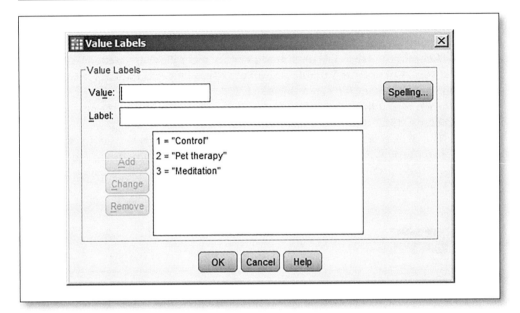

Pretest Checklist

ANOVA Pretest Checklist

☑ 1. Normality*

☑ 2. *n* quota*

☑ 3. Homogeneity of Variance **

*Run prior to ANOVA test

**Results produced upon ANOVA test run

NOTE: If any of the pretest checklist criteria are not satisfied, rerun the analysis using the nonparametric version of this test: the Kruskal-Wallis test (p. 125).

The statistical pretest checklist for the ANOVA is similar to the *t* test: (1) normality, (2) *n,* and (3) homogeneity of variance, except that you will assess the data for more than two groups.

Pretest Checklist Criterion 1—Normality

Check for normality by inspecting the histogram with a normal curve for each of the three groups. Begin by using the *Select Cases* icon to select the records pertaining to the *Control* group (*Group = 1*); the selection criteria would be *Group = 1*. Next, run a histogram (with normal curve) on the variable *Pulse*. For more details on this procedure, refer to **Chapter 3: Descriptive Statistics**, and the following section: SPSS—Descriptive Statistics: Continuous Variable (Age) Select by Categorical Variable (Gender)—Females Only; see the star (★) icon on page 62.

Then repeat the process for the *Pet therapy* group (*Group = 2*), and finally, repeat the process a third time for the *Meditation* group (*Group = 3*).

This will produce three histograms with normal curves—one for the scores in the *Control* group, a second for the scores in the *Pet therapy* group, and a third for the *Meditation* group. The histograms should resemble the graphs shown in Figures 5.2, 5.3, and 5.4.

Figure 5.2 Histogram of *Pulse* for Group 1: *Control.*

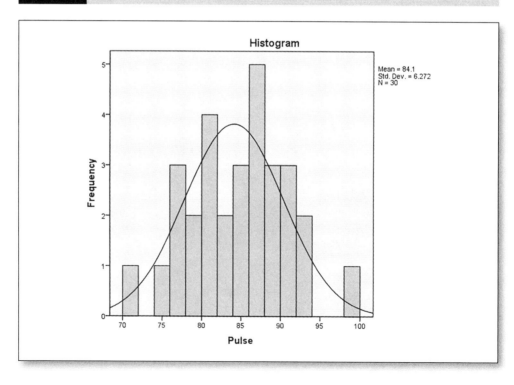

Figure 5.3   Histogram of *Pulse* for Group 2: *Pet therapy.*

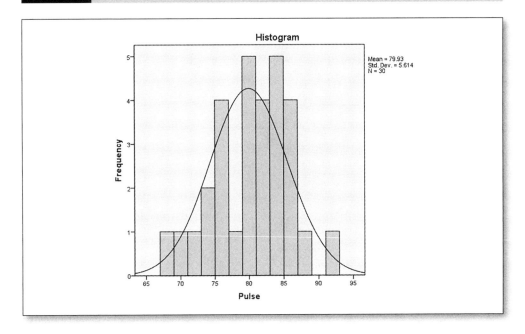

Figure 5.4   Histogram of *Pulse* for Group 3: *Meditation.*

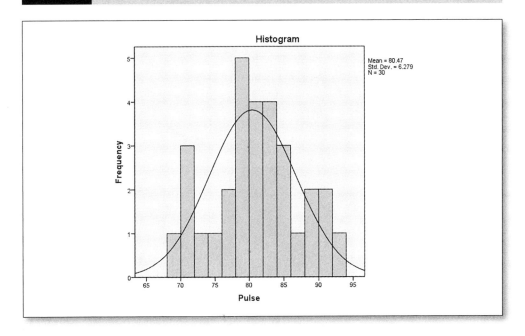

As we read these three histograms, our focus is primarily on the *normality of the curve,* as opposed to the characteristics of the individual bars. Although the height and width of each curve are unique, we see that each is bell shaped and shows good symmetry with no substantial *skewing.* On the basis of the inspection of these three figures, we would conclude that the criteria of *normality* are satisfied for all three groups.

Next, (re)activate all records for further analysis. You can either delete the temporary variable *filter_$* or click on the *Select Cases* icon and select the *All cases* button. For more details on this procedure, please refer to **Chapter 3: Descriptive statistics**, and the following section: SPSS—(Re)Selecting All Variables; see the star (★) icon on page 68.

Pretest Checklist Criterion 2—*n* Quota

As with the *t* test, technically, you can run an ANOVA test with an *n* of any size in each group, but when *n* is at least 30 in each group, the ANOVA is considered more robust. The histograms with normal curves (Figures 5.2, 5.3, and 5.4) include *n*s associated with each group; in this case *n* = 30 for each group. Normality is considered a more important criterion than the *n* quota; if a group is showing a normal distribution but the n is low, you can proceed with confidence.

Pretest Checklist Criterion 3—Homogeneity of Variance

Homogeneity pertains to sameness. The homogeneity of variance criterion involves checking that the variances among the groups are similar to each other. As a rule of thumb, homogeneity of variance is likely to be achieved if the variance (standard deviation squared) from one group is not more than twice the variance of the other groups. In this case, the variance for *Pulse* in the *Control* group is 39.3 (derived from Figure 5.2: $6.272^2 = 39.338$), the variance for *Pulse* in the *Pet therapy* group is 31.7 (derived from Figure 5.3: $5.614^2 = 31.517$), and the variance for *Pulse* in the *Meditation* group is 39.4 (derived from Figure 5.4: $6.279^2 = 39.426$). When looking at the *Pulse* variances from these three groups (39.3, 31.7, and 39.4), clearly none of these figures are more than twice any of the others, so we would expect that the homogeneity of variance test would pass.

The *homogeneity of variance test* is an option selected during the ANOVA run. If the homogeneity of variance test renders a significance (*p*) value that is greater than .05, then this suggests that there are no statistically significant differences among the variances of the groups. This would mean that the data pass the homogeneity of variance test.

Test Run

To run an ANOVA test (for the most part, this is *t* test déjà vu time), complete the following steps:

1. First, be sure to reactivate all of the records; the easiest way to do this is to delete the *filter_$* variable, or click on the *Select Cases* icon and under *Select,* click on *All cases.*

2. On the main screen, click on *Analyze, Compare Means, One-Way ANOVA* (Figure 5.5).

| Figure 5.5 | Running an ANOVA test. |

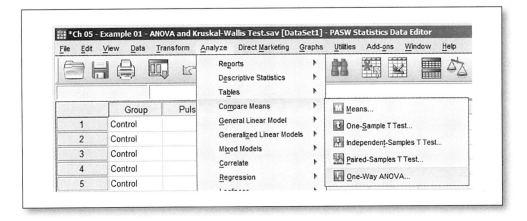

3. On the *One-Way ANOVA* menu, move the continuous variable that you wish to analyze (*Pulse*) into the *Dependent List* window, and move the variable that contains the categorical variable that specifies the group (*Group*) into the *Factor* window (Figure 5.6).

| Figure 5.6 | The *One-Way ANOVA* menu. |

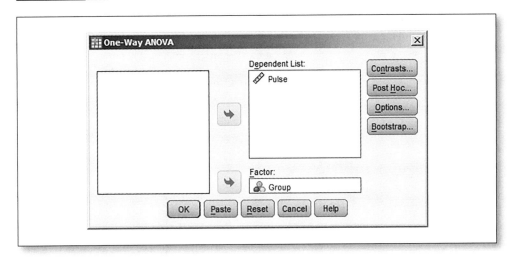

4. Click on the *Options* button. On the *One-Way ANOVA: Options* menu, check *Descriptive* and *Homogeneity of variance test;* then click on the *Continue* button (Figure 5.7). This will take you back to the *One-Way ANOVA* menu.

Figure 5.7   The *One-Way ANOVA: Options* menu.

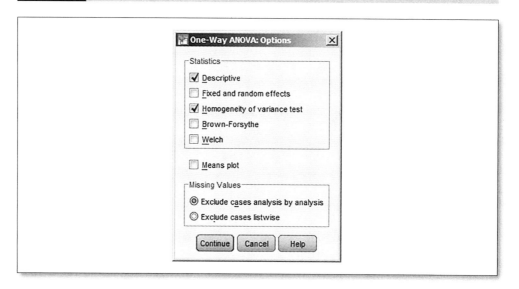

5. Click on the *Post Hoc* button.

6. This will take you to the *One-Way ANOVA: Post Hoc Multiple Comparisons* menu (Figure 5.8).

Figure 5.8   The *One-Way ANOVA: Post Hoc Multiple Comparisons* menu.

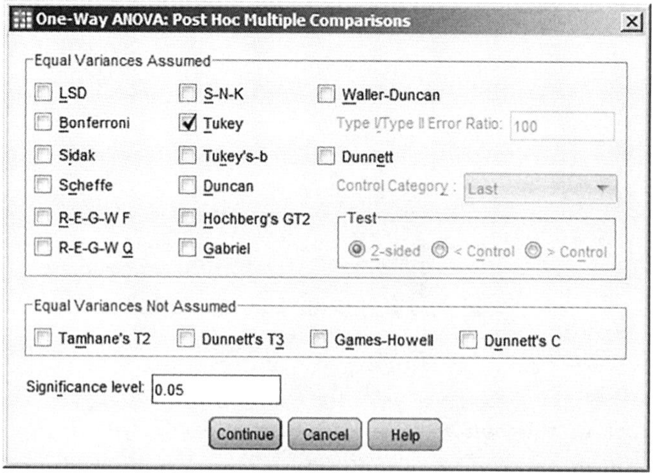

7. If you were to run the ANOVA test without selecting a post hoc test, then all it would return is a single *p* value; if that *p* is statistically significant, then that would tell you that somewhere among the groups processed, the mean for at least one group is statistically significantly different from the mean of at least one other group, but it would not tell you specifically *which* group is different from *which*. The post hoc test produces a table comparing the mean of each group with the mean of every other group, along with the *p* values for each pair of comparisons. This will become clearer in the Results section when we read the post hoc multiple comparisons table.

8. On the *One-Way ANOVA* menu (Figure 5.6), click on the *OK* button, and the ANOVA test will process.

As for which post hoc test to select, there are a lot of choices. We will focus on only two options: Tukey and Sidak. **Tukey** is appropriate when each group has the *same n*s; in this case, each group has an *n* of 30, so check the *Tukey* checkbox; then click on the *Continue* button (this will take you back to the *One-Way ANOVA* menu, see Figure 5.6). If the groups had *different n*s (e.g., *n*(Group 1) = 40, *n*(Group 2) = 55, *n*(Group 3) = 36), then the **Sidak** post hoc test would be appropriate. If you do not know the *n*s for each group in advance, then just select either *Tukey* or *Sidak* and observe the *n*s on the resulting report; if you chose wrong, then go back and rerun the analysis using the appropriate post hoc test.

ANOVA Post Hoc Summary

- If all groups have the same *n*s, then select *Tukey*.
- If the groups have different *n*s, then select *Sidak*.

Results

Pretest Checklist Criterion 3—Homogeneity of Variance

For the final item on the pretest checklist, Table 5.1 shows that the homogeneity of variance test produced a significance (*p*) value of .689. Because this is greater than the α level of .05, this tells us that there are *no statistically significant differences among the variances of the* Pulse *variable for the three groups analyzed*. In other words, the variances for *Pulse* are similar enough among the three groups: *Control*, *Pet therapy*, and *Meditation*; hence, we would conclude that the criteria of the homogeneity of variance has been satisfied.

Table 5.1 Homogeneity of variance test results.

Test of Homogeneity of Variances

Pulse

Levene Statistic	df1	df2	Sig.
.374	2	87	.689

Table 5.2 ANOVA test results comparing *Pulse* of *Control, Pet therapy,* and *Meditation.*

ANOVA

Pulse

	Sum of Squares	df	Mean Square	F	Sig.
Between Groups	308.467	2	154.233	4.196	.018
Within Groups	3198.033	87	36.759		
Total	3506.500	89			

Next, we look at the ANOVA table (Table 5.2) and find a significance (*p*) value of .018. This is less than the α level of .05, so this tells us that there is a statistically significant difference somewhere among the (three) group means for *Pulse,* but unlike reading the results of the *t* test, we are not done yet.

Remember that in the realm of the *t* test, there are only *two* groups involved, so interpreting the *p* value is fairly straightforward: If *p* is ≤ .05, there is no question as to which group is different from which—clearly, the mean from Group 1 is statistically significantly different from the mean of Group 2, but when there are *three or more groups,* we need more information to determine *which* group is different from which; that is what the post hoc test answers.

Consider this: Suppose you have *two* kids, Aaron and Blake. You are in the living room, and someone calls out from the den, "The kids are fighting again!" Because there are only *two* kids, you immediately know that the fight is between Aaron and Blake. This is akin to the *t* test, which involves comparing the means of *two* groups.

Now suppose you have *three* kids—Aaron, Blake, and Claire.

This time when someone calls out, "The kids are fighting again!" you can no longer simply know that the fight is between Aaron and Blake; when there are *three* kids, you need more information. Instead of just *one* possibility, there are now *three* possible pairs of fighters:

| Aaron : Blake | Aaron : Claire | Blake : Claire |
| Pair 1 | Pair 2 | Pair 3 |

Back to our example: The ANOVA table (Table 5.2) produced a statistically significant *p* value (Sig. = .018), which indicates that there is a statistically significant difference detected somewhere among the three groups (*The kids are fighting!*); the post hoc table will tell us precisely *which pairs* are statistically significantly different from each other (which pair of kids is fighting). Specifically, it will reveal which group(s) outperformed which.

This brings us to the (Tukey Post Hoc) Multiple Comparisons table (Table 5.3). As with the three kids fighting, in this three-group design, there are three possible pairs of comparisons that we can assess in terms of (mean) *Pulse* for the groups. NOTE: Mean scores are drawn from the histograms with normal curves (Figures 5.2, 5.3, and 5.4); these figures are also on the *Descriptives* table produced in the ANOVA output report (not shown here).

Group 1 : Group 2	Group 1 : Group 3	Group 2 : Group 3
84.10 : 79.93	84.10 : 80.47	79.93 : 80.47
Pair 1	**Pair 2**	**Pair 3**

Pairs of means shown for Group 1—Control, Group 2—Pet therapy, and Group 3—Meditation

We will use means shown previously and Table 5.3 (*Multiple Comparisons*) to analyze the ANOVA test results. To summarize, the mean *Pulse* for each of the three groups: *Control* (M = 84.10), *Pet therapy* (M = 79.93), and *Meditation* (M = 80.47). We will assess each of the three pairwise score comparisons separately.

Comparison 1—*Control* : *Pet Therapy*

Table 5.3 compares the mean *Pulse* for the *Control* group with the mean *Pulse* rate for the *Pet therapy* group, which produces a Sig.(nificance) (*p*) of .025. Because the *p* is less than the .05 α level, this tells us that for *Pulse,* there is a statistically significant difference between *Control* (M = 84.10) and *Pet therapy* (M = 79.93).

Table 5.3	*ANOVA Post Hoc Multiple Comparisons* table shows a statistically significant difference between *Control* and *Pet therapy* (p = .025).

Multiple Comparisons

Pulse
Tukey HSD

(I) Group	(J) Group	Mean Difference (I-J)	Std. Error	Sig.	95% Confidence Interval	
					Lower Bound	Upper Bound
Control	Pet therapy	4.167*	1.565	.025	.43	7.90
	Meditation	3.633	1.565	.058	-.10	7.37
Pet therapy	Control	-4.167*	1.565	.025	-7.90	-.43
	Meditation	-.533	1.565	.938	-4.27	3.20
Meditation	Control	-3.633	1.565	.058	-7.37	.10
	Pet therapy	.533	1.565	.938	-3.20	4.27

*. The mean difference is significant at the 0.05 level.

Comparison 2—*Control : Meditation*

The second comparison in Table 5.4 is between *Control* and *Meditation*, which produces a Sig.(nificance) (p) of .058. Because the p is greater than the .05 α level, this tells us that for *Pulse,* there is no statistically significant difference between *Control* (M = 84.10) and *Meditation* (M = 80.47).

Table 5.4	*ANOVA Post Hoc Multiple Comparisons* table shows a statistically insignificant difference between *Control* and *Meditation* (p = .058).

Multiple Comparisons

Pulse
Tukey HSD

(I) Group	(J) Group	Mean Difference (I-J)	Std. Error	Sig.	95% Confidence Interval	
					Lower Bound	Upper Bound
Control	Pet therapy	4.167*	1.565	.025	.43	7.90
	Meditation	3.633	1.565	.058	-.10	7.37
Pet therapy	Control	-4.167*	1.565	.025	-7.90	-.43
	Meditation	-.533	1.565	.938	-4.27	3.20
Meditation	Control	-3.633	1.565	.058	-7.37	.10
	Pet therapy	.533	1.565	.938	-3.20	4.27

*. The mean difference is significant at the 0.05 level.

Comparison 3—*Pet Therapy : Meditation*

The third comparison in Table 5.5 is between *Pet therapy* and *Meditation*, which produces a Sig.(nificance) (*p*) of .938. Since the *p* is greater than the .05 α level, this tells us that for *Pulse,* there is no statistically significant difference between *Pet therapy* (M = 79.93) and *Meditation* (M = 80.47).

Table 5.5 *ANOVA Post Hoc Multiple Comparisons* table shows no statistically significant difference between *Pet therapy* and *Meditation* (*p* = .938).

Multiple Comparisons

Pulse
Tukey HSD

(I) Group	(J) Group	Mean Difference (I-J)	Std. Error	Sig.	95% Confidence Interval Lower Bound	Upper Bound
Control	Pet therapy	4.167*	1.565	.025	.43	7.90
	Meditation	3.633	1.565	.058	-.10	7.37
Pet therapy	Control	-4.167*	1.565	.025	-7.90	-.43
	Meditation	-.533	1.565	.938	-4.27	3.20
Meditation	Control	-3.633	1.565	.058	-7.37	.10
	Pet therapy	.533	1.565	.938	-3.20	4.27

*. The mean difference is significant at the 0.05 level.

This concludes the analysis of the *Multiple Comparisons* (post hoc) table. You have probably noticed that we skipped analyzing half of the rows; this is because there is a double redundancy among the figures in the Sig. column. This is the kind of double redundancy that you would expect to see in a typical two-dimensional table. For example, in a multiplication table, you would see two 32s in the table because 4 × 8 = 32 and 8 × 4 = 32. Similarly, the Sig. column of the *Multiple Comparisons* table (Table 5.6) contains two *p* values of .025: one comparing *Control* to *Pet therapy* and the other comparing *Pet therapy* to *Control*. In addition, there are two .058 *p* values (*Control : Meditation* and *Meditation : Control*) and two .938 *p* values (*Pet therapy : Meditation* and *Meditation : Pet therapy*).

The ANOVA test can process any number of groups, provided the pretest criteria are met. As the number of groups increases, the number of (multiple) pairs of comparisons increases as well (see Table 5.7).

Table 5.6	*ANOVA Post Hoc Multiple Comparisons* table containing double-redundant Sig. (*p*) values: *Control : Pet therapy* produces the same *p* value as *Pet therapy : Control* (*p* = .025).

Multiple Comparisons

Pulse
Tukey HSD

(I) Group	(J) Group	Mean Difference (I-J)	Std. Error	Sig.	95% Confidence Interval	
					Lower Bound	Upper Bound
Control	Pet therapy	4.167*	1.565	.025	.43	7.90
	Meditation	3.633	1.565	.058	-.10	7.37
Pet therapy	Control	-4.167*	1.565	.025	-7.90	-.43
	Meditation	-.533	1.565	.938	-4.27	3.20
Meditation	Control	-3.633	1.565	.058	-7.37	.10
	Pet therapy	.533	1.565	.938	-3.20	4.27

*. The mean difference is significant at the 0.05 level.

Table 5.7	Increasing groups substantially increases ANOVA post hoc multiple comparisons.

2 Groups Renders 1 Comparison	*3 Groups Renders 3 Comparisons*	*4 Groups Renders 6 Comparisons*
$G_1{:}G_2$	$G_1{:}G_2$ $G_2{:}G_3$	$G_1{:}G_2$ $G_2{:}G_3$ $G_3{:}G_4$
	$G_1{:}G_3$	$G_1{:}G_3$ $G_2{:}G_4$
		$G_1{:}G_4$

NOTE: G = group.

You can easily calculate the number of (unique) pairwise comparisons the post hoc test will produce:

Unique Pairs Formula

G = Number of groups

Number of ANOVA post hoc unique pairs = **G! ÷ [2 × (G − 2)!]**

The preceding formula uses the **factorial** function denoted by the exclamation mark (!). If your calculator does not have a factorial (!) button, you can calculate it manually: Simply multiply all of the integers between 1 and the specified number. For example, $3! = 1 \times 2 \times 3$, which equals 6.

H₀ Hypothesis Resolution

To clarify the hypothesis resolution process, it is helpful to organize the findings in a table and use an asterisk to flag statistically significant difference(s) (Table 5.8).

NOTE: SPSS does not generate this table (Table 5.8) directly; you can assemble this table by gathering the means from the *Descriptives* table or the histograms with normal curves (Figures 5.2, 5.3, and 5.4) and the p values from the Sig. column in the *Multiple Comparisons* table (Table 5.3).

With this results table assembled, we can now revisit and resolve our pending hypotheses, which focuses on identifying the best way to reduce anxiety. To finalize this process, we will assess each hypothesis per the statistics contained in Table 5.8.

REJECT: H_0: There is no difference in pulse rates across the groups.

ACCEPT: H_1: There is a difference in pulse rates across the groups.

Table 5.8   Results summary of ANOVA for pulse.

Groups	p
Control (M = 84.10) : Pet therapy (M = 79.93)	.025*
Control (M = 84.10) : Mediation (M = 80.47)	.058
Pet therapy (M = 79.93) : Mediation (M = 80.47)	.938

*Statistically significant difference detected between groups ($p \le .05$).

Because we discovered a statistically significant difference among at least one pair of the relaxation techniques, we reject H_0 and accept H_1. Specifically, when it comes to reducing the pulse rates of these participants, *Pet therapy* outperformed *Control* group ($p = .025$).

Incidentally, if all of the pairwise comparisons had produced p values that were greater than .05, then we would have accepted H_0 and rejected H_1.

Abstract

We recruited 90 participants who were diagnosed with acute stress disorder. We randomly assigned participants to one of three groups: Participants in Group 1 (the control group) received no supplemental treatment (for 30 minutes), those in Group 2 were provided a 30-minute pet therapy session with a certified therapy dog, and those in Group 3 engaged in a 30-minute guided meditation. After 30 minutes, the researcher recorded the pulse rate (beats per minute) of each participant.

The pulse rates were as follows: control group (M = 84.10, SD = 6.27), pet therapy group (M = 79.93, SD = 5.61), and meditation (M = 80.47, SD = 6.28).

The mean pulse rate of those in the pet therapy group was 4.17 lower than those in the control group (p = .025, α = .05). This statistically significant finding suggests that pet therapy is a viable nonpharmaceutical supplemental treatment for those diagnosed with acute stress disorder. Considering that the meditation group had a pulse rate that was 3.63 lower than the control group (p = .058, α = .05), we intend to retain meditation in our next study.

Occasionally, as in this example, a *p* value may be close to .05 (e.g., *p* = .058). In such instances, you may be tempted to comment that the .058 *p* level is *approaching* statistical significance. While the optimism may be commendable, this is a common mistake. The term *approaching* wrongly implies that the *p* value is a *dynamic* variable—that it is in motion, and somehow on its way to crossing the .05 finish line, but this is not at all the case. The .058 *p* value is actually a *static* variable, meaning that it is not in motion—the .058 *p* value is no more *approaching* .05 than it is *approaching* .06. Think of the .058 *p* value as *parked;* it is not going anywhere, in the same way that a parked car is neither *approaching* nor *departing* from the car parked in front of it, no matter how close those cars are parked to each other. At best, one could state that it (the .058 *p* value) is *close* to the .05 α level, and that it would be interesting to consider monitoring this variable should this experiment be repeated at some future point.

Here is a simpler way to think about this: Consider the Number 4 parked right where it belongs on a number line. It is not *drifting* in any direction; it is not *approaching* 3 or 5.

OVERVIEW—KRUSKAL-WALLIS TEST

One of the pretest criteria that must be met prior to running an ANOVA states that the data from each group must be normally distributed (Figure 5.9); minor variations in the normal distribution are acceptable. Occasionally, you may encounter data that are substantially skewed (Figure 5.10), bimodal (Figure 5.11), flat (Figure 5.12), or may have some other atypical distribution. In such instances, the **Kruskal-Wallis statistic test** is an appropriate alternative to the ANOVA test.

Figure 5.9   Normal.

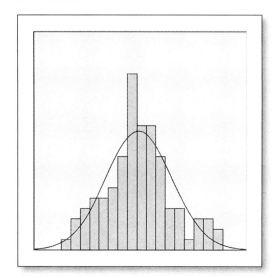

Figure 5.10   Skewed.

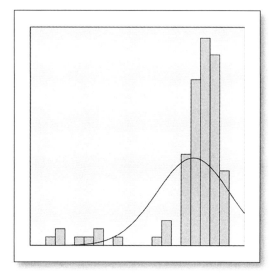

Figure 5.11   Bimodal.

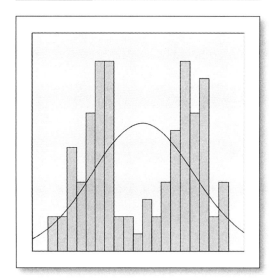

Figure 5.12   Flat.

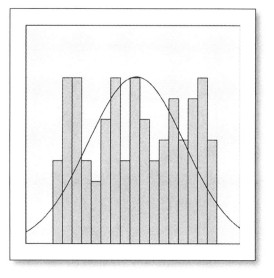

Test Run

For exemplary purposes, we will run the Kruskal-Wallis test using the same data set (**Ch 05 – Example 01 – ANOVA and Kruskal-Wallis Test.sav**) even though the data are normally distributed. This will enable us to compare the results of an ANOVA test to the results produced by the Kruskal-Wallis test.

1. On the main screen, click on *Analyze, Nonparametric Tests, Legacy Dialogs, K Independent Samples* (Figure 5.13).

Figure 5.13	Ordering the Kruskal-Wallis test: Click on *Analyze, Nonparametric Tests, Legacy Dialogs, K Independent Samples.*

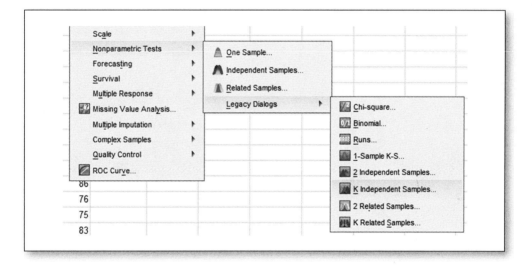

2. On the *Test for Several Independent Samples* menu, move *Pulse* to the *Test Variable List* window.

3. Move *Group* to the *Grouping Variable* box (Figure 5.14).

4. Click on *Group(? ?)*; then click on *Define Range*.

5. On the *Several Independent* Samples: Define Range submenu, for *Minimum,* enter *1;* for *Maximum,* enter *3* (since the groups are numbered 1 [for *Control*] through 3 [for *Meditation*]) (Figure 5.15).

6. Click *Continue;* this will close this submenu.

7. On the *Tests for Several Independent Samples* menu, click on *OK*.

Figure 5.14 On the *Tests for Several Independent Samples* menu, move *Time* to *Test Variable List*, and move *Group* to the *Grouping Variable* box.

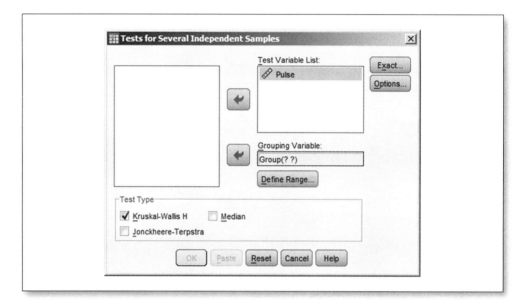

Figure 5.15 On the *Tests for Several Independent Samples* submenu, for *Minimum*, enter 1; for *Maximum*, enter 3.

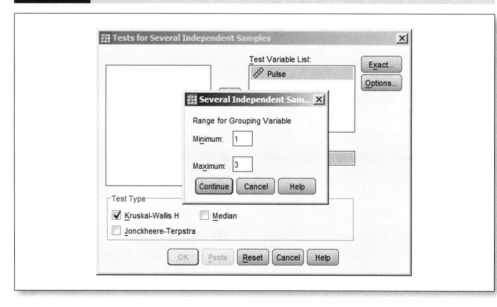

Results

The Kruskal-Wallis result is found in the Test Statistics table (Table 5.9); the *Asymp. Sig.* statistic rendered a *p* value of .030; this is less than α (.05), so we would conclude that there is a statistically significant difference (somewhere) among the performances of the three *times*, but we still need to conduct pairwise (post hoc type) analyses to determine which group(s) outperformed which.

Table 5.9   Kruskal-Wallis *p* value = .030.

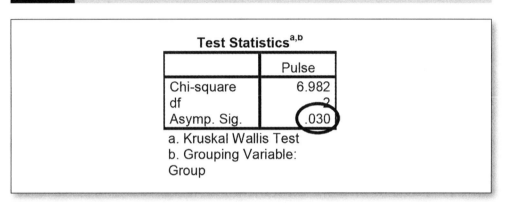

The ANOVA test provides a variety of post hoc options (e.g., Tukey, Sidak). Although the Kruskal-Wallis test does not include a post hoc menu, we can take a few extra steps to process pairwise comparisons among the groups using the Kruskal-Wallis test. We will accomplish this using the *Select Cases* function to select two groups at a time and run separate Kruskal-Wallis tests for each pair. First, we will select and process *Control : Pet therapy,* then *Control : Meditation,* and finally *Pet therapy : Meditation.*

8. Click on the *Select Cases* icon.

9. On the *Select Cases* menu, click on ⊙ *If condition is satisfied* (Figure 5.16).

10. Click on *If.*

11. On the *Select Cases: If* menu, specify the pair of groups that you want selected (Figure 5.17):

   - *On the first pass* through this process, enter *Group = 1 or Group = 2.*
   - *On the second pass,* enter *Group = 1 or Group = 3.*
   - *On the third pass,* enter *Group = 2 or Group = 3.*

| Figure 5.16 | On the *Select Cases* menu, click on ⊙ *If condition is satisfied*, then click on *If*. |

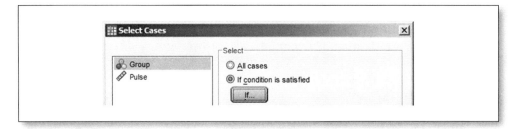

| Figure 5.17 | On the *Select Cases* menu, click on ⊙ *If condition is satisfied*, then click on *If*. |

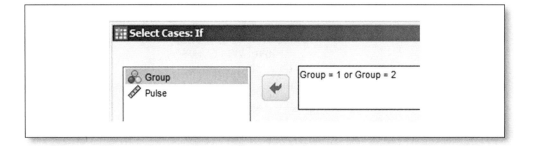

12. Click *OK*.

13. Now that only two groups are selected, run the Kruskal-Wallis procedure from Step 1 and record the *p* value produced by each run; upon gathering these figures, you will be able to assemble a Kruskal-Wallis post hoc table (Table 5.10). NOTE: You can keep using the parameters specified from the previous run(s).

| Table 5.10 | Pairwise *p* values for the Kruskal-Wallis test (manually assembled). |

Groups	*p*
Control : Pet therapy	.012*
Control : Meditation	.042*
Pet therapy : Meditation	.847

*Statistically significant difference detected between groups ($p \leq .05$).

To finalize this discussion, consider Table 5.11, which shows the p values produced by the ANOVA Tukey post hoc test compared alongside the p values produced by the Kruskal-Wallis test.

In addition to noting the differences in the pairwise p values (Table 5.11), remember that the ANOVA test produced an initial p value of .018 (which we read before the paired post hoc tests), whereas the Kruskal-Wallis produced an initial (overall) p value of .030. The differences in these p values are due to the internal transformations that the Kruskal-Wallis test conducts on the data. If one or more substantial violations are detected when running the pretest checklist for the ANOVA, then the Kruskal-Wallis test is considered a viable alternative.

Table 5.11 ANOVA and Kruskal-Wallis pairwise post hoc p values.

Groups	ANOVA p	Kruskal-Wallis p
Control : Pet therapy	.025*	.012*
Control : Meditation	.058	.042*
Pet therapy : Meditation	.938	.847

*Statistically significant difference detected between groups ($p \le .05$).

GOOD COMMON SENSE

When carrying statistical results into the real world, there are some practical considerations to take into account. Using this example, pet therapy stood out as the best treatment with a mean pulse rate of 79.93; however, the meditation group came in as a close second with a mean pulse rate of 80.47. The .054 difference in mean pulse rates between these two groups is statistically insignificant ($p = .938$). This suggests that these two treatments produced very similar results when it comes to reducing the pulse rate of anxious participants. Despite the appeal of the therapy dogs, it may not be feasible or affordable to issue such pets to each participant. However, it would be fairly simple and affordable to provide each participant with a copy of the meditation recording so that they can practice meditation at home to facilitate longitudinal home care.

The point is that statistical analysis can provide precise results that can be used in making (more) informed decisions, yet in addition to statistical results, other factors may be considered when it comes to making decisions in the real world.

Another issue involves the capacity of the ANOVA model. Table 5.7 and the combinations formula (Unique pairs = G! ÷ [2 × (G − 2)!]) reveal that as more groups are included, the number of ANOVA post hoc paired comparisons increases substantially. A 5-group design would render 10 unique comparisons, 6 groups would render 15, and a 10-group design would render 45 unique comparisons along with their corresponding p values.

While SPSS or any statistical software would have no problem processing these figures, there would be some real-world challenges to address. Consider the pretest criteria—in order for the results of an ANOVA test to be considered robust, there should be a suitably (large) sample to facilitate normal distributions among all of the groups. Another consideration involves the documentation process. For example, a 10-group study would render 45 unique pairwise comparisons in the ANOVA post hoc table, which, depending on the nature of the data, may be a bit unwieldy when it comes to interpretation and overall comprehension of the results.

Key Concepts

- ANOVA
- Pretest checklist

    ○ Normality
    ○ Homogeneity of variance
    ○ n

- Post hoc tests

    ○ Tukey
    ○ Sidak

- Hypothesis resolution
- Documenting results
- Kruskal-Wallis test
- Good common sense

Practice Exercises

Use the prepared SPSS data sets (download from **study.sagepub.com/intermediatestats**).

NOTE: These practice exercises and data sets are the same as those in **Chapter 5: *t* Test and Mann-Whitney U test** except instead of the two-group designs, additional data has been included to facilitate ANOVA processing: Exercises 5.1 through 5.8 have three groups, and exercises 5.9 and 5.10 have four groups.

Exercise 5.1

You want to determine the optimal tutor-to-student ratio. Students seeking tutoring will be randomly assigned to one of three groups: Group 1 will involve each tutor working with only one student; in Group 2, each tutor will work with two students; and in Group 3, each tutor will work with five students. At the end of the term, students will be asked to complete the Tutor Satisfaction Survey, which renders a score from 0 to 100.

Data set: **Ch 05 – Exercise 01A.sav**

Codebook

Variable:	Group
Definition:	Group number (1 = One-to-one, 2 = Two-to-one, 3 = Five-to-one)
Type:	Categorical

Variable:	TSS
Definition:	Tutor Satisfaction Survey score (0 = Very unsatisfied . . . 100 = Very satisfied)
Type:	Continuous

a. Write the hypotheses.

b. Run each criterion of the pretest checklist (normality, homogeneity of variance, and *n*) and discuss your findings.

c. Run the ANOVA test and document your findings (*n*s, means, and Sig. [*p* value], hypotheses resolution).

d. Write an abstract under 200 words detailing a summary of the study, the ANOVA test results, hypothesis resolution, and implications of your findings.

Repeat this exercise using data set: **Ch 05 – Exercise 01B.sav.**

Exercise 5.2

Clinicians at a nursing home facility want to see if giving residents a plant to tend to will help lower depression. To test this idea, the residents are randomly assigned to one of three groups: Those assigned to Group 1 will serve as the control group and will not be given a plant. Members of Group 2 will be given a small bamboo plant along with a card detailing care instructions. Members of Group 3 will be given a small cactus along with a card detailing care instructions. After 90 days, all participants will complete the Acme Depression Scale, which renders a score between 1 and 100 (1 = Low depression . . . 100 = High depression).

Data set: **Ch 05 – Exercise 02A.sav**

Codebook

Variable:	Group
Definition:	Group number
Type:	Categorical (1 = No plant, 2 = Bamboo, 3 = Cactus)

Variable: Depress

Definition: Acme Depression Scale

Type: Continuous (1 = Low depression . . . 100 = High depression)

a. Write the hypotheses.

b. Run each criterion of the pretest checklist (normality, homogeneity of variance, and n) and discuss your findings.

c. Run the ANOVA test and document your findings (ns, means, and Sig. [p value], hypotheses resolution).

d. Write an abstract under 200 words detailing a summary of the study, the ANOVA test results, hypothesis resolution, and implications of your findings.

Repeat this exercise using **Ch 05 – Exercise 02B.sav.**

Exercise 5.3

A judge mandates that juvenile offenders who have priors be assigned to a trained delinquency prevention mentor. To assess this intervention, offenders will be randomly assigned to one of three groups: No mentor, a peer mentor who is 3 to 5 years older than the offender, or an adult mentor who is 10 or more years older than the offender. The following data will be gathered on each participant: Probation officer's compliance evaluation (0% . . . 100%).

Data set: **Ch 05 – Exercise 03A.sav**

Codebook

Variable: Group

Definition: Mentor group assignment

Type: Categorical (1 = No mentor, 2 = Peer mentor, 3 = Adult mentor)

Variable: Probation_compliance

Definition: Probation officer's overall assessment of the youth's probation compliance

Type: Continuous (0 = Completely non-compliant . . . 100 = Completely compliant)

a. Write the hypotheses.

b. Run each criterion of the pretest checklist (normality, homogeneity of variance, and n) and discuss your findings.

c. Run the ANOVA test and document your findings (*n*s, means, and Sig. [*p* value], hypotheses resolution).

d. Write an abstract under 200 words detailing a summary of the study, the ANOVA test results, hypothesis resolution, and implications of your findings.

Repeat this exercise using **Ch 05 – Exercise 03B.sav.**

Exercise 5.4

In an effort to determine the effectiveness of light therapy to alleviate depression, you recruit a group of individuals who have been diagnosed with depression. The participants are randomly assigned to one of three groups: Group 1 will be the control group— members of this group will receive no light therapy. Members of Group 2 will get light therapy for 1 hour on even-numbered days over the course of 1 month. Members of Group 3 will get light therapy every day for 1 hour over the course of 1 month. After 1 month, all participants will complete the Acme Mood Scale, consisting of 10 questions; this instrument renders a score between 1 and 100 (1 = Extremely bad mood . . . 100 = Extremely good mood).

Data set: **Ch 05 – Exercise 04A.sav**

Codebook

Variable:	Group
Definition:	Group number
Type:	Categorical (1 = No light therapy, 2 = Light therapy: even days, 3 = Light therapy: every day)
Variable:	Mood
Definition:	Acme Mood Scale
Type:	Continuous (1 = Extremely bad mood . . . 100 = Extremely good mood)

a. Write the hypotheses.

b. Run each criterion of the pretest checklist (normality, homogeneity of variance, and *n*) and discuss your findings.

c. Run the ANOVA test and document your findings (*n*s, means, and Sig. [*p* value], hypotheses resolution).

d. Write an abstract under 200 words detailing a summary of the study, the ANOVA test results, hypothesis resolution, and implications of your findings.

Repeat this exercise using **Ch 05 – Exercise 04B.sav.**

Exercise 5.5

To assess the workplace benefits of providing paid time off (PTO), the Human Resources (HR) Department implements and evaluates different PTO plans at each of the company's three sites: Site 1 will serve as the control group; employees at this site will continue to receive 2 weeks of PTO per year. Employees at Site 2 will receive 2 weeks of PTO per year plus the fourth Friday of each month off (with pay). Employees at Site 3 will receive 3 weeks of PTO per year. The HR Department will use a web-based survey to gather the following data from all employees: score on the Acme Morale Scale (1 = extremely low morale . . . 25 = extremely high morale).

Data set: **Ch 05 – Exercise 05A.sav**

Codebook

Variable:	Site
Definition:	Work site
Type:	Categorical (1 = 2 Weeks PTO, 2 = 2 Weeks PTO + fourth Fridays off, 3 Weeks PTO)
Variable:	Morale
Definition:	Score on Acme Morale Scale
Type:	Continuous (1 = Extremely low morale . . . 25 = Extremely high morale)

a. Write the hypotheses.

b. Run each criterion of the pretest checklist (normality, homogeneity of variance, and n) and discuss your findings.

c. Run the ANOVA test and document your findings (ns, means, and Sig. [p value], hypotheses resolution).

d. Write an abstract under 200 words detailing a summary of the study, the ANOVA test results, hypothesis resolution, and implications of your findings.

Repeat this exercise using **Ch 05 – Exercise 5B.sav.**

Exercise 5.6

It is thought that exercising early in the morning will provide better energy throughout the day. To test this idea, participants are recruited and randomly assigned to one of three groups: Members of Group 1 will constitute the control group and not be assigned any walking. Members of Group 2 will walk from 7:00 to 7:30 a.m., Monday through Friday, over the course of 30 days. Members of Group 3 will walk from 7:00 to 8:00 a.m., Monday through Friday, over the course of 30 days. At the conclusion of the study, each participant will answer the 10 questions on the Acme End-of-the-Day Energy Scale. This instrument produces a score between 1 and 100 (1 = Extremely low energy . . . 100 = Extremely high energy).

Data set: **Ch 05 – Exercise 06A.sav**

Codebook

Variable:	Group
Definition:	Walking group assignment
Type:	Categorical (1 = No walking, 2 = Walking: 30 Minutes, 3 = Walking: 60 minutes)
Variable:	Energy
Definition:	Acme End-of-the-Day Energy Scale
Type:	Continuous (1 = Extremely low energy . . . 100 = Extremely high energy)

a. Write the hypotheses.

b. Run each criterion of the pretest checklist (normality, homogeneity of variance, and *n*) and discuss your findings

c. Run the ANOVA test and document your findings (*n*s, means, and Sig. [*p* value], hypotheses resolution).

d. Write an abstract under 200 words detailing a summary of the study, the ANOVA test results, hypothesis resolution, and implications of your findings.

Repeat this exercise using **Ch 05 – exercise 06B.sav**.

Exercise 5.7

A political consulting firm wants to determine the characteristics of voters when it comes to issues involving alternative energy. The researchers recruit a group of participants and randomly assign them to one of three groups: Group 1 will be the control group, and they will not be exposed to any advertising materials; Group 2 will be shown a print advertisement that will be used in a postal mailing; and Group 3 will be shown a video advertisement that will be aired on television. Finally, each participant will indicate his or her voting intentions for Proposition 86, which involves tax deductions for hybrid cars on a 1 to 7 scale (1 = Will definitely vote no . . . 7 = will definitely vote yes).

Data set: **Ch 05 – Exercise 07A.sav**

Codebook

> Variable: Group
>
> Definition: Advertising media
>
> Type: Categorical (1 = Control, 2 = Print, 3 = Video)

> Variable: Prop_86
>
> Definition: Likely voting decision on tax deductions for hybrid cars
>
> Type: Continuous (1 = Will definitely vote no . . . 7 = Will definitely vote yes)

a. Write the hypotheses.

b. Run each criterion of the pretest checklist (normality, homogeneity of variance, and n) and discuss your findings.

c. Run the ANOVA test and document your findings (ns, means, and Sig. [p value], hypotheses resolution).

d. Write an abstract under 200 words detailing a summary of the study, the ANOVA test results, hypothesis resolution, and implications of your findings.

Repeat this exercise using **Ch 05 – exercise 07B.sav**.

Exercise 5.8

A team of educational researchers wants to assess traditional classroom instruction compared to online options. Students who are enrolled in a course will be randomly assigned to one of three sections: Students in Section 1 will take the class in a traditional classroom. Students in Section 2 will take the course online with an interactive video cast of the instructor wherein students can ask the instructor questions during the session. Students in Section 3 will take the course online and view a prerecorded video of the professor delivering the lecture. The researchers will gather the course grade of each student (0% . . . 100%).

Data set: **Ch 05 – Exercise 08A.sav**

Codebook

> Variable: Section
>
> Definition: Learning modality
>
> Type: Categorical (1 = Classroom, 2 = Online live interactive, 3 = Online prerecorded video)

Variable: Grade

Definition: Final grade in course

Type: Continuous (0 . . . 100)

a. Write the hypotheses.

b. Run each criterion of the pretest checklist (normality, homogeneity of variance, and *n*) and discuss your findings.

c. Run the ANOVA test and document your findings (*n*s, means, and Sig. [*p* value], hypotheses resolution).

d. Write an abstract under 200 words detailing a summary of the study, the ANOVA test results, hypothesis resolution, and implications of your findings.

Repeat this exercise using **Ch 05 – Exercise 08B.sav**.

NOTE: Exercises 9 and 10 involve four groups each.

Exercise 5.9

The Acme Company claims that its new reading lamp increases reading speed, and you want to test this. You will record how long (in seconds) it takes for participants to read a 1,000-word essay. Participants will be randomly assigned to one of four groups: Group 1 will be the control group; they will read the essay using regular room lighting. Those in Group 2 will read the essay using the Acme lamp. Those in Group 3 will read the essay using a generic reading lamp. Those in Group 4 will read the essay using a flashlight.

Data set: **Ch 05 – Exercise 09A.sav**

Codebook

Variable: Group

Definition: Lighting group assignment

Type: Categorical (1 = Room lighting, 2 = Acme lamp, 3 = Generic lamp, 4 = Flashlight)

Variable: Seconds

Definition: The time it takes to read the essay

Type: Continuous

a. Write the hypotheses.

b. Run each criterion of the pretest checklist (normality, homogeneity of variance, and *n*) and discuss your findings.

c. Run the ANOVA test and document your findings (*n*s, means, and Sig. [*p* value], hypotheses resolution).

d. Write an abstract under 200 words detailing a summary of the study, the ANOVA test results, hypothesis resolution, and implications of your findings.

Repeat this exercise using **Ch 05 – Exercise 09B.sav.**

Exercise 5.10

Due to numerous complications involving missed medication dosages, you implement a study to determine the best strategy for enhancing medication adherence. Patients who are on a daily medication regime will be recruited, will receive a complimentary 1-month dosage of their regular medication(s), and will be randomly assigned to one of four groups. Group 1 will serve as the control group (no treatment); Group 2 will participate in a 1-hour in-person pharmacist-administered medication adherence workshop; Group 3 will receive a text message reminder with a picture of the drug (e.g., *It's time to take one tablet of Drug A*); Group 4 will attend the medication adherence workshop and also receive text messages. At the end of 1 month, participants will present their prescription bottle(s); you will count the remaining pills and calculate the dosage adherence percentage (e.g., 0 pills remaining = 100% adherence).

Data set: **Ch 05 – Exercise 10A.sav**

Codebook

Variable:	Group
Definition:	Group number
Type:	Categorical (1 = Control, 2 = Rx workshop, 3 = Texts, 4 = Rx workshop and texts)

Variable:	RxAdhere
Definition:	Percentage of medication adherence
Type:	Continuous (0 . . . 100)

a. Write the hypotheses.

b. Run each criterion of the pretest checklist (normality, homogeneity of variance, and *n*) and discuss your findings.

c. Run the ANOVA test and document your findings (*n*s, means, and Sig. [*p* value], hypotheses resolution).

d. Write an abstract under 200 words detailing a summary of the study, the ANOVA test results, hypothesis resolution, and implications of your findings.

Repeat this exercise using **Ch 05 – Exercise 10B.sav.**

C H A P T E R 6

ANCOVA

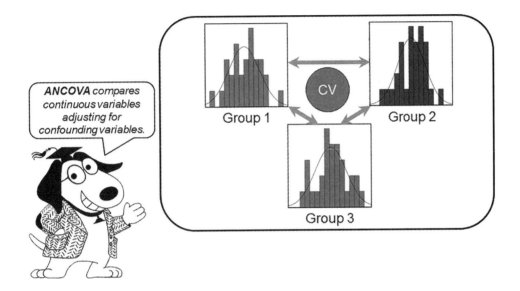

ANCOVA compares continuous variables adjusting for confounding variables.

Group 1   CV   Group 2

Group 3

Timing has a lot to do with the outcome of a rain dance.

—Cowboy proverb

Learning Objectives

Upon completing this chapter, you will be able to do the following:

- Determine when it is appropriate to run an ANCOVA test.
- Comprehend the characteristics of confounding variables (covariates).
- Verify that the data meet the criteria for ANCOVA processing: homogeneity of regression slopes and homogeneity of variance (Levene's test).
- Order an ANCOVA test.
- Derive results from the estimates and pairwise comparisons tables.
- Resolve the hypotheses.
- Write an appropriate abstract.

WHEN TO USE THIS STATISTIC

Guidelines for Selecting the ANCOVA Test

Overview: This statistic is for designs that involve more than two groups to determine which group(s) (if any) outperformed another taking into account the covariate that is expected to influence the outcome.

Variables: This statistic requires three variables for each record: (1) a categorical variable to designate the group, (2) a continuous variable to contain the outcome or score, (3) the continuous covariate. NOTE: There may be more than one covariate.

Results: Among those diagnosed with anxiety, we separated our participants into three groups and measured their pulse rates after 30 minutes of treatment. Because smoking is known to affect the pulse rate, we also gathered the mean daily smoking rate of each participant. Taking smoking into account, the (adjusted) mean pulse rates were 84.1 for the control group, 79.9 for the pet therapy group, and 80.5 for the meditation group. The pulse rate for the pet therapy group is statistically significantly lower than the control group ($p = .029$, $\alpha = .05$).

VIDEO

The tutorial video for this chapter is **Ch 06 – ANCOVA.mp4**. This video provides an overview of the ANCOVA (analysis of covariance) statistic, followed by the SPSS procedures for processing the pretest checklist, ordering the statistical run, and interpreting the results of this test using the data set: **Ch 06 – Example 01 – ANCOVA.sav**.

LAYERED LEARNING

The notion of ANCOVA is conceptually so similar to ANOVA (Chapter 5) that the same data sets will be used in the example and exercises, with one variable added to each data set. Notice that the example data set for this chapter (**Ch 06 – Example 01 – ANCOVA.sav**) is exactly the same as the example data set used for the ANOVA chapter (**Ch 05 – Example 01 – ANOVA .sav**), except it has a third variable (*Smoking*) included (Figure 6.1).

OVERVIEW—ANCOVA

The **ANCOVA** is similar to the ANOVA test, except ANCOVA allows us to include a covariate into the model to adjust the results for a known confounding variable.

| Figure 6.1 | Excerpt from **Ch 06 – Example – ANCOVA.sav.** |

Ch 06 - Example 01 - ANCOVA.sav [DataSet1] - PASW S

File Edit View Data Transform Analyze Direct Mar

	Group	Pulse	Smoking
1	Control	76	0
2	Control	84	0
3	Control	86	0
4	Control	78	60
5	Control	71	0

To recap, the experimental model used in this example involves administering one of three treatments for 30 minutes: a control condition, pet therapy, or meditation to individuals who have been diagnosed with acute anxiety disorder, and then measuring their pulse rate. In terms of the variables, the treatment (control, pet therapy, or meditation) is the independent variable (IV) and the pulse rate is the outcome variable, technically referred to as the dependent variable (DV). In a perfect world, the experimental design could look like Figure 6.2.

| Figure 6.2 | Independent variable (IV) propagates change in the dependent variable (DV). |

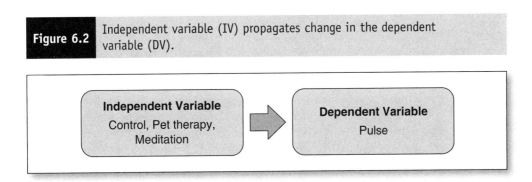

Independent Variable
Control, Pet therapy, Meditation

Dependent Variable
Pulse

As you might expect, we do not live in a perfect world; in fact, science actively acknowledges this. It is expected that extraneous factors may influence scores as they travel from the independent variable to the dependent variable. In the language of experimental design, these factors are referred to as **confounding variables (CV)**, as they can influence the results contained in the dependent variable. In statistical language, confounding variables are referred to as **covariates**.

In the ANOVA example, we did not identify a confounding variable, as symbolized in Figure 6.2. For the ANCOVA example, a confounding variable (*Smoking*) has been introduced: Suppose we discovered that some of the participants in the relaxation experiment smoke cigarettes. Cigarette smoking could be considered a confounding variable as smoking influences the pulse rate. Now instead of just the independent variable (control, pet therapy, or meditation) influencing changes in the dependent variable (pulse), there is an additional *confounding* variable (smoking) that can alter the data in the dependent variable (Figure 6.3).

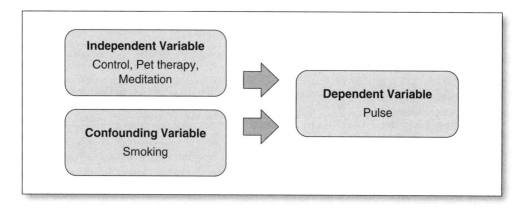

Figure 6.3 Independent variable (IV) and confounding variable (CV) both propagate change in the dependent variable (DV).

As stated, ANCOVA is similar to an ANOVA-type model; however, ANCOVA adjusts the results according to the influence that the confounding variable (covariate) introduced. In other words, if we have data pertaining to a known confounding variable, such as the influence of smoking on pulse rate, ANCOVA can statistically adjust the results so as to neutralize the effects of the identified confounding factor. This provides a cleaner image of the effect that the independent variable (Control, Pet therapy, Meditation) has on the dependent variable (pulse rate)—as if the confounding variable (smoking) has been (statistically) removed from the picture. The results will look as if you had ordered an ANOVA test, except the figures will be adjusted to account for the influence of the covariate (*Smoking*).

The covariate must be a *continuous* variable. Notice that in the codebook for this example, the variable *Smoking* is a continuous variable, defined as the *Number of cigarettes the participant smokes in a typical day (0 = nonsmoker)*.

In order to facilitate the integrity of this analysis, there should be a reasonable rationale for including a covariate—there needs to be some reason to expect that the covariate can be gathered accurately, and that the proposed covariate is rationally associated with the dependent variable. Such findings may emerge from such sources as evidence based literature, expert consultation, prior experience, or even common sense.

Example

A research team has recruited a group of individuals who have been diagnosed with acute stress disorder to determine the effectiveness of supplemental nonpharmaceutical treatments for reducing stress: (1) no supplemental therapy, (2) pet therapy with certified therapy dogs, or (3) meditation.

Research Question

Is pet therapy or meditation effective in reducing stress among those diagnosed with acute stress disorder?

GROUPS

A researcher recruits a total of 90 participants who meet the diagnostic criteria for acute stress disorder. Participants will be scheduled to come to the research center one at a time. Upon arriving, each participant will be assigned to one of three groups on a sequential basis (first assigned to Group 1, second assigned to Group 2, third assigned to Group 3, fourth assigned to Group 1, etc.). Those assigned to Group 1 will constitute the control group and will be instructed to sit and relax for 30 minutes (with no treatment). Those in Group 2 will receive 30 minutes of pet therapy, and those in Group 3 will meditate for 30 minutes.

PROCEDURE

Each participant will be guided to a room with a comfortable sofa. Those in the control group will be instructed to just sit and relax. Those in the pet therapy group will be introduced to the therapy dog by name and instructed that the participant may hold the dog in his or her lap, pet the dog on the sofa, brush the dog, or give the dog the allotted treats in whatever combination they wish. Those in the meditation group will listen to a recording of gentle music with a narrative taking the participant through a guided meditation. After 30 minutes, the researcher will return to each participant to measure the participant's pulse rate, ask the participant the average number of cigarettes he or she smokes per day, and then dismiss them. The lower pulse rate would reflect more relaxation, controlling for smoking.

NOTE: This study will rule out those who use other forms of smoking (e.g., e-cigarettes, pipes, hookahs) due to the difficulty in quantifying the smoking rates of such devices.

HYPOTHESES

The null hypothesis (H_0) is phrased to anticipate that the experiment/intervention fails, indicating that *no treatment outperformed any of the others*. The alternative hypothesis (H_1) states that *at least one treatment did outperform another.*

H_0:   There is no difference in pulse rates across the groups.

H_1:   There is a difference in pulse rates across the groups.

 ## DATA SET

Use the following data set: **Ch 06 – Example – ANCOVA.sav.**

Codebook

Variable:	Group
Definition:	Group assignment
Type:	Categorical (1 = Control, 2 = Pet therapy, 3 = Meditation)

Variable:	Pulse
Definition:	Heartbeats per minute measured 30 minutes after start
Type:	Continuous

Variable:	Smoking
Definition:	Number of cigarettes the participant smokes in a typical day (0 = nonsmoker)
Type:	Continuous

 ## PRETEST CHECKLIST

ANCOVA Pretest Checklist

☑ 1. Homogeneity of regression slopes*

☑ 2. Homogeneity of variance (Levene's test)**

*Run prior to ANCOVA test

**Results produced upon ANCOVA test run

NOTE: If any of the pretest checklist criteria are not satisfied, proceed with the analysis, but concisely discuss such anomalies in the *Results* or *Limitations* sections of the documentation so the reader can more plausibly interpret the precision of the findings.

The statistical pretest checklist for the ANCOVA involves two criteria: (1) homogeneity of regression slopes and (2) homogeneity of variance (Levene's test).

Pretest Checklist Criterion 1—Homogeneity of Regression Slopes

The **homogeneity of regressions slopes** test checks that the slopes of the regression lines of the variables involved are similar to each other.

1. On the main SPSS menu, click on *Analyze, General Linear Model, Univariate.* (Figure 6.4)

Figure 6.4 *Analyze, General Linear Model, Univariate.*

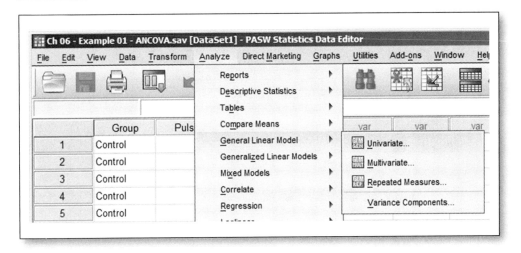

2. Move the *Group* variable into the *Fixed Factor(s)* window. (Figure 6.5)

3. Move the *Pulse* variable into the *Dependent Variable* window.

4. Move the *Smoking* variable into the *Covariate(s)* window.

5. Click on *Model.*

6. Select ⊙ *Custom.* (Figure 6.6)

7. Move *Group* and *Smoking* (in *Factors & Covariates* box) into *Model* box.

8. Hold down *Shift* key, click on *Group* and *Smoking* (this will select both *Group* and *Smoking* together to signify the interaction term), and move them into the *Model* box (this should show as *Smoking*Group*).

9. Click *Continue* (this will take you back to the *Univariate* menu).

10. Click *OK.*

Figure 6.5   *Univariate* menu.

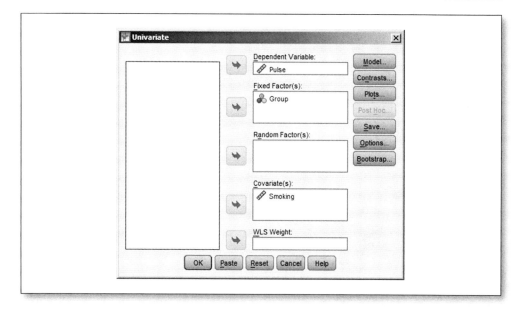

Figure 6.6   *Univariate: Model* menu.

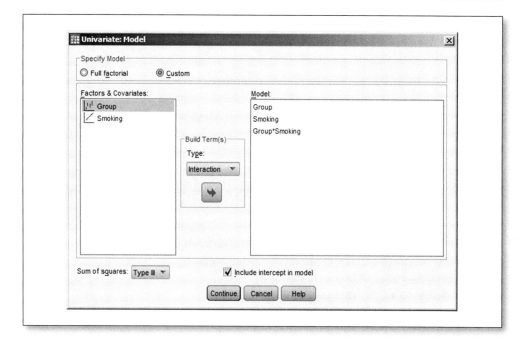

Inspect the *Test of Between-Subjects Effects* table (Table 6.1). The *Sig.* (*p* value) for the *Group*Smoking* (interaction) term is .488. This is greater than α (.05), indicating that there is no statistically significant difference in the regression slopes among the variables involved in this model. Hence, the assumption of *homogeneity of regression slopes* is satisfied. In other words, the trend of the values contained in each variable concurs (runs virtually parallel) with each other.

Table 6.1 Tests of between-subjects effects.

Tests of Between-Subjects Effects

Dependent Variable:Pulse

Source	Type III Sum of Squares	df	Mean Square	F	Sig.
Corrected Model	362.659ª	5	72.532	1.938	.097
Intercept	543567.131	1	543567.131	14523.520	.000
Group	348.280	2	174.140	4.653	.012
Smoking	.890	1	.890	.024	.878
Group * Smoking	54.137	2	27.069	.723	.488
Error	3143.841	84	37.427		
Total	601309.000	90			
Corrected Total	3506.500	89			

a. R Squared = .103 (Adjusted R Squared = .050)

The remaining pretest criterion, (2) homogeneity of variance (Levene's test), will be processed during the Test Run and finalized in the Results section.

TEST RUN

1. On the main SPSS menu, click on *Analyze, General Linear Model, Univariate.*

   Steps 2 to 4 may be bypassed; the variables should still reside in the proper windows from the prior procedure where we checked for the *Homogeneity of Regression Slopes.*

2. Move the *Group* variable into the *Fixed Factor(s)* window.

3. Move the *Pulse* variable into the *Dependent Variable* window.

4. Move the *Smoking* variable into the *Covariate(s)* window.

5. Click on *Model*.

6. Select ⊙ *Full factorial*. This will discard the model that involved the *Group*Smoking* interaction term specified earlier (Figure 6.8).

7. Click on *Continue*. This will take you back to the *Univariate* menu (Figure 6.7).

Figure 6.7 *Univariate* menu.

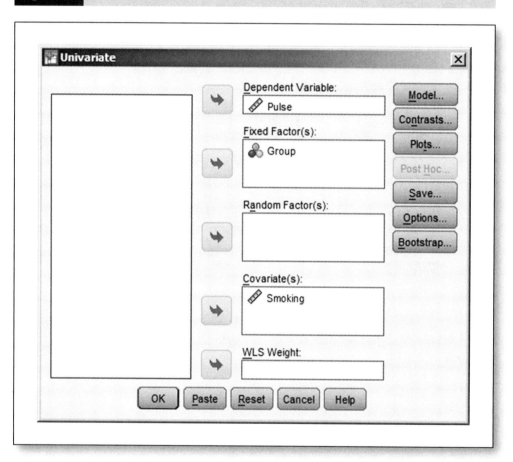

8. On the *Univariate* menu, click on *Options*.

9. In the *Factor(s) and Factor Interactions* window, move *Group* into the *Display Means for* window (Figure 6.9).

10. Check the ☑ *Compare main effects* checkbox.

Figure 6.8   *Univariate: Model* menu.

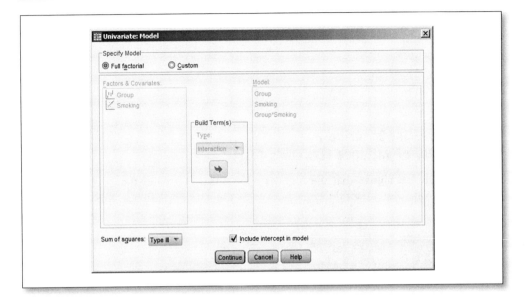

Figure 6.9   *Univariate: Options* menu.

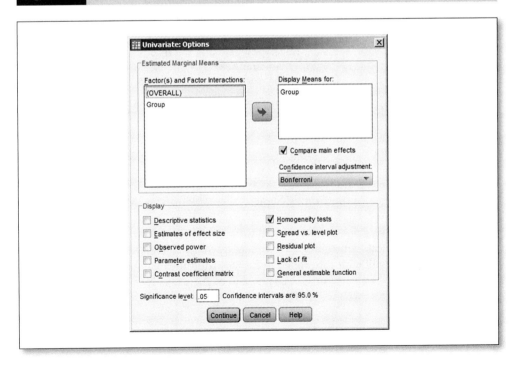

11. In the *Confidence interval adjustment* pull-down menu, select *Bonferroni*.

12. In the *Display* options, check the ☑ *Homogeneity tests*.

13. Click on *Continue*.

14. Click on *OK*.

RESULTS

Pretest Checklist Criterion 2— Homogeneity of Variance (Levene's Test)

Table 6.2 shows that the Sig. (*p*) = .691; this is greater than α (.05), indicating that there is no significant difference between the variances; hence, this criterion is satisfied.

Table 6.2	Levene's test of equality of error variances shows no statistically significant difference among the variances (*p* = .691, α = .05).

Levene's Test of Equality of Error Variances[a]
Dependent Variable:Pulse

F	df1	df2	Sig.
.371	2	87	.691

Tests the null hypothesis that the error variance
of the dependent variable is equal across groups.
a. Design: Intercept + Smoking + Group

Next, we look to the *Tests of Between-Subjects Effects* table (Table 6.3); the Sig. (*p*) value of .020 on the *Group* row indicates that a statistically significant difference has been detected among (the adjusted means for) the groups. For specific details on which group(s) outperformed which, we look to the *Pairwise Comparisons* table (Table 6.4).

The *Pairwise Comparisons* table (Table 6.4) is read in the same way as the *Multiple Comparisons* table produced by the ANOVA post hoc tests. These results reveal a statistically significant difference in the adjusted means between Control and Pet therapy (*p* = .029). The actual adjusted means of the *Pulse* rates for each *Group* are shown in the *Estimates* table (Table 6.5).

Table 6.3
Tests of Between-Subjects Effects table shows that a significant difference has been detected among the *Group*s ($p = .020$, $\alpha = .05$).

Tests of Between-Subjects Effects

Dependent Variable:Pulse

Source	Type III Sum of Squares	df	Mean Square	F	Sig.
Corrected Model	308.522[a]	3	102.841	2.766	.047
Intercept	547240.431	1	547240.431	14716.385	.000
Smoking	.055	1	.055	.001	.969
Group	306.124	2	153.062	4.116	.020
Error	3197.978	86	37.186		
Total	601309.000	90			
Corrected Total	3506.500	89			

a. R Squared = .088 (Adjusted R Squared = .056)

Table 6.4
Pairwise Comparisons table shows statistically significant differences between *control* and *pet therapy* ($p = .029$).

Pairwise Comparisons

Dependent Variable:Pulse

(I) Group	(J) Group	Mean Difference (I-J)	Std. Error	Sig.[a]	95% Confidence Interval for Difference[a]	
					Lower Bound	Upper Bound
Control	Pet therapy	4.165*	1.575	.029	.320	8.011
	Meditation	3.625	1.589	.075	-.254	7.505
Pet therapy	Control	-4.165*	1.575	.029	-8.011	-.320
	Meditation	-.540	1.585	1.000	-4.410	3.329
Meditation	Control	-3.625	1.589	.075	-7.505	.254
	Pet therapy	.540	1.585	1.000	-3.329	4.410

Based on estimated marginal means
*. The mean difference is significant at the .05 level.
a. Adjustment for multiple comparisons: Bonferroni.

| Table 6.5 | *Estimates* table shows adjusted values for each group per the influence of the *Smoking* covariate. |

Estimates

Dependent Variable:Pulse

Group	Mean	Std. Error	95% Confidence Interval	
			Lower Bound	Upper Bound
Control	84.097[a]	1.116	81.878	86.316
Pet therapy	79.931[a]	1.114	77.716	82.147
Meditation	80.472[a]	1.121	78.243	82.700

a. Covariates appearing in the model are evaluated at the following values: Smoking = 3.43.

H₀ HYPOTHESIS RESOLUTION

To clarify the hypothesis resolution process, it is helpful to organize the findings in a table and use an asterisk to flag statistically significant difference(s) (Table 6.6).

NOTE: SPSS does not generate this table (Table 6.6) directly; you can assemble this table by gathering the means from the *Estimates* table (Table 6.5) and the *p* values from the Sig. column in the *Pairwise Comparisons* table (Table 6.4).

| Table 6.6 | Results of ANCOVA for Pulse. |

Groups	*p*
Control (M = 84.10) : Pet therapy (M = 79.93)	.029*
Control (M = 84.10) : Meditation (M = 80.47)	.075
Pet therapy (M = 79.93) : Meditation (M = 80.47)	1.000

NOTE: Figures adjusted to account for cigarettes smoked per day among participants (M = 3.4, SD = 11.5).

*Statistically significant difference detected between groups ($p \leq .05$).

With this results table assembled, we can now revisit and resolve our pending hypotheses, which focus on the best method for reducing anxiety. To finalize this process, we will assess each hypothesis per the statistics contained in Table 6.6.

REJECT: H_0: There is no difference in pulse rates across the groups.

ACCEPT: H_1: There is a difference in pulse rates across the groups.

Because we discovered a statistically significant difference among at least one pair of the (mean) pulses, we reject H_0 and accept H_1. Specifically, pet therapy outperformed the control group in lowering the pulse rate (p = .029).

Incidentally, if all of the pairwise comparisons had produced p values that were greater than .05, then we would have accepted H_0 and rejected H_1.

ABSTRACT

We recruited 90 participants who were diagnosed with acute stress disorder. We randomly assigned participants to one of three groups: Participants in Group 1 (the control group) received no supplemental treatment (for 30 minutes), those in Group 2 were provided a 30-minute pet therapy session with a certified therapy dog, and those in Group 3 engaged in a 30-minute guided meditation. After 30 minutes, the researcher recorded the pulse rate (beats per minute) of each participant. Per concerns that smoking could influence pulse rate, we asked each participant how many cigarettes he or she smoked in a typical day and included that figure as a covariate.

The pulse rates were as follows: Control group (M = 84.10, SD = 6.27), pet therapy group (M = 79.93, SD = 5.61), and meditation group (M = 80.47, SD = 6.28).

The mean pulse rate of those in the pet therapy group was 4.17 lower than those in the control group (p = .029, α = .05). This statistically significant finding suggests that pet therapy is a viable nonpharmaceutical supplemental treatment for those diagnosed with acute stress disorder. Considering that the meditation group had a pulse rate that was 3.63 lower than the control group (p = .075, α = .05), we intend to retain meditation in our next study.

GOOD COMMON SENSE

The ANCOVA statistic provides a system for efficiently coping with the effects of identified (measured) covariates within a multigroup design, but keep in mind that the adjusted results are considered *estimated* (not perfect) values, based on the covariate data.

While it is valuable to anticipate, measure, and load a critical covariate into the ANCOVA model, it is not possible to account for and accurately measure the effects of all possible confounding variables, such as threats to internal validity, distractions, environmental impurities, and so forth.

Statistics is not about achieving perfection or proving anything; overall, it is about increasing our understanding by reducing uncertainty. ANCOVA helps to control for the effects of potential confounds, which brings us closer to achieving a clearer understanding of the IV → DV model, but it may not be possible to create a completely "clean" experiment, which would comprehensively identify and eliminate all effects that confounding variables could be having on the dependent variable.

Key Concepts

- ANCOVA
- Confounding variable/Covariate
- Pretest checklist

  - Homogeneity of regression slopes
  - Homogeneity of variance (Levene's test)

- Hypothesis resolution
- Documenting results
- Good common sense

Practice Exercises

Use the prepared SPSS data sets (download from **study.sagepub.com/intermediatestats**).

NOTE: These practice exercises and data sets are the same as those in **Chapter 6: ANOVA** except an extra (covariate) variable has been included to enable ANCOVA processing. All of the exercises involve three groups, except for Exercises 9 and 10, which involve four groups.

Exercise 6.1

You want to determine the optimal tutor-to-student ratio. Students seeking tutoring will be randomly assigned to one of three groups: Group 1 will involve each tutor working with only one student; in Group 2, each tutor will work with two students; and in Group 3, each tutor will work with five students. At the end of the term, students will be asked to complete the Tutor Satisfaction Survey, which renders a score from 0 to 100, and the number of months that the tutor has been providing tutoring service (as the covariate).

Data set: **Ch 06 – Exercise 01A.sav**

Codebook

Variable:	Group
Definition:	Group number
Type:	Categorical (1 = One-to-one, 2 = Two-to-one, 3 = Five-to-one)

Variable:	TSS
Definition:	Tutor Satisfaction Survey score
Type:	Continuous (0 = very unsatisfied . . . 100 = very satisfied)

Variable:	Tutor_months
Definition:	Number of months the tutor has been providing tutor service
Type:	Continuous

a. Write the hypotheses.

b. Run each criterion of the pretest checklist (homogeneity of regression slopes, homogeneity of variance [Levene's test]) and discuss your findings.

c. Run the ANCOVA test and document your findings (*ns*, means, and Sig. [*p* value], hypotheses resolution).

d. Write an abstract under 200 words detailing a summary of the study, the ANCOVA test results, hypothesis resolution, and implications of your findings.

Repeat this exercise using data set: **Ch 06 – Exercise 01B.sav.**

Exercise 6.2

Clinicians at a nursing home facility want to see if giving residents a plant to tend to will help lower depression. To test this idea, the residents are randomly assigned to one of three groups: Those assigned to Group 1 will serve as the control group and will not be given a plant. Members of Group 2 will be given a small bamboo plant along with a card detailing care instructions. Members of Group 3 will be given a small cactus along with a card detailing care instructions. After 90 days, all participants will complete the Acme Depression Scale, which renders a score between 1 and 100 (1 = Low depression . . . 100 = High depression). Daily antidepressant medication dosages will also be recorded (as the covariate).

Data set: **Ch 06 – Exercise 02A.sav**

Codebook

Variable:	Group
Definition:	Group number
Type:	Categorical (1 = No plant, 2 = Bamboo, 3 = Cactus)

Variable:	Depress
Definition:	Acme Depression Scale
Type:	Continuous (1 = Low depression . . . 100 = High depression)

Variable:	Antidepressant_Rx
Definition:	Antidepressant medication take per day (in milligrams)
Type:	Continuous

a. Write the hypotheses.

b. Run each criterion of the pretest checklist (homogeneity of regression slopes, homogeneity of variance [Levene's test]) and discuss your findings.

c. Run the ANCOVA test and document your findings (*n*s, means, and Sig. [*p* value], hypotheses resolution).

d. Write an abstract under 200 words detailing a summary of the study, the ANCOVA test results, hypothesis resolution, and implications of your findings.

Repeat this exercise using **Ch 06 – Exercise 02B.sav**.

Exercise 6.3

A judge mandates that juvenile offenders who have priors be assigned to a trained delinquency prevention mentor. To assess this intervention, offenders will be randomly assigned to one of three groups: No mentor, a peer mentor who is 3 to 5 years older than the offender, or an adult mentor who is 10 or more years older than the offender. The following data will be gathered on each participant: Probation officer's compliance evaluation (0% . . . 100%), and the age of the offender (as the covariate).

Data set: **Ch 06 – Exercise 03A.sav**

Codebook

Variable:	Group
Definition:	Mentor group assignment
Type:	Categorical (1 = No mentor, 2 = Peer mentor, 3 = Adult mentor)
Variable:	Probation_compliance
Definition:	Probation officer's overall assessment of the youth's probation compliance (0 = Completely noncompliant . . . 100 = Completely compliant)
Type:	Continuous
Variable:	Age
Definition:	Age of offender (e.g., 16.5 years)
Type:	Continuous

a. Write the hypotheses.

b. Run each criterion of the pretest checklist (homogeneity of regression slopes, homogeneity of variance [Levene's test]) and discuss your findings.

c. Run the ANCOVA test and document your findings (*ns*, means, and Sig. [*p* value], hypotheses resolution).

d. Write an abstract under 200 words detailing a summary of the study, the ANCOVA test results, hypothesis resolution, and implications of your findings.

Repeat this exercise using **Ch 06 – Exercise 03B.sav.**

Exercise 6.4

In an effort to determine the effectiveness of light therapy to alleviate depression, you recruit a group of individuals who have been diagnosed with depression. The participants are randomly assigned to one of three groups: Group 1 will be the control group—members of this group will receive no light therapy. Members of Group 2 will get light therapy for 1 hour on even-numbered days over the course of 1 month. Members of Group 3 will get light therapy every day for 1 hour over the course of 1 month. After 1 month, all participants will complete the Acme Mood Scale, consisting of 10 questions; this instrument renders a score between 1 and 100 (1 = Extremely bad mood . . . 100 = Extremely good mood). Each participant's age will also be recorded (as the covariate).

Data set: **Ch 06 – Exercise 04A.sav**

Codebook

Variable:	Group
Definition:	Group number
Type:	Categorical (1 = No light therapy, 2 = Light therapy: even days, 3 = Light therapy: every day)
Variable:	Mood
Definition:	Acme Mood Scale
Type:	Continuous (1 = Extremely bad mood . . . 100 = Extremely good mood)
Variable:	Age
Definition:	Age
Type:	Continuous

a. Write the hypotheses.

b. Run each criterion of the pretest checklist (homogeneity of regression slopes, homogeneity of variance [Levene's test]) and discuss your findings.

c. Run the ANCOVA test and document your findings (*ns*, means, and Sig. [*p* value], hypotheses resolution).

d. Write an abstract under 200 words detailing a summary of the study, the ANCOVA test results, hypothesis resolution, and implications of your findings.

Repeat this exercise using **Ch 06 – Exercise 04B.sav**.

Exercise 6.5

To assess the workplace benefits of providing paid time off (PTO), the Human Resources (HR) Department implements and evaluates different PTO plans at each of the company's three sites: Site 1 will serve as the control group; employees at this site will continue to receive 2 weeks of PTO per year. Employees at Site 2 will receive 2 weeks of PTO per year plus the fourth Friday of each month off (with pay). Employees at Site 3 will receive 3 weeks of PTO per year. The HR Department will use a web-based survey to gather the following data from all employees: Score on the Acme Morale Scale (1 = Extremely low morale . . . 25 = Extremely high morale). Additionally, seniority (the number of years at the company) will be recorded (as the covariate).

Data set: **Ch 06 – Exercise 05A.sav**

Codebook

Variable:	Site
Definition:	Work site
Type:	Categorical (1 = 2 Weeks PTO, 2 = 2 Weeks PTO + fourth Fridays off, 3 Weeks PTO)
Variable:	Morale
Definition:	Score on Acme Morale Scale
Type:	Continuous (1 = Extremely low morale . . . 25 = Extremely high morale)
Variable:	Seniority
Definition:	Number of years at the company
Type:	Continuous

a. Write the hypotheses.

b. Run each criterion of the pretest checklist (homogeneity of regression slopes, homogeneity of variance [Levene's test]) and discuss your findings.

c. Run the ANCOVA test and document your findings (*n*s, means, and Sig. [*p* value], hypotheses resolution).

d. Write an abstract under 200 words detailing a summary of the study, the ANCOVA test results, hypothesis resolution, and implications of your findings.

Repeat this exercise using **Ch 06 – Exercise 05B.sav**.

Exercise 6.6

It is thought that exercising early in the morning will provide better energy throughout the day. To test this idea, participants are recruited and randomly assigned to one of three groups: Members of Group 1 will constitute the control group and not be assigned any walking. Members of Group 2 will walk from 7:00 to 7:30 a.m., Monday through Friday, over the course of 30 days. Members of Group 3 will walk from 7:00 to 8:00 a.m., Monday through Friday, over the course of 30 days. At the conclusion of the study, each participant will answer the 10 questions on the Acme End-of-the-Day Energy Scale. This instrument produces a score between 1 and 100 (1 = Extremely low energy . . . 100 = Extremely high energy). The researcher will also record the number of hours that each participant spent sitting in a typical work day (as the covariate).

Data set: **Ch 06 – Exercise 06A.sav**

Codebook

Variable:	Group
Definition:	Walking group assignment
Type:	Categorical (1 = No walking, 2 = Walking: 30 Minutes, 3 = Walking: 60 minutes)
Variable:	Energy
Definition:	Acme End-of-the-Day Energy Scale
Type:	Continuous (1 = Extremely low energy . . . 100 = Extremely high energy)
Variable:	Sitting
Definition:	Mean number of hours sitting per day
Type:	Continuous

a. Write the hypotheses.

b. Run each criterion of the pretest checklist (homogeneity of regression slopes, homogeneity of variance [Levene's test]) and discuss your findings.

c. Run the ANCOVA test and document your findings (*n*s, means, and Sig. [*p* value], hypotheses resolution).

d. Write an abstract under 200 words detailing a summary of the study, the ANCOVA test results, hypothesis resolution, and implications of your findings.

Repeat this exercise using **Ch 06 – Exercise 06B.sav**.

Exercise 6.7

A political consulting firm wants to determine the characteristics of voters when it comes to issues involving alternative energy. The researchers recruit a group of participants and randomly assign them to one of three groups: Group 1 will be the control group, and they will not be exposed to any advertising materials; Group 2 will be shown a print advertisement that will be used in a postal mailing; and Group 3 will be shown a video advertisement that will be aired on television. Finally, each participant will indicate his or her voting intentions for Proposition 86, which involves tax deductions for hybrid cars on a 1 to 7 scale (1 = Will definitely vote no . . . 7 = will definitely vote yes). Additionally, participants will be asked to indicate their gross annual household income (as the covariate).

Data set: **Ch 06 – Exercise 07A.sav**

Codebook

Variable:	Group
Definition:	Advertising media
Type:	Categorical (1 = Control, 2 = Print, 3 = Video)
Variable:	Prop_86
Definition:	Likely voting decision on tax deductions for hybrid cars
Type:	Continuous (1 = Will definitely vote no . . . 7 = Will definitely vote yes)
Variable:	Income
Definition:	Annual gross household income
Type:	Continuous

a. Write the hypotheses.

b. Run each criterion of the pretest checklist (homogeneity of regression slopes, homogeneity of variance [Levene's test]) and discuss your findings.

   c. Run the ANCOVA test and document your findings (*n*s, means, and Sig. [*p* value], hypotheses resolution).

   d. Write an abstract under 200 words detailing a summary of the study, the ANCOVA test results, hypothesis resolution, and implications of your findings.

Repeat this exercise using **Ch 06 – Exercise 07B.sav**.

Exercise 6.8

A team of educational researchers wants to assess traditional classroom instruction compared to online options. Students who are enrolled in a course will be randomly assigned to one of three sections: Students in Section 1 will take the class in a traditional classroom. Students in Section 2 will take the course online with an interactive video cast of the instructor wherein students can ask the instructor questions during the session. Students in Section 3 will take the course online and view a prerecorded video of the professor delivering the lecture. The researchers will gather the course grade of each student (0% . . . 100%). Additionally, students will be asked to indicate their age (as the covariate).

Data set: **Ch 06 – Exercise 08A.sav**

Codebook

Variable:	Section
Definition:	Learning modality
Type:	Categorical (1 = Classroom, 2 = Online live interactive, 3 = Online prerecorded video)
Variable:	Grade
Definition:	Final grade in course
Type:	Continuous (0 . . . 100)
Variable:	Age
Definition:	Student's age
Type:	Continuous

   a. Write the hypotheses.

   b. Run each criterion of the pretest checklist (homogeneity of regression slopes, homogeneity of variance [Levene's test]) and discuss your findings.

   c. Run the ANCOVA test and document your findings (*n*s, means, and Sig. [*p* value], hypotheses resolution).

d. Write an abstract under 200 words detailing a summary of the study, the ANCOVA test results, hypothesis resolution, and implications of your findings.

Repeat this exercise using **Ch 06 – Exercise 08B.sav**.

NOTE: Exercises 9 and 10 involve four groups each.

Exercise 6.9

The Acme Company claims that its new reading lamp increases reading speed, and you want to test this. You will record how long (in seconds) it takes for participants to read a 1,000-word essay. Participants will be randomly assigned to one of four groups: Group 1 will be the control group; they will read the essay using regular room lighting. Those in Group 2 will read the essay using the Acme lamp. Those in Group 3 will read the essay using a generic reading lamp. Those in Group 4 will read the essay using a flashlight. Additionally, you will record the age of each participant (as the covariate).

Data set: **Ch 06 – Exercise 09A.sav**

Codebook

Variable:	Group
Definition:	Lighting group assignment
Type:	Categorical (1 = Room lighting, 2 = Acme lamp, 3 = Generic lamp, 4 = Flashlight)
Variable:	Seconds
Definition:	The time it takes to read the essay
Type:	Continuous
Variable:	Age
Definition:	Age
Type:	Continuous

a. Write the hypotheses.

b. Run each criterion of the pretest checklist (homogeneity of regression slopes, homogeneity of variance [Levene's test]) and discuss your findings.

c. Run the ANCOVA test and document your findings (*n*s, means, and Sig. [*p* value], hypotheses resolution).

d. Write an abstract under 200 words detailing a summary of the study, the ANCOVA test results, hypothesis resolution, and implications of your findings.

Repeat this exercise using **Ch 06 – Exercise 09B.sav**.

Exercise 6.10

Due to numerous complications involving missed medication dosages, you implement a study to determine the best strategy for enhancing medication adherence. Patients who are on a daily medication regime will be recruited, will receive a complimentary 1-month dosage of their regular medication(s), and will be randomly assigned to one of four groups. Group 1 will serve as the control group (no treatment); Group 2 will participate in a 1-hour in-person pharmacist-administered medication adherence workshop; Group 3 will receive a text message reminder with a picture of the drug (e.g., *It's time to take one tablet of Drug A*); Group 4 will attend the medication adherence workshop and receive text messages. At the end of 1 month, participants will present their prescription bottle(s); you will count the remaining pills and calculate the dosage adherence percentage (e.g., 0 pills remaining = 100% adherence). Additionally, you'll record the total number of pills prescribed for the month (as the covariate).

Data set: **Ch 06 – Exercise 10A.sav**

Codebook

Variable:	Group
Definition:	Group number
Type:	Categorical (1 = Control, 2 = Rx workshop, 3 = Texts, 4 = Rx workshop and texts)
Variable:	RxAdhere
Definition:	Percentage of medication adherence
Type:	Continuous (0 – 100)
Variable:	TotalRx
Definition:	Total number of pills prescribed for the month
Type:	Continuous

a. Write the hypotheses.

b. Run each criterion of the pretest checklist (homogeneity of regression slopes, homogeneity of variance [Levene's test]) and discuss your findings.

c. Run the ANCOVA test and document your findings (*n*s, means, and Sig. [*p* value], hypotheses resolution).

d. Write an abstract under 200 words detailing a summary of the study, the ANCOVA test results, hypothesis resolution, and implications of your findings.

Repeat this exercise using **Ch 06 – Exercise 10B.sav.**

C H A P T E R 7

MANOVA

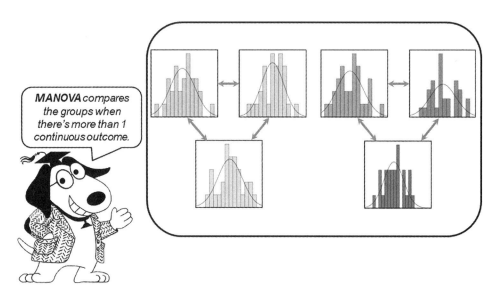

Forget about style; worry about results.

—Bobby Orr

Learning Objectives

Upon completing this chapter, you will be able to do the following:

- Determine when it is appropriate to run a MANOVA test.
- Verify that the data meet the criteria for MANOVA processing: sample size, normality, moderate correlation, homogeneity of variance-covariance (Box's *M* test), and homogeneity of variance (Levene's test).
- Order a MANOVA test.
- Derive results from the estimates and pairwise comparisons tables.
- Resolve the hypotheses.
- Write an appropriate abstract.

WHEN TO USE THIS STATISTIC

Guidelines for Selecting the MANOVA Test

Overview: This statistic is for designs that involve more than two groups and more than one outcome variable to determine which group(s) (if any) outperformed another for each outcome variable.

Variables: This statistic requires three variables for each record: (1) a categorical variable to designate the group, (2) a continuous variable to contain the score for the first outcome, and (3) a continuous variable to contain the score for the second outcome.

Results: Among those diagnosed with anxiety, we separated our participants into three groups and measured their pulse rates and sense of well-being after 30 minutes of treatment. The mean pulse rates were 84.1 for the control group, 79.9 for the pet therapy group, and 80.1 for the meditation group. The pulse rate for the pet therapy group is statistically significantly lower than the control group ($p = .025$, $\alpha = .05$). The mean sense-of-well-being score was 22.9 for the control group, 25.2 for the pet therapy group, and 27.2 for the meditation group. Those in the meditation group scored significantly higher than those in the control group (.039, $\alpha = .05$).

VIDEO

The tutorial video for this chapter is **Ch 07 – MANOVA.mp4**. This video provides an overview of the MANOVA (multiple analysis of variance) statistic, followed by the SPSS procedures for processing the pretest checklist, ordering the statistical run, and interpreting the results of this test using the data set: **Ch 07 – Example 01 – MANOVA.sav**.

LAYERED LEARNING

The notion of MANOVA builds on the concept of ANOVA (Chapter 5); hence, the same data sets will be used in the example and exercises, with one variable added to each data set. Notice that the example data set for this chapter (**Ch 07 – Example 01 – MANOVA.sav**) is exactly the same as the example data set used for the ANOVA chapter (**Ch 05 – Example 01 – ANOVA.sav**), except it has a third variable (*Well_being*) included (Figure 7.1).

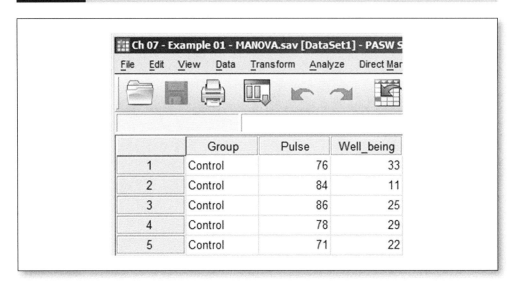

Figure 7.1 Excerpt from **Ch 07 – Example – MANOVA.sav.**

OVERVIEW—MANOVA

The **MANOVA** is similar to the ANOVA test, except MANOVA allows us to assess more than one outcome (dependent) variable.

To recap, the experimental model used in the ANOVA example involved three treatment groups (Control, Pet therapy, or Meditation) to participants diagnosed with acute stress disorder and then measuring *one* outcome—their *Pulse* to compare the effectiveness of each treatment. Suppose, in addition to assessing the effect that each intervention had on pulse rate, we also wanted to compare these treatment methods to determine if they may have an effect on a *second* outcome variable, such as the participant's sense of well-being (*Well_being*). Basically, this MANOVA would be akin to running two separate ANOVAs:

- ANOVA$_1$: *(Control, Pet therapy, Meditation)* : *(Pulse)*
- ANOVA$_2$: *(Control, Pet therapy, Meditation)* : *(Well_being)*

The disadvantage of running two separate ANOVAs (one for *Pulse* and another for *Well_being*) is that doing so would substantially increase the likelihood of committing a Type I error (as detailed in Chapter 4, at the ★ icon with the Type I Error section on page 93). To review, a Type I error occurs when the findings indicate that there is a statistically significant difference between two variables (or groups) when, in fact, on the whole, there actually is not, which would prompt you to (wrongly) reject the null hypothesis. This would lead you to conclude that a treatment was effective when, in fact, on the whole, it was not.

In this example, the MANOVA will basically perform these two ANOVA tests as a single procedure. The results will look as if you had ordered two separate ANOVA tests: (1) comparing the three treatments in terms of their effects on *Pulse* and (2) comparing the three treatments in terms of their effect on *Well_being*. For a preview of the MANOVA results, see pages 183 and 184.

Example

A research team has recruited a group of individuals who have been diagnosed with acute stress disorder to determine the effectiveness of supplemental nonpharmaceutical treatments for reducing stress: (1) no supplemental therapy, (2) pet therapy with certified therapy dogs, or (3) meditation.

Research Questions

Because this example involves two outcome (dependent) variables, it is appropriate to have two research questions:

Q_1: Is pet therapy or meditation effective in reducing stress among those diagnosed with acute stress disorder?

(NOTE: Q_1 is the same research question as was used in the ANOVA example.)

Q_2: Is pet therapy or meditation effective in enhancing personal sense of well-being among those diagnosed with acute stress disorder?

GROUPS

A researcher recruits a total of 90 participants who meet the diagnostic criteria for acute stress disorder. Participants will be scheduled to come to the research center one at a time. Upon arriving, each participant will be assigned to one of three groups on a sequential basis (first assigned to Group 1, second assigned to Group 2, third assigned to Group 3, fourth assigned to Group 1, etc.). Those assigned to Group 1 will constitute the control group and will be instructed to sit and relax for 30 minutes (with no treatment). Those in Group 2 will receive 30 minutes of pet therapy, and those in Group 3 will meditate for 30 minutes.

PROCEDURE

Each participant will be guided to a room with a comfortable sofa. Those in the control group will be instructed to just sit and relax. Those in the pet therapy group will be introduced to the therapy dog by name and instructed that the participant may hold the dog in his or her lap, pet the dog on the sofa, brush the dog, or give the dog the allotted treats in whatever combination they wish. Those in the meditation group will listen to a recording of gentle music with a narrative taking the participant through a guided meditation. After 30 minutes, the researcher will return to each participant to measure the participant's pulse rate, ask the participant to complete the Acme Well-Being Inventory (AWBI), and dismiss them. The lower pulse rate would reflect more relaxation.

NOTE: Gathering the pulse rate will provide an indication of the *physical* effect of each treatment, whereas administering the Acme Well-Being Inventory assess the *emotional* effect of each treatment.

HYPOTHESES

This study involves two outcome (dependent) variables (*Pulse* and *Well_being*), so two sets of hypotheses are constructed: H_0 and H_1 pertain to pulse rate; H_0 and H_2 pertain to well-being.

H_0:   There is no difference in pulse rates or sense of well-being across the groups.

H_1:   There is a difference in pulse rates across the groups.

H_2:   There is a difference in sense of well-being across the groups.

 ## DATA SET

Use the following data set: **Ch 07 – Example 01 – MANOVA.sav.**

Codebook

  Variable: Group

  Definition: Group assignment

  Type: Categorical (1 = Control, 2 = Pet therapy, 3 = Meditation)

  Variable: Pulse

  Definition: Heartbeats per minute measured 30 minutes after start

  Type: Continuous

  Variable: Well_being

  Definition: Score on Acme Well-Being Inventory (AWBI)

  Type: Continuous (8 = Low sense of well-being . . . 40 = High sense of well-being)

(NOTE: The AWBI is a self-administered survey consisting of eight 5-point Likert-scale questions.)

PRETEST CHECKLIST

MANOVA Pretest Checklist

☑ 1. *n* quota*

☑ 2. Normality*

☑ 3. Moderate correlation*

☑ 4. Homogeneity of variance-covariance (Box's *M* test)**

☑ 5. Homogeneity of variance (Levene's test)**

*Run prior to MANOVA test

**Results produced upon MANOVA test run

NOTE: If any of the pretest checklist criteria are not satisfied, proceed with the analysis, but concisely discuss such anomalies in the *Results* or *Limitations* sections of the documentation so the reader can more plausibly interpret the precision of the findings.

Considering the (behind-the-scenes) internal complexity of the MANOVA statistic, five pretest criteria need to be assessed to better ensure the robustness of the findings: (1) *n* quota, (2) normality, (3) moderate correlation, (4) homogeneity of variance-covariance (Box's *M* test), and (5) homogeneity of variance (Levene's test).

Pretest Checklist Criterion 1—*n* Quota

As with the *t* test and ANOVA, the MANOVA becomes more stable with a larger sample. An *n* of at least 30 per group is advised.

1. On the SPSS main menu, click on *Analyze, Descriptive Statistics, Frequencies* (Figure 7.2).

2. Move the *Group* variable into the *Variable(s)* window.

3. Click on *OK* (Figure 7.3).

The *Frequency* table indicates 30 participants per group (Table 7.1); hence, this criterion is satisfied.

Figure 7.2 *Analyze, Descriptive Statistics, Frequencies.*

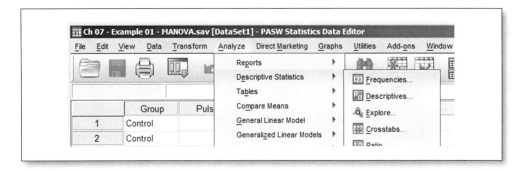

Figure 7.3 *Frequencies* menu.

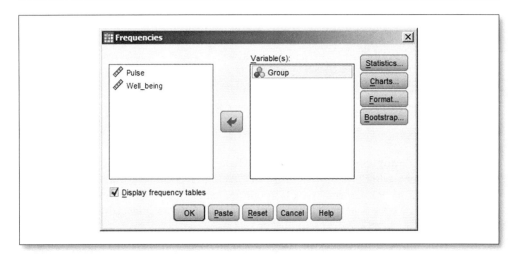

Table 7.1 *Frequencies* table for *Group*; *n* (Frequency) ≥ 30 for each group.

		Frequency	Percent	Valid Percent	Cumulative Percent
				Group	
Valid	Control	30	33.3	33.3	33.3
	Pet therapy	30	33.3	33.3	66.7
	Meditation	30	33.3	33.3	100.0
	Total	90	100.0	100.0	

Pretest Checklist Criterion 2—Normality

When assessing the normality criteria for ANOVA, it involved examining three separate normal curves: *Pulse* for *Control, Pulse* for *Pet therapy,* and *Pulse* for *Meditation.* Considering that an additional outcome variable (*Well_being*) is included in the MANOVA model, we need to examine three additional histograms to check for normality: *Well_being* for *Control, Well_being* for *Pet therapy,* and *Well_being* for *Meditation:*

1. Use the *Select Cases* icon to select the records pertaining to *Control;* the selection criteria would be *Group = 1.*

   For more details on this procedure, refer to **Chapter 4: t Test and Mann-Whitney *U* Test**, and the following section: SPSS—Descriptive Statistics: Continuous Variable (Age) Select by Categorical Variable (Gender)—Females Only; see the star (★) icon on page 62—instead of Gender = *1,* specify *Group = 1.*

2. Run a histogram (with normal curve) on the variables *Pulse* and *Well_being;* SPSS can process charts for several variables in a single order (see Figure 7.4).

   For more details on this procedure, refer to **Chapter 4: t Test and Mann-Whitney *U* Test**, and the following section: SPSS—Descriptive Statistics: Continuous Variables (Age); see the star (★) icon on page 52—on the *Frequencies* menu; instead of moving *Age* into the *Variable(s)* window, move *Pulse* and *Well_being* (Figure 7.4).

Figure 7.4   On the *Frequencies* menu, load *Pulse* and *Well_being* into the *Variable(s)* window to produce (separate histograms with normal curve) *Charts* for these two variables.

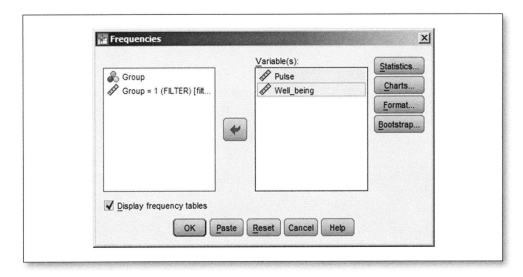

3. Repeat the process for the *Pet therapy* group (*Group* = 2).

4. Repeat the process a final time for the *Meditation* group (*Group* = 3).

This will produce six histograms with normal curves (Figures 7.5–7.10). The symmetry of the bell-shaped curve on each of these histograms satisfies the criterion of normality among these variables.

Figure 7.5	Histogram of *Pulse* for *Control*.

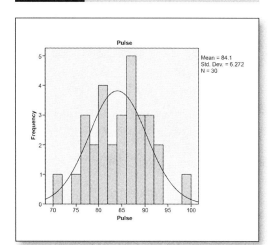

Figure 7.6	Histogram of *Well_being* for *Control*.

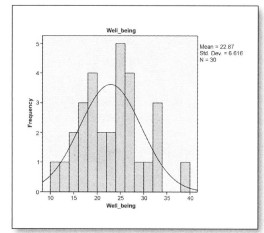

Figure 7.7	Histogram of *Pulse* for *Pet therapy*.

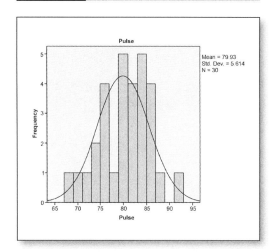

Figure 7.8	Histogram of *Well_being* for *Pet therapy*.

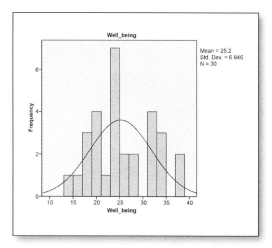

Figure 7.9	Histogram of *Pulse* for *Meditation*.

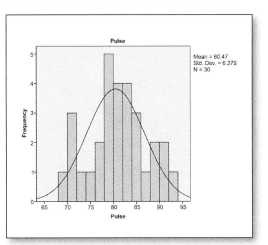

Figure 7.10	Histogram of *Well_being* for *Meditation*.

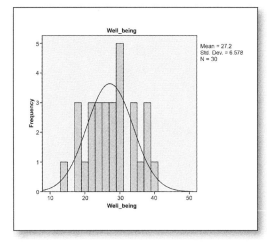

Pretest Checklist Criterion 3—Moderate Correlation

The variables (*Pulse* and *Well_being*) must have a **moderate correlation**. This concept is covered thoroughly in **Chapter 11: Correlation and Regression**, but for now, consider correlation, which ranges from –1 to +1 and indicates the extent to which two variables are associated with each other. A correlation score that is further from 0 (near –1 or +1) indicates a stronger association between the variables, whereas a correlation score nearer to 0 indicates a weaker association.

To run a correlational analysis between *Pulse* and *Well_being*, complete the following steps:

1. First, be sure to reactivate all of the records; the easiest way to do this is to delete the *filter_$* variable, or click on the *Select Cases* icon and, under *Select*, click on *All cases*.

2. On the main screen, click on *Analyze, Correlate, Bivariate* (Figure 7.11).

3. On the *Bivariate Correlations* menu, move *Pulse* and *Well_being* into the *Variables* window.

4. Click on *OK* (Figure 7.12).

This criterion specifies that there must be a moderate correlation between the variables, meaning that the correlation needs to be between –.9 and –.3 or between .3 and .9 (Figure 7.13). Correlations that are between –.3 and .3 are considered too weak, whereas

Figure 7.11 To order the correlation between *Pulse* and *Well_being,* click on *Analyze, Correlate, Bivariate.*

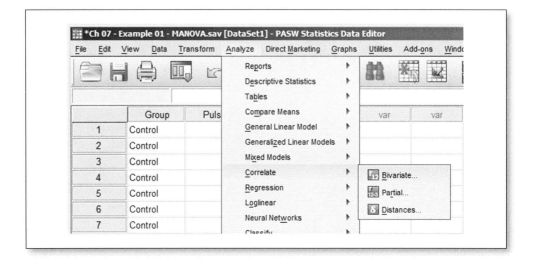

Figure 7.12 On the *Bivariate Correlation* menu, load *Pulse* and *Well_being* into the *Variables* window.

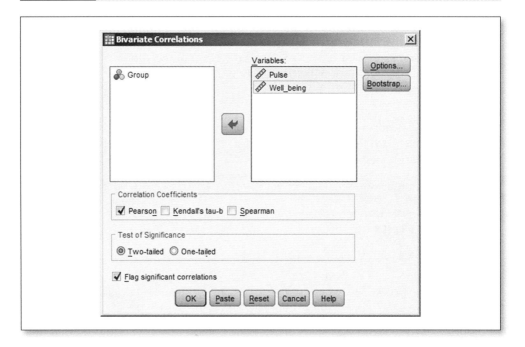

correlations that are less than –.9 or greater than .9 are considered too strongly correlated, which is referred to as **multicollinearity** (pronounced *multi-coe-lyn-ee-air-it-tee*). When variables are very highly correlated with each other (e.g., glove size : hand size), including both in the statistical model basically constitutes double-loading the formula. The rule of thumb for handling multicollinearity is that because the two variables contain such similar values, just select one of them to process, and leave the other out of the model. Typically, the decision as to which one to keep and which to leave out involves considering the characteristics of the variables in question (e.g., reliability, ease of access to the data, time/economic costs of gathering the variables).

Table 7.2	*Correlations* table shows a –.621 (Pearson) correlation for the two outcome variables, *Pulse* : *Pulse.*

Correlations

		Pulse	Well_being
Pulse	Pearson Correlation	1	-.621
	Sig. (2-tailed)		.000
	N	90	90
Well_being	Pearson Correlation	-.621**	1
	Sig. (2-tailed)	.000	
	N	90	90

**. Correlation is significant at the 0.01 level (2-tailed).

Figure 7.13	Moderate correlation is –9 . . . –.3, and +.3 . . . +.9.

The remaining two pretest criteria, (4) homogeneity of variance-covariance (Box's *M* test) and (5) homogeneity of variance (Levene's test), will be processed during the Test Run and finalized in the Results section.

TEST RUN

1. On the SPSS main menu, click on *Analyze, General Linear Model, Multivariate* (Figure 7.14).

Figure 7.14 To order a MANOVA test, click on *Analyze, General Linear Model, Multivariate.*

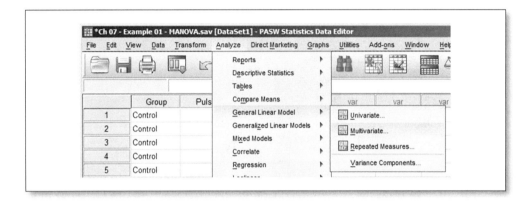

2. On the *Multivariate* menu (Figure 7.15), move *Pulse* and *Well_being* to the *Dependent Variables* window.

Figure 7.15 Move *Pulse* and *Well_being* to the *Dependent Variables* window and *Group* to the *Fixed Factor(s)* window.

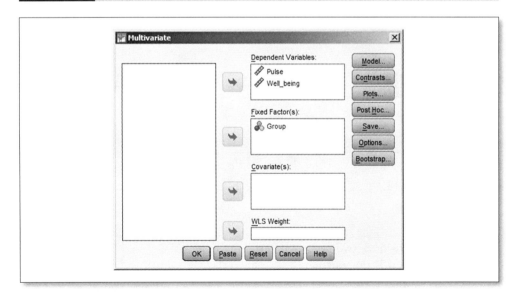

3. Move *Group* to the *Fixed Factor(s)* window.

4. Click on *Post Hoc*.

5. On the *Multivariate: Post Hoc* menu (Figure 7.16), move *Group* from the *Factor(s)* window to the *Post Hoc Tests for* window.

Figure 7.16   Move *Group* to the *Post Hoc Tests for* window, and check ☑ *Bonferroni*.

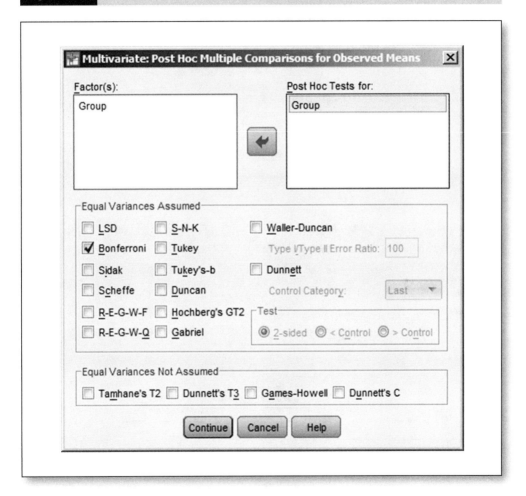

6. On the *Equal Variances Assumed* options, check ☑ *Bonferroni*.

7. Click on *Continue* to return to the *Multivariate* menu.

8. On the *Multivariate* menu, click on *Options*.

Figure 7.17 On the *Multivariates: Options* menu, move *Group* into the *Display Means for* window, and check ☑ *Homogeneity tests*.

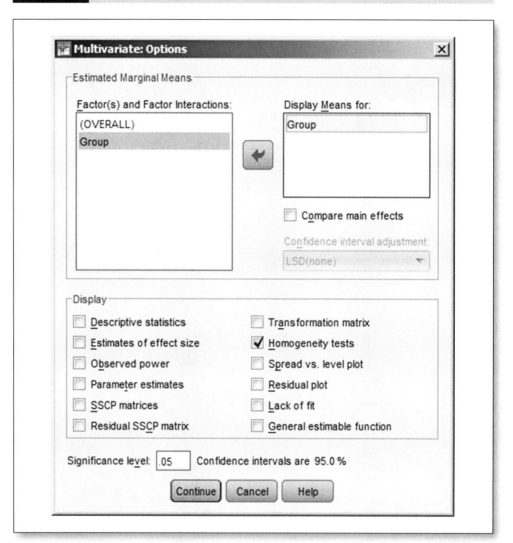

9. On the *Multivariate: Options* menu (Figure 7.17), move *Group* into the *Display Means for* window.

10. Check ☑ *Homogeneity tests*.

11. Click on *Continue* to return to the *Multivariate* menu.

12. On the *Multivariate* menu, click on *OK*.

RESULTS

Pretest Checklist Criterion 4—Homogeneity of Variance-Covariance (Box's *M* Test)

To assess the **homogeneity of variance-covariance**, we look to *Box's Test of Equality of Covariance Matrices* (Table 7.3), which rendered a Sig. (*p*) = .901; because this is greater than the α (.001) associated with this test, this indicates that there is no significant difference between the variance-covariances in this model, and hence, this pretest criterion is satisfied. Another way to think about this is to see that the *p* value (.901) suggests that no statistically significant difference was detected among the values in question; hence, these values are similar to each other. In other words, detecting no statistically significant differences tells us that the values are homogeneous.

Table 7.3	Box's *M* Test (*Box's Test of Equality of Covariance Matrices* table) shows no statistically significant difference among the variances (*p* = .901, α = .001).

Box's Test of Equality of Covariance Matrices[a]

Box's M	2.268
F	.365
df1	6
df2	188642.769
Sig.	.901

Tests the null hypothesis that the observed covariance matrices of the dependent variables are equal across groups.

a. Design: Intercept + Group

Pretest Checklist Criterion 5— Homogeneity of Variance (Levene's Test)

Next, the homogeneity of variance test checks to see that there is no statistically significant difference in the variances among the three groups (*Control, Pet therapy,* and *Meditation*) for each of the two outcome variables: *Pulse* and *Well_being*.

Levene's Test of Equality of Error Variances (Table 7.4) shows a Sig. (*p*) of .689 for *Pulse* and 1.000 for *Well_being*. These *p* values are greater than α (.05), indicating that there is no statistically significant difference among the groups (*Control, Pet therapy, Meditation*) for the two outcome variables (*Pulse* and *Well_being*), and hence, this criterion is satisfied.

Proceeding with the results of the MANOVA test, the first table to inspect is the *Multivariate Tests* (Table 7.5); notice the four statistics pertaining to the *Group* variable: *Pillai's Trace* (symbol is "V"), *Wilks' Lambda* (symbol is "Λ"—the Greek letter, lambda), *Hotelling's Trace* (symbol is "T"), and *Roy's Largest Root* (symbol is "Θ"—the Greek letter, theta). Usually, these four will produce fairly similar *p* values; of these four, Pillai's trace is considered to be preferred in that it is the most conservative and the most robust in terms of possible violations to the pretest checklist criteria (assumptions).

Pillai's Trace indicates Sig. (*p*) = .023, which is less than the .05 α level, indicating that a statistically significant difference has been detected among the pairs of groups (*Control, Pet therapy, Meditation*) for the outcome (dependent) variables *Pulse* and *Well_being*.

To finalize this analysis, we look to the *Multiple Comparisons* table (Table 7.6) to determine which group(s) performed statistically significantly different from which and the *Estimates* table for the means (Table 7.7). Notice that the *Multiple Comparisons* table (Table 7.6) resembles two ANOVA Multiple Comparisons tables, wherein the top half of the table shows the three pairwise comparisons (*Control, Pet therapy, Meditation*) for *Pulse,* and the bottom half shows a separate set of comparisons for those three groups for *Well_being*.

Table 7.4	*Levene's Test of Equality of Error Variances* shows a Sig. (*p*) of .689 for *Pulse* and 1.000 for *Pulse.*

Levene's Test of Equality of Error Variances[a]

	F	df1	df2	Sig.
Pulse	.374	2	87	.689
Well_being	.000	2	87	1.000

Tests the null hypothesis that the error variance of the dependent variable is equal across groups.

a. Design: Intercept + Group

NOTE: Since these *p* values are greater than α (.05), this indicates that there is no statistically significant difference in the variances among the groups (*Control, Pet therapy, Meditation*) for the two outcome variables (*Pulse* and *Well_being*).

Table 7.5	*Multivariate Tests: Pillai's Trace* rendered a Sig. (*p*) = .023 (α = ▨ 5), indicating that at least one statistically significant difference has been detected among the pairs of variables.

Multivariate Tests^c

Effect		Value	F	Hypothesis df	Error df	Sig.
Intercept	Pillai's Trace	.998	17976.779ᵃ	2.000	86.000	.000
	Wilks' Lambda	.002	17976.779ᵃ	2.000	86.000	.000
	Hotelling's Trace	418.065	17976.779ᵃ	2.000	86.000	.000
	Roy's Largest Root	418.065	17976.779ᵃ	2.000	86.000	.000
Group	Pillai's Trace	.125	2.907	4.000	174.000	.023
	Wilks' Lambda	.878	2.894ᵃ	4.000	172.000	.024
	Hotelling's Trace	.136	2.881	4.000	170.000	.024
	Roy's Largest Root	.100	4.350ᵇ	2.000	87.000	.016

a. Exact statistic
b. The statistic is an upper bound on F that yields a lower bound on the significance level.
c. Design: Intercept + Group

Table 7.6	*Multiple Comparisons* table shows pairwise group comparisons (*Control, Pet therapy, Meditation*) for each of the two outcome variables (*Pulse* at the top and *Well_being* at the bottom).

Multiple Comparisons

Bonferroni

Dependent Variable	(I) Group	(J) Group	Mean Difference (I-J)	Std. Error	Sig.	95% Confidence Interval	
						Lower Bound	Upper Bound
Pulse	Control	Pet therapy	4.17*	1.565	.028	.35	7.99
		Meditation	3.63	1.565	.068	-.19	7.45
	Pet therapy	Control	-4.17*	1.565	.028	-7.99	-.35
		Meditation	-.53	1.565	1.000	-4.35	3.29
	Meditation	Control	-3.63	1.565	.068	-7.45	.19
		Pet therapy	.53	1.565	1.000	-3.29	4.35
Well_being	Control	Pet therapy	-2.33	1.708	.526	-6.50	1.84
		Meditation	-4.33*	1.708	.039	-8.50	-.16
	Pet therapy	Control	2.33	1.708	.526	-1.84	6.50
		Meditation	-2.00	1.708	.734	-6.17	2.17
	Meditation	Control	4.33*	1.708	.039	.16	8.50
		Pet therapy	2.00	1.708	.734	-2.17	6.17

Based on observed means.
The error term is Mean Square(Error) = 43.736.
*. The mean difference is significant at the .05 level.

Table 7.7	Group *Estimates* table shows the means from each *Group* (*Control, Pet therapy, Meditation*) for each of the outcome variables (*Pulse* at the top and *Well_being* at the bottom).

		Group			
Dependent Variable	Group			95% Confidence Interval	
		Mean	Std. Error	Lower Bound	Upper Bound
Pulse	Control	84.100	1.107	81.900	86.300
	Pet therapy	79.933	1.107	77.733	82.133
	Meditation	80.467	1.107	78.267	82.667
Well_being	Control	22.867	1.207	20.467	25.267
	Pet therapy	25.200	1.207	22.800	27.600
	Meditation	27.200	1.207	24.800	29.600

Despite all of these data being presented on a single table, this does not compound the complexity of the documentation process. The results will be documented as if we had conducted two separate ANOVA tests: one for *Pulse* (wherein pairs that are significantly different are identified with ovals) and another for *Well_being* (where rectangles are used).

H_0 HYPOTHESIS RESOLUTION

To clarify the hypothesis resolution process, it is helpful to organize the findings in a table and use an asterisk to flag statistically significant difference(s) (Table 7.8).

With this results table assembled, consider the hypothesis resolution as if you had run two separate ANOVA tests.

REJECT: H_0: There is no difference in pulse rates or sense of well-being across the groups.

ACCEPT: H_1: There is a difference in pulse rates across the groups.

ACCEPT: H_2: There is a difference in sense of well-being across the groups.

Because a statistically significant difference was discovered among at least one pair of the treatments, we reject H_0 and accept H_1. Specifically, pet therapy outperformed the control group in lowering the pulse rate ($p = .028$).

Additionally, it was found that the participants in the meditation group had a significantly different sense of personal well-being compared to those in the control group ($p = .039$); hence, we reject H_0 (which is already rejected) and accept H_2.

Table 7.8	Results of MANOVA for *Pulse* and *Well_being*.	

	MANOVA Summary Table	*p*
Pulse	Control (M = 84.10) : Pet therapy (M = 79.93)	.028*
Pulse	Control (M = 84.10) : Meditation (M = 80.47)	.068
Pulse	Pet therapy (M = 79.93) : Meditation (M = 80.47)	1.000
Well_being	Control (M = 22.87) : Pet therapy (M = 25.20)	.526
Well_being	Control (M = 22.87) : Meditation (M = 27.20)	.039*
Well_being	Pet therapy (M = 25.20) : Meditation (M = 27.20)	.734

NOTE: SPSS does not generate this table (Table 7.8) directly; you can assemble this table by gathering the means from the *Estimates* table (Table 7.7) and the *p* values from the Sig. column in the *Multiple Comparisons* table (Table 7.6).

*Statistically significant (*p* < .05).

ABSTRACT

We recruited 90 participants who were diagnosed with acute stress disorder. We randomly assigned participants to one of three groups: Participants in Group 1 (the control group) received no supplemental treatment (for 30 minutes), those in Group 2 were provided a 30-minute pet therapy session with a certified therapy dog, and those in Group 3 engaged in a 30-minute guided meditation. After 30 minutes, the researcher returned to each participant to measure his or her pulse rate, ask the participant to complete the Acme Well-Being Inventory (self-administered survey consisting of eight 5-point Likert-scale questions that renders a score between 8 and 40, wherein 40 indicates highest sense of well-being), and dismiss them. The lower pulse rate would reflect more relaxation.

Those in the pet therapy group had a lower pulse rate (M = 79.93) compared to those in the control group (M = 84.10); this difference of 4.17 is statistically significant (p = .028, α = .05).

Additionally, members of the meditation group showed a higher sense of well-being (M = 27.20) compared to those in the control group (M = 22.87); this 4.33 difference is statistically significant (M = .039, α = .05). These findings suggest that pet therapy and guided meditation, either individually or together, may serve as effective ancillary treatment(s) for such individuals.

NOTE: In the above abstract, notice that the second paragraph addresses the *Pulse* rate results, and the third paragraph discusses the *Well_being* results. Also, notice that *lower Pulse* signifies better functioning, whereas a *higher Well_being* signifies better functioning.

GOOD COMMON SENSE

One of the pretest criteria for running a quality MANOVA involves checking that the outcome (dependent) variables (*Pulse* and *Well_being*) are moderately correlated; they also need to be *conceptually* correlated. In the example that we processed, it is reasonable to consider the possible effect that a relaxation technique may have on the pulse rate; hence, the decision to include *Pulse* in this MANOVA conceptually makes sense. Conversely, gathering data on *Pulse* and *Foot size* would constitute an implausible MANOVA model: It is unreasonable to presume that administering a relaxation technique would have any effect on the size of the individual's foot. Despite the obvious implausibility of this model, it may be that *Pulse* and *Foot size* pass the moderate correlation test, but any such correlation should be reasonably dismissed as spurious (coincidental, but not pertinent).

Another point worth considering is that at the onset of this study, the participants were screened; all of the participants were properly diagnosed with acute anxiety disorder. However, this design did not specify gathering a baseline pulse rate (although it could have). As such, the documentation of the results involving the pulse rate needs to be handled appropriately: The MANOVA revealed that those who were in the pet therapy group had the lowest mean pulse rate (M = 79.93) compared to those in the control group (M = 84.10) and those in the meditation group (M = 80.47); however, because baseline pulse data were not gathered, it is not possible to determine precisely what effect the treatment(s) had on the pulse rate. There are a variety of possibilities:

1. Pet therapy lowered pulse; the control condition and meditation lowered pulse but not as much as pet therapy.

2. Pet therapy lowered pulse; the control condition and meditation had no effect on pulse.

3. Pet therapy lowered pulse; the control condition and meditation increased pulse.

4. Pet therapy had no effect on pulse; the control condition and meditation increased pulse.

5. Pet therapy increased pulse; the control condition and meditation increased pulse more than pet therapy.

Given the experimental design and the data that are available, the preceding (pulse rate) possibilities are unresolvable; take appropriate care when phrasing such results. Alternatively, consider the advantage of gathering pretest data on outcome (dependent) variables, when feasible, to help reduce potentially ambiguous results.

Key Concepts

- MANOVA
- Pretest checklist
  - Sample size
  - Normality

○ Moderate correlation
○ Homogeneity of variance-covariance (Box's *M* test)
○ Homogeneity of variance (Levene's test)

- Hypothesis resolution
- Documenting results
- Good common sense

Practice Exercises

Use the prepared SPSS data sets (download from **study.sagepub.com/intermediatestats**).

NOTE: These practice exercises and data sets are the same as those in **Chapter 6: ANOVA** except an extra outcome (dependent) variable has been included to enable MANOVA processing. All the exercises involve three groups, except for Exercises 9 and 10, which involve four groups.

Exercise 7.1

You want to determine the optimal tutor-to-student ratio. Students seeking tutoring will be randomly assigned to one of three groups: Group 1 will involve each tutor working with only one student; in Group 2, each tutor will work with two students; and in Group 3, each tutor will work with five students. At the end of the term, students will be asked to complete the Tutor Satisfaction Survey, which renders a score from 0 to 100, and the average number of homework errors or incomplete questions made over the course of the term.

Data set: **Ch 07 – Exercise 01A.sav**

Codebook

Variable:	Group
Definition:	Group number
Type:	Categorical (1 = One-to-one, 2 = Two-to-one, 3 = Five-to-one)
Variable:	TSS
Definition:	Tutor Satisfaction Survey score
Type:	Continuous (0 = Very unsatisfied . . . 100 = Very satisfied)
Variable:	HW_errors
Definition:	Number of homework errors or incomplete questions
Type:	Continuous

a. Write the hypotheses.

b. Run each criterion of the pretest checklist (*n* quota, normality, moderate correlation, homogeneity of variance-covariance [Box's *M* test], and homogeneity of variance [Levene's test]) and discuss your findings.

c. Run the MANOVA test and document your findings (*n*s, means, and Sig. [*p* value], hypotheses resolution).

d. Write an abstract under 200 words detailing a summary of the study, the MANOVA test results, hypothesis resolution, and implications of your findings.

Repeat this exercise using data set: **Ch 07 – Exercise 01B.sav**.

Exercise 7.2

Clinicians at a nursing home facility want to see if giving residents a plant to tend to will help lower depression. To test this idea, the residents are randomly assigned to one of three groups: Those assigned to Group 1 will serve as the control group and will not be given a plant. Members of Group 2 will be given a small bamboo plant along with a card detailing care instructions. Members of Group 3 will be given a small cactus along with a card detailing care instructions. After 90 days, all participants will complete the Acme Depression Scale, which renders a score between 1 and 100 (1 = Low depression . . . 100 = High depression). The staff will also keep track of the socialization of each participant (number of hours per day each resident is outside his or her room).

Data set: **Ch 07 – Exercise 02A.sav**

Codebook

Variable:	Group
Definition:	Group number
Type:	Categorical (1 = No plant, 2 = Bamboo, 3 = Cactus)
Variable:	Depress
Definition:	Acme Depression Scale
Type:	Continuous (1 = Low depression . . . 100 = High depression)
Variable:	Social_Hours
Definition:	The mean number of hours per day the resident is out of his or her room (rounded to half-hour)
Type:	Continuous

a. Write the hypotheses.

b. Run each criterion of the pretest checklist (*n* quota, normality, moderate correlation, homogeneity of variance-covariance [Box's *M* test], and homogeneity of variance [Levene's test]) and discuss your findings.

c. Run the MANOVA test and document your findings (*n*s, means, and Sig. [*p* value], hypotheses resolution).

d. Write an abstract under 200 words detailing a summary of the study, the MANOVA test results, hypothesis resolution, and implications of your findings.

Repeat this exercise using **Ch 07 – Exercise 02B.sav**.

Exercise 7.3

A judge mandates that juvenile offenders who have priors be assigned to a trained delinquency prevention mentor. To assess this intervention, offenders will be randomly assigned to one of three groups: No mentor, a peer mentor who is 3 to 5 years older than the offender, or an adult mentor who is 10 or more years older than the offender. The following data will be gathered on each participant: Probation officer's compliance evaluation (0% . . . 100%), and truancy (number of unexcused missed classes for the semester: 0–6 per day).

Data set: **Ch 07 – Exercise 03A.sav**

Codebook

Variable:	Group
Definition:	Mentor group assignment
Type:	Categorical (1 = No mentor, 2 = Peer mentor, 3 = Adult mentor)
Variable:	Probation_compliance
Definition:	Probation officer's overall assessment of the youth's probation compliance
Type:	Continuous (0 = Completely noncompliant . . . 100 = Completely compliant)
Variable:	Truancy
Definition:	Total number of unexcused missed classes for the semester
Type:	Continuous

a. Write the hypotheses.

b. Run each criterion of the pretest checklist (n quota, normality, moderate correlation, homogeneity of variance-covariance [Box's M test], and homogeneity of variance [Levene's test]) and discuss your findings.

c. Run the MANOVA test and document your findings (ns, means, and Sig. [p value], hypotheses resolution).

d. Write an abstract under 200 words detailing a summary of the study, the MANOVA test results, hypothesis resolution, and implications of your findings.

Repeat this exercise using **Ch 07 – Exercise 03B.sav**.

Exercise 7.4

In an effort to determine the effectiveness of light therapy to alleviate depression, you recruit a group of individuals who have been diagnosed with depression. The participants are randomly assigned to one of three groups: Group 1 will be the control group— members of this group will receive no light therapy. Members of Group 2 will get light therapy for 1 hour on even-numbered days over the course of 1 month. Members of Group 3 will get light therapy every day for 1 hour over the course of 1 month. After 1 month, all participants will complete the Acme Mood Scale, consisting of 10 questions; this instrument renders a score between 1 and 100 (1 = Extremely bad mood . . . 100 = Extremely good mood). Additionally, each participant will respond to the Acme Self Care Survey, a self-administered survey (5 = Strong self-neglect . . . 30 = Strong self-care).

Data set: **Ch 07 – Exercise 04A.sav**

Codebook

Variable:	Group
Definition:	Group number
Type:	Categorical (1 = No light therapy, 2 = Light therapy: even days, 3 = Light therapy: every day)

Variable:	Mood
Definition:	Acme Mood Scale
Type:	Continuous (1 = Extremely bad mood . . . 100 = Extremely good mood)

Variable:	Self_care
Definition:	Acme Self Care Survey
Type:	Continuous (5 = Strong self-neglect . . . 30 = Strong self-care)

a. Write the hypotheses.

b. Run each criterion of the pretest checklist (*n* quota, normality, moderate correlation, homogeneity of variance-covariance [Box's *M* test], and homogeneity of variance [Levene's test]) and discuss your findings.

c. Run the MANOVA test and document your findings (*n*s, means, and Sig. [*p* value], hypotheses resolution).

d. Write an abstract under 200 words detailing a summary of the study, the MANOVA test results, hypothesis resolution, and implications of your findings.

Repeat this exercise using **Ch 07 – Exercise 04B.sav**.

Exercise 7.5

To assess the workplace benefits of providing paid time off (PTO), the Human Resources (HR) Department implements and evaluates different PTO plans at each of the company's three sites: Site 1 will serve as the control group; employees at this site will continue to receive 2 weeks of PTO per year. Employees at Site 2 will receive 2 weeks of PTO per year plus the fourth Friday of each month off (with pay). Employees at Site 3 will receive 3 weeks of PTO per year. The HR Department will use a web-based survey to gather the following data from all employees: score on the Acme Morale Scale (1 = Extremely low morale . . . 25 = Extremely high morale) and productivity rating as assigned by their supervisor (1 = Extremely poor productivity . . . 100 = Extremely strong productivity).

Data set: **Ch 07 – Exercise 05A.sav**

Codebook

Variable:	Site
Definition:	Work site
Type:	Categorical (1 = 2 Weeks PTO, 2 = 2 Weeks PTO + fourth Fridays off, 3 Weeks PTO)
Variable:	Morale
Definition:	Score on Acme Morale Scale
Type:	Continuous (1 = Extremely low morale . . . 25 = Extremely high morale)
Variable:	Productivity
Definition:	Productivity score per supervisor's evaluation
Type:	Continuous (1 = Extremely poor productivity . . . 100 = Extremely strong productivity)

a. Write the hypotheses.

b. Run each criterion of the pretest checklist (*n* quota, normality, moderate correlation, homogeneity of variance-covariance [Box's *M* test], and homogeneity of variance [Levene's test]) and discuss your findings.

c. Run the MANOVA test and document your findings (*n*s, means, and Sig. [*p* value], hypotheses resolution).

d. Write an abstract under 200 words detailing a summary of the study, the MANOVA test results, hypothesis resolution, and implications of your findings.

Repeat this exercise using **Ch 07 – Exercise 05B.sav**.

Exercise 7.6

It is thought that exercising early in the morning will provide better energy throughout the day. To test this idea, participants are recruited and randomly assigned to one of three groups: Members of Group 1 will constitute the control group and not be assigned any walking. Members of Group 2 will walk from 7:00 to 7:30 a.m., Monday through Friday, over the course of 30 days. Members of Group 3 will walk from 7:00 to 8:00 a.m., Monday through Friday, over the course of 30 days. At the conclusion of the study, each participant will answer the 10 questions on the Acme End-of-the-Day Energy Scale. This instrument produces a score between 1 and 100 (1 = Extremely low energy . . . 100 = Extremely high energy). The researcher will also record the number of sick days each participant had over the past 30 days.

Data set: **Ch 07 – Exercise 06A.sav**

Codebook

Variable:	Group
Definition:	Walking group assignment
Type:	Categorical (1 = No walking, 2 = Walking: 30 Minutes, 3 = Walking: 60 minutes)
Variable:	Energy
Definition:	Acme End-of-the-Day Energy Scale
Type:	Continuous (1 = Extremely low energy . . . 100 = Extremely high energy)
Variable:	Sick_days
Definition:	Number of sick days over the past 30 days
Type:	Continuous

a. Write the hypotheses.

b. Run each criterion of the pretest checklist (n quota, normality, moderate correlation, homogeneity of variance-covariance [Box's M test], and homogeneity of variance [Levene's test]) and discuss your findings.

c. Run the MANOVA test and document your findings (ns, means, and Sig. [p value], hypotheses resolution).

d. Write an abstract under 200 words detailing a summary of the study, the MANOVA test results, hypothesis resolution, and implications of your findings.

Repeat this exercise using **Ch 07 – Exercise 06B.sav**.

Exercise 7.7

A political consulting firm wants to determine the characteristics of voters when it comes to issues involving alternative energy. The researchers recruit a group of participants and randomly assign them to one of three groups: Group 1 will be the control group, and they will not be exposed to any advertising materials; Group 2 will be shown a print advertisement that will be used in a postal mailing; and Group 3 will be shown a video advertisement that will be aired on television. Finally, each participant will indicate his or her voting intentions for Proposition 86, which involves tax deductions for hybrid cars on a 1 to 7 scale (1 = Will definitely vote no . . . 7 = will definitely vote yes). Additionally, participants will indicate their voting intentions for Proposition 99, which involves rebates for installing home solar energy using the same type of (1 to 7) scale.

Data set: **Ch 07 – Exercise 07A.sav**

Codebook

Variable:	Group
Definition:	Advertising media
Type:	Categorical (1 = Control, 2 = Print, 3 = Video)
Variable:	Prop_86
Definition:	Likely voting decision on tax deductions for hybrid cars
Type:	Continuous (1 = Will definitely vote no . . . 7 = Will definitely vote yes)
Variable:	Prop_99
Definition:	Likely voting decision on rebates for installing home solar energy
Type:	Continuous (1 = Will definitely vote no . . . 7 = Will definitely vote yes)

a. Write the hypotheses.

b. Run each criterion of the pretest checklist (n quota, normality, moderate correlation, homogeneity of variance-covariance [Box's M test], and homogeneity of variance [Levene's test]) and discuss your findings.

c. Run the MANOVA test and document your findings (ns, means, and Sig. [p value], hypotheses resolution).

d. Write an abstract under 200 words detailing a summary of the study, the MANOVA test results, hypothesis resolution, and implications of your findings.

Repeat this exercise using **Ch 07 – Exercise 07B.sav**.

Exercise 7.8

A team of educational researchers want to assess traditional classroom instruction compared to online options. Students who are enrolled in a course will be randomly assigned to one of three sections: Students in Section 1 will take the class in a traditional classroom. Students in Section 2 will take the course online with an interactive video cast of the instructor wherein students can ask the instructor questions during the session. Students in Section 3 will take the course online and view a prerecorded video of the professor delivering the lecture. The researchers will gather the course grade of each student (0% . . . 100%). Additionally, students will be asked to complete a course satisfaction survey (1 = Extremely unsatisfied . . . 10 = Extremely satisfied).

Data set: **Ch 07 – Exercise 08A.sav**

Codebook

Variable:	Section
Definition:	Learning modality
Type:	Categorical (1 = Classroom, 2 = Online live interactive, 3 = Online prerecorded video)
Variable:	Grade
Definition:	Final grade in course
Type:	Continuous (0 . . . 100)
Variable:	Satisfaction
Definition:	Course satisfaction
Type:	Continuous (1 = Extremely unsatisfied . . . 10 = Extremely satisfied)

a. Write the hypotheses.

b. Run each criterion of the pretest checklist (n quota, normality, moderate correlation, homogeneity of variance-covariance [Box's M test], and homogeneity of variance [Levene's test]) and discuss your findings.

c. Run the MANOVA test and document your findings (ns, means, and Sig. [p value], hypotheses resolution).

d. Write an abstract under 200 words detailing a summary of the study, the MANOVA test results, hypothesis resolution, and implications of your findings.

Repeat this exercise using **Ch 07 – Exercise 08B.sav**.

NOTE: Exercises 9 and 10 involve four groups each.

Exercise 7.9

The Acme Company claims that its new reading lamp increases reading speed; you want to test this. You will record how long (in seconds) it takes for participants to read a 1,000-word essay. Participants will be randomly assigned to one of four groups: Group 1 will be the control group; they will read the essay using regular room lighting. Those in Group 2 will read the essay using the Acme lamp. Those in Group 3 will read the essay using a generic reading lamp. Those in Group 4 will read the essay using a flashlight. You will also administer a one-question survey wherein each participant indicates his or her level of satisfaction with the lighting that he or she were provided (1 = Strongly dislike . . . 10 = Strongly like).

Data set: **Ch 07 – Exercise 09A.sav**

Codebook

Variable:	Group
Definition:	Lighting group assignment
Type:	Categorical (1 = Room lighting, 2 = Acme lamp, 3 = Generic lamp, 4 = Flashlight)
Variable:	Seconds
Definition:	The time it takes to read the essay
Type:	Continuous
Variable:	Lighting_satisfaction
Definition:	Participant's satisfaction with assigned lighting
Type:	Continuous (1 = Strongly dislike . . . 10 = Strongly like)

Repeat this exercise using **Ch 07 – Exercise 09B.sav**.

Exercise 7.10

Due to numerous complications involving missed medication dosages, you implement a study to determine the best strategy for enhancing medication adherence. Patients who are on a daily medication regime will be recruited, receive a complimentary 1-month dosage of their regular medication(s), and randomly assigned to one of four groups: Group 1 will serve as the control group (no treatment); Group 2 will participate in a 1-hour in-person pharmacist-administered medication adherence workshop; Group 3 will receive a text message reminder with a picture of the drug (e.g., *It's time to take one tablet of Drug A*); Group 4 will attend the medication adherence workshop and also receive text messages. At the end of 1 month, participants will present their prescription bottle(s); you will count the remaining pills and calculate the dosage adherence percentage (e.g., 0 pills remaining = 100% adherence). At the conclusion of the month, each participant will answer the Acme Health Outlook Survey, a self-administered instrument to measure how pessimistic/optimistic one feels about his or her health (1 = Strong negative outlook . . . 20 = Strong positive outlook).

Data set: **Ch 07 – Exercise 10A.sav**

Codebook

Variable:	Group
Definition:	Group number
Type:	Categorical (1 = Control, 2 = Rx workshop, 3 = Texts, 4 = Rx workshop and texts)

Variable:	RxAdhere
Definition:	Percentage of medication adherence
Type:	Continuous (0 . . . 100)

Variable:	Health_outlook
Definition:	Score on Acme Health Outlook Survey
Type:	Continuous (1 = Strong negative outlook . . . 20 = Strong positive outlook)

a. Write the hypotheses.

b. Run each criterion of the pretest checklist (*n* quota, normality, moderate correlation, homogeneity of variance-covariance [Box's *M* test], and homogeneity of variance [Levene's test]) and discuss your findings.

c. Run the MANOVA test and document your findings (*ns*, means, and Sig. [*p* value], hypotheses resolution).

d. Write an abstract under 200 words detailing a summary of the study, the MANOVA test results, hypothesis resolution, and implications of your findings.

Repeat this exercise using **Ch 07 – Exercise 10B.sav**.

PART IV

Measuring Differences Over Time

These chapters provide statistics for detecting change(s) in a continuous variable over time using a single group.

Chapter 8: Paired *t* Test and Wilcoxon Test illustrates how the paired *t* test is generally used to gather data on a variable before and after an intervention to determine if the performance on the posttest is significantly better than the pretest. In the event that the data are not fully suitable to run a paired *t* test, the Wilcoxon test provides an alternative.

Chapter 9: ANOVA Repeated Measures is similar to the paired *t* test, but it is capable of assessing a variable over *more than two time points*.

CHAPTER 8

Paired *t* Test and Wilcoxon Test

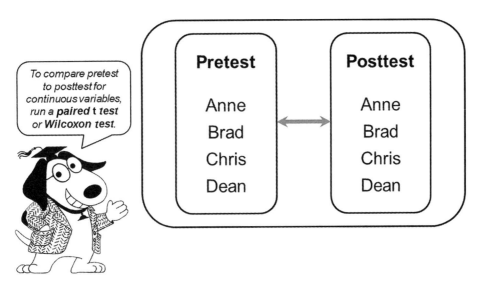

To compare pretest to posttest for continuous variables, run a **paired** *t* test or **Wilcoxon** test.

Things never happen the same way twice.

—C. S. Lewis

Learning Objectives

Upon completing this chapter, you will be able to do the following:

- Determine when it is appropriate to run a paired *t* test.
- Verify that the data meet the criteria for paired *t* test processing: normality of differences.
- Order a paired *t* test.
- Interpret test results.
- Resolve the hypotheses.
- Write an appropriate abstract.
- Calculate and document the Δ% formula.
- Know when and how to run and interpret the Wilcoxon test.

WHEN TO USE THIS STATISTIC

Guidelines for Selecting the Paired *t* Test and Wilcoxon Tests

Overview: This statistic detects if a measurement changes from one time point to another time point.

Variables: This statistic requires two continuous variables for each record: (1) the score at an initial time point and (2) the score at a later time point.

Results: In March, the mean crime rate in the 26 communities of Anytown was 408. On April 1, brighter street lighting was installed. In April, the mean crime rated dropped to 343. This decrease in the crime rate is statistically significant ($p < .001$, $\alpha = .05$).

VIDEOS

The tutorial videos for this chapter are **Ch 08 – Paired t Test.mp4** and **Ch 08 – Wilcoxon Test.mp4**. These videos provide an overview of these tests, followed by the SPSS procedures for processing the pretest checklist, ordering the statistical run, and interpreting the results using the data set: **Ch 08 – Example 01 – Paired t Test.sav**.

OVERVIEW—PAIRED *t* TEST

The *t* test and ANOVA test were appropriate for conducting research using a classic experimental model, which involves random assignment of participants to a control group and at least one other (treatment) group. There will be times when such rigorous designs are not feasible due to limited resources (e.g., low *n,* limited staff, lack of facilities, budget constraints, etc.). The **paired *t* test** provides an alternate approach that can be used to test the effectiveness of an implementation using a single group (pretest/posttest) design that does not require a sizable *n*.

In cases where the pretest criterion is not satisfied for the paired *t* test, the Wilcoxon test, which is conceptually similar to the paired *t* test, is the better option; this alternate test is explained near the end of this chapter.

Pretest/Posttest Design

The design associated with the paired *t* test is typically referred to as a **pretest/posttest design**, also known as a **simple time-series design**, or **O X O design** (O = observation, X = treatment) (Figure 8.1).

Figure 8.1   Pretest/posttest design.

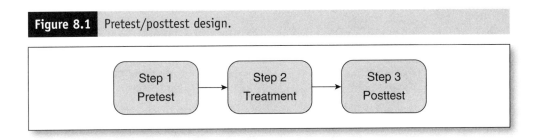

This design consists of one group and three steps.

Step 1: Pretest

Begin by gathering a quantitative metric, and attach each participant's name or ID to the score. The score needs to be a continuous variable. This could be an existing score or a test that you administer. This will be the *pretest* score, sometimes referred to as the *baseline* score, indicating the level that each participant was at prior to exposing him or her to the *treatment*. For the *t* test processing, it is important that the participant's name or ID is included with his or her responses (the *pretest* score for each participant will need to be paired with his or her *posttest* score). Essentially, each subject acts as his or her own control group.

Step 2: Treatment

Execute the treatment (e.g., intervention, change in condition, training, etc.).

Step 3: Posttest

Administer the same test that was used in Step 1 (pretest) to the same people and record the participant's name or ID with the score.

The paired *t* test analysis produces three critical pieces of information: (1) the mean pretest score, (2) the mean posttest score, and (3) the *p* value. If the *p* value is less than or equal to the specified α level (.05), then this indicates that there is a statistically significant difference between the pretest score and the posttest score, suggesting that the treatment made an impact.

Example

Anytown city council has voted to replace the old-style light bulbs in residential street lighting in all 26 districts with new energy-efficient lights that last longer, require less power, and are substantially brighter. The Anytown Police Department wants to determine if this change in lighting influences residential crime rates.

Research Question

Does the brighter energy-efficient lighting have an effect on crime rates?

Groups

As stated earlier, part of the utility of the paired *t* test is that it can function with just one group. The (one) group will consist of monthly crime data collected over the 26 districts of Anytown. Although data will be collected from 26 different sources, the point is that all 26 will be receiving the same treatment (brighter lighting).

Procedure

Step 1: Pretest

The new street lighting will be activated on April 1, so pretest (baseline) will consist of the monthly crime reports filed in all 26 districts for March.

NOTE: March has 31 days, whereas April has 30 days; hence, to keep the monthly crime reports comparable, we will not count data gathered on March 31.

Step 2: Treatment

The new brighter street lighting will be activated on April 1.

Step 3: Posttest

You will gather the total number of crime reports from each of the 26 districts for April.

Hypotheses

H_0: Brighter street lighting has no effect on crime rates.

H_1: Brighter street lighting has an effect on crime rates.

Data Set

Use the following data set: **Ch 08 – Example 01 – Paired t Test.sav and Wilcoxon Test**.

Codebook

Variable:	District
Definition:	Community district
Type:	Alphanumeric (D-1 . . . D-26)

Variable:	March
Definition:	Total number of crime reports filed in March
Type:	Continuous

Variable: April

Definition: Total number of crime reports filed in April

Type: Continuous

Pretest Checklist

Paired *t* Test Pretest Checklist

☑ 1. Normality of differences *

*Run prior to paired *t* test

NOTE: If the pretest checklist criterion is not satisfied, rerun the analysis using the nonparametric version of this test, later in this chapter, found within the Overview—Wilcoxon Test section (p. 209).

Pretest Checklist Criterion 1—Normality of Differences

To run a paired *t* test, only one pretest criterion must be satisfied: The difference between the pretest (*March*) scores and the posttest (*April*) scores must be normally distributed. Follow this procedure:

1. We will have SPSS compute a new variable (*Diff*), which will contain the difference between each *pretest* score and the corresponding *posttest* score for each record (*Diff* = *April* – *March*).

2. We will run a histogram with a normal curve for *Diff* and inspect the curve for normality.

3. On the main screen, click on *Transform, Compute Variable* (Figure 8.2).

Figure 8.2   Select *Transform, Compute Variable.*

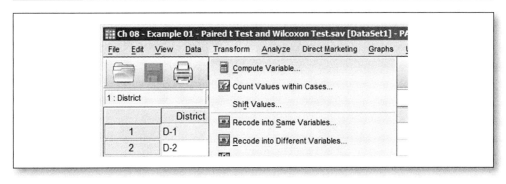

4. On the *Compute Variable* menu (Figure 8.3). Enter *Diff* in the *Target Variable* box. Enter *April–March* in the *Numeric Expression* box. You can type in the variables *March* and *April*, double-click on them or use the arrow key to copy them from the left box to the right box.

NOTE: For this procedure, you can enter *April–March* or *March–April*; either is fine.

5. Click the *OK* button to process this menu.

Figure 8.3 *Compute Variable* menu.

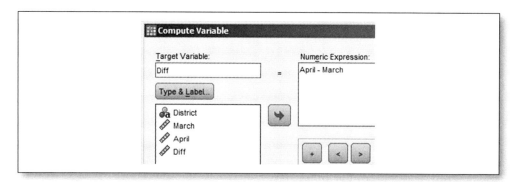

Notice that this operation created a new variable, *Diff* (Figure 8.4), which equals the *posttest–pretest* for each row. We can now order the **histogram with a normal curve** for the *Diff* variable. This is the same procedure used as part of the pretest checklist for the *t* test and ANOVA. For more details on this procedure, refer to **Chapter 4: *t* Test and Mann-Whitney *U* Test**, and the following section: SPSS—Descriptive Statistics: Continuous Variables (Age); see the star (★) icon on page 52.

Figure 8.4 *Data View* reveals new variable: *Diff* (derived from *April–March*).

	District	March	April	Diff
1	D-1	315	241	-74.00
2	D-2	427	324	-103.00
3	D-3	511	388	-123.00
4	D-4	343	277	-66.00
5	D-5	441	388	-53.00

Alternatively, the following steps will produce a histogram with a normal curve for *Diff*:

1. From the main screen, select *Analyze, Descriptive Statistics, Frequencies*; this will take you to the *Frequencies* menu.

2. On the *Frequencies* menu, move *Diff* from the left window to the right (*Variables*) window.

3. Click on the *Charts* button; this will take you to the *Charts* menu.

4. Click on the *Histograms* button, and check the ☑ *Show normal curve on histogram* checkbox.

5. Click on the *Continue* button; this will return you to the *Frequencies* menu.

6. Click on the *OK* button, and the system will produce a histogram with a normal curve for the *Diff* variable (Figure 8.5).

The normal curve for *Diff* (Figure 8.5) presents as a reasonably symmetrical bell shape—hence, we would say that the difference between the *March* and *April* scores meets the criteria of normality.

Figure 8.5   Histogram with normal curve for *Diff*.

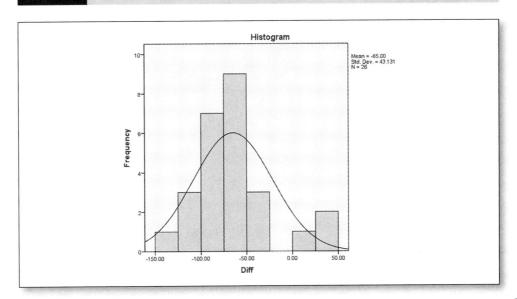

Test Run

To run the paired t test from the main screen, complete the following steps:

1. Click on *Analyze, Compare Means, Paired-Samples T Test* (Figure 8.6).

Figure 8.6 Order paired *t* test.

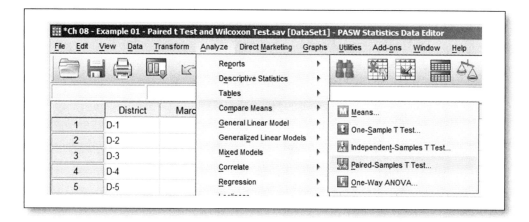

This will take you to the *Paired-Samples T Test* menu (Figure 8.7).

Figure 8.7 *Paired-Samples T Test* menu.

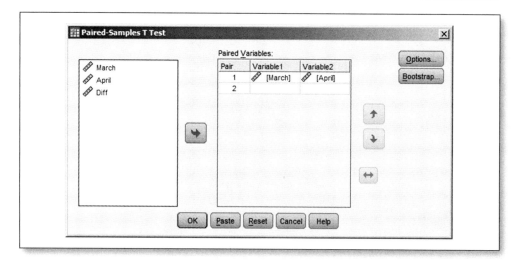

2. On the *Paired-Samples T Test* menu (Figure 8.7), copy the pretest variable (*March*) from the left window to the right window (under *Variable1*); next, copy the posttest variable (*April*) from the left window to the right window (under *Variable2*).

3. Click on *OK*.

Results

The results of the paired *t* test are read from two tables: The *paired-samples statistics test* (Table 8.1) reports the means for each month: March (M = 407.88) and April (M = 342.88). The table also shows the corresponding *ns* (26) and standard deviations.

Table 8.1   Paired-samples (summary) statistics for *pretest* and *posttest.*

Paired Samples Statistics

		Mean	N	Std. Deviation	Std. Error Mean
Pair 1	March	407.88	26	62.916	12.339
	April	342.88	26	72.727	14.263

The *paired-samples test* (Table 8.2) focuses on the difference between the mean number of crimes reported in each district for *March* (M = 407.88) and *April* (M = 342.88) scores, which is 65.00 (407.88 − 342.88 = 65.00). The last column (Sig.) shows that the *p* value is .000 for this comparison; because the *p* value is less than the specified α level of .05, we would conclude that there is a statistically significant difference between the mean reported crimes for March and April.

Table 8.2   Paired-samples test results.

Paired Samples Test

		Paired Differences							
					95% Confidence Interval of the Difference				
		Mean	Std. Deviation	Std. Error Mean	Lower	Upper	t	df	Sig. (2-tailed)
Pair 1	March - April	65.000	43.131	8.459	47.579	82.421	7.684	25	.000

Hypothesis Resolution

REJECT: H_0: Brighter street lighting has no effect on crime rates.

ACCEPT: H_1: Brighter street lighting has an effect on crime rates.

Because the *p* value (.000) is less than the specified α level (.05), this suggests that the 65-point decrease in mean crime rate (from 407.88 to 342.88) is statistically significant. In terms of the hypotheses, we would reject H_0 and not reject H_1.

Abstract

The paired *t* test is a fairly straightforward process; as such, the documentation is typically concise:

> *In order to determine if brighter energy-efficient street lighting would have an effect on crime rates in Anytown, we gathered the total number of crimes reported in each of the 26 districts for the month before the lighting was installed (March). The new lighting was activated on April 1, and we continued gathering data through April. Analysis revealed that in March, the monthly mean district crime rate was 407.88 (SD = 62.92), whereas this figure dropped significantly to 342.88 (SD = 72.73) in April. This reduction of 65 was found to be a statistically significant decrease (p < .001, α = .05).*

NOTE: Because the *p* value never really goes to 0, when the *p* value is shown as ".000" in the output reports, it is customary to document it as "*p* < .001"

The change from *pretest* to *posttest* (*March* to *April*) can also be expressed clearly as a percentage using the **Δ%** formula (Δ is the Greek letter delta, which symbolizes *change*). SPSS does not provide the Δ%, but you can easily process this formula on any calculator, simply by plugging two variables into the equation: **Δ% = (New − Old) ÷ Old × 100**, where the *Old* value is the *pretest* mean (407.88), and the *New* value is the *posttest* mean (342.88) (Table 8.3).

Table 8.3 Δ% formula computes change percentage.

Δ% Formula
Δ% = (New − Old) ÷ Old × 100
Δ% = (342.88 − 407.88) ÷ 407.88 × 100
Δ% = (−65) ÷ 407.88 × 100
Δ% = −.1594 × 100
Δ% = −15.94

NOTE: In this example, the Δ% formula produced a *negative* result (Δ% = −15.94), which translates to a 15.94% *decrease* from *pretest* to *posttest*. Conversely, a *positive* Δ% (e.g., Δ% = 15.94), would indicate a 15.94% *increase* from *pretest* to *posttest*.

In terms of documentation, you could include the "*Δ% = −15.94*" as is or express it verbosely: *". . . we observed a 15.94% decrease in mean monthly community crime reports from an average of 407.88 per district in March down to 342.88 in April."*

OVERVIEW—WILCOXON TEST

Remember that the pretest criteria that must be assessed prior to running a paired *t* test require that the difference between each pair of scores must be computed (which produced the *diff* variable) and that those differences (contained in the *diff* variable) must be normally distributed (Figure 8.8); minor variations in the normal distribution are acceptable. Occasionally, you may encounter data that are substantially skewed (Figure 8.9), bimodal (Figure 8.10), or flat (Figure 8.11) or that may have some other atypical distribution. In such instances, the **Wilcoxon test** is an appropriate alternative to the paired *t* test.

Figure 8.8 Normal.

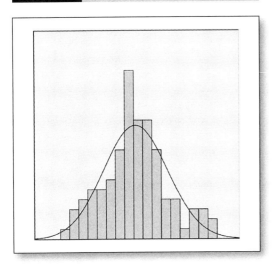

Figure 8.9 Skewed.

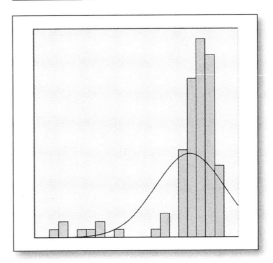

Figure 8.10 Bimodal.

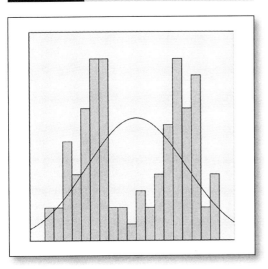

Figure 8.11 Flat.

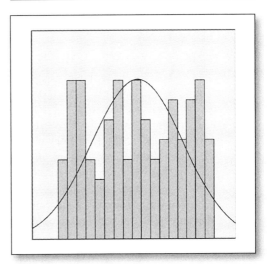

Test Run

For exemplary purposes, we will run the Wilcoxon test using the same data set (**Ch 08 – Example 01 – Paired t Test and Wilcoxon Test.sav**) even though the (*pretest–posttest*) data are normally distributed. This will enable us to compare the results of a paired *t* test to the results produced by the Wilcoxon test.

1. On the main screen, click on *Analyze, Nonparametric Tests, Legacy Dialogs, 2 Related Samples* (Figure 8.12).

| **Figure 8.12** | Ordering the Wilcoxon: Click on *Analyze, Nonparametric Tests, Legacy Dialogs, 2 Related Samples*. |

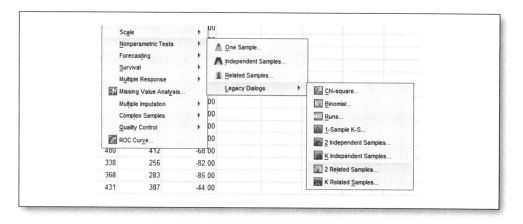

2. On the *Two-Related-Samples Tests* menu (Figure 8.13), move *March* to *Variable1*.

3. Move *April* to *Variable2*.

4. Click on *OK*.

 Results

The Wilcoxon test result is found on the *Test Statistics* table (Table 8.4); the *Asymp. Sig. (2-tailed)* statistic rendered a *p* value of .000; because this is less than α (.05), we would conclude that there is a statistically significant difference between the scores of the pretest (March) and the posttest (April).

Referring back, remember that the paired *t* test also produced a *p* value of .000; however, given a different data set, the Wilcoxon test could produce a *p* value that is different from the paired *t* test due to the internal transformations that the Wilcoxon test conducts on the data. If a substantial violation in the *normality of differences* criteria is detected when running the pretest checklist for the paired *t* test, then the Wilcoxon test is considered a viable alternative.

Figure 8.13 On the *Two-Related-Samples Tests* menu, move *March* to *Variable1* and *April* to *Variable 2.*

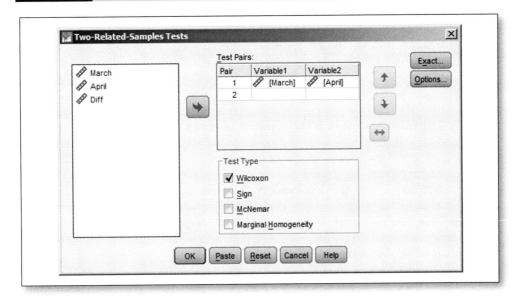

Table 8.4 Wilcoxon *p* value = .018.

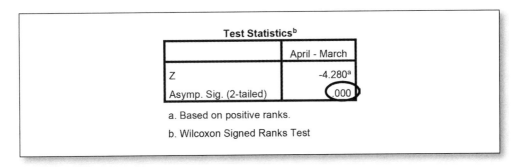

Test Statistics[b]

	April - March
Z	-4.280[a]
Asymp. Sig. (2-tailed)	.000

a. Based on positive ranks.

b. Wilcoxon Signed Ranks Test

GOOD COMMON SENSE

When opting for the pretest/posttest design and corresponding paired *t* test, it is important to consider potential threats to internal validity that are endemically present when using this one-group quasi-experimental design.

In a classic experimental design, the control group and treatment group(s) are processed during the same time frame, but when using the paired *t* test, the pretest (control/baseline) data and posttest (treatment) data are collected at different time points.

Although the example presented in this chapter took place over two 30-day blocks of time, it is possible to run a pretest/posttest intervention wherein there is considerably more time between the pretest and the posttest, depending on the study design. During this time, history does not stand still; things outside your investigation can change over time either in the individual or in the environment (e.g., personal issues, sociopolitical events, season, etc.), which could potentially affect the pretest or posttest scores.

Another factor (outside of our procedure) that could have influenced the pulse rates is that each participant was measured on only one day. We do not know how stressful that day was (e.g., perhaps stress levels are higher during weekdays compared to weekends), so it is not possible to know if we gathered a representative sample from the participants.

In instances wherein participants are asked to complete a test twice (once at pretest and again at posttest), repeated testing can be an issue; there is a chance that participants may show improvement in the *posttest*, partly because they are familiar with it—they remember it from the *pretest* phase.

Maturation may also influence the outcome, specifically in pretest/posttest designs wherein there is considerable time between the pretest and the posttest. Prior to the posttest, the participants' condition/problem may resolve or become less burdensome, or the participants may become more proficient at selected skills due to influences other than (only) the treatment.

One must also take into account the potential influence of reactivity, specifically, the *Hawthorne effect*, wherein people's performance improves merely because they know that they are being monitored.

Any one, or combination of these threats to internal validity must be considered when using quasi-experimental implementations such as the pretest/posttest design. Because there is no formal control group, it can be challenging to detect and control for such extraneous influences which may alter the findings of your study.

Key Concepts

- Paired *t* test
- Paired *t* test designs (synonyms):

  - Pretest/treatment/posttest
  - Pretest/posttest design
  - Simple time-series design
  - O-X-O design

- Histogram with a normal curve
- Paired *t* test with multiple metrics
- Δ%
- Wilcoxon test
- Good common sense

  - Internal validity
  - History

○ Testing

○ Maturation

○ Hawthorne effect

Practice Exercises

Exercise 8.1

Acme Industries has implemented a new website for employees to enter their weekly hours (e.g., start time, end time, sick hours, vacation hours, holiday hours, family leave hours). Upon clicking Save, the system checks the validity of the entries and points the user to correct any errors or omissions before saving the data. To evaluate the efficiency of this new website, the system journals the access time (in seconds) indicating how long it took for each employee to file their daily entries. A manager will assess the mean access times starting at the initial launch of the website (Week1), and continue to gather data for the next week (Week2).

Data set: **Ch 08 – Exercise 01A.sav**

Codebook

Variable:	ID
Definition:	Employee ID
Type:	Alphanumeric
Variable:	Week1
Definition:	Average time (in seconds) required to fill out webpage for first week
Type:	Continuous
Variable:	Week2
Definition:	Average time (in seconds) required to fill out webpage for second week
Type:	Continuous

a. Write the hypotheses.

b. Run the criteria of the pretest checklist (normality for posttest–pretest) and discuss your findings.

c. Run the paired *t* test and document your findings (means and Sig. [*p* value], hypothesis resolution).

d. Write an abstract under 200 words detailing a summary of the study, the paired *t* test results, hypothesis resolution, and implications of your findings.

Repeat this exercise using data set: **Ch 08 – Exercise 01B.sav**.

Exercise 8.2

Prior to a Heart Health presentation, you administer a survey asking participants to indicate how many times they used the stairs (as opposed to the elevator) in the past week. A week after the lecture, you resurvey the attendees.

Data set: **Ch 08 – Exercise 02A.sav**

Codebook

Variable:	ID
Definition:	Participant ID
Type:	Alphanumeric
Variable:	Time1
Definition:	Number of times the steps were used in the week before the seminar
Type:	Continuous
Variable:	Time2
Definition:	Number of times the steps were used in the week after the seminar
Type:	Continuous

a. Write the hypotheses.

b. Run the criteria of the pretest checklist (normality for posttest–pretest) and discuss your findings.

c. Run the paired t test and document your findings (means and Sig. [p value], hypothesis resolution).

d. Write an abstract under 200 words detailing a summary of the study, the paired t test results, hypothesis resolution, and implications of your findings.

Repeat this exercise using data set: **Ch 08 – Exercise 02B.sav**.

Exercise 8.3

The staff at a mental health clinic wants to determine if their current form of short-term therapy substantially reduces depression. Prior to the first treatment, each patient will be asked to complete the Acme Depression Inventory (ADI), which renders a score from 0 to 75 (0 = Low depression . . . 75 = High depression). Patients will be asked to complete the same instrument at the conclusion of their appointment on Week 5.

Data set: **Ch 08 – Exercise 03A.sav**

Codebook

Variable:	ID
Definition:	Participant ID
Type:	Alphanumeric

Variable:	Baseline
Definition:	Acme Depression Inventory score at baseline
Type:	Continuous

Variable:	Week05
Definition:	Acme Depression Inventory score at Week 5
Type:	Continuous

a. Write the hypotheses.

b. Run the criteria of the pretest checklist (normality for posttest–pretest) and discuss your findings.

c. Run the paired *t* test and document your findings (means and Sig. [*p* value], hypothesis resolution).

d. Write an abstract under 200 words detailing a summary of the study, the paired *t* test results, hypothesis resolution, and implications of your findings.

Repeat this exercise using data set: **Ch 08 – Exercise 03B.sav**.

Exercise 8.4

The staff of the Physical Education Department wants to know if providing a single 15-minute individual coaching session with an expert bowler will enhance students' bowling scores. Each participant will bowl one game, during which time the coach will unobtrusively observe his or her bowling style. Then, the coach will provide a 15-minute coaching session. Immediately following the coaching, the student will bowl a second game. The scores of each student will be recorded and evaluated to determine the effectiveness of this form of coaching.

Data set: **Ch 08 – Exercise 04A.sav**

Codebook

Variable:	Student
Definition:	Student's last name
Type:	Alphanumeric

Variable: Game1

Definition: Bowling score on first (baseline) game

Type: Continuous

Variable: Game2

Definition: Bowling score on second game

Type: Continuous

a. Write the hypotheses.

b. Run the criteria of the pretest checklist (normality for posttest–pretest) and discuss your findings.

c. Run the paired t test and document your findings (means and Sig. [p value], hypothesis resolution).

d. Write an abstract under 200 words detailing a summary of the study, the paired t test results, hypothesis resolution, and implications of your findings.

Repeat this exercise using data set: **Ch 08 – Exercise 04B.sav**.

Exercise 8.5

In an effort to affordably boost productivity, the Acme Company has started providing free unlimited gourmet coffee to all employees. The manager will track the weekly total productivity (units produced) of each employee before and after the coffee machine is installed.

Data set: **Ch 08 – Exercise 05A.sav**

Codebook

Variable: Name

Definition: Employee name

Type: Alphanumeric

Variable: Productivity_1

Definition: Number of units produced during week 1 (baseline)

Type: Continuous

Variable: Productivity_2

Definition: Number of units produced during week 2

Type: Continuous

a. Write the hypotheses.

b. Run the criteria of the pretest checklist (normality for posttest–pretest) and discuss your findings.

c. Run the paired *t* test and document your findings (means and Sig. [*p* value], hypothesis resolution).

d. Write an abstract under 200 words detailing a summary of the study, the paired *t* test results, hypothesis resolution, and implications of your findings.

Repeat this exercise using data set: **Ch 08 – Exercise 05B.sav**.

Exercise 8.6

On Tuesday morning, the student council at a middle school announced its plan to combat the chronic litter problem in the outdoor lunch area: The 16 large trash cans in the lunch area now each have the name of a popular band on them—they are now referred to as *Band-Cans*. The Band-Can containing the most trash at the end of each day wins; music from that band's latest release will be played on the school's public address system in between classes for the next day. The Band-Cans are 42 inches tall; at the end of each day, starting on Monday (to gather baseline data), the members of the student council will use a tape measure to record how full each Band-Can is (0 = Empty . . . 42 = Full).

Data set: **Ch 08 – Exercise 06A.sav**

Codebook

Variable:	Band
Definition:	Name of band on trashcan
Type:	Alphanumeric

Variable:	Monday
Definition:	Inches of trash in trashcan (baseline)
Type:	Continuous

Variable:	Tuesday
Definition:	Inches of trash in trashcan
Type:	Continuous

a. Write the hypotheses.

b. Run the criteria of the pretest checklist (normality for posttest–pretest) and discuss your findings.

c. Run the paired *t* test and document your findings (means and Sig. [*p* value], hypothesis resolution).

d. Write an abstract under 200 words detailing a summary of the study, the paired *t* test results, hypothesis resolution, and implications of your findings.

Repeat this exercise using data set: **Ch 08 – Exercise 06B.sav**.

Exercise 8.7

A political consultant convened a focus group to evaluate the effectiveness of a commercial promoting a candidate. Prior to running any media, the participants are asked to answer one question: *Do you intend to vote for Jones in the upcoming election?* The participants will respond using a scale ranging from 1 to 7 (1 = Absolutely will not vote for Jones . . . 7 = Absolutely will vote for Jones). Next, the facilitator runs a 30-second radio advertisement, promoting the candidate, after which, the participants are asked to respond to the same question using the 1 to 7 scale.

Data set: **Ch 08 – Exercise 07A.sav**

Codebook

Variable:	ID
Definition:	Name
Type:	Alphanumeric

Variable:	Opinion1_Baseline
Definition:	Likelihood of voting for Jones (baseline)
Type:	Continuous

Variable:	Opinion2_Audio
Definition:	Likelihood of voting for Jones after hearing the radio advertisement
Type:	Continuous

a. Write the hypotheses.

b. Run the criteria of the pretest checklist (normality for posttest–pretest) and discuss your findings.

c. Run the paired *t* test and document your findings (means and Sig. [*p* value], hypothesis resolution).

d. Write an abstract under 200 words detailing a summary of the study, the paired *t* test results, hypothesis resolution, and implications of your findings.

Repeat this exercise using data set: **Ch 08 – Exercise 07B.sav**.

Exercise 8.8

In an effort to improve customer satisfaction, the manager at the Acme Customer Support Call Center installed a large-screen monitor in the front of the room to run classic movies with the sound off during work hours. At the conclusion of each call, the caller is routed to respond to an automated one-question customer satisfaction survey, where the caller is prompted with the following instructions: *Please use the buttons on your phone to rate your satisfaction with this call on a scale of 1 to 9, where 1 is for low satisfaction and 9 is for high satisfaction.* The manager will gather weekly mean customer satisfaction scores for each employee before and after the activation of the movies.

Data set: **Ch 08 – Exercise 08A.sav**

Codebook

Variable:	Name
Definition:	Employee name
Type:	Alphanumeric
Variable:	Satisfaction1
Definition:	Customer satisfaction score for baseline week
Type:	Continuous
Variable:	Satisfaction2
Definition:	Customer satisfaction score for first week of video
Type:	Continuous

a. Write the hypotheses.

b. Run the criteria of the pretest checklist (normality for posttest–pretest) and discuss your findings.

c. Run the paired *t* test and document your findings (means and Sig. [*p* value], hypothesis resolution).

d. Write an abstract under 200 words detailing a summary of the study, the paired *t* test results, hypothesis resolution, and implications of your findings.

Repeat this exercise using data set: **Ch 08 – Exercise 08B.sav**.

Exercise 8.9

The *Zzzleep Zzzound* app provides audio selections (e.g., gentle rain, ocean waves, soothing music) to help induce peaceful sleep. During the night, the app uses the camera and motion sensor to gather sleep data. If the user wakes during the night, the app senses it and plays the selected sound for 10 minutes. For the first week, the app runs without any audio to gather baseline data. Once a week, the software transmits the mean sleep time per night for that week to the sleep researcher's database.

Data set: **Ch 08 – Exercise 09A.sav**

Codebook

Variable:	CellPhone
Definition:	Cell phone number
Type:	Alphanumeric

Variable:	Sleep1
Definition:	Mean sleep minutes per night for Week 1 (baseline)
Type:	Continuous

Variable:	Sleep2
Definition:	Mean sleep minutes per night for Week 2
Type:	Continuous

a. Write the hypotheses.

b. Run the criteria of the pretest checklist (normality for posttest–pretest) and discuss your findings.

c. Run the paired *t* test and document your findings (means and Sig. [*p* value], hypothesis resolution).

d. Write an abstract under 200 words detailing a summary of the study, the paired *t* test results, hypothesis resolution, and implications of your findings.

Repeat this exercise using data set: **Ch 08 – Exercise 09B.sav**.

Exercise 8.10

To assess the effect that chocolate may have on attitude, a researcher recruits a group of participants to complete the Acme Attitude Survey (AAS), which renders a 0 to 100 score (0 = very bad attitude . . . 100 = very good attitude). After giving the pretest, the researcher gives each participant a large bar of chocolate. Five minutes after the participant eats the chocolate, the researcher readministers the AAS.

Data set: **Ch 08 – Exercise 10A.sav**

Codebook

Variable:	ID
Definition:	Participant ID
Type:	Alphanumeric

Variable: Attitude_0

Definition: Attitude before eating chocolate (baseline)

Type: Continuous

Variable: Attitude_1

Definition: Attitude 5 minutes after eating chocolate

Type: Continuous

a. Write the hypotheses.

b. Run the criteria of the pretest checklist (normality for posttest–pretest) and discuss your findings.

c. Run the paired *t* test and document your findings (means and Sig. [*p* value], hypothesis resolution).

d. Write an abstract under 200 words detailing a summary of the study, the paired *t* test results, hypothesis resolution, and implications of your findings.

Repeat this exercise using data set: **Ch 08 – Exercise 10B.sav**.

CHAPTER 9

ANOVA Repeated Measures

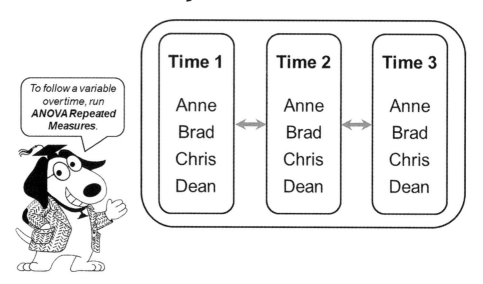

To follow a variable overtime, run **ANOVA Repeated Measures**.

Time 1	Time 2	Time 3
Anne	Anne	Anne
Brad	Brad	Brad
Chris	Chris	Chris
Dean	Dean	Dean

The only reason for time is so that everything doesn't happen at once.

—Albert Einstein

Learning Objectives

Upon completing this chapter, you will be able to do the following:

- Determine when it is appropriate to run an ANOVA repeated-measures test.
- Verify that the data meet the criteria for ANOVA repeated-measures test processing: Mauchly's test of sphericity.
- Order an ANOVA repeated-measures test.
- Interpret test results.
- Resolve the hypotheses.
- Write an appropriate abstract.
- Comprehend the versatility of repeated-measures designs.

WHEN TO USE THIS STATISTIC

Guidelines for Selecting the ANOVA Repeated Measures Test

Overview: This statistic detects if a measurement changes over more than two time points.

Variables: A continuous measurement that is gathered at three time points requires three variables: *Measurement1*, *Measurement2*, and *Measurement3*.

Results: In March, the mean crime rate in the 26 communities of Anytown was 408. On April 1, brighter street lighting was installed. In April, the mean crime rated significantly decreased to 343 ($p < .001$, $\alpha = .05$). In May, the mean crime rate showed a further decrease to 330; however, compared to April, this reduction was a statistically insignificant ($p = .116$, $\alpha = .05$).

VIDEO

The tutorial video for this chapter is **Ch 09 – ANOVA Repeated Measures.mp4**. This video provides an overview of the ANOVA repeated-measures statistic, followed by the SPSS procedures for processing the pretest checklist, ordering the statistical run, and interpreting the results of this test using the data set: **Ch 09 – Example 01 – ANOVA Repeated Measures.sav**.

LAYERED LEARNING

If you mastered the paired *t* test, then you can consider yourself more than halfway there when it comes to comprehending the ANOVA repeated-measures test. Whereas the paired *t* test involves measuring the same thing at *two* time points (*pretest* vs. *posttest*), the ANOVA repeated-measures test does exactly the same thing, except it accommodates more than *two* time points—for example, (1) a score gathered at 7:00 a.m. to establish a baseline, followed immediately by the treatment; (2) a score gathered at 9:00 a.m. to detect the initial effectiveness of the treatment; and (3) a score gathered at 11:00 a.m. to check for sustainability—this will tell us if the effects of the treatment endured over time, beyond the (first) 9:00 a.m. posttest. The ANOVA repeated measures test is a versatile upgrade to the paired *t* test, as it lends itself to more elaborate longitudinal designs involving any number of measures gathered over any duration. This will be discussed more thoroughly at the conclusion of the chapter, but first we will begin with a more detailed overview of the ANOVA repeated-measures test.

OVERVIEW—ANOVA REPEATED MEASURES

Before embarking on the ANOVA repeated-measures test, we will briefly revisit the paired *t* test. The paired *t* test is typically thought of as the statistic used to measure change from *pretest* to *posttest,* which can render some valuable information regarding the effect of the treatment, situated (in time) between the *pretest* and *posttest.* Another way to think about the labels *pretest* and *posttest* is to conceive them in terms of time: The variable labeled *pretest* could plausibly be renamed as $Time_1$, and the variable *posttest* could be renamed as $Time_2$. With this in mind, we can move into the ANOVA repeated-measures test.

Essentially, the findings of the paired *t* test end at the *posttest* ($Time_2$), but what if we wanted to know *what happens next?* In the example used in Chapter 8, the paired *t* test revealed that the mean monthly crime rates dropped significantly across the 26 districts of Anytown in the month after the installation of brighter street lighting, but that is *all* we know. Considering that crime is an ongoing issue, it would be useful if we had a way to track the crime rates over time—beyond the posttest; ANOVA repeated measures enables us to do just that.

Just as the ANOVA test compares the mean from each group to every other group ($Group_1$: $Group_2$, $Group_1$: $Group_3$, $Group_2$: $Group_3$) and produces corresponding *p* values for each pair of groups, the ANOVA repeated-measures test compares the mean from each time point to every other time point ($Time_1$: $Time_2$, $Time_1$: $Time_3$, $Time_2$: $Time_3$) and produces corresponding *p* values for each pair of times.

To build on the similarity between the *paired t test* and the *ANOVA repeated-measures test,* this chapter will use the same example that was used in Chapter 8 with one enhancement: In addition to the $Time_1$ pretest variable (*March*), and the $Time_2$ posttest variable (*April*), a new variable for *Time3,* is now included (*May*).

We will use the **treatment effect and sustainability O X O O** (O = observation, X = treatment) (quasi-)experimental design for this example, which will consist of the monthly reported crime rates from each of the 26 districts covering $Time_1$ (*March*), $Time_2$, (*April*), and $Time_3$ (*May*) (Figure 9.1).

This design will enable us to determine

- the baseline monthly mean crime rate across the 26 districts (*March*);
- the initial effectiveness of the new brighter street lighting (comparing *March* to *April*);
- if the effect of the treatment is sustained over time (comparing *April* to *May*); and
- if, over time, the decrease in crime rate was maintained or if the crime rate reverted back to the baseline rate (comparing *March* to *May*).

Figure 9.1   Repeated-measures design (0 X 0 0) to assess sustainability. 0 = observation; X = treatment.

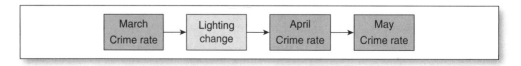

Example

Anytown city council has voted to replace the old-style light bulbs in residential street lighting in all 26 districts with new energy-efficient lights that last longer, require less power, and are substantially brighter. Anytown has a fairly steady crime rate from month to month in each district.

Research Question

The Anytown Police Department wants to determine if this change in lighting influences residential crime rates.

Groups

The (one) group will consist of 26 residential districts in Anytown.

Procedure

Step 1—*March* (Time$_1$): The new street lighting will be activated on April 1, so pretest (baseline) will consist of the monthly crime reports filed in all 26 districts for March.

NOTE: March and May each have 31 days, whereas April has 30 days; hence, to keep the monthly crime reports comparable, we will only gather data from the first 30 days of each month.

Step 2—Treatment: The new brighter street lighting will be activated on April 1.

Step 3—*April* (Time$_2$): You will gather the total number of crime reports from each of the 26 districts for April.

Step 4—*May* (Time$_3$): You will gather the total number of crime reports from each of the 26 districts for May.

Hypotheses

H$_0$: Brighter street lighting has no effect on crime rates.

H$_1$: Brighter street lighting has an effect on crime rates.

Data Set

Use the following data set: **Ch 09 – Example 01 – ANOVA Repeated Measures.sav**.

Codebook

Variable:	District
Definition:	Community district
Type:	Alphanumeric (D-1 . . . D-26)

Variable: March

Definition: Total number of crime reports filed in March

Type: Continuous

Variable: April

Definition: Total number of crime reports filed in April

Type: Continuous

Variable: May

Definition: Total number of crime reports filed in May

Type: Continuous

 Pretest Checklist

ANOVA Repeated-Measures Pretest Checklist

☑   1. Mauchly's test of sphericity*

*Results produced upon ANOVA repeated-measures test run

NOTE: If this pretest checklist criterion is not satisfied, proceed with the analysis, but concisely discuss such anomalies in the *Results* or *Limitations* sections of the documentation so the reader can more plausibly interpret the precision of the findings.

 ### Pretest Checklist Criterion 1—Mauchly's Test of Sphericity

To run an ANOVA repeated-measures test, we need to check that the variances from each of the time points are similar. We check for this using **Mauchly's test of sphericity**. If this test produces a p value that is greater than .05, then this tells us that there is no statistically significant difference among the variances from the data gathered at the (three) time points, indicating that this criterion is satisfied.

This test will be processed during the Test Run and finalized in the Results section.

NOTE: Occasionally, this test renders a p value that is less than .05; in such cases, proceed with the ANOVA repeated-measures test, and include a statement pertaining to this (imperfect) finding when documenting the results.

 Test Run

1. To run the ANOVA repeated measures, from the *Data View* screen, click on *Analyze, General Linear Model, Repeated Measures* (Figure 9.2).

| **Figure 9.2** | Order ANOVA repeated-measures test. |

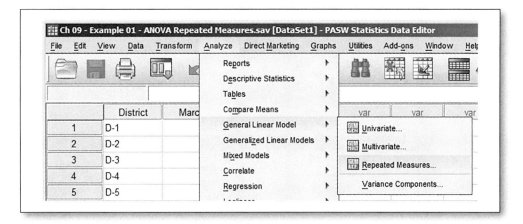

2. This will take you to the *Repeated Measure Define Factor(s)* menu (Figure 9.3).

| **Figure 9.3** | *Repeated Measures Define Factor(s)* menu. |

3. In the *Within-Subject Factor Name* box, erase *factor1* and type in *Month* (because our time frame is in months). In the *Number of Levels* box, enter *3*, indicating that we will be comparing measurements taken from *three* time points (*March*, *April* and *May*). Click on *Add;* then click on *Define*. This will take you to the *Repeated Measures* menu (Figure 9.4).

Figure 9.4   *Repeated Measures menu.*

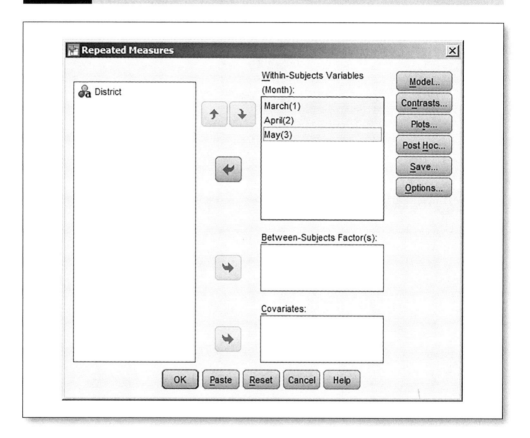

4. On the *Repeated Measures* menu, move the variables *March, April,* and *May* from the left box to the *Within-Subjects Variables (Month)* box; be sure to keep them in order; then click on *Options* (Figure 9.4). This will take you to the *Repeated Measures: Options* menu (Figure 9.5).

5. Move *Month* from the *Factor(s) and Factor Interactions* box to the *Display Means for* box. Check the ☑ *Compare main effects* option and the ☑ *Descriptive statistics* option; then click *Continue*. This will take you back to the *Repeated Measures* menu (Figure 9.6).

| Figure 9.5 | *Repeated Measures: Options* menu. |

| Figure 9.6 | *Repeated Measures* menu. |

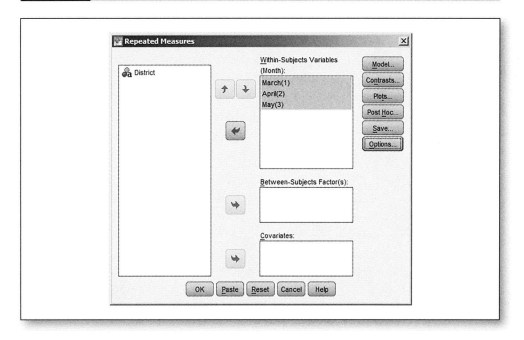

6. On the *Repeated Measures* menu, click on *Plots*. This will take you to the *Repeated Measures: Profile Plots* menu (Figure 9.7).

Figure 9.7   *Repeated Measures: Profile Plots* menu.

7. Next, we will order a line graph that will show how the data changed over the three time points (*March* to *April* to *May*). On the *Repeated Measures: Profile Plots* menu, move *Month* from the *Factors* box to the *Horizontal Axis* box; then click on *Add*. Finally, click on *Continue*. This will take you back to the *Repeated Measures* menu (Figure 9.8).

8. On the *Repeated Measures* menu, click on *OK,* and the data will be processed.

Figure 9.8 *Repeated Measures* menu.

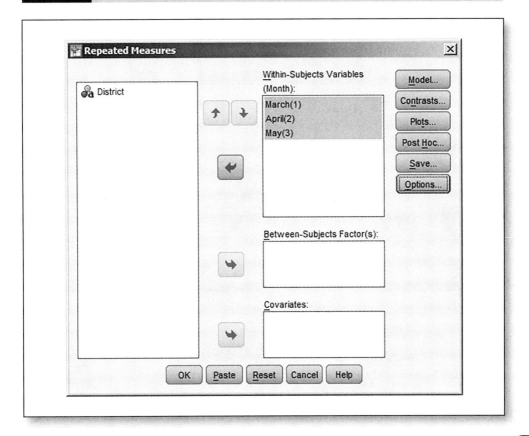

Results

Pretest Checklist Criterion 1—Mauchly's Test of Sphericity

We can now finalize the pretest checklist; look at the *Mauchly's Test of Sphericity* table (Table 9.1), specifically, focus on the Sig. (*p*) value, which is .231. Because this is greater than the α level of .05, this tells us that there is no statistically significant difference between the variances of the data gathered at the three time points; hence, this pretest criterion is satisfied.

Next, inspect the *Tests of Within-Subjects Effects* table (Table 9.2), focusing on the *Month, Sphericity Assumed Sig.* (*p*) value, .000. Since this is less than the α level (.05), this indicates that the mean of one of the *Months* is significantly different from the mean of one of the other *Months*.

Table 9.1   *Mauchly's Test of Sphericity* table [Sig. (*p*) > α (.05)] indicates a pass.

Mauchly's Test of Sphericity[b]

Measure:MEASURE_1

Within Subjects Effect	Mauchly's W	Approx. Chi-Square	df	Sig.	Epsilon[a]		
					Greenhouse-Geisser	Huynh-Feldt	Lower-bound
– Month	.885	2.929	2	.231	.897	.962	.500

Tests the null hypothesis that the error covariance matrix of the orthonormalized transformed dependent variables is proportional to an identity matrix.

a. May be used to adjust the degrees of freedom for the averaged tests of significance. Corrected tests are displayed in the Tests of Within-Subjects Effects table.

b. Design: Intercept
 Within Subjects Design: Month

Table 9.2   Tests of Within-Subjects Effects table.

Tests of Within-Subjects Effects

Measure:MEASURE_1

Source		Type III Sum of Squares	df	Mean Square	F	Sig.
Month	Sphericity Assumed	90930.769	2	45465.385	60.006	.000
	Greenhouse-Geisser	90930.769	1.794	50688.028	60.006	.000
	Huynh-Feldt	90930.769	1.924	47267.986	60.006	.000
	Lower-bound	90930.769	1.000	90930.769	60.006	.000
Error(Month)	Sphericity Assumed	37883.897	50	757.678		
	Greenhouse-Geisser	37883.897	44.848	844.713		
	Huynh-Feldt	37883.897	48.093	787.718		
	Lower-bound	37883.897	25.000	1515.356		

NOTE: For *Month, Sphericity Assumed* Sig. (*p*) < α (.05), indicating that there is a statistically

significant difference (somewhere) among the pairs of *Months*.

The mean for each *Month* is shown in the *Descriptive Statistics* table (Table 9.3). The *Pairwise Comparisons* table (Tables 9.4, 9.5, and 9.6) indicates which *Month* outperformed which (other) *Month*(s) as indicated by the *p* values.

The best way to comprehend the story of how the brighter street lighting changed the crime rates over the three time points is to (manually) build a *Longitudinal Results* table (Table 9.7). This is the same sort of results table that we assembled to comprehend ANOVA results. SPSS does not produce this table directly, but you can derive it from key figures in the output that we ordered SPSS to generate. To bring all the

Table 9.3 Descriptive Statistics table provides the mean for each month.

Descriptive Statistics

	Mean	Std. Deviation	N
March	407.88	62.916	26
April	342.88	72.727	26
May	329.81	60.368	26

Table 9.4 Pairwise Comparisons table—Month$_1$ (*March*) : Month$_2$ (*April*), p = .000.

Pairwise Comparisons

Measure:MEASURE_1

(I) Month	(J) Month	Mean Difference (I-J)	Std. Error	Sig.^{a}	95% Confidence Interval for Difference^a	
					Lower Bound	Upper Bound
1	2	65.000*	8.459	.000	47.579	82.421
	3	78.077*	6.243	.000	65.219	90.935
2	1	-65.000*	8.459	.000	-82.421	-47.579
	3	13.077	8.020	.116	-3.441	29.595
3	1	-78.077*	6.243	.000	-90.935	-65.219
	2	-13.077	8.020	.116	-29.595	3.441

Based on estimated marginal means
*. The mean difference is significant at the .05 level.
a. Adjustment for multiple comparisons: Least Significant Difference (equivalent to no adjustments).

critical figures together into one comprehensive table, assemble the *Longitudinal Results* table (Table 9.7): Draw the *Means* from the *Descriptive Statistics* table (Table 9.3) and the *p* values (Sig.) from the *Pairwise Comparisons* tables (Table 9.4, 9.5, and 9.6).

NOTE: Tables 9.4, 9.5, and 9.6 are the same table but with different circle placements to point out the pairs being compared along with their corresponding *p* values.

To comprehend the results of this 3-month study, we will discuss findings in the *Longitudinal Results* table, one row at a time.

The first comparison shows a decline in crime from *March* (M = 407.88) to *April* (M = 342.88); this change is statistically significant (*p* = .000).

The next comparison shows a further decline in crime from *April* (M = 342.88) to *May* (M = 329.81); however, this change is not statistically significant (*p* = .116).

Table 9.5 Pairwise Comparisons table—Month$_2$ (*April*) : Month$_3$ (*May*), *p* = .116.

Pairwise Comparisons

Measure:MEASURE_1

(I) Month	(J) Month	Mean Difference (I-J)	Std. Error	Sig.[a]	95% Confidence Interval for Difference[a]	
					Lower Bound	Upper Bound
1	2	65.000*	8.459	.000	47.579	82.421
	3	78.077*	6.243	.000	65.219	90.935
2	1	-65.000*	8.459	.000	-82.421	-47.579
	3	13.077	8.020	.116	-3.441	29.595
3	1	-78.077*	6.243	.000	-90.935	-65.219
	2	-13.077	8.020	.116	-29.595	3.441

Based on estimated marginal means
*. The mean difference is significant at the .05 level.
a. Adjustment for multiple comparisons: Least Significant Difference (equivalent to no adjustments).

Table 9.6 Pairwise Comparisons—Month$_1$ (*March*) : Month$_3$ (*May*), *p* = .000.

Pairwise Comparisons

Measure:MEASURE_1

(I) Month	(J) Month	Mean Difference (I-J)	Std. Error	Sig.[a]	95% Confidence Interval for Difference[a]	
					Lower Bound	Upper Bound
1	2	65.000*	8.459	.000	47.579	82.421
	3	78.077*	6.243	.000	65.219	90.935
2	1	-65.000*	8.459	.000	-82.421	-47.579
	3	13.077	8.020	.116	-3.441	29.595
3	1	-78.077*	6.243	.000	-90.935	-65.219
	2	-13.077	8.020	.116	-29.595	3.441

Based on estimated marginal means
*. The mean difference is significant at the .05 level.
a. Adjustment for multiple comparisons: Least Significant Difference (equivalent to no adjustments).

Whereas the first two rows compare the scores at adjacent time points (*March* : *April* and *April* : *May*), the last row compares the first measurement to the last to assess the overall performance of the lighting in terms of crime rates. This row compares *March* (M = 407.88) to *May* (M = 329.81), which is a statistically significant change in reported crime rates (*p* = .000).

Table 9.7	Manually Built Longitudinal Results table: *Means* drawn from *Descriptive Statistics* (Table 9.3) and *p* values (Sig.) drawn from *Pairwise Comparisons* (Tables 9.4, 9.5, and 9.6).

Months	*p*
March (M = 407.88) : April (M = 342.88)	.000*
April (M = 342.88) : May (M = 329.81)	.116
March (M = 407.88) : May (M = 329.81)	.000*

*Statistically significant difference detected between groups ($p \leq .05$).

The plot that we ordered clearly graphs these three findings (Figure 9.9). Notice the steep slope of the line between $Month_1$ and $Month_2$, indicating the statistically significant reduction in crime rates. Also notice the less steep line between $Month_2$ and $Month_3$, indicating the insignificant drop in reported crimes between $Month_2$ and $Month_3$.

Figure 9.9	A graphical representation of the mean number of reported crimes (Y-axis) at each of the three time points (X-axis).

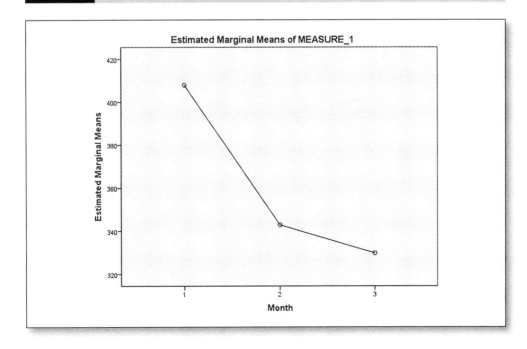

Hypothesis Resolution

H_0: Brighter street lighting has no effect on crime rates.

H_1: Brighter street lighting has an effect on crime rates.

Because we detected a statistically significant reduction in mean reported crimes between $Month_1$ (March) and $Month_2$ (April), as well as between $Month_1$ (March) and $Month_3$ (May), we would reject H_0.
For the same reasons, we would not reject H_1.

 Abstract

The abstract for the ANOVA repeated measures is similar to the paired t test; however, more variables are involved, so the Results section is typically a bit longer:

In order to determine if brighter energy-efficient street lighting would have an effect on crime rates in Anytown, we gathered the total number of crimes reported in each of the 26 districts for the month before the lighting was installed (March). The new lighting was activated on April 1, and we continued gathering monthly data through May. Analysis revealed that in March (the baseline month), the monthly mean district crime rate was 407.88 (SD = 62.92), whereas this figure dropped significantly to 342.88 (SD = 72.73) in April. This reduction of 65 was found to be a statistically significant decrease (p < .001, α = .05). The monthly district crime rate continued to decrease to 329.81 (SD = 60.37) in May, however, this drop (from April to May) was not statistically significant (p = .116, α = .05).

Over the course of this 3-month study, we detected a significant 19.1% reduction in monthly district crime rates (p < .001, α = .05). Based on these findings, we intend to continue monitoring monthly crime rates in the 26 districts of Anytown to determine if the change associated with the brighter lighting is sustainable.

VARIATIONS ON LONGITUDINAL DESIGN

Whereas the ANOVA repeated-measures statistic can assess measurements taken over three or more time points, the test is essentially oblivious to anything (treatment/interventions) that may be occurring in between the specified time points; it only computes the data gathered in each variable. This characteristic lends this test to a variety of research designs. Although the following examples demonstrate three unique longitudinal research designs, each involving data gathered over three time points ($Time_1$, $Time_2$, and $Time_3$), they would all be coded and processed exactly the same way—from a statistical processing standpoint, each design merely focuses on the data gathered at each of the three time points.

Design A—Treatment Effect and Sustainability (O X O O)

Treatment effect and sustainability (O X O O) is the design that we used for the example in this chapter. Comparing $Time_1$ (*March*) to $Time_2$ (*April*) detects the initial *effectiveness* of the treatment. Comparing $Time_2$ (*April*) to $Time_3$ (*May*) allows us to check for *sustainability*, answering the question, *At this point (Time$_3$), do crime rates go up/down/stabilize?* Finally, one could compare $Time_1$ (*March*) to $Time_3$ (*May*) to detect the overall *effect* of the treatment (Figure 9.10).

Figure 9.10 Design to detect initial treatment effectiveness ($Time_1 : Time_2$), sustainability ($Time_2 : Time_3$), and start-to-end performance ($Time_1 : Time_3$).

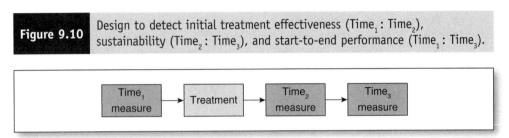

NOTE: O = observation (measurement); X = treatment.

Design B—Incremental Monitoring (O X O X O)

Incremental monitoring (O X O X O) design involves ongoing treatment; repeated measures placed along the treatment timeline allows us to *incrementally* assess the effectiveness of the intervention (Figure 9.11).

Figure 9.11 Design to assess progressive performance metrics ($Time_1 : Time_2$, $Time_2 : Time_3$) and start-to-end performance ($Time_1 : Time_3$).

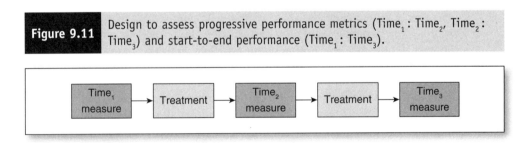

Design C—Stable Baseline and Treatment Effect (O O X O)

In cases where it is essential to establish a **stable baseline and treatment effect (O O X O)**, optimal results would render no statistically significant difference between $Time_1$ and $Time_2$, followed by the treatment, and last, the posttreatment data would be gathered at $Time_3$, wherein a statistically significant difference between measurements gathered at $Time_2$ and $Time_3$ would suggest the effectiveness of the treatment (Figure 9.12).

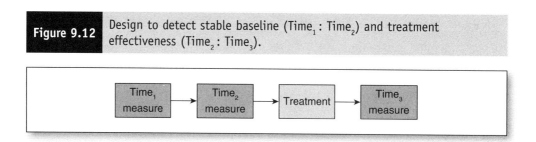

Figure 9.12   Design to detect stable baseline (Time$_1$: Time$_2$) and treatment effectiveness (Time$_2$: Time$_3$).

Despite the conceptual diversity of these designs, when it comes to the ANOVA repeated-measures coding and processing, SPSS would see all of them identically—as a data set simply consisting of three variables: *Time1, Time2,* and *Time3.*

As we have discussed, the ANOVA repeated-measures statistic is not limited to measurements taken over (only) three time points, gathered over 3 weeks. The ANOVA repeated-measures test can process data gathered from any number of time points spanning minutes, hours, days, weeks, months, or even years. Additionally, as shown in Designs A, B, and C, the ANOVA repeated-measures test can accommodate designs where treatments and measurements are placed anywhere they are needed.

As versatile as these designs are, one needs to adhere to the fundamental rule of consistency when it comes to gathering data that are to be analyzed with the ANOVA repeated-measures method: The same metric (e.g., survey, self-administered questionnaire, archival data, etc.) must be used consistently among the same participants.

GOOD COMMON SENSE

While the ANOVA repeated-measures statistic lends itself to tracking the progress of a variety of longitudinal models, it is important to remember that because the data are being gathered from a single group of participants, these models are classified as quasi-experimental because there is no random assignment to two or more groups. Such models can be vulnerable to threats to internal validity, specifically the following: history, test–retest reliability, and attrition/mortality—more so in studies that span longer time frames.

This is a one-group design wherein measurements are taken over time, one must therefore consider the **historical threat to internal validity**. Specifically speaking, changes taking place outside of the realm of the study (e.g., social events, political changes, changes in the personal lives of the participants, etc.) may act as confounding variables, bringing change(s) to the data that are being gathered over the course of a study. This is a particular vulnerability involving designs that span longer periods.

If the data are being gathered via survey or skill test, as opposed to biometrics (e.g., pulse rate, blood count), the data can be vulnerable to *test-retest reliability* issues; upon (repeated) retesting, the participant's score may improve merely due to the participant becoming progressively more familiar and proficient at responding to the question(s). Naturally, as the number of measurement iterations increases, so increases the risk of test–retest reliability issues.

Additionally, studies that take place over extended periods are also vulnerable to participant *attrition/mortality*—over time, some participants may opt to drop out of the study, or the researcher may rule out participants who no longer meet the criteria for this study (e.g., a study focusing on pregnant women may specify ruling out the participant upon giving birth). When launching such a study, it is advised that you recruit a sufficient number of participants in anticipation of such (expected) attrition.

Key Concepts

- Time-series designs

  - Treatment effect and sustainability: O X O O
  - Incremental monitoring: O X O X O
  - Stable baseline and treatment effect: O O X O

- Mauchly's test of sphericity
- Confounds/threats to internal validity

  - History
  - Testing (test/retest)
  - Attrition/mortality

Practice Exercises

Exercise 9.1

Acme Industries has implemented a new website for employees to enter their weekly hours (e.g., start time, end time, sick hours, vacation hours, holiday hours, family leave hours). Upon clicking Save, the system checks the validity of the entries and points the user to correct any errors or omissions before saving the data. To evaluate the efficiency of this new website, the system journals the access time (in seconds) indicating how long it took for each employee to file their daily entries. A manager will assess the mean access times starting at the initial launch of the website (Week1) and continue to gather data for an additional 2 weeks (Week2 and Week3).

Data set: **Ch 09 – Exercise 01A.sav**

Codebook

Variable:	ID
Definition:	Employee ID
Type:	Alphanumeric

Variable:	Week1
Definition:	Average time (in seconds) required to fill out webpage for first week
Type:	Continuous

Variable:	Week2
Definition:	Average time (in seconds) required to fill out webpage for second week
Type:	Continuous

Variable:	Week3
Definition:	Average time (in seconds) required to fill out webpage for third week
Type:	Continuous

a. Write the hypotheses.

b. Run the criteria of the pretest checklist (Mauchly's test of sphericity) and discuss your findings.

c. Run the ANOVA repeated measures and document your findings (means and Sig. [p value]), graphical plot, and hypothesis resolution.

d. Write an abstract under 200 words detailing a summary of the study, the ANOVA repeated-measures test results, hypothesis resolution, and implications of your findings.

Repeat this exercise using data set: **Ch 09 – Exercise 01B.sav**.

Exercise 9.2

Prior to a Heart Health presentation, you administer a survey asking participants to indicate how many times they used the stairs (as opposed to the elevator) in the past week. A week after the lecture, you resurvey the attendees. Finally, 2 weeks after the lecture, you resurvey the attendees (a third time).

Data set: **Ch 09 – Exercise 02A.sav**

Codebook

Variable:	ID
Definition:	Participant ID
Type:	Alphanumeric

Variable:	Time1
Definition:	Number of times the steps were used in the week before the seminar
Type:	Continuous

Variable: Time2

Definition: Number of times the steps were used in the week after the seminar

Type: Continuous

Variable: Time3

Definition: Number of times the steps were used in the week 2 weeks after the seminar

Type: Continuous

a. Write the hypotheses.

b. Run the criteria of the pretest checklist (Mauchly's test of sphericity) and discuss your findings.

c. Run the ANOVA repeated measures and document your findings (means and Sig. [*p* value]), graphical plot, and hypothesis resolution.

d. Write an abstract under 200 words detailing a summary of the study, the ANOVA repeated-measures test results, hypothesis resolution, and implications of your findings.

Repeat this exercise using data set: **Ch 09 – Exercise 02B.sav**.

Exercise 9.3

The staff at a mental health clinic wants to determine if their current form of short-term therapy substantially reduces depression. Prior to the first treatment, each patient will be asked to complete the Acme Depression Inventory (ADI), which renders a score from 0 to 75 (0 = Low depression . . . 75 = High depression). Patients will be asked to complete the same instrument at the conclusion of their appointment on Week 5 and at the end of their final appointment on Week 10.

Data set: **Ch 09 – Exercise 03A.sav**

Codebook

Variable: ID

Definition: Participant ID

Type: Alphanumeric

Variable: Baseline

Definition: Acme Depression Inventory score at baseline

Type: Continuous

Variable: Week05

Definition: Acme Depression Inventory score at Week 5

Type: Continuous

Variable: Week10

Definition: Acme Depression Inventory score at Week 10

Type: Continuous

a. Write the hypotheses.

b. Run the criteria of the pretest checklist (Mauchly's test of sphericity) and discuss your findings.

c. Run the ANOVA repeated measures and document your findings (means and Sig. [p value]), graphical plot, and hypothesis resolution.

d. Write an abstract under 200 words detailing a summary of the study, the ANOVA repeated-measures test results, hypothesis resolution, and implications of your findings.

Repeat this exercise using data set: **Ch 09 – Exercise 03B.sav**.

Exercise 9.4

The staff of the Physical Education Department wants to know if providing a single 15-minute individual coaching session with an expert bowler will enhance students' bowling scores. Each participant will bowl one game, during which time the coach will unobtrusively observe his or her bowling style. Then, the coach will provide a 15-minute coaching session. Immediately following the coaching, the student will bowl a second game. One week later, the student will return to bowl a third game. The scores from all three games of each student will be recorded and evaluated to determine the effectiveness of this form of coaching.

Data set: **Ch 09 – Exercise 04A.sav**

Codebook

Variable: Student

Definition: Student's last name

Type: Alphanumeric

Variable: Game1

Definition: Bowling score on first (baseline) game

Type: Continuous

Variable: Game2

Definition: Bowling score on second game

Type: Continuous

Variable: Game3

Definition: Bowling score on third game

Type: Continuous

a. Write the hypotheses.

b. Run the criteria of the pretest checklist (Mauchly's test of sphericity) and discuss your findings.

c. Run the ANOVA repeated measures and document your findings (means and Sig. [p value]), graphical plot, and hypothesis resolution.

d. Write an abstract under 200 words detailing a summary of the study, the ANOVA repeated-measures test results, hypothesis resolution, and implications of your findings.

Repeat this exercise using data set: **Ch 09 – Exercise 04B.sav**.

Exercise 9.5

In an effort to affordably boost productivity, the Acme Company has started providing free unlimited gourmet coffee to all employees. The manager will track the weekly total productivity (units produced) of each employee before and after the coffee machine is installed.

Data set: **Ch 09 – Exercise 05A.sav**

Codebook

Variable: Name

Definition: Employee name

Type: Alphanumeric

Variable: Productivity_1

Definition: Number of units produced during Week 1 (baseline)

Type: Continuous

Variable: Productivity_2

Definition: Number of units produced during Week 2

Type: Continuous

Variable: Productivity_3

Definition: Number of units produced during Week 3

Type: Continuous

a. Write the hypotheses.

b. Run the criteria of the pretest checklist (Mauchly's test of sphericity) and discuss your findings.

c. Run the ANOVA repeated measures and document your findings (means and Sig. [p value]), graphical plot, and hypothesis resolution.

d. Write an abstract under 200 words detailing a summary of the study, the ANOVA repeated-measures test results, hypothesis resolution, and implications of your findings.

Repeat this exercise using data set: **Ch 09 – Exercise 05B.sav**.

Exercise 9.6

On Tuesday morning, the student council at a middle school announced its plan to combat the chronic litter problem in the outdoor lunch area: The 16 large trash cans in the lunch area now each have the name of a popular band on them—they are now referred to as *Band-Cans*. The Band-Can containing the most trash at the end of each day wins; music from that band's latest release will be played on the school's public address system in between classes for the next day. The Band-Cans are 42 inches tall; at the end of each day, starting on Monday (to gather baseline data), the members of the student council will use a tape measure to record how full each Band-Can is (0 = Empty . . . 42 = Full).

Data set: **Ch 09 – Exercise 06A.sav**

Codebook

Variable: Band

Definition: Name of band on trash can

Type: Alphanumeric

Variable: Monday

Definition: Inches of trash in trash can (baseline)

Type: Continuous

Variable: Tuesday

Definition: Inches of trash in trash can

Type: Continuous

Variable: Wednesday

Definition: Inches of trash in trash can

Type: Continuous

a. Write the hypotheses.

b. Run the criteria of the pretest checklist (Mauchly's test of sphericity) and discuss your findings.

c. Run the ANOVA repeated measures and document your findings (means and Sig. [p value]), graphical plot, and hypothesis resolution.

d. Write an abstract under 200 words detailing a summary of the study, the ANOVA repeated-measures test results, hypothesis resolution, and implications of your findings.

Repeat this exercise using data set: **Ch 09 – Exercise 06B.sav**.

Exercise 9.7

A political consultant convened a focus group to evaluate the effectiveness of two commercials promoting a candidate. Prior to running any media, the participants are asked to answer one question: *Do you intend to vote for Jones in the upcoming election?* The participants will respond using a scale ranging from 1 to 7 (1 = Absolutely will not vote for Jones . . . 7 = Absolutely will vote for Jones). Next, the facilitator runs a 30-second radio advertisement, promoting the candidate, after which, the participants are asked to respond to the same question using the 1 to 7 scale. Finally, the facilitator runs a 30-second video advertisement for the candidate, after which, the participants will respond to the voting intentions using the 1 to 7 scale.

Data set: **Ch 09 – Exercise 07A.sav**

Codebook

Variable: ID

Definition: Name

Type: Alphanumeric

Variable: Opinion1_Baseline

Definition: Likelihood of voting for Jones

Type: Continuous

Variable: Opinion2_Audio

Definition: Likelihood of voting for Jones after hearing the radio advertisement

Type: Continuous

Variable: Opinion3_Video

Definition: Likelihood of voting for Jones after viewing the video advertisement

Type: Continuous

a. Write the hypotheses.

b. Run the criteria of the pretest checklist (Mauchly's test of sphericity) and discuss your findings.

c. Run the ANOVA repeated measures and document your findings (means and Sig. [p value]), graphical plot, and hypothesis resolution.

d. Write an abstract under 200 words detailing a summary of the study, the ANOVA repeated-measures test results, hypothesis resolution, and implications of your findings.

Repeat this exercise using data set: **Ch 09 – Exercise 07B.sav**.

Exercise 9.8

In an effort to improve customer satisfaction, the manager at the Acme Customer Support Call Center installed a large-screen monitor in the front of the room to run classic movies with the sound off during work hours. At the conclusion of each call, the caller is routed to respond to an automated one-question customer satisfaction survey, where the caller is prompted to do the following: *Please use the buttons on your phone to rate your satisfaction with this call on a scale of 1 to 9, where 1 is for low satisfaction and 9 is for high satisfaction.* The manager will gather weekly mean customer satisfaction scores for each employee before and after the activation of the movies.

Data set: **Ch 09 – Exercise 08A.sav**

Codebook

Variable: Name

Definition: Employee name

Type: Alphanumeric

Variable: Satisfaction1

Definition: Customer satisfaction score for baseline week

Type: Continuous

Variable: Satisfaction2

Definition: Customer satisfaction score for first week of video

Type: Continuous

Variable: Satisfaction3

Definition: Customer satisfaction score for second week of video

Type: Continuous

a. Write the hypotheses.

b. Run the criteria of the pretest checklist (Mauchly's test of sphericity) and discuss your findings.

c. Run the ANOVA repeated measures and document your findings (means and Sig. [p value]), graphical plot, and hypothesis resolution.

d. Write an abstract under 200 words detailing a summary of the study, the ANOVA repeated-measures test results, hypothesis resolution, and implications of your findings.

Repeat this exercise using data set: **Ch 09 – Exercise 08B.sav**.

Exercise 9.9

The *Zzzleep Zzzound* app provides audio selections (e.g., gentle rain, ocean waves, soothing music) to help induce peaceful sleep. During the night, the app uses the camera and motion sensor to gather sleep data. If the user wakes during the night, the app senses it and plays the selected sound for 10 minutes. For the first week, the app runs without any audio to gather baseline data. Once a week, the software transmits the mean sleep time per night for that week to the sleep researcher's database.

Data set: **Ch 09 – Exercise 09A.sav**

Codebook

Variable: CellPhone

Definition: Cell phone number

Type: Alphanumeric

Variable: Sleep1

Definition: Mean sleep minutes per night for Week 1 (baseline)

Type: Continuous

Variable: Sleep2

Definition: Mean sleep minutes per night for Week 2

Type: Continuous

Variable: Sleep3

Definition: Mean sleep minutes per night for Week 3

Type: Continuous

Variable: Sleep4

Definition: Mean sleep minutes per night for Week 4

Type: Continuous

a. Write the hypotheses.

b. Run the criteria of the pretest checklist (Mauchly's test of sphericity) and discuss your findings.

c. Run the ANOVA repeated measures and document your findings (means and Sig. [*p* value]), graphical plot, and hypothesis resolution.

d. Write an abstract under 200 words detailing a summary of the study, the ANOVA repeated-measures test results, hypothesis resolution, and implications of your findings.

Repeat this exercise using data set: **Ch 09 – Exercise 09B.sav**.

Exercise 9.10

To assess the effect that chocolate may have on attitude over time, a researcher recruits a group of participants to complete the Acme Attitude Survey (AAS), which renders a 0 to 100 score (0 = Very bad attitude . . . 100 = Very good attitude). After giving the pretest, the researcher gives each participant a large bar of chocolate. The researcher readministers the AAS three more times: 5 minutes after the participant eats the chocolate, 1 hour later, and 4 hours later.

Data set: **Ch 09 – Exercise 10A.sav**

Codebook

Variable: ID

Definition: Participant ID

Type: Alphanumeric

Variable: Attitude_0

Definition: Attitude before eating chocolate (baseline)

Type: Continuous

Variable: Attitude_1

Definition: Attitude 5 minutes after eating chocolate

Type: Continuous

Variable: Attitude_2

Definition: Attitude 1 hour after eating chocolate

Type: Continuous

Variable: Attitude_3

Definition: Attitude 4 hours after eating chocolate

Type: Continuous

a. Write the hypotheses.

b. Run the criteria of the pretest checklist (Mauchly's test of sphericity) and discuss your findings.

c. Run the ANOVA repeated measures and document your findings (means and Sig. [*p* value]), graphical plot, and hypothesis resolution.

d. Write an abstract under 200 words detailing a summary of the study, the ANOVA repeated-measures test results, hypothesis resolution, and implications of your findings.

Repeat this exercise using data set: **Ch 09 – Exercise 10B.sav**.

PART V

Measuring Relationship Between Variables

These chapters compute statistics that describe the nature of the relationship(s) between the variables.

Chapter 10: Chi-Square assesses the relationship between categorical variables.

Chapter 11: Correlation and Regression: Pearson and Spearman demonstrates how to use the Pearson statistic to assess the relationship between two continuous variables. Similarly, the Spearman statistic is generally used to assess the relationship between two ordered lists.

Chapter 12: Multiple Regression indicates the relative weight that each variable has in terms of predicting the value of a continuous outcome variable.

Chapter 13: Logistic Regression predicts the odds of a dichotomous outcome occurring (or not) based on data from continuous and/or categorical predictors.

Chi-Square

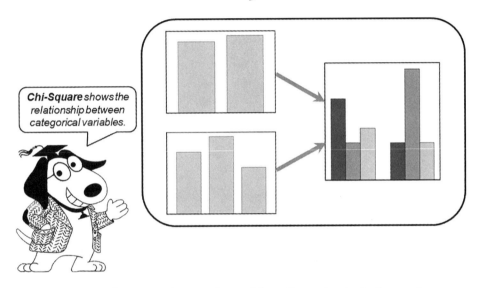

Chi-Square shows the relationship between categorical variables.

Some people are passionate about aisles, others about window seats.

—Terry Jones

Learning Objectives

Upon completing this chapter, you will be able to do the following:

- Determine when it is appropriate to run a chi-square test.
- Identify dichotomous and polychotomous variables.
- Verify that the data meet the criteria for running a chi-square test: $n \geq 5$ per cell.
- Order a chi-square test: table and bar chart.
- Interpret the test results.
- Resolve the hypotheses.
- Write an appropriate abstract.
- Calculate the % formula.

WHEN TO USE THIS STATISTIC

Guidelines for Selecting the Chi-Square Test

Overview: This statistic indicates if there is an association between two categorical variables.

Variables: This statistic requires two categorical variables for each record.

Results: In a survey of favorite ice cream flavors, we found that girls favored chocolate (48% chocolate, 22% strawberry, 30% vanilla), whereas boys favored strawberry (20% chocolate, 60% strawberry, 20% vanilla). These results indicate that girls and boys have statistically significantly different ice cream flavor preferences ($p = .001$, $\alpha = .05$).

VIDEO

The tutorial video for this chapter is **Ch 10 – Chi-Square.mp4**. This video provides an overview of chi-square, followed by the SPSS procedures for processing the pretest checklist, ordering the statistical run, and interpreting the results of this test using the data set: **Ch 10 – Example 01 – Chi-Square.sav**.

OVERVIEW—CHI-SQUARE

As we have seen, variables can be *continuous*, such as temperature, distance, weight, bank account balance, mood score, height, and test score. Alternatively, variables may be *categorical*, such as gender, race, religion, blood type, and marital status.

A categorical variable may consist of any number of categories. Variables that contain two categories are **dichotomous** (pronounced *die-cot-uh-muss*), such as these:

- Gender: Female, Male
- Voter status: Registered, Not registered
- Opinion: Yes, No
- Attendance: Present, Absent
- Dwelling: House, Apartment
- Grade: Pass, Fail

A categorical variable that contains more than two categories is **polychotomous** (pronounced *poly-cot-uh-muss*):

- Appointment status: On time, Late, Canceled, No-show, Rescheduled
- Marital status: Single, Married, Separated, Divorced, Widowed
- Ice cream flavor preference: Chocolate, Strawberry, Vanilla
- Visual aids: None, Glasses, Contact lenses, Surgical correction
- Transportation: Train, Plane, Car, Bus, Taxi, Motorcycle, Bicycle, Walk
- Blood type: A+, A−, B+, B−, AB+, AB−, O+, O−

The statistical function for comparing categorical variables to each other is the **chi-square** (*chi* is pronounced *kai*—rhymes with *eye*), sometimes written as χ^2 (χ is the Greek letter *chi*). Fortunately, the chi-square does not need you to specify how many categories are in each variable; SPSS will automatically derive that as part of the process. Chi-square can efficiently handle a mix of dichotomous and polychotomous variables.

The chi-square organizes the data from each categorical variable into a table, compares the categories to each other, and produces a *p* value. If the chi-square produces a *p* value that is less than α (.05), this indicates that there is a statistically significant difference among the categories; alternatively, a *p* value greater than a (.05) indicates that no statistically significant differences among the categories exist.

Chi-square can be used to answer questions involving categorical variables, such as *Is gender (Female, Male) associated with ice cream preference (Chocolate, Strawberry, Vanilla)?* In other words, *Do girls and boys tend to select the same ice cream flavors, or do girls tend to prefer different flavors from boys?* If the *p* value is less than α (.05), then we would say that there is a statistically significant difference between girls' ice cream preference and boys' ice cream preference (girls like different ice cream flavors than boys do). Alternatively, if the *p* value is greater than the a (.05), then we would say that there is no statistically significant difference between the genders when it comes to ice cream selection (chocolate can be pretty compelling to both genders).

The chi-square calculation is fairly liberal in terms of the sample sizes; it can work properly even if the sample contains unbalanced strata (categories). For example, suppose the sample consists of 71 boys and 308 girls; naturally, we would expect that each of the ice cream flavor categories would be loaded with more girls than boys; however the chi-square can still work because instead of focusing exclusively on the *ns*, the formula assesses *proportions*. Specifically, chi-square would be comparing the *percentage* of boys who selected chocolate, to the *percentage* of girls who selected chocolate to determine how similar the gender proportions are within that flavor (then it would process all of the other flavors).

To recap, chi-square can be used to compare categorical variables with the same number of categories in each variable, such as *gender* (Female, Male) to *opinion* (Yes, No), which would render a 2 × 2 chi-square table. Chi-square can also analyze categorical variables that have different category counts without having to specify any additional processing parameters, such as gender (Female, Male) to blood type (A+, A−, B+, B−, AB+, AB−, O+, O−). This chi-square test would produce a 2 × 8 or an 8 × 2 chi-square table, depending on how you choose to load the variables into rows and columns—either way, the analysis would produce equivalent results.

Example

Acme Creamery wants to create advertisements showing boys and girls enjoying Acme Ice Cream. They have consulted with you to discover if boys and girls have the same or different ice cream flavor preferences.

Research Question

Does gender have a bearing on ice cream flavor preference, or are girls and boys fairly evenly distributed among the ice cream flavor preferences?

Groups

When it comes to chi-square, it is not so much a matter of *groups* as *categories* within the variables. This inquiry involves two categorical variables: *Gender*, which has two categories (Girl, Boy), and *IceCream* which has three categories (Chocolate, Strawberry, Vanilla), which has three categories. Notice that *Gender* is dichotomous and *IceCream* is polychotomous.

Procedure

You recruit a group of volunteers and gather two pieces of information from each participant (*Gender* and *Ice cream flavor preference*) using this self-administered survey card:

Ice Cream Preference Survey

Please check <u>one</u> answer for each question:

1. What is your gender?
   - ☐ Girl
   - ☐ Boy
2. What is your favorite ice cream flavor?
   - ☐ Chocolate
   - ☐ Strawberry
   - ☐ Vanilla

Thank you for participating in our survey.

Hypotheses

H_0: There is no association between gender and ice cream flavor preference.

H_1: There is an association between gender and ice cream flavor preference.

Data Set

Use the following data set: **Ch 10 – Example 01 – Chi-Square.sav**.

Codebook

Variable:	Gender
Definition:	Gender
Type:	Categorical (1 = Girl, 2 = Boy)

Variable:	IceCream
Definition:	Ice cream flavor preference
Type:	Categorical (1 = Chocolate, 2 = Strawberry, 3 = Vanilla)

Pretest Checklist

Chi-Square Pretest Checklist

☑ *1. n > 5 per cell minimum**

*Results produced upon chi-square test run.

NOTE: If this pretest checklist criterion is not satisfied, proceed with the analysis, but concisely discuss such anomalies in the *Results* or *Limitations* sections of the documentation so the reader can more plausibly interpret the precision of the findings.

Pretest Checklist Criterion 1 – $n \geq 5$ per Cell Minimum

The chi-square will organize the categorical data from the variables into a table. It is easy to anticipate the dimensions of the table simply by multiplying the number of categories in each variable. In this case, *Gender* has two categories (Girl, Boy), and *IceCream* has three categories (Chocolate, Strawberry, Vanilla); hence, the chi-square table will consist of ($2 \times 3 =$) 6 cells (Table 10.1).

| **Table 10.1** | Chi-square table basic structure for *Gender* and *Ice Cream* contains six cells. |

	Chocolate	Strawberry	Vanilla
Girl			
Boy			

The pretest checklist rule for chi-square states that each cell should have at least five entries; initially, one might anticipate that the total n for this study should be 30 (6 cells × 5 per cell = 30). Actually, the total n will need to be more than 30, because a total n of 30 would presume that participants' responses will fill the six cells evenly (five per cell). This is implausible, so we should thus consider 30 as the *minimum* total n; we will require a total n of more than 30.

The chi-square report will show these counts for each cell in the form of a **cross-tabulation** table, and hence, we will be able to verify these criteria when we inspect the table in the Results section.

Test Run

1. From the main screen, click on *Analyze, Descriptive Statistics, Crosstabs* (Figure 10.1); this will bring you to the *Crosstabs* menu (Figure 10.2).

| **Figure 10.1** | Run the chi-square analysis; click on *Analyze, Descriptive Statistics, Crosstabs.* |

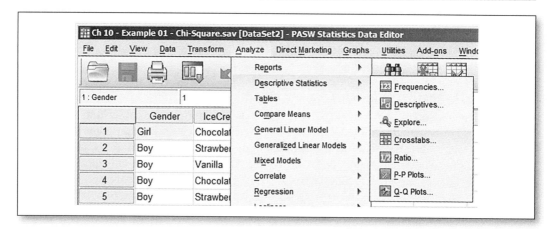

| **Figure 10.2** | Crosstabs menu: Load *Gender* into *Row(s)* and *IceCream* into *Column(s)* and check ☑ *Display clustered bar charts*. |

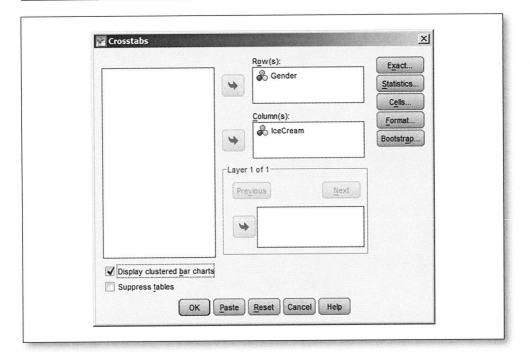

2. On the *Crosstabs* menu (Figure 10.2), move *Gender* from the left window to the *Row(s)* window, and move *IceCream* from the left window to the *Column(s)* window.

3. Check the ☑ *Display clustered bar charts* checkbox.

4. Click on the *Statistics* button; this will take you to the *Crosstabs: Statistics* menu.

5. Check the ☑ *Chi-square* checkbox.

6. Click on the *Continue* button. This will take you back to the *Crosstabs* menu.

7. Click the *OK* button, and the chi-square will process.

Results

Pretest Checklist Criterion 1 – $n \geq 5$ Per Cell Minimum

Observe the (six) circled cells in the *Gender * IceDream Crosstabulation* table (Table 10.2) and note that each cell has a count (*n*) of at least five; hence, the pretest criteria are satisfied.

Figure 10.3 *Crosstabs: Statistics* menu: Check the *Chi-square* checkbox.

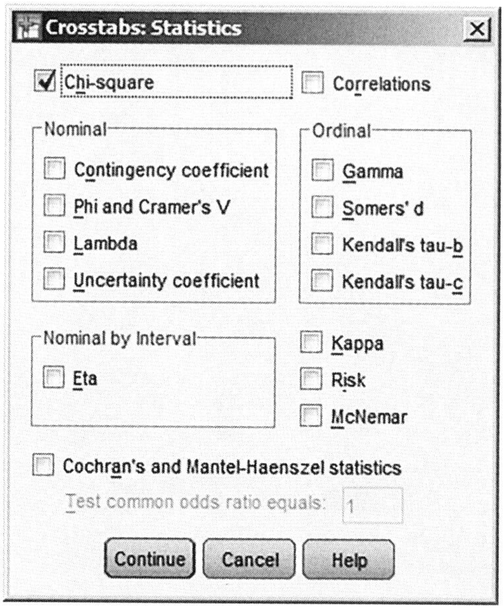

Table 10.2 *Gender * IceCream* Crosstabulation.

Gender * IceCream Crosstabulation

Count

		IceCream			Total
		Chocolate	Strawberry	Vanilla	
Gender	Girl	22	10	14	46
	Boy	10	30	10	50
Total		32	40	24	96

Next, observe the Sig. (*p*) value in the *Chi-Square Tests* table (Table 10.3) on the *Pearson Chi-Square* row; it indicates a Sig. (*p*) value of .001; because this is less than the specified .05 α level, we conclude that *there is a statistically significant difference among genders when it comes to ice cream flavor preference.*

Table 10.3 Chi-square tests results: Sig. (*p*) = .001.

Chi-Square Tests

	Value	df	Asymp. Sig. (2-sided)
Pearson Chi-Square	15.026ᵃ	2	.001
Likelihood Ratio	15.580	2	.000
Linear-by-Linear Association	1.244	1	.265
N of Valid Cases	96		

a. 0 cells (.0%) have expected count less than 5. The minimum expected count is 11.50.

The *Gender * IceCream Crosstabulation* (Table 10.2) provides clear enough results detailing how many girls and how many boys favor each ice cream flavor; even a cursory overview of this table helps us to see that the numbers for the girls look very different from those of the boys, which is confirmed by the .001 *p* value (Table 10.3), but to get a more intuitive grasp of these data, inspect the corresponding bar chart (Figure 10.4).

Figure 10.4 Chi-square bar chart—row(s): *Gender,* and column(s) *IceCream.*

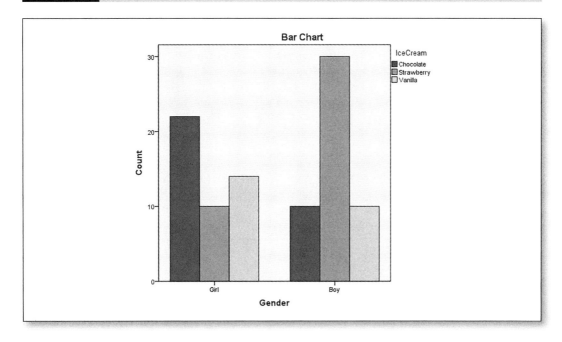

It can be useful to run the chi-square test a second time. Swapping the variables (rows/columns) will reconfigure the presentation of the chi-square results, which may offer a different perspective (Figure 10.5).

| **Figure 10.5** | Crosstabs menu: Load *IceCream* into *Row(s)* and *Gender* into *Column(s)* and Check ☑ *Display clustered bar charts*. |

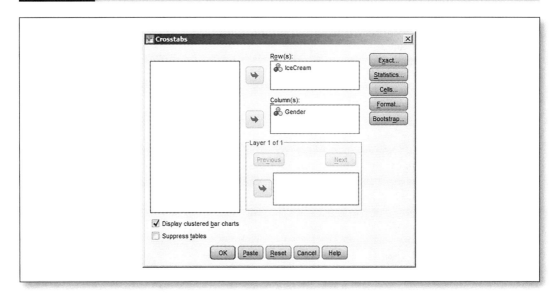

This will produce the same statistical results as the initial run, but they are arranged slightly differently; notice that the *IceCream * Gender Crosstabulation* table (Table 10.4) is merely a slightly different layout of the results in the *Gender * IceCream Crosstabulation* table (Table 10.2).

| **Table 10.4** | *IceCream * Gender* Crosstabulation. |

IceCream * Gender Crosstabulation

Count

		Gender		Total
		Girl	Boy	
IceCream	Chocolate	22	10	32
	Strawberry	10	30	40
	Vanilla	14	10	24
Total		46	50	96

Also, notice that the *Chi-Square Tests* table (Table 10.5) produced exactly the same result as the prior run (Table 10.3).

Table 10.5 Chi-Square test results: Sig. (*p*) = .001.

Chi-Square Tests

	Value	df	Asymp. Sig. (2-sided)
Pearson Chi-Square	15.026ª	2	.001
Likelihood Ratio	15.580	2	.000
Linear-by-Linear Association	1.244	1	.265
N of Valid Cases	96		

a. 0 cells (.0%) have expected count less than 5. The minimum expected count is 11.50.

Finally, observe that the bar chart is drawn differently (Figure 10.6) compared to the prior chart (Figure 10.4).

Figure 10.6 Chi-square bar chart—*Row(s): IceCream,* and *Column(s) : Gender.*

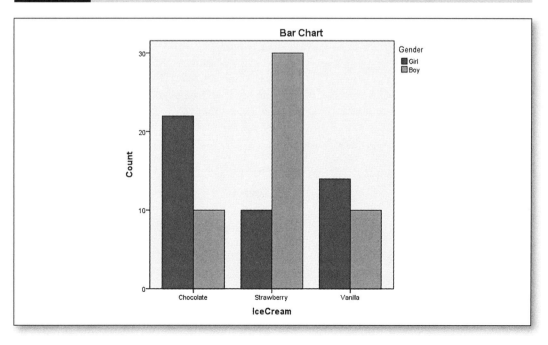

Running the chi-square both ways (swapping the rows and columns) offers alternative representations of the results without changing the outcome. You may find that one version provides more clarity in comprehending the results. The better you can conceptualize the data, the better prepared you will be to write a cogent Results section detailing your findings.

In addition to discussing that the *p* value indicates a statistically significant difference in ice cream flavor preference among the genders, the bar chart can help provide additional meaning to the discussion. You may include narrative explaining that the findings indicate that girls tend to prefer chocolate and boys tend to prefer strawberry, whereas vanilla seems relatively balanced among girls and boys.

Hypothesis Resolution

REJECT: H_0: There is no association between gender and ice cream flavor preference.

ACCEPT: H_1: There is an association between gender and ice cream flavor preference.

The chi-square produced a *p* of .001, which is less than the specified .05 α level, which indicates that there is a statistically significant difference between the genders with respect to ice cream flavor preference. As such, we would reject H_0 and not reject H_1.

Abstract

According to a survey of 96 children, we detected a statistically significant difference (p = .001, α = .05) in ice cream flavor preference based on gender. Of the 46 girls surveyed, most preferred chocolate (22 Chocolate, 10 Strawberry, and 14 Vanilla), whereas the 50 boys in our sample predominately selected Strawberry (10 Chocolate, 30 Strawberry, and 10 Vanilla).

Another way of documenting chi-square results involves discussing percentages. With respect to chi-square crosstabulation results (Table 10.2 or 10.5), percentages are fairly easy to calculate; just divide the *part* (smaller number) by the *total* (larger number) and multiply by 100. For example, to compute the percentage of girls who prefer chocolate, *Part = 22* and *Total = 46* (Table 10.4).

% Formula

% = Part ÷ Total × 100

% = 22 ÷ 46 × 100

% = .4783 × 100

% = 47.83

Consider this documentation variation (the bracketed portions in the proceeding section are included to clarify the **percentage calculations** but would not typically be included in the write-up):

In an effort to discover if gender is associated with ice cream flavor preference (Chocolate, Strawberry, or Vanilla), we surveyed 96 children (46 girls and 50 boys); 48% [22 ÷ 46 = .4783] of the girls preferred Chocolate, whereas 60% [30 ÷ 50 = .6000] of boys preferred Strawberry. Chi-square analysis revealed a statistically significant difference (p = .001, α = .05) between the genders when it comes to ice cream flavor preference.

GOOD COMMON SENSE

You may find it useful to order that the chi-square crosstabulation data be presented using percentages instead of (just) the *n*. To try this, go to the *Crosstabs* menu (Figure 10.2) and click on the *Cells* button. This will take you to the *Crosstabs: Cell Display* menu (Figure 10.7), where you can selectively order percentages for *Row*, *Column*, and *Total*.

Figure 10.7   Crosstabs: Cell Display—Check Percentages.

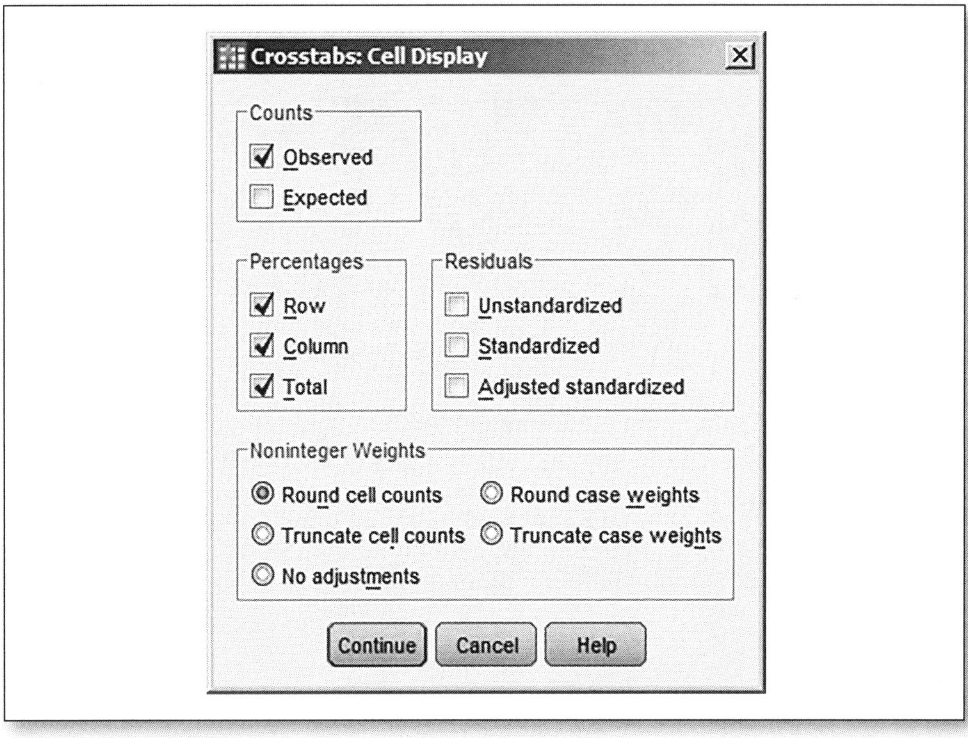

Occasionally, a continuous variable can be reduced to a categorical variable, thereby facilitating chi-square analyses. For example, *Age* is a continuous variable (ranging from 0 . . . 100), but *Age* could be reduced to two categories: 1 = *Minor* and 2 = *Adult*. SPSS includes an easy-to-use *Recode* feature that helps automate such processes.

Recoding would leave the continuous variable *Age* as is, but based on the age, we could generate values for a new categorical variable, *Age2* (1 = Minor, 2 = Adult), using the following criteria:

If *Age* is less than 18, then *Age2* = 1.

If *Age* is 18 or greater, then *Age2* = 2.

The procedure for recoding variables in this way is detailed in Chapter 14, specifically the sections on *recoding*.

Key Concepts

- Continuous variables
- Categorical variables
- Chi-square (χ^2)
- Pretest checklist ($n \geq 5$ per cell)
- Overall *n* actually required
- Crosstabs
- Percentage calculation

Practice Exercises

Exercise 10.1

Acme Bank wants to determine if a person's age (group) is associated with a preferred bill paying method. The research team gathers data using this self-administered survey card:

Bill Paying Survey

Please check <u>one</u> answer for each question:

1. How old are you?

   ☐ 18–25

   ☐ 26–35

   ☐ 36–55

   ☐ 56–99

2. What method do you use most often to pay bills?

   ☐ Check

   ☐ E-pay

   ☐ Other

Thank you for participating in our survey.

Data set: **Ch 10 – Exercise 01A.sav**

Codebook

    Variable: Age

    Definition: Age of the respondent

    Type: Categorical (1 = 18 – 25, 2 = 26 – 26, 3 = 36 – 55, 4 = 56 – 99)

    Variable: BillPay

    Definition: Preferred method for paying bills

    Type: Categorical (1 = Check, 2 = E-pay, 3 = Other)

a. Write the hypotheses.

b. Run the criteria of the pretest checklist (*n* is at least 5 per cell in the Crosstabs) and discuss your findings.

c. Run the chi-square test and document your findings (*n*s and/or percentages, Sig. [*p* value]).

d. Write an abstract under 200 words detailing a summary of the study, the chi-square test results, hypothesis resolution, and implications of your findings.

Repeat this exercise using data set: **Ch 10 - Exercise 01B.sav**.

Exercise 10.2

You notice that some bus riders wear headphones while others do not, but with so many passengers on so many different buses, it is hard to estimate if gender is a factor when it comes to wearing or not wearing headphones. To address this question, you spend the day riding city buses as you unobtrusively record your observations of each passenger on the following data sheet:

Gender		Headphones	
☐ F ☐ M		☐ Headphones	☐ No headphones
☐ F ☐ M		☐ Headphones	☐ No headphones
☐ F ☐ M		☐ Headphones	☐ No headphones
☐ F ☐ M		☐ Headphones	☐ No headphones

Data set: **Ch 10 – Exercise 02A.sav**

Codebook

    Variable: Gender

    Definition: Gender of bus rider

    Type: Categorical (1 = Female, 2 = Male)

Variable: Headphone

Definition: Headphone status

Type: Categorical (1 = Headphones, 2 = No headphones)

a. Write the hypotheses.

b. Run the criteria of the pretest checklist (n is at least 5 per cell in the Crosstab) and discuss your findings.

c. Run the chi-square test and document your findings (ns and/or percentages, Sig. [p value]).

d. Write an abstract under 200 words detailing a summary of the study, the chi-square test results, hypothesis resolution, and implications of your findings.

Repeat this exercise using data set: **Ch 10 - Exercise 02B.sav**.

Exercise 10.3

The clinicians at Anytown Health Clinic want to determine how useful the flu shot is in their community. The researcher approaches patients as they exit the clinic; those who are willing to partake in this study are asked to sign an informed consent document and complete and submit the following card:

Flu Shot Survey

1. Did you have a flu shot this season?

   ☐ Yes

   ☐ No

2. Phone number or email ID: _____

A member of our staff will contact you in 60 days.

Thank you for participating in our survey.

FOR ADMINISTRATIVE USE ONLY

☐ Got sick with flu

☐ Did not get sick with flu

The researcher will contact each participant in 60 days to ask if he or she contracted the flu in the past 60 days and mark the bottom of each card accordingly.

Data set: **Ch 10 – Exercise 03A.sav**

Codebook

Variable:	FluShot	
Definition:	Flu shot status	
Type:	Categorical (1 = Had a flu shot, 2 = Did not have a flu shot)	

Variable:	FluSick	
Definition:	Flu status	
Type:	Categorical (1 = Got sick with flu, 2 = Did not get sick with flu)	

a. Write the hypotheses.

b. Run the criteria of the pretest checklist (n is at least 5 per cell in the Crosstabs) and discuss your findings.

c. Run the chi-square test and document your findings (ns and/or percentages, Sig. [p value]).

d. Write an abstract under 200 words detailing a summary of the study, the chi-square test results, hypothesis resolution, and implications of your findings.

Repeat this exercise using data set: **Ch 10 – Exercise 03B.sav**.

Exercise 10.4

The administrative staff of Acme College wants to optimize the availability of student resources (e.g., website content, library hours, support staffing, etc.) to better fit the needs of students. You have been asked to determine if the degree students are working on (bachelor's vs. master's) is associated with the type of learning (in classroom vs. remote learning) students have opted for; you are given a sample drawn from the student enrollment database to analyze.

Data set: **Ch 10 – Exercise 04A.sav**

Codebook

Variable:	Degree	
Definition:	Degree that the student is currently working on	
Type:	Categorical (1 = Bachelor's, 2 = Master's)	

Variable: Location

Definition: Learning modality

Type: Categorical (1 = In classroom, 2 = Remote learning)

a. Write the hypotheses.

b. Run the criteria of the pretest checklist (*n* is at least 5 per cell in the Crosstabs) and discuss your findings.

c. Run the chi-square test and document your findings (*n*s and/or percentages, Sig. [*p* value]).

d. Write an abstract under 200 words detailing a summary of the study, the chi-square test results, hypothesis resolution, and implications of your findings.

Repeat this exercise using data set: **Ch 10 - Exercise 04B.sav**.

Exercise 10.5

To determine if *how* data are gathered has any bearing on responses to a question involving substance abuse (*Have you ever used an illegal drug?*), you recruit willing participants and randomly assign them to one of three groups: Those in Group 1 will be asked the question via face-to-face interview, those in Group 2 will respond using a standard pencil-and-paper mail-in survey, and those in Group 3 will be directed to an online survey; no names or identifying information will be gathered from any of the participants.

Data set: **Ch 10 – Exercise 05A.sav**

Codebook

Variable: Media

Definition: Media used to administer survey

Type: Categorical (1 = Face-to-face interview, 2 = Mail-in survey, 3 = Online survey)

Variable: Drug

Definition: Have you ever used an illegal drug?

Type: Categorical (1 = Yes, 2 = No)

a. Write the hypotheses.

b. Run the criteria of the pretest checklist (*n* is at least 5 per cell in the Crosstabs) and discuss your findings.

c. Run the chi-square test and document your findings (*n*s and/or percentages, Sig. [*p* value]).

d. Write an abstract under 200 words detailing a summary of the study, the chi-square test results, hypothesis resolution, and implications of your findings.

Repeat this exercise using data set: **Ch 10 - Exercise 05B.sav**.

Exercise 10.6

In an effort to better accommodate students, Acme University wants to find out if students pursuing different degrees (bachelor's, master's, doctorate) have the same or different preferences when it comes to class time (day, night). To determine this, you are commissioned to administer the following survey to a sample of the students currently enrolled.

Course Schedule Preference Survey

Please check one answer for each question.

1. When do you prefer to take the majority of your courses?

   ☐ Day (8.00 a.m.–5:00 p.m.)

   ☐ Night (5.00 p.m.–10:00 p.m.)

2. What degree are you currently working on?

   ☐ Bachelor's

   ☐ Master's

   ☐ Doctorate

   Thank you for participating in our survey.

Data set: **Ch 10 – Exercise 06A.sav**

Codebook

Variable:	Time
Definition:	Time when student takes most courses
Type:	Categorical (1 = Day, 2 = Night)

Variable:	Degree
Definition:	Degree that the student is currently working on
Type:	Categorical (1 = Bachelor's, 2 = Master's, 3 = Doctorate)

a. Write the hypotheses.

b. Run the criteria of the pretest checklist (n is at least 5 per cell in the Crosstabs) and discuss your findings.

c. Run the chi-square test and document your findings (ns and/or percentages, Sig. [p value]).

d. Write an abstract under 200 words detailing a summary of the study, the chi-square test results, hypothesis resolution, and implications of your findings.

Repeat this exercise using data set: **Ch 10 - Exercise 06B.sav**.

Exercise 10.7

A political scientist expects that how a person votes (or does not vote) may be associated with his or her age. To investigate this, the scientist gathers a convenience sample, asking voluntary participants to anonymously complete the following card:

Voter Survey

Please check one answer for each question:

1. How old are you?

    ☐ 18–35

    ☐ 36–64

    ☐ 65 and older

2. How did you vote in the last election?

    ☐ I voted in person at a polling precinct.

    ☐ I voted by mail.

    ☐ I did not vote.

Thank you for participating in our survey.

Data set: **Ch 10 – Exercise 07A.sav**

Codebook

Variable:	Age
Definition:	Age classification of respondent
Type:	Categorical (1 = 18–64, 2 = 36–64, 3 = 65 and older)

Variable:	Vote
Definition:	Method of voting
Type:	Categorical (1 = Vote in person, 2 = Vote by mail, 3 = Not vote)

a. Write the hypotheses.

b. Run the criteria of the pretest checklist (*n* is at least 5 per cell in the Crosstabs) and discuss your findings.

c. Run the chi-square test and document your findings (*n*s and/or percentages, Sig. [*p* value]).

d. Write an abstract under 200 words detailing a summary of the study, the chi-square test results, hypothesis resolution, and implications of your findings.

Repeat this exercise using data set: **Ch 10 - Exercise 07B.sav**.

Exercise 10.8

The Acme Veterinary Nutrition Laboratory wants to find out if its three dog foods appeal to all dogs equally or if breed is a factor in a dog's food preference. Per the research criteria specified, you recruit 90 pets: 30 cocker spaniels, 30 beagles, and 30 keeshonds. Owners are asked not to feed their pets for 4 hours prior to the test. Each dog is tested individually; the dog is placed 5 feet (1.5 meters) away from three clear bowls of dog food, all with equal weights. On cue, the leash is removed, and the dog is free to eat from any bowl(s). After dismissing each participant, you weigh the bowls; the lightest bowl wins (meaning that the dog ate the most food from that bowl). In case of a tie, the winning bowl is the one that the dog went to first.

Data set: **Ch 10 – Exercise 08A.sav**

Codebook

Variable:	Dog
Definition:	Dog breed
Type:	Categorical (1 = Cocker Spaniel, 2 = Beagle, 3 = Keeshond)

Variable:	Food
Definition:	Dog food preference (the lightest bowl by weight)
Type:	Categorical (1 = Food A, 2 = Food B, 3 = Food C)

a. Write the hypotheses.

b. Run the criteria of the pretest checklist (n is at least 5 per cell in the Crosstabs) and discuss your findings.

c. Run the chi-square test and document your findings (ns and/or percentages, Sig. [p value]).

d. Write an abstract under 200 words detailing a summary of the study, the chi-square test results, hypothesis resolution, and implications of your findings.

Repeat this exercise using data set: **Ch 10 – Exercise 08B.sav**.

Exercise 10.9

Each year, the Department of Education in Anytown publishes a report of college-bound high school seniors. You have been recruited to compare data gathered from seniors at the Acme Academy, a local private school, with seniors at Anytown High School, a public school.

Data set: **Ch 10 – Exercise 09A.sav**

Codebook

    Variable: HighSchool

    Definition: High school

    Type: Categorical (1 = Acme Academy, 2 = Anytown High School)

    Variable: College

    Definition: College attendance

    Type: Categorical (1 = Not attending university, 2 = Attending university)

a. Write the hypotheses.

b. Run the criteria of the pretest checklist (n is at least 5 per cell in the Crosstabs) and discuss your findings.

c. Run the chi-square test and document your findings (ns and/or percentages, Sig. [p value]).

d. Write an abstract under 200 words detailing a summary of the study, the chi-square test results, hypothesis resolution, and implications of your findings.

Repeat this exercise using data set: **Ch 10 – Exercise 09B.sav**.

Exercise 10.10

A political analyst is conducting a survey aimed at tuning campaign messages; the question of interest is, "Do women and men tend to vote the same or differently when it comes to electing the mayor?" The analyst gathered responses from willing participants using self-administered survey cards:

Voter Survey—City Mayor

Please check one answer for each question:

1. What is your gender?

    ☐ Female

    ☐ Male

2. Who will you vote for?

    ☐ Smith

    ☐ Jones

    ☐ Undecided

Thank you for participating in our survey.

Data set: **Ch 10 – Exercise 10A.sav**

Codebook

    Variable: Gender

    Definition: Respondent's gender

    Type: Categorical (1 = Female, 2 = Male)

    Variable: Mayor

    Definition: Vote choice for mayor

    Type: Categorical (1 = Smith, 2 = Jones, 3 = Undecided)

a. Write the hypotheses.

b. Run the criteria of the pretest checklist (n is at least 5 per cell in the Crosstabs) and discuss your findings.

c. Run the chi-square test and document your findings (ns and/or percentages, Sig. [p value]).

d. Write an abstract under 200 words detailing a summary of the study, the chi-square test results, hypothesis resolution, and implications of your findings.

Repeat this exercise using data set: **Ch 10 – Exercise 10B.sav**.

CHAPTER 11

Correlation and Regression
Pearson and Spearman

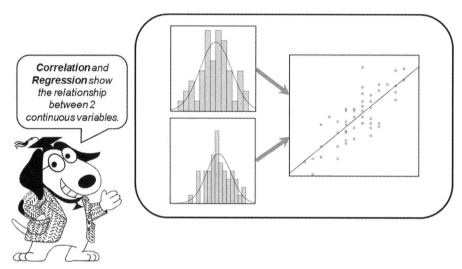

Correlation and *Regression* show the relationship between 2 continuous variables.

He who laughs most, learns best.

—John Cleese

Learning Objectives

Upon completing this chapter, you will be able to do the following:

- Determine when it is appropriate to run Pearson regression and Spearman correlational analyses.
- Interpret the direction and strength of a correlation.
- Verify that the data meet the criteria for running regression and correlational analyses: normality, linearity, and homoscedasticity.
- Order a regression analysis: correlation and scatterplot with regression line.
- Interpret the test results.
- Resolve the hypotheses.
- Write an appropriate abstract.
- Understand the criteria for causation: association/correlation, temporality, and nonspurious.
- Differentiate between correlation and causation

WHEN TO USE THIS STATISTIC

Guidelines for Selecting the Pearson Test

Overview: This statistic indicates if there is a correlation between two continuous variables.

Variables: This statistic requires two continuous variables for each record.

Results: To determine if there is a correlation between the time spent taking an academic test and the grade, we recorded the submission time on each test. After the tests were graded, we conducted a Pearson analysis which revealed a strong positive correlation ($r = .815$, $p < .001$), suggesting that the longer students spent taking the test, the higher the grade, and vice versa.

Guidelines for Selecting the Spearman Test

Overview: This statistic indicates if there is a correlation between the order of two ranked lists.

Variables: This statistic requires two categorical variables for each record.

Results: In a dietary consultation, the dietician and the patient each sorted five food cards (Fish, Vegetables, Poultry, Beef, Pork) in order of preference. Spearman analysis produced a statistically significant positive correlation of .900 ($p = .037$, $\alpha = .05$) indicating a strong concurrence between the order of the two lists, suggesting that it should be fairly plausible to assemble a healthy dietary plan that is suitable to this patient's tastes.

TUTORIAL VIDEOS

The videos for this chapter are **Ch 11 – Correlation and Regression – Pearson.mp4** and **Ch 11 – Correlation and Regression – Spearman.mp4**. These videos provide overviews of these tests, instructions for carrying out the pretest checklist, run, and interpreting the results of the tests using the data sets: **Ch 11 – Example 01 – Correlation and Regression - Pearson.sav** and **Ch 11 – Example 02 – Correlation and Regression - Spearman.sav**.

OVERVIEW—PEARSON CORRELATION

Regression involves assessing the **correlation** between two variables. Before proceeding, let us deconstruct the word *correlation*: The prefix *co* means *two*—hence, correlation is about *the relationship between two things*. Regression is about *statistically assessing the correlation between two continuous variables.*

Correlation involving two variables, sometimes referred to as *bivariate correlation*, is notated using the lowercase *r* and has a value between −1 and +1. Correlations have two primary attributes: direction and strength.

Direction is indicated by the sign of the *r* value: − or +. **Positive correlations** ($r = 0 \ldots +1$) emerge when the two variables move in the same direction. For example, we would expect that low homework hours would correlate with low grades, and high homework hours would correlate with high grades. **Negative correlations** ($r = −1 \ldots 0$) emerge when the two variables move in different directions. For example, we would expect that high alcohol consumption would correlate with low grades, just as we would expect that low alcohol consumption would correlate with high grades (see Table 11.1).

Table 11.1 Correlation direction summary.

Correlation	r	Variable Directions
Positive	0 . . . +1	X↑ Y↑ or X↓ Y↓
Negative	−1 . . . 0	X↑ Y↓ or X↓ Y↑

Figure 11.1 Correlation strength.

Strong	Weak	Strong
-1	0	+1

Correlation strength is indicated by the numeric value. A correlation wherein the *r* is close to 0 is considered weaker than those nearer to −1 or +1 (see Figure 11.1). Continuing with the prior example, we would expect to find a strong positive correlation between homework hours and grade (e.g., $r = +.80$); conversely, we would expect to find a strong negative correlation between alcohol consumption and grade (e.g., $r = −.80$). However, we would not expect that a variable such as height would have much to do with academic performance, and hence we would expect to find a relatively weak correlation between height and grade (e.g., $r = +.02$ or $r = −.02$).

The concepts of correlation direction and strength will become clearer as we examine the test results, specifically upon inspecting the graph of the scatterplot with the regression line in the Results section.

In cases where the three pretest criteria are not satisfied for the Pearson test, the Spearman test, which is conceptually similar to the Pearson test, is the better option. Additionally, the Spearman test has some other uses which are explained near the end of this chapter.

Example 1—Pearson Regression

An instructor wants to determine if there is a relationship between how long students spend taking a final exam (2 hours allotted) and their grade on the exam (students are free to depart upon completion).

Research Question

Is there a correlation between how long it takes for a student to complete an exam and the grade on that exam?

GROUPS

Bivariate regression/correlation involves only one group, but two different continuous variables are gathered from each participant: In this case, the variables are (1) *Time* taking the exam and (2) the *Grade* on the exam.

Notice that in correlation analysis, you can mix apples and oranges; *Time* is a measure of *minutes*, whereas *Grade* is a measure of *academic performance*. The only constraints in this respect are that the two metrics must both be continuous variables, and of course, the comparison needs to inherently make sense. Whereas it is reasonable to consider the correlation between the amount of *Time* a student spent taking an exam and the *Grade* on that exam, it is implausible to assess the correlation between *shoe size,* and exam *Grade*, even though *shoe size* is a continuous variable.

Procedure

The instructor briefs the students that they are welcome to quietly leave the room upon completing the exam. At the start of the exam, the instructor will start a stopwatch. When each student hands in his or her exam, the instructor refers to the stopwatch and records the time (in minutes) on the back of each exam.

Hypotheses

H_0: There is no correlation between the length of time spent taking the exam and the grade on the exam.

H_1: There is a correlation between the length of time spent taking the exam and the grade on the exam.

Data Set

Use the following data set: **Ch 11 – Example 01 – Correlation and Regression - Pearson.sav**.

Codebook

Variable:	Name
Definition:	Student's last name
Type:	Alphanumeric

Variable:	Time
Definition:	Number of minutes the student spent taking the exam
Type:	Continuous (0 . . . 120) [2 hours = 120 minutes]

Variable:	Grade
Definition:	Grade on exam
Type:	Continuous (0 . . . 100)

Pretest Checklist

Correlation and Regression Pretest Checklist

☑ 1. Normality*

☑ 2. Linearity**

☑ 3. Homoscedasticity**

*Run prior to correlation and regression test

**Results produced upon correlation and regression test run

NOTE: If any of the pretest checklist criteria are not satisfied, rerun the analysis using the nonparametric version of this test: the Spearman test (p. 292).

The pretest criteria for running a correlation/regression involve checking the data for (1) *normality*, (2) *linearity*, and (3) *homoscedasticity* (pronounced *hoe-moe-skuh-daz-tis-city*).

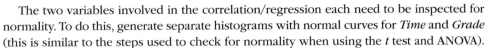

Pretest Checklist Criterion 1—Normality

The two variables involved in the correlation/regression each need to be inspected for normality. To do this, generate separate histograms with normal curves for *Time* and *Grade* (this is similar to the steps used to check for normality when using the *t* test and ANOVA).

For more details on this procedure, refer to **Chapter 3: Descriptive Statistics**; see the star (★) icon on page 52 and follow the procedure in the following section: SPSS—Descriptive Statistics: Continuous Variables (Age); instead of processing *Age,* load the two variables: *Time* and *Grade*. Alternatively, the following steps will produce histograms with a normal curve for *Time* and *Grade*:

1. From the main screen, select *Analyze, Descriptive Statistics, Frequencies*; this will take you to the *Frequencies* menu.

2. On the *Frequencies* menu, move *time* and *grade* from the left window to the right (*Variables*) window. This will order histograms for both variables at the same time.

3. Click on the *Charts* button; this will take you to the *Charts* menu.

4. Click on the *Histograms* button, and check the ☑ *Show normal curve on histogram* checkbox.

5. Click on the *Continue* button; this will return you to the *Frequencies* menu.

6. Click on the *OK* button, and the system will produce (two) histograms with normal curves for *Time* and *Grade* (Figures 11.2 and 11.3).

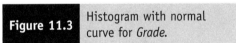

Figure 11.2	Histogram with normal curve for *Time*.

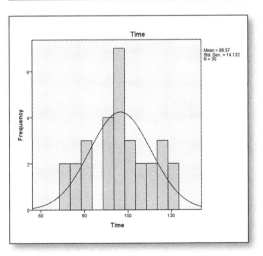

Figure 11.3	Histogram with normal curve for *Grade*.

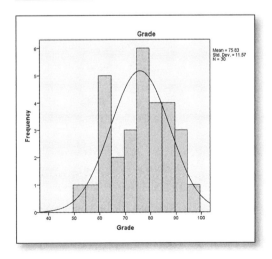

The curves on each histogram are reasonably symmetrically bell shaped; there is no notable skewing, and hence, these criteria are satisfied.

The remaining two pretest criteria, *(2) linearity and (3) homoscedasticity*, are graphical in nature; they will be processed during the Test Run and finalized in the Results section.

Test Run

The test run for correlation and regression involves two steps: First we will process the correlation table, which will render the correlation value (*r*) and the corresponding *p* value. Next, we will order a scatterplot, which will provide a clear graph showing the paired points from both variables on a chart along with the **regression line**, sometimes referred to as a *trend line*, which can be thought of as the average pathway through the points.

Correlation

1. To run a correlation, starting from the main screen, click on *Analyze, Correlate, Bivariate*. (Figure 11.4).

Figure 11.4 Accessing the *Correlation* menu: *Analyze, Correlate, Bivariate.*

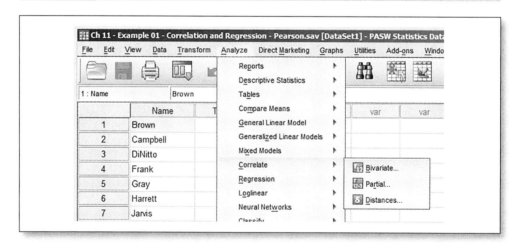

2. On the *Bivariate Correlations* menu (Figure 11.5), move the *Time* and *Grade* variables from the left window to the right (*Variables*) window. Make sure that the ☑ *Pearson* checkbox is checked.

3. Click the *OK* button, and the correlation will process. For now, set aside the correlations table that is produced; we will interpret it in the Results section.

4. To order a scatterplot with a regression line, from the main menu, click on *Graph, Chart Builder* (Figure 11.6).

Figure 11.5   Accessing the *Correlation* menu: *Analyze, Correlate, Bivariate.*

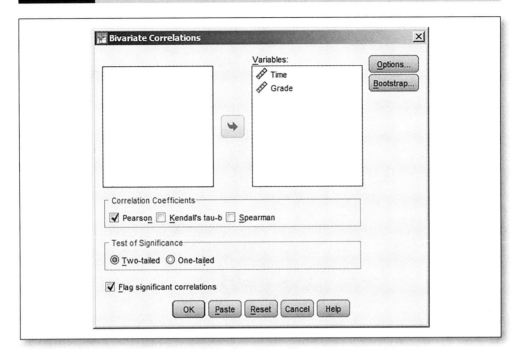

Figure 11.6   Accessing the *Chart Builder* menu: *Graphics, Chart Builder.*

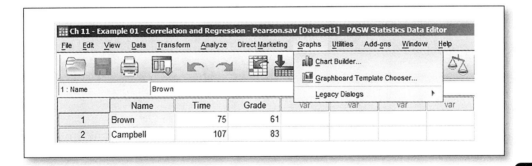

Regression (Scatterplot With Regression Line)

NOTE: SPSS graphics processing menus tend to differ across versions. If these instructions do not fit your version of the software, use the *Help* menu to guide you to order a scatterplot with the regression line. Indicate that you want the *Time* variable on the X-axis and the *Grade* variable on the Y-axis.

5. In the *Choose from*: list, click on *Scatter/Dot* (Figure 11.7).

Figure 11.7   *Chart Builder* menu.

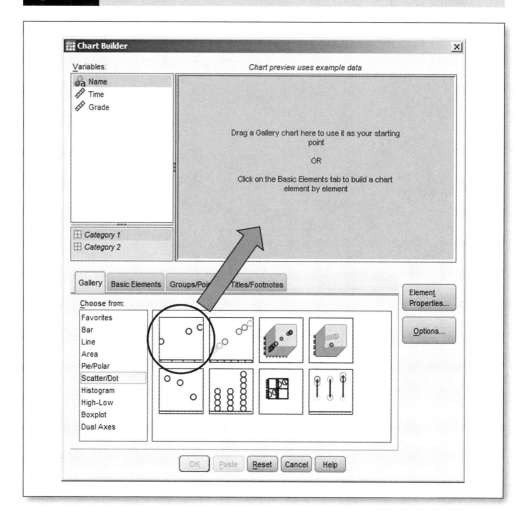

6. Double-click on the (circled) first choice, or click and drag this icon to the *Chart preview uses example data* window.

7. Click and drag *Time* from the *Variables* window to the *X-Axis* box (Figure 11.8).

8. Click and drag *Grade* from the *Variables* window to the *Y-Axis* box.

9. Click on the *OK* button, and the system will produce the scatterplot.

When the scatterplot emerges, you will need to order the regression line: In the *Output* window, double-click on the scatterplot. This will bring you to the *Chart Editor* (Figure 11.9).

Figure 11.8   *Chart Builder* menu—assign *Time* to X-axis and *Grade* to Y-axis.

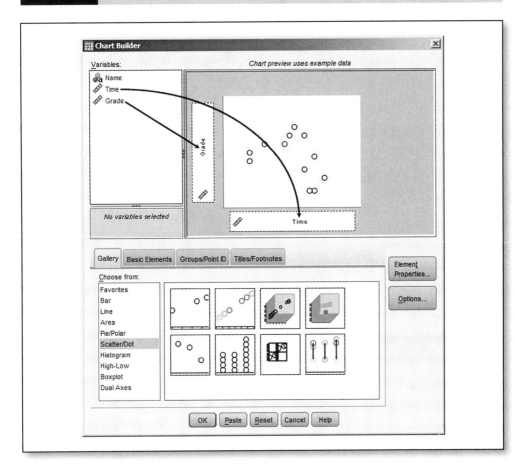

10. Click on the *Add Fit Line at Total* icon to include the regression line on the scatterplot.

11. When you see the regression line emerge on the scatterplot, close the *Chart Editor* and you will see that the regression line is now included on the scatterplot in the *Output* window.

Results

In this section, we will begin by explaining the two elements on the **scatterplot**: (1) the points and (2) the regression line. Next, we will finalize the two remaining pretest criteria (linearity and homoscedasticity), and finally, we will discuss the overall meaning of the scatterplot and correlation findings.

Figure 11.9	*Chart Editor* menu—click on *Add Fit Line* to include the regression line on the scatterplot.

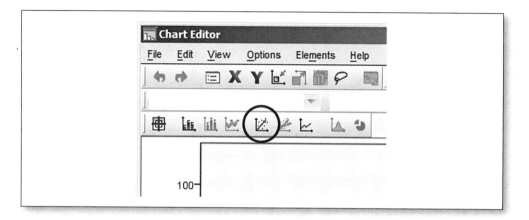

Scatterplot Points

The coordinates of each point on the scatterplot are derived from the two variables: *Time* and *Grade* for each record (individual).

Figure 11.10	Source data for scatterplot: *Time* and *Grade*.

The first record of the data set shows that Brown spent 75 minutes (*Time*) taking the exam and earned a *Grade* of 61 on that exam (Figure 11.10). When we ordered the scatterplot, we placed *Time* on the X-axis and *Grade* on the Y-axis—hence,

Brown's dot on the (X,Y) scatterplot is at coordinates (75, 83), Campbell's dot on the scatterplot is at (107, 83), and so on (Figure 11.11).

Figure 11.11 Scatterplot with regression line for the *Time : Grade* correlation.

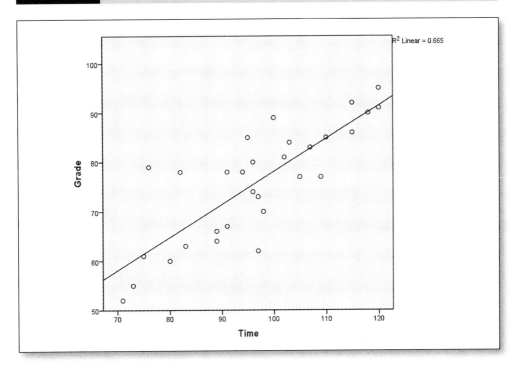

Scatterplot Regression Line

The simplest way to conceive the **regression line**, without presenting the formula, is to think of it as the average straight-line pathway through the cloud of points, based on their positions. Just as the descriptive statistics provide a summary of a single variable, the regression line provides a sort of graphical summary of the relationship between pairs of continuous variables—in this case, *Time* and *Grade*.

Pretest Checklist Criterion 2—Linearity

For **linearity**, the points on the scatterplot should form a relatively straight line (Figure 11.12); the regression line should take a middle-of-the-road path through the cloud of points. If the overall shape of the points departs into some other shape(s) that is not conducive to drawing a straight (regression) line through it (Figure 11.13), then this would constitute a violation of the linearity assumption.

Figure 11.12 Linearity satisfied.

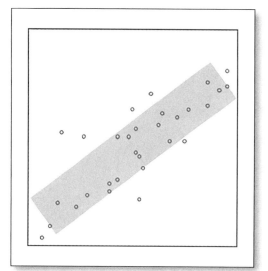

Figure 11.13 Linearity violated.

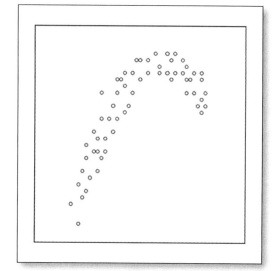

Pretest Checklist Criterion 3—Homoscedasticity

Homoscedasticity pertains to the density of the points along the regression line. The criterion of homoscedasticity is satisfied when the cloud of points is densest in the middle and tapers off at the ends (Figure 11.14) as opposed to the points being concentrated in some other way (Figure 11.15). The rationale for this distribution of points on the scatterplot follows the same notion as the shape of the normal curve of the histogram—the majority of the values are gathered around the mean, which accounts for the height of the normal bell-shaped curve on the histogram, whereas the tapered tails signify that there are considerably fewer very low and very high values. The positions of the points on the scatterplot are derived from the same data that rendered the normally distributed histograms for the two variables (Figure 11.14), so it follows that the middle of the cloud should contain considerably more points (and be denser) than the ends.

Correlation

Table 11.2 shows a positive correlation ($r = .815$) between *Time* and *Grade*, with a (Sig.) p value of .000. As mentioned in Chapter 4, the p value never really goes to zero; in this case, $p = .0000000409310999$. When the p value is less than .001, it is typically notated as "$p < .001$." Because the p value is less than the α level of .05, and the r is greater than zero, we would say that there is a statistically significant positive correlation ($p < .001$, $\alpha = .05$) between *Time* and *Grade*. The positive correlation ($r = .815$) pertains to the positive slope of the regression line.

Notice that the correlations table (Table 11.2) is double-redundant; there are two .815s and two .000s in the table. This is because the correlation between *Time* and *Grade* is the same as the correlation between *Grade* and *Time*.

Figure 11.14   Homoscedasticity satisfied.

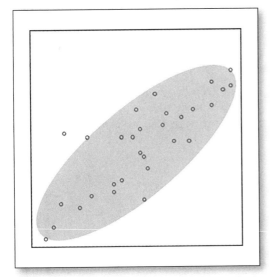

Figure 11.15   Homoscedasticity violated.

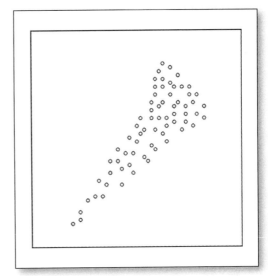

Table 11.2   Correlations between *Time* and *Grade*.

Correlations

		Time	Grade
Time	Pearson Correlation	1	.815**
	Sig. (2-tailed)		.000
	N	30	30
Grade	Pearson Correlation	.815**	1
	Sig. (2-tailed)	.000	
	N	30	30

**. Correlation is significant at the 0.01 level (2-tailed).

Hypothesis Resolution

REJECT: H_0: There is no correlation between the length of time spent taking the exam and the grade on the exam.

ACCEPT: H_1: There is a correlation between the length of time spent taking the exam and the grade on the exam.

The correlation calculation produced a *p* (*p* < .001) that is less than the specified .05 α level, so we would therefore say that there is a statistically significant (positive) correlation between the length of time that students spent taking the exam and the associated grade. As such, we would reject H_0 and not reject H_1.

Abstract

Prior to writing the abstract, it can be helpful to run descriptive statistics for the two variables (*Time* and *Grade*) involved in the correlation (the procedure for running descriptive statistics can be found at the ★ icon on page 52; you can load *Time* and *Grade* into the *Variables* window together) (Table 11.3).

Table 11.3 Descriptive statistics for *Time* and *Grade*.

Statistics

		Time	Grade
N	Valid	30	30
	Missing	0	0
Mean		96.57	75.83
Median		96.50	78.00
Mode		89[a]	78
Std. Deviation		14.132	11.570
Variance		199.702	133.868
Range		49	43
Minimum		71	52
Maximum		120	95

a. Multiple modes exist. The smallest value is shown

Discussing the *n*, means, and standard deviations of each variable along with the regression results can add to the substance of the abstract:

We were interested in discovering if there was a correlation between how long students spent taking an exam and the associated grade. The 30 students were allotted 2 hours to take their final exam. Students spent a mean of 96.6 (SD = 14.1) minutes taking the exam and earned mean of 78.0 (SD = 11.6) on the exam. Correlation analysis revealed a strong positive correlation between these two variables (r = .815), which was statistically significant (p < .001, α = .05) *suggesting that the more time students spend on their exams, the higher the grade and vice versa.*

Before concluding this discussion of the Pearson statistic, wherein the example resulted in a statistically significant positive correlation between exam *Time* and *Grade*, let us take a brief look at two more examples: one that produces a *negative* correlation between *Time* and *Grade* and another wherein there is *no* (significant) correlation.

Negative Correlation

Consider this result, where the data produced a statistically significant negative correlation (r = -.803, p < .001). The scatterplot would resemble Figure 11.16.

Figure 11.16 Scatterplot reflecting a statistically significant negative correlation between *Time* and *Grade* (r = −.803, p < .001).

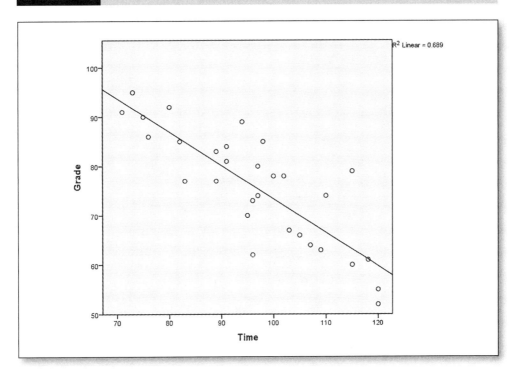

These findings reflect a negative (inverse) relationship between exam *Time* and exam *Grade*, suggesting that students who spent less time completing the exam scored higher, and vice versa.

No Correlation

Finally, it is possible that there is no statistically significant correlation between the two variables ($r = -.072$, $p = .704$), as shown in the scatterplot (Figure 11.17).

Figure 11.17	Scatterplot reflecting a statistically insignificant negative correlation between *Time* and *Grade* ($r = -.072$, $p = .704$).

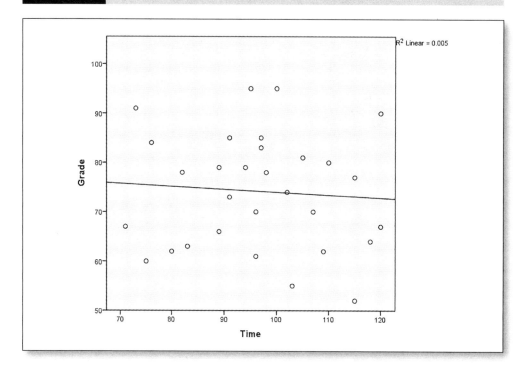

Notice that as the r gets closer to 0, the relationship between the variables starts to break down. This is typically reflected in the scatterplot, wherein the points are scattered further from the regression line, and the regression line becomes more horizontal (less of a negative or positive slope).

Basically, this graph shows that there are about as many high and low grades among the students who spent a little time on the exam as those who spent a lot of time on the exam. In other words, knowing how long a student spent taking the exam has nothing to do with how well he or she did on it.

OVERVIEW—SPEARMAN CORRELATION

The **Spearman correlation**, formally referred to as **Spearman's rho** (pronounced *row*), symbolized by the Greek letter ρ, can be thought of as a close cousin of the more commonly used Pearson regression; however, whereas the Pearson statistic assesses the relationship between two continuous variables gathered from a data sample (e.g., height and weight), the Spearman correlation assesses the relationship between two rankings (ordered lists) using the same –1 . . . +1 value range as the Pearson regression. The most common use of Spearman's rho is to determine how similarly two lists are sequenced.

For example, suppose you want to determine how similar Alice's color preferences are compared to Bill's. You could write the names of the colors on the front of each card with the corresponding code number on the back (in this demonstration, the code numbers are shown on the front of each card for easy reference). Next, ask Alice and Bill to independently arrange their cards in their order of preference, with their favorite color at the top (Figure 11.18).

Figure 11.18   Two lists ranked identically produces a Spearman's rho of +1.

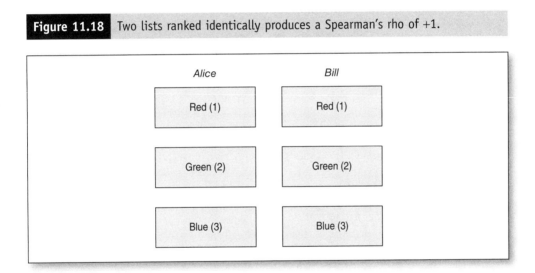

Because Alice and Bill arranged their cards in exactly the *same* order, this would produce a Spearman rho of +1, signifying a perfectly positive correlation between the two prioritized lists (Figure 11.18).

If instead, Jane sorted the colors the same way: *Red, Green Blue* (1, 2, 3), but John sequenced them: *Blue, Green, Red* (3, 2, 1), then these two rankings would be exactly *opposite* of each other, which would produce a Spearman rho of –1, signifying a (perfectly) negative correlation between the two lists (Figure 11.19).

In this concise example, three items (colors) were used; however, there is no limit to the number of items that can constitute these lists. As you might expect, a variety of rankings of the items are possible, producing Spearman rho values anywhere between –1 and +1. As with the Pearson correlation, the corresponding p value indicates if there is (or is not) a statistically significant difference between the (two) rankings.

Example 2—Spearman Correlation

A patient is referred to confer with a dietician to collaboratively build a healthful eating plan. Part of this process involves ascertaining the patient's food preferences.

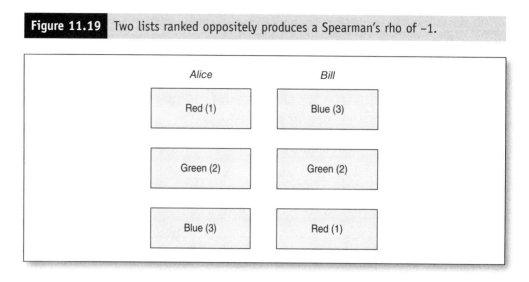

Figure 11.19 Two lists ranked oppositely produces a Spearman's rho of −1.

Research Question

Is there a statistically significant correlation between the dietician's recommended food ranking and the patient's current food preferences?

Groups

Unlike the Pearson regression, which gathers two continuous variables from each sample, the Spearman correlation gathers a sequence of ranked data from each of the two participants—in this case, food rankings from the dietician and the patient.

Procedure

At the initial consultation meeting, the dietician issues the patient five cards and asks the patient to arrange them in order of preference, with the most favorite food at the top. The dietician will then use another set of cards to demonstrate the recommended diet in terms of which foods should be considered best (to worst) nutritional choices. The dietician will record the two card sequences and compare them using Spearman's rho.

Hypotheses

H_0: There is no correlation between the dietician's recommended food ranking and the patient's food preferences.

H_1: There is a correlation between the dietician's recommended food ranking and the patient's food preferences.

Data Set

Use the following data set: **Ch 11 – Example 02 – Correlation and Regression – Pearson.sav**.

Codebook

Variable:	Dietician
Definition:	Dietician's recommended food ranking
Type:	Categorical (1 = Vegetables, 2 = Fish, 3 = Poultry, 4 = Beef, 5 = Pork)

Variable:	Patient
Definition:	Patient's food preferences
Type:	Categorical (1 = Vegetables, 2 = Fish, 3 = Poultry, 4 = Beef, 5 = Pork)

The dietician and the patient independently arrange their five cards with the most preferable food at the top (Figure 11.20). On the *Data View* screen, you can click on the *Value Labels* icon to toggle between the numeric values and the corresponding assigned value labels.

Figure 11.20   Food rankings for dietician and patient.

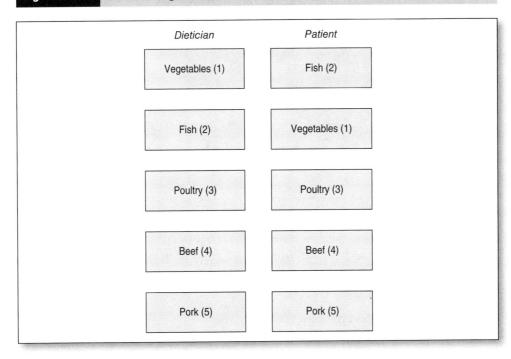

Pretest Checklist

The Spearman's rho (symbolized by the Greek letter ρ) is a nonparametric (pronounced *non-pair-uh-metric*) test, meaning that the data are not expected to be normally distributed, and hence, the pretest criteria for the Pearson regression (normality, linearity, and homoscedasticity) are not pertinent when it comes to running the Spearman's correlation. Because each item is only present once per variable, a bar chart, or a histogram with a normal curve, would render all the bars at the same height, signifying one entry per value, which would be unrevealing.

The only real pretest criterion for Spearman's rho is to be certain that both lists consist of the same items—in this case, both the dietician and the patient ranked the same five food items, each in their own way.

Test Run

The test run for the Spearman test involves the same order menu and results table as the Pearson correlation.

1. Click on *Analyze, Correlate, Bivariate* (Figure 11.21); this will take you to the *Bivariate Correlations* menu (Figure 11.22).

Figure 11.21 Accessing the *Bivariate Correlations* menu: *Analyze, Correlate, Bivariate.*

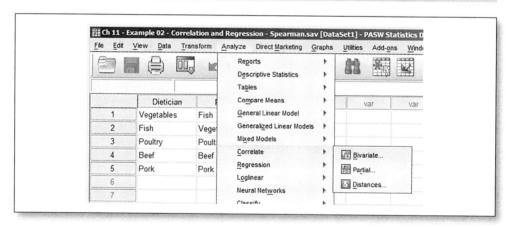

2. On the *Bivariate Correlations* menu (Figure 11.22), move both variables (*Dietician* and *Patient*) from the left window to the right *Variables* window.

3. On the *Correlation Coefficients* options, uncheck ☐ *Pearson* and check ☑ *Spearman.*

4. Click *OK,* and the correlation will run.

Figure 11.22	On the bivariate *Correlations* table, move the two variables into the right Variables window; then uncheck ☐ *Pearson* and check ☑ *Spearman*.

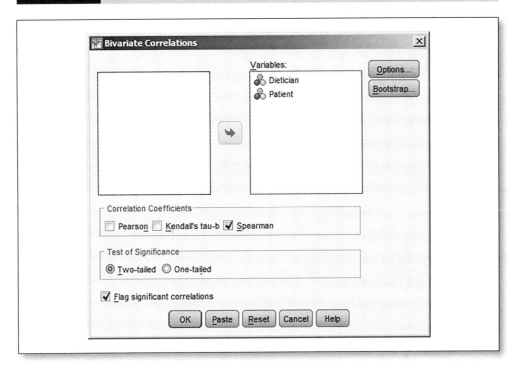

Results

The results are presented in a single *Correlations* table (Table 11.4) indicating a Spearman rho of .900 with a corresponding p (Sig.) value of .037. This indicates a statistically significant positive correlation in the ranking of the two food lists. In other words, there is a strong similarity in the order of the foods on these two lists.

Hypothesis Resolution

REJECT: H_0: There is no correlation between the dietician's recommended food ranking and the patient's food preferences.

ACCEPT: H_1: There is a correlation between the dietician's recommended food ranking and the patient's food preferences.

Table 11.4	Correlations table showing the Spearman's rho of .900 and corresponding statistically significant p (Sig.) value of .037.

Correlations

			Dietician	Patient
Spearman's rho	Dietician	Correlation Coefficient	1.000	.900*
		Sig. (2-tailed)	.	.037
		N	5	5
	Patient	Correlation Coefficient	.900*	1.000
		Sig. (2-tailed)	.037	.
		N	5	5

*. Correlation is significant at the 0.05 level (2-tailed).

The Spearman rho is .900, indicating a strong positive correlation between the two lists; because the *p* value of .037 is less than the specified .05 α level, we would say that there is a statistically significant (positive) correlation between the food rankings of the dietician and the patient. As such, we would reject H$_0$ and not reject H$_1$.

Abstract

To work collaboratively with the patient in building a palatable healthy eating plan, as part of the initial encounter, the dietician asks the patient to sequence five food cards from favorite to least favorite without prompting. The dietician compared the patient's food preference (Fish, Vegetables, Poultry, Beef, Pork) to the recommended optimal nutrition for this patient (Vegetables, Fish, Poultry, Beef, Pork); Spearman's rho produced a statistically significant positive correlation of .900 (p = .037, α = .05) indicating a strong concurrence between the two lists, suggesting that it should be fairly plausible to assemble a healthy dietary plan that is suitable to this patient's tastes.

ALTERNATE USE FOR SPEARMAN CORRELATION

The Spearman statistic is a viable alternative to the Pearson statistic when there is one or more substantial violation of the (Pearson) pretest criteria (normality, linearity, homoscedasticity).

Correlation Versus Causation

Correlation only means that two variables appear to move in a predictable direction with respect to each other (e.g., when one goes up, the other goes up; when one goes down, the other goes down; or when one goes up, the other goes down), but keep in mind, this is not necessarily due to **causation**, which would involve the change in one variable *causing* the change in the other. To make the leap from *correlation* to *causation,* three criteria must be met: (1) association/correlation, (2) temporality (timing), and (3) nonspurious (authentic) (Table 11.5).

Table 11.5	Three criteria for satisfying causality: association/correlation, temporality, nonspurious.

Causality Criteria		
Criteria	**Rule**	**Example**
1. Association/correlation	Variable A and variable B must be empirically related; there must be a (scientific) logical relationship between A and B.	Taking a dose of aspirin lowers fever.
2. Temporality	A (cause [independent variable]) precedes B (effect [dependent variable]).	The person took aspirin, and *then* the fever went down, not the other way around.
3. Nonspurious	The relationship between A and B is not caused by other variable(s).	The drop in fever is not due to the room getting colder, submerging the person in an ice bath, or other factors.

Admittedly, the criteria to claim causation are strict, but without this rigor, numerous spurious (bogus) correlations could be wrongly attributed to causality, leading to inappropriate conclusions and potentially misguided interventions.

For example, one might find a positive correlation between chocolate milk consumption and automobile theft—as chocolate milk sales go up, so do car thefts. Instead of concluding that chocolate milk causes people to steal cars or that car theft causes one to crave chocolate milk, anyone reasonable would continue his or her investigation and probably discover that *population* may be a variable worth consideration: In a town with a population of 2,000, we would find low chocolate milk sales and few car thefts, whereas in a city with a population of 2,000,000, chocolate milk sales and car thefts would both be considerably higher. In this case, we would be free to notice the positive correlation between chocolate milk consumption and car theft, but the causal criteria between these two variables clearly breaks down at all three levels.

GOOD COMMON SENSE

Reflecting back on the Pearson regression example involving homework hours and grade, even if a statistically significant, strong positive correlation was found between these two variables, it would be presumptuous to simply claim that homework hours (and nothing else) caused the grade. One or more underlying unaccounted-for factors that would not be revealed by correlation analysis may be responsible for affecting the homework hours, which, in turn, may have affected the grade. For example, an adverse factor (e.g., household stress, health problem, adverse social issue, etc.) may be cutting into the student's ability to engage in longer homework hours; conversely, a pleasurable factor may be detracting from homework time (e.g., great social circle, multiple extracurricular activities, compelling video games, etc.). Alternatively, an overarching factor may affect both homework and grade, such as an undiagnosed learning disability, depression, exhaustion, effective tutor, and so forth.

The point is that correlation, no matter what the *r* or the *p,* is just that—an overall *correlation*; try to avoid jumping to conclusions regarding *causation*.

Key Concepts

- Pearson regression (*r*)

  - Correlation
  - Strength

- Direction
- Normality
- Linearity
- Homoscedasticity
- Bivariate correlation
- Scatterplot
- Regression
- Spearman's rho correlation (ρ)
- Correlation vs. causation

Practice Exercises

NOTE: Exercises 11.1 to 11.8 involve continuous data; use the Pearson statistic for these.

Exercises 11.9 and 11.10 involve ordinal (categorical) data; as such, use the Spearman's rho statistic.

Exercise 11.1

An exercise advocate wants to determine the effect that walking rigorously has on weight loss. The researcher recruits participants to engage in a weeklong study. The researcher instructs participants to take a brisk walk as many days of the week as possible for as long as they can. Participants will record the following data: weight prior to engaging in the walking regimen, the amount of time walked each day, and their weight at the end of the week. Participants will submit their data to the researcher at the end of the week. The researcher will preprocess the data to derive the total number of hours walked (WalkHrs) and the change in weight for each participant (WtLoss = weight at the end of the week – weight at the beginning of the week).

Data set: **Ch 11 – Exercise 01A.sav**

Codebook

Variable: WalkHours

Definition: Total hours walked in a week

Type: Continuous

Variable: WeightLoss

Definition: Total weight loss in a week

Type: Continuous

NOTE: In Data Set A, Record 3, notice that the weight loss (WeightLoss) is –1.00; this indicates that the participant gained 1 pound. Data Set B, Record 16 also signifies a half-pound weight gain (WeightLoss = –0.50) for that participant.

a. Write the hypotheses.

b. Run the criteria of the pretest checklist (normality [for both variables], linearity, homoscedasticity) and discuss your findings.

c. Run the bivariate correlation, scatterplot with regression line, and descriptive statistics for both variables and document your findings (r and Sig. [p value], ns, means, standard deviations) and hypothesis resolution.

d. Write an abstract under 200 words detailing a summary of the study, the bivariate correlation, hypothesis resolution, and implications of your findings.

Repeat this exercise using data set: **Ch 11 – Exercise 01B.sav**.

Exercise 11.2

A social scientist has noticed that people seem to be spending a lot of nonwork hours on computers and wants to determine if this may, in some way, be associated with social relationship satisfaction (satisfaction derived from interacting with others). To determine if there is a correlation between nonwork computer hours and social satisfaction, the scientist recruited a group of participants and asked them to indicate (about) how many nonwork hours they spend on the computer each week. Next, each participant was given the Acme Social Satisfaction Inventory (ASSI); this self-administered instrument renders a score between 0 and 80 (0 = very low social satisfaction . . . 80 = very high social satisfaction).

Data set: **Ch 11 – Exercise 02A.sav**

Variable:	CompHrs
Definition:	Number of nonwork hours spent on the computer per week
Type:	Continuous

Variable:	ASSI
Definition:	Acme Social Satisfaction Inventory
Type:	Continuous (0 = Very low social satisfaction . . . 80 = Very high social satisfaction)

a. Write the hypotheses.

b. Run the criteria of the pretest checklist (normality [for both variables], linearity, homoscedasticity) and discuss your findings.

c. Run the bivariate correlation, scatterplot with regression line, and descriptive statistics for both variables and document your findings (r and Sig. [p value], ns, means, standard deviations) and hypothesis resolution.

d. Write an abstract under 200 words detailing a summary of the study, the bivariate correlation, hypothesis resolution, and implications of your findings.

Repeat this exercise using data set: **Ch 11 – Exercise 02B.sav**.

Exercise 11.3

A social scientist and an economist working together want to discover if there is a correlation between income and happiness. The researchers recruit a group of participants and ask them to complete a confidential survey. This self-administered survey asks for the participant's annual income; it also includes the Acme Life Happiness Scale (ALHS), which renders a score between 0 and 100 (0 = Very unhappy . . . 100 = Very happy).

Data set: **Ch 11 – Exercise 03A.sav**

Variable:	Income
Definition:	Annual income in dollars rounded to the nearest thousand
Type:	Continuous

Variable:	ALHS
Definition:	Score on the Acme Life Happiness Scale
Type:	Continuous (0 = Very unhappy . . . 100 = Very happy)

a. Write the hypotheses.

b. Run the criteria of the pretest checklist (normality [for both variables], linearity, homoscedasticity) and discuss your findings.

c. Run the bivariate correlation, scatterplot with regression line, and descriptive statistics for both variables and document your findings (*r* and Sig. [*p* value], *ns*, means, standard deviations) and hypothesis resolution.

d. Write an abstract under 200 words detailing a summary of the study, the bivariate correlation, hypothesis resolution, and implications of your findings.

Repeat this exercise using data set: **Ch 11 – Exercise 03B.sav**.

Exercise 11.4

A political scientist wants to find out if there is a correlation between listening to a newscast and an individual's mood. This researcher recruits a group of participants and has them listen to a newscast that was recorded earlier that morning. Participants are instructed to listen for as long as they want; when they are finished listening, the researcher writes down the listening duration and then asks each participant to complete the Acme Mood Report (AMR), a self-administered instrument that renders a score between 0 and 100 (0 = Very bad mood . . . 100 = Very good mood).

Data set: **Ch 11 – Exercise 04A.sav**

Variable:	MinNews
Definition:	Number of minutes of news listened to
Type:	Continuous

Variable:	AMR
Definition:	Acme Mood Report
Type:	Continuous (0 = Very bad mood . . . 100 = Very good mood)

a. Write the hypotheses.

b. Run the criteria of the pretest checklist (normality [for both variables], linearity, homoscedasticity) and discuss your findings.

c. Run the bivariate correlation, scatterplot with regression line, and descriptive statistics for both variables and document your findings (*r* and Sig. [*p* value], *ns*, means, standard deviations) and hypothesis resolution.

d. Write an abstract under 200 words detailing a summary of the study, the bivariate correlation, hypothesis resolution, and implications of your findings.

Repeat this exercise using data set: **Ch 11 – Exercise 04B.sav**.

Exercise 11.5

An educational scientist wants to examine the correlation between years of education and job satisfaction. To address this question, the scientist recruits a group of participants and has each complete a self-administered survey; the first question asks how many years of education the participant has (e.g., 12 = high school diploma, 14 = associate's degree,

16 = bachelor's degree, 18 = master's degree). The remaining questions consist of the Acme Job Satisfaction Index (AJSI), which produces a score between 0 and 60 (0 = Very unsatisfied with job . . . 60 = Very satisfied with job).

Data set: **Ch 11 – Exercise 05A.sav**

Variable:	YearsEd
Definition:	Number of years of education
Type:	Continuous

Variable:	AJSI
Definition:	Acme Job Satisfaction Index
Type:	Continuous (0 = Very unsatisfied with job . . . 60 = Very satisfied with job)

a. Write the hypotheses.

b. Run the criteria of the pretest checklist (normality [for both variables], linearity, homoscedasticity) and discuss your findings.

c. Run the bivariate correlation, scatterplot with regression line, and descriptive statistics for both variables and document your findings (*r* and Sig. [*p* value], *ns*, means, standard deviations) and hypothesis resolution.

d. Write an abstract under 200 words detailing a summary of the study, the bivariate correlation, hypothesis resolution, and implications of your findings.

Repeat this exercise using data set: **Ch 11 – Exercise 05B.sav**.

Exercise 11.6

A dietician wants to discover if there is a correlation between age and number of meals eaten outside the home. The dietician recruits participants and administers a two-question survey: (1) *How old are you?* and (2) *How many times do you eat out (meals not eaten at home) in an average month?*

Data set: **Ch 11 – Exercise 06A.sav**

Variable:	Age
Definition:	Age of participant
Type:	Continuous

Variable:	MealsOut
Definition:	Number of means out participant eats per month
Type:	Continuous

a. Write the hypotheses.

b. Run the criteria of the pretest checklist (normality [for both variables], linearity, homoscedasticity) and discuss your findings.

c. Run the bivariate correlation, scatterplot with regression line, and descriptive statistics for both variables and document your findings (*r* and Sig. [*p* value], *n*s, means, standard deviations) and hypothesis resolution.

d. Write an abstract under 200 words detailing a summary of the study, the bivariate correlation, hypothesis resolution, and implications of your findings.

Repeat this exercise using data set: **Ch 11 – Exercise 06B.sav**.

Exercise 11.7

A social scientist wants to determine if a person's height might be correlated with his or her sense of self-confidence. To explore this, the scientist recruits a group of participants and gathers two metrics: First the researcher administers the Acme Self-Confidence Instrument (ASCI), a self-administered survey that produces a score between 0 and 50 (0 = Very low self-confidence . . . 50 = Very high self-confidence). Second, the scientist measures the height (in inches) of each participant.

Data set: **Ch 11 – Exercise 07A.sav**

Variable:	Height
Definition:	Height of participant (in inches)
Type:	Continuous

Variable:	ASCI
Definition:	Acme Self-Confidence Instrument
Type:	Continuous (0 = Very low self-confidence . . . 50 = Very high self-confidence)

a. Write the hypotheses.

b. Run the criteria of the pretest checklist (normality [for both variables], linearity, homoscedasticity) and discuss your findings.

c. Run the bivariate correlation, scatterplot with regression line, and descriptive statistics for both variables and document your findings (*r* and Sig. [*p* value], *n*s, means, standard deviations) and hypothesis resolution.

d. Write an abstract under 200 words detailing a summary of the study, the bivariate correlation, hypothesis resolution, and implications of your findings.

Repeat this exercise using data set: **Ch 11 – Exercise 07B.sav**.

Exercise 11.8

A sociologist has learned from a prior study that there is a strong positive correlation between time spent playing a video game and the score the player earns on that game (practice makes perfect). Because achieving such proficiency is time-consuming, this sociologist expects that there may be a (negative) correlation between game score and overall academic performance (grade: 0 . . . 100). To determine if there is such an inverse correlation, the sociologist recruits a group of participants to play a popular video game for 15 minutes, at which time the researcher records the score. Participants will also be asked to provide a copy of their most recent transcript.

Data set: **Ch 11 – Exercise 08A.sav**

Variable:	Score
Definition:	Score on video game
Type:	Continuous

Variable:	Grade
Definition:	Overall academic grade
Type:	Continuous (0 . . . 100)

a. Write the hypotheses.

b. Run the criteria of the pretest checklist (normality [for both variables], linearity, homoscedasticity) and discuss your findings.

c. Run the bivariate correlation, scatterplot with regression line, and descriptive statistics for both variables and document your findings (*r* and Sig. [*p* value], *ns*, means, standard deviations) and hypothesis resolution.

d. Write an abstract under 200 words detailing a summary of the study, the bivariate correlation, hypothesis resolution, and implications of your findings.

Repeat this exercise using data set: **Ch 11 – Exercise 08B.sav**.

NOTE: Exercises 11.9 and 11.10 involve categorical data; as such, use the Spearman's rho statistic.

Exercise 11.9

In order to better control inventory, Acme Motors wants to assess how similar customer car color preference is comparing the Pico Boulevard dealership to the Sepulveda Boulevard dealership (in the data sets, the most popular car color choice is at the top of the list for each dealership).

Data set: **Ch 11 – Exercise 09A.sav**

Variable:	Pico
Definition:	Customer car color preference at the Pico Blvd. dealership
Type:	Categorical (1 = Black, 2 = Blue, 3 = Red, 4 = Silver, 5 = White, 6 = Yellow)

Variable: Sepulveda

Definition: Customer car color preference at the Sepulveda Blvd. dealership

Type: Categorical (1 = Black, 2 = Blue, 3 = Red, 4 = Silver, 5 = White, 6 = Yellow)

a. Write the hypotheses.

b. Verify the pretest checklist (both independently ranking the same set of items).

c. Run the bivariate correlation for Spearman's rho, and document your findings (Spearman rho and Sig. [*p* value]) and hypothesis resolution.

d. Write an abstract under 200 words detailing a summary of the study, the bivariate correlation, hypothesis resolution, and implications of your findings.

Repeat this exercise using data set: **Ch 11 – Exercise 09B.sav.**

Exercise 11.10

Ariel and Dusty want to determine how similar their movie preferences are. They independently rank the 13 movie categories with their favorite at the top.

Data set: **Ch 11 – Exercise 10A.sav**

Variable: Ariel

Definition: Ariel's movie type preference

Type: Categorical (1 = Action / Adventure, 2 = Animation=, 3 = Comedy, 4 = Cult Movie, 5 = Documentary, 6 = Fantasy, 7 = Film Noir, 8 = Horror, 9 = Romantic, 10 = Sci-Fi, 11 = Spy, 12 = Western, 13 = Zombies)

Variable: Dusty

Definition: Dusty's movie type preference

Type: Categorical (1 = Action / Adventure, 2 = Animation =, 3 = Comedy, 4 = Cult Movie, 5 = Documentary, 6 = Fantasy, 7 = Film Noir, 8 = Horror, 9 = Romantic, 10 = Sci-Fi, 11 = Spy, 12 = Western, 13 = Zombies)

a. Write the hypotheses.

b. Verify the pretest checklist (both independently ranking the same set of items).

c. Run the bivariate correlation for Spearman's rho and document your findings (Spearman rho and Sig. [*p* value]) and hypothesis resolution.

d. Write an abstract under 200 words detailing a summary of the study, the bivariate correlation, hypothesis resolution, and implications of your findings.

Repeat this exercise using data set: **Ch 11 – Exercise 10B.sav.**

CHAPTER 12

Multiple Regression

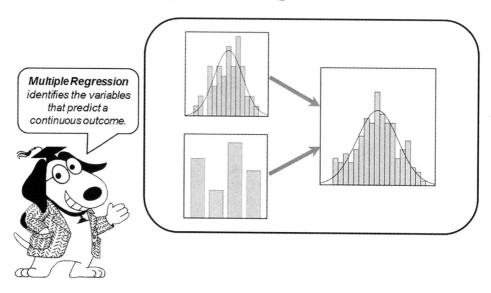

Multiple Regression identifies the variables that predict a continuous outcome.

What we see depends mainly on what we look for.

—John Lubbock

Learning Objectives

Upon completing this chapter, you will be able to do the following:

- Determine when it is appropriate to run a multiple regression analysis.
- Verify that the data meet the criteria for multiple regression processing: sample size, linearity, homoscedasticity, multicollinearity, and normality.
- Understand the procedure for handling polychotomous categorical variables.
- Order a multiple regression test.
- Comprehend the R^2 statistic.
- Derive results from the Model Summary table.
- Resolve the hypotheses.
- Write an appropriate abstract.

WHEN TO USE THIS STATISTIC

Guidelines for Selecting the Multiple Regression Test

Overview: This statistic indicates which variables predict a continuous outcome.

Variables: This statistic can accommodate multiple continuous and categorical predictor variables with one continuous outcome variable for each record.

Results: After a group of smokers engaged in a smoking cessation program, we gathered data detailing their daily smoking rates before and after the intervention along with their age, gender, race, and income. Multiple regression analysis revealed that age accounts for 53.1% of the variability observed in the current smoking rate, baseline smoking rate accounts for an additional 4.5%, and gender accounts for 2.1% ($\alpha = .05$).

VIDEO

The tutorial video for this chapter is **Ch 12 – Multiple Regression.mp4**. This video provides an overview of the multiple regression statistic, followed by the SPSS procedures for processing the pretest checklist, ordering the statistical run, and interpreting the results of this test using the data set: **Ch 12 – Example 01 – Multiple Regression.sav**.

OVERVIEW—MULTIPLE REGRESSION

As we saw in Chapter 11, the Pearson *r* correlation, sometimes referred to as *bivariate correlation*, is useful for assessing the relationship between two continuous variables when we have two such scores for each participant. In the example for that chapter, we explored the extent to which test taking *time* predicts the *grade* on the exam. **Multiple regression**, symbolized by $\mathbf{R}^2$, is an extension of this kind of (bivariate) correlation; whereas bivariate correlation involves assessing the (co)relationship between one continuous predictor variable (amount of *time* taking a test) paired with one continuous outcome variable (exam *grade*), multiple regression enables more complex analyses to understand the (possible) multiple predictors correlated with a continuous outcome variable.

For example, suppose instead of only considering the (co)relationship between *time* (the number of minutes spent taking the exam) and the *grade* on the exam, we expect that some other variables (e.g., age, academic year, gender, major) may also be significant when it comes to predicting the outcome (grade on the exam). The multiple regression processor does a series of things: (1) It identifies which of the predictor variables (time, age, academic year, gender, and major) are statistically significantly correlated ($p \leq .05$) to the outcome variable (grade), (2) it then assigns a percentage value to each statistically significant predictor variable, and (3) it eliminates any predictor variables that are statistically insignificant ($p > .05$), and therefore (statistically) irrelevant when it comes to predicting the outcome variable. You can think of a *predictor* as a variable that you think may influence the value of the outcome variable.

Often, the goal of multiple regression is to assemble a parsimonious (pronounced *par-suh-moe-nee-us*) model, meaning that the fewest number of variables are identified that are relevant in predicting the outcome variable. The following excerpt demonstrates how the results of such an analysis would be documented:

> *In order to better understand the variables that predict the outcome on an exam, Professor Smith gathered the following data on 188 students: exam grade, time spent taking the exam, age, academic year, gender, and academic major. Multiple regression analysis revealed an overall $R^2 = 38.4$ ($p < .05$), wherein academic year accounts for 22.5 percent of the variability observed in the grade, time spent taking the exam accounted for an additional 9.7 percent, and academic major accounted for 6.2 percent.*

Notice that in the documentation of this hypothetical example, *age* and *gender* have no percentages assigned to them; this is because the regression processor determined that they are not statistically significantly correlated to the outcome variable (*grade*). Also notice that the overall R^2 only accounts for 38.4% (22.5 + 9.7 + 6.2) of the variability observed in the outcome variable, so the question stands: *What about the other 61.6% (100 − 38.4 = 61.6)?* The answer is *error*. In this context, "error" does not imply that somebody made a mistake; rather, this model is saying that three of the predictor variables (academic year, time spent taking the exam, and academic major) account for 38.4% of the variability observed in the outcome variable (grade), leaving 61.6% unaccounted for. Basically, this is saying that other predictors pertain to the outcome variable, which are not included in this model. If this study were to be repeated, we might consider retaining the three statistically significant predictors (academic year, time spent taking the exam, and academic major), dropping the statistically insignificant predictors (age and gender), and include some other, hopefully more relevant, predictor variables to increase the overall R^2 (e.g., family size, educational level of parents, household income).

Before proceeding notice that multiple regression involves one continuous outcome variable (*grade*), and a variety of predictor variables: *time, age,* and *academic year* are continuous variables; *gender* is a dichotomous (two categories) categorical variable; and *academic major* is a polychotomous (more than two categories) categorical variable.

Example

A nurse has conducted a smoking cessation workshop for a wide variety of patients who wish to quit smoking. At the conclusion of the series, instead of simply calculating the percentage of the participants who quit smoking, logistic regression is used to better comprehend the characteristics of those who succeeded.

Research Question

What influences do (predictive) variables such as age, income, baseline mean number of cigarettes smoked daily, gender, and race have when it comes to quitting (or not quitting) smoking?

Groups

In this example, all of the members are included in a single group—everyone receives the same smoking cessation intervention.

Procedure

As a public service, the Acme Health Center advertises and offers a free 90-day smoking cessation program, consisting of nurse-facilitated psychoeducational meetings, peer support from those who have been smoke free for more than 1 year, and multimedia resources designed to promote smoking cessation.

At the conclusion of the intervention, each participant is requested to respond to a self-administered anonymous Smoking Cessation Survey card (Figure 12.1).

| Figure 12.1 | Smoking Cessation Survey card, anonymously completed by each participant at the conclusion of the intervention. |

Smoking Cessation Survey

1. What is your age? _____

2. What is your annual (gross) income? _____

3. Prior to this intervention, how many cigarettes did you smoke in an average day? _____

4. What is your gender?
   ☐ Female ☐ Male

5. What is your race?
   ☐ African American ☐ Asian ☐ Caucasian ☐ Latino ☐ Other

6. How many cigarettes do you now smoke in an average day? _____

Please drop this card into the survey box.
Thank you for your participation.

Hypotheses

Considering that this is the first run of this intervention, we have no plausible basis for presuming that any of the predictors will produce statistically significant findings (e.g., females will smoke more [or less] than males, those with higher income will smoke more [or less] than those with lower income, etc.). Naturally, such hypotheses could be drafted; however, for this initial run, we will take a less specific exploratory approach:

H_0: There is no correlation between age, income, baseline smoking, gender, or race and postintervention smoking rates.

H_1: There is a correlation between age, income, baseline smoking, gender, or race and postintervention smoking rates.

Data Set

Use the following data set: **Ch 12 – Example 01 – Multiple Regression.sav**.

Codebook

Variable:	Gender
Definition:	[Predictor] Gender
Type:	Categorical (0 = Female, 1 = Male)

Variable:	Race
Definition:	[Predictor] Race
Type:	Categorical (0 = African American, 1 = Asian, 2 = Caucasian, 3 = Latino, 4 = Other)

Variable:	Age
Definition:	[Predictor] Age
Type:	Continuous

Variable:	Income
Definition:	[Predictor] Annual gross income (in dollars)
Type:	Continuous

Variable:	Cigarettes
Definition:	[Predictor] Baseline mean number of cigarettes smoked daily
Type:	Continuous

Variable: Smoking_status

Definition: [Outcome] Mean number of cigarettes smoked at conclusion of the
               treatment

Type: Continuous

Dummy Variables

In addition to the above variables, notice that this data set contains four additional **dummy variables**: *Race.01*, *Race.02*, *Race.03*, and *Race.04*; (together) they contain a binary representation of the *Race* variable:

Race	Race.01	Race.02	Race.03	Race.04
0 (African American)	0	0	0	0
1 (Asian)	1	0	0	0
2 (Caucasian)	0	1	0	0
3 (Latino)	0	0	1	0
4 (Other)	0	0	0	1

This is the traditional way that polychotomous predictors are (re)coded and used in multiple regression as opposed to using *Race* as is. Considering that *Race* is a nominal categorical variable, there is no inherent order to these categories, and as such the numbering is arbitrary. In this case, the numbers were assigned to the races in alphabetical order: 0 = African American, 1 = Asian, 2 = Caucasian, 3 = Latino, 4 = Other. If *Race* was loaded into the multiple regression processor in this way, it would produce one set of results; however, if instead we had assigned the numbers in some other way (e.g., 0 = Latino, 1 = Other, 2 = African American, 3 = Asian, 4 = Caucasian), this would produce a different set of results. The use of the dummy-coded binary matrix controls for the effect that the categorical values (0, 1, 2, 3, and 4) for *Race* would have on the multiple regression processor.

NOTE: This type of **dummy coding** is not required for dichotomous (two category) variables such as *Gender*, wherein 0 = Female and 1 = Male.

The Test Run section of this chapter will explain how to load these dummy variables into the regression processor.

For the example and exercises in this chapter, the provided data sets include the supplemental dummy coding for all polychotomous variables. Chapter 14 includes a section explaining how to create dummy variables to represent polychotomous variables manually; however, because such data sets tend to be sizable, it is preferable to use the SPSS Syntax language to generate these dummy variables quickly and accurately (see the ★ on page 428).

Pretest Checklist

Multiple Regression Pretest Checklist

☑ 1. *n* quota*

☑ 2. Linearity*

☑ 3. Homoscedasticity**

☑ 4. Multicollinearity**

☑ 5. Normality**

*Run prior to multiple regression test.

**Results produced upon multiple regression test run.

NOTE: If any of the pretest checklist criteria are not satisfied, proceed with the analysis, but concisely discuss such anomalies in the Results or Limitations sections of the documentation so the reader can more plausibly interpret the precision of the findings.

Five pretest criteria need to be assessed to better ensure the robustness of the findings: (1) n *quota*, (2) *linearity*, (3) *homoscedasticity*, (4) *multicollinearity*, and (5) *normality*.

Pretest Checklist Criterion 1—*n* Quota

Considering that the multiple regression statistic is unique in that it accommodates both continuous and categorical predictor variables, there are several steps involved in determining the minimum required sample size.

NOTE: The process for determining *n* quota for logistic regression (Chapter 13) is the same as multiple regression:

1. Count the total number of continuous predictor variables (*Age, Income, Cigarettes*) = **3**.

2. Count the number of categories contained within each categorical variable (*Gender* and *Race*) and subtract 1 from each:

   - *Gender* has two categories (*Female, Male*): 2 – 1 = **1.**
   - *Race* has five categories (*African American, Asian, Caucasian, Latino, Other*): 5 – 1 = **4.**

3. Add the (**bold**) figures together: **3 + 1 + 4 = 8.**

4. Multiply that sum by 10: **8** × 10 = 80. The minimum *n* required to run this multiple regression is 80.

You may find it clearer to organize the variables in a table (Table 12.1).

- For each continuous variable, *n* = 10.
- For each categorical variable, *n* = (number of categories − 1) × 10.

Table 12.1	Assess the variables to determine the minimum *n* required (in this case, *n* = 80).

Variable	Type	Categorical (Categories − 1) × 10	Continuous 10
Age	Continuous		10
Income	Continuous		10
Cigarettes	Continuous		10
Gender	Categorical	10	
Race	Categorical	40	
Total *n* quota = 80		**50**	**30**

Proceed by verifying that the data set contains the minimum required *n* (80):

1. On the SPSS main menu, click on *Analyze, Descriptive Statistics, Frequency* (Figure 12.2).

Figure 12.2	To determine the *n* of the data set, click on *Analyze, Descriptive Statistics, Frequencies.*

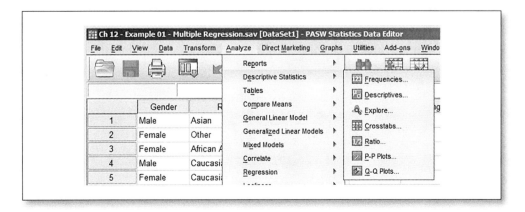

2. Move the outcome variable (*Smoking_Status*) into the *Variable(s)* window (Figure 12.3).

3. Click on *OK*.

Figure 12.3 On the *Frequencies* menu, move the outcome variable (*Smoking_status*) into the *Variable(s)* window.

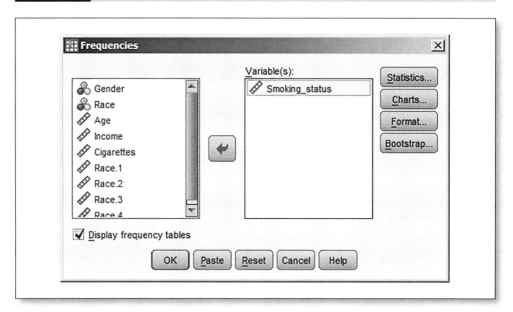

The *Smoking_status* table shows a *Total Frequency* (n) of 218, which is greater than the minimum required ($n = 80$); hence, this pretest criterion is satisfied (Table 12.2).

Table 12.2 Descriptive statistics for *Smoking_status*: Total (n) = 218.

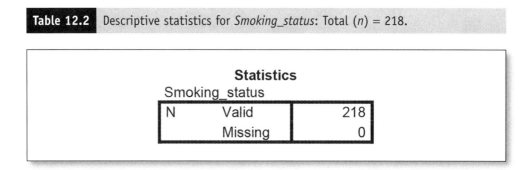

Statistics

Smoking_status

N	Valid	218
	Missing	0

Pretest Checklist Criterion 2—Linearity

To assess for possible violations of linearity among the continuous variables, we will order three separate scatterplots (one at a time) for each of the continuous predictor variables (*Age*, *Income*, and *Smoking*) paired with the outcome variable (*Smoking_status*).

1. Click on *Graphs*, *Chart Builder* (Figure 12.4).

Figure 12.4 Click on *Graphs, Chart Builder.*

		Ch 12 - Example 01 - Multiple Regression.sav [DataSet1] - PASW Statistics Data Editor					
File Edit View Data Transform Analyze Direct Marketing Graphs Utilities Add-ons Window Help							
	Gender	Race	Age	Income	Cigarettes	Smoking_status
1	Male	Asian	27	$93,000	33	4
2	Female	Other	56	$46,000	54	37

Menu items shown: Chart Builder..., Graphboard Template Chooser..., Legacy Dialogs

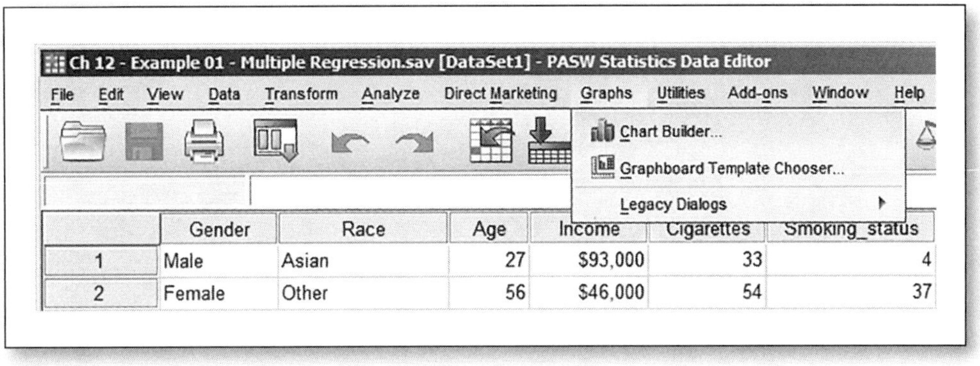

2. In the *Choose from*: list, click on *Scatter/Dot* (Figure 12.5).

3. Double-click on the (circled) first choice, or click and drag this icon to the *Chart preview uses example data* window.

4. Click and drag *Age* from the *Variables* window to the *X-Axis* box (Figure 12.5).

5. Click and drag *Smoking_status* from the *Variables* window to the *Y-Axis* box.

6. Click on the *OK* button, and the system will produce the scatterplot.

7. Repeat Steps 1 through 9, but at Step 7, click and drag *Income* to the *X-Axis* box.

8. Finally, repeat Steps 1 through 9, but at Step 7, click and drag *Cigarettes* to the *X-Axis* box.

Observe the corresponding scatterplots (Figures 12.6, 12.7, and 12.8). Remember, we are not necessarily looking for a perfect straight line shape in the arrangement of the points per se; we are actually looking for possible *violations of linearity*. For example, Figure 12.7 does not depict a particularly linear scatterplot, suggesting a relatively insignificant correlation between the variables; however, this does not constitute a violation

Figure 12.5 *Chart Builder* menu.

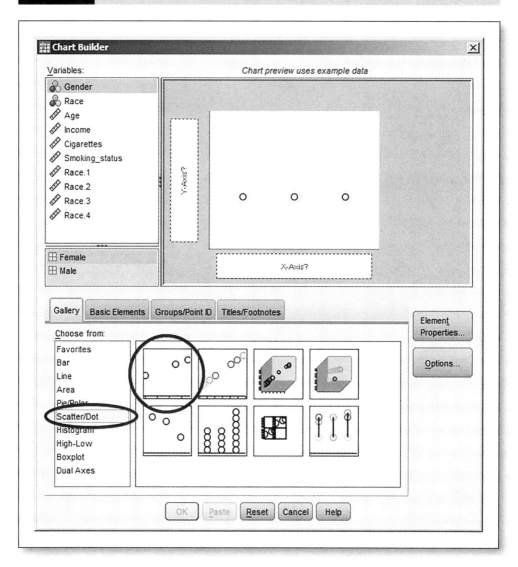

of the linearity criterion. A violation would involve a scatterplot that shows an unexpected curve or nonlinear arrangement of the cloud of points that might be shaped like a U, a J, or an S. Per the scatterplots in Figures 12.6, 12.7, and 12.8, this criterion passes.

The remaining three pretest criteria for multiple regression (*homoscedasticity*, *multicollinearity*, and *normality*) will be assessed when we inspect the results of the multiple regression run.

Figure 12.6   Scatterplot for *Age* : *Smoking_status*.

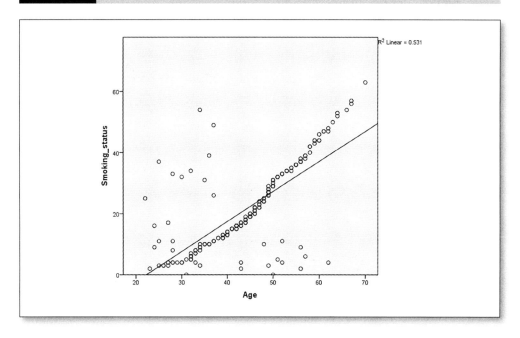

Figure 12.7   Scatterplot for *Income* : *Smoking_status*.

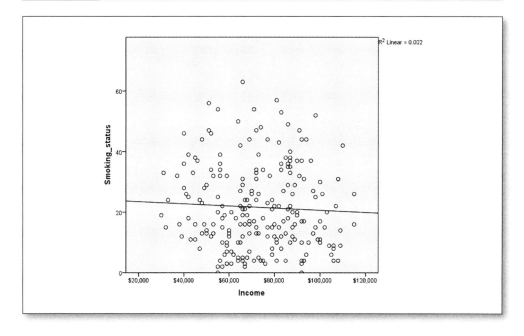

Figure 12.8 Scatterplot for *Cigarettes* : *Smoking_status*.

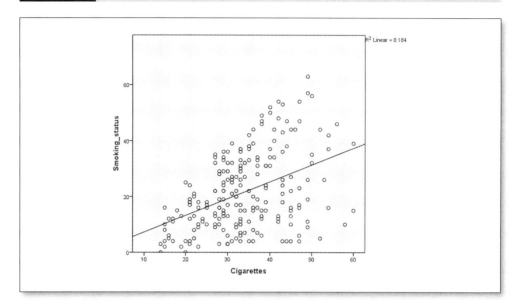

Test Run

1. On the main SPSS menu, click on *Analyze, Regression, Linear* (Figure 12.9).

2. On the *Linear Regression* menu (Figure 12.10), move the outcome variable *(Smoking_status)* into the *Dependent box.*

Figure 12.9 To run a multiple regression, click on *Analyze, Regression, Linear.*

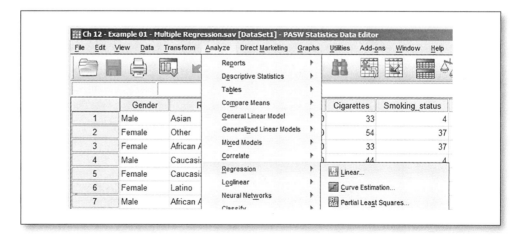

3. Move *Gender*, *Age*, *Income*, and *Cigarettes*) into the *Independent(s)* window.

4. Set *Method* to *Forward*.

Figure 12.10 *Linear Regression* menu—move outcome variable (*Smoking_status*) into the *Dependent* box and the continuous predictor variables (*Age*, *Income*, and *Cigarettes*) and dichotomous predictor variable (*Gender*) into the *Independent(s)* window.

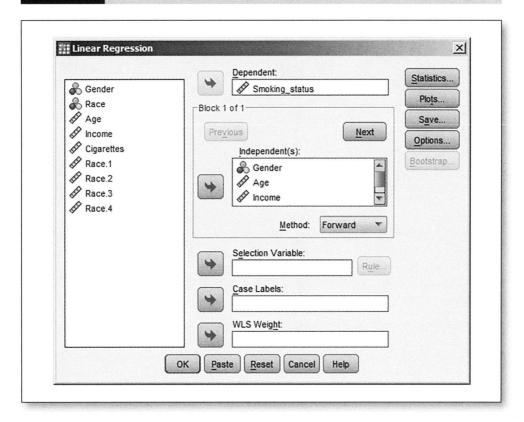

At this point, all of the variables are loaded into the model except for *Race*, which is a polychotomous variable. As discussed earlier, we will now load the dummy-coded variables (*Race.1*, *Race.2*, *Race.3*, and *Race.4*) into the multiple regression processor together as a group to represent *Race*.

5. On the *Linear Regression* menu, click on *Next*. Move *Race.1*, *Race.2*, *Race.3*, and *Race.4* into the *Independent(s)* window (Figure 12.11). NOTE: Due to the small window size, only the first three variables are showing in the *Independent(s)* window, but you can scroll down to see the fourth (*Race.4*).

Figure 12.11 *Linear Regression* menu—move the dummy-coded variables (*Race.1, Race.2, Race.3,* and *Race.4*) into the *Independent(s)* window.

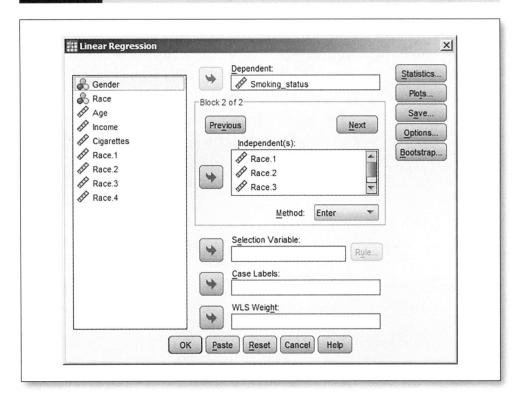

6. If there were more polychotomous variables that had been dummy coded, then you would repeat Step 5 for each variable. For example, suppose this data set also included *Marital_status*, which had the following dummy variables associated with it: *Marital_status.1*, *Marital_status.2*, and *Marital_status.3*. You would click *Next* and then move those three variables into the *Independent(s)* window. You can do this as many time as you need to, but make sure that all of the dummy variables are loaded together in each (*Next*) *Block* of data.

7. Click on *Statistics*.

8. On the *Linear Regression: Statistics* menu, check ☑ *R squared change* and ☑ *Collinearity diagnostics* (Figure 12.12).

9. Click *Continue*; this will take you back to the *Linear Regression* menu.

10. On the *Linear Regression* menu, click on *Save*.

11. On the *Linear Regression: Save* menu, under *Residuals*, check ☑ *Unstandardized* (Figure 12.13).

Figure 12.12

On the *Linear Regression: Statistics* menu, check ☑ *R squared change*, and ☑ *Collinearity diagnostics*.

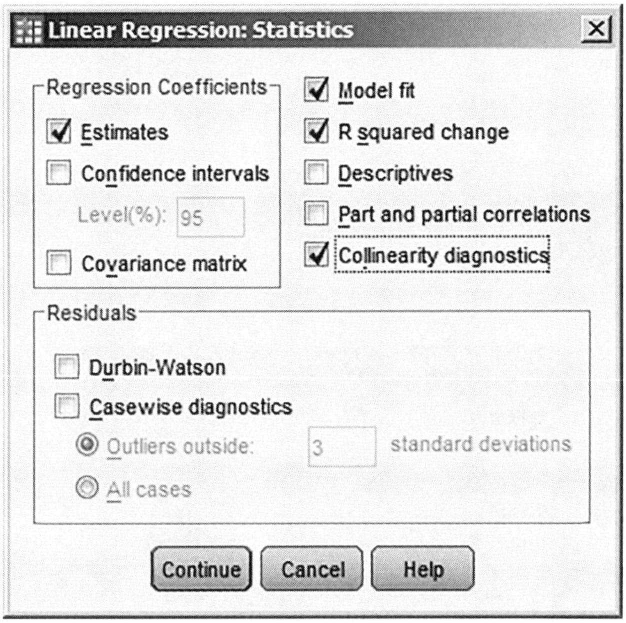

Figure 12.13

On the *Linear Regression: Save* menu, under *Residuals*, check ☑ *Unstandardized*.

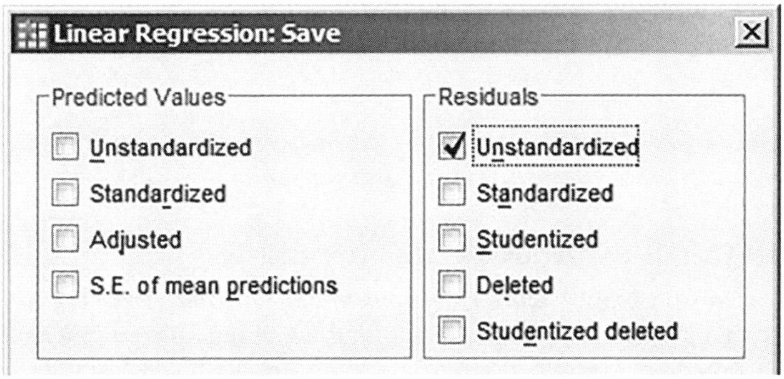

12. Click *Continue*. This will generate the temporary variable *RES_1*, which we will later assess using a histogram with a normal curve.

13. On the *Linear Regression* menu, click on *Plots*.

14. On the *Linear Regression: Plots* menu, move *ZPRED* (predicted) to *Y* and *ZRESID* (residual) to *X* (Figure 12.14).

15. Click *Continue*.

16. On the *Linear Regression* menu, click *OK*.

Figure 12.14.	On the *Linear Regression: Plots* menu, move *ZPRED* to *Y* and move *ZRESID* to *X*.

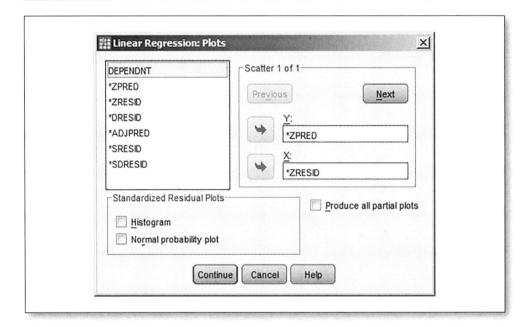

Results

Before inspecting the results, we will first assess the remaining three pretest criteria: *homoscedasticity*, *multicollinearity*, and *normality*.

Pretest Checklist Criterion 3—Homoscedasticity

Observe the graph: *Scatterplot Dependent Variable: Smoking_status* (Figure 12.15). Notice that most of the points are within the ±2 range. This signifies the *predicted* values in the outcome variable (*Smoking_status*) are within ±2 standard deviations of the *residuals* for this variable. This satisfies the homoscedasticity criterion.

Figure 12.15 Scatterplot of Dependent Variable graph: *Smoking_status*.

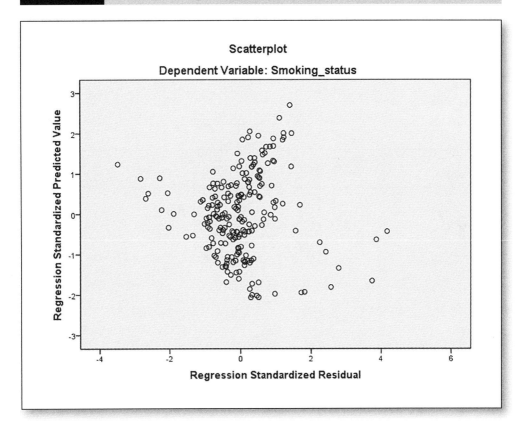

Pretest Checklist Criterion 4—Multicollinearity

The term *multicollinearity* describes two continuous variables that are very highly correlated such as *hand-size* and *glove-size*, which would produce a strong positive correlation. Loading two such variables into a multiple regression model essentially constitutes double-loading the processor; *checking that we do not have multicollinearity* assures us that each continuous variable that we intend to load into the logistic regression model is (statistically) unique.

To assess for multicollinearity, refer to the Coefficients table (Table 12.3), focusing on the last block of figures in the VIF (variance inflation factor) column. If the VIF is less than or equal to 5, this indicates that multicollinearity is not an issue for a variable. If the VIF for a row (variable) is between 5 and 10, this suggests that multicollinearity may be a problem. If the VIF for a variable is greater than 10, this indicates a problem with multicollinearity for that variable. In such cases, the recommended strategy is to remove one of the problematic (predictor) variables and rerun the analysis to see if this resolved the multicollinearity issue. This may require more than one pass, depending on the amount of predictor variables and the possible (strong) correlation(s) among them. Alternatively, in some cases, multicollinearity may be resolved by increasing the sample size. Depending on the nature of the data and the characteristics of the study, this may be a less feasible approach than eliminating predictor variables (one at a time).

Table 12.3 Observe that the VIF scores in the last Model (4) are less than 5.

Coefficients^a

Model		Unstandardized Coefficients		Standardized Coefficients			Collinearity Statistics	
		B	Std. Error	Beta	t	Sig.	Tolerance	VIF
1	(Constant)	-21.854	2.853		-7.661	.000		
	Age	.982	.063	.729	15.634	.000	1.000	1.000
2	(Constant)	-28.278	3.035		-9.318	.000		
	Age	.889	.063	.659	14.096	.000	.903	1.108
	Cigarettes	.312	.065	.223	4.767	.000	.903	1.108
3	(Constant)	-22.196	3.472		-6.393	.000		
	Age	.850	.063	.631	13.572	.000	.873	1.146
	Cigarettes	.243	.067	.174	3.621	.000	.819	1.221
	Gender	-4.410	1.311	-.159	-3.365	.001	.838	1.193
4	(Constant)	-21.096	3.712		-5.684	.000		
	Age	.852	.063	.632	13.537	.000	.870	1.149
	Cigarettes	.228	.070	.163	3.272	.001	.769	1.301
	Gender	-5.100	1.460	-.184	-3.492	.001	.680	1.470
	Race.1	.124	2.453	.002	.050	.960	.792	1.263
	Race.2	.808	1.713	.026	.472	.638	.604	1.655
	Race.3	-1.599	1.679	-.052	-.952	.342	.629	1.591
	Race.4	-1.204	2.259	-.028	-.533	.595	.696	1.436

a. Dependent Variable: Smoking_status

Pretest Checklist Criterion 5—Normality

In multiple regression, *normality* pertains to the distribution of the residuals in the outcome (Y) variable, in this case, *Smoking_status*. We ordered the regression process to calculate a temporary variable (*RES_1*) to contain the *Smoking_status* residual score for each record. This is the first time we have seen SPSS include a new variable in the data set; *RES_1* is the last variable and may be deleted after this criterion is processed. Order a histogram with a normal curve on *RES_1* to assess for normality.

1. Click on *Analyze, Descriptive Statistics, Frequency* (Figure 12.16).

2. On the *Frequencies* menu, move *Unstandardized Residual [RES_1]* to the *Variable(s)* window (Figure 12.17).

3. Click *Charts*.

Figure 12.16 Click on *Analyze, Descriptive Statistics, Frequencies.*

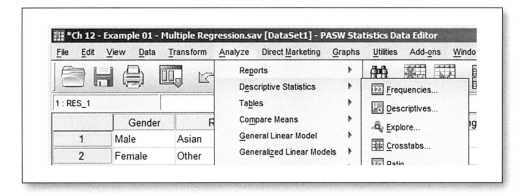

Figure 12.17 Move *Unstandardized Residual [RES_1]* to the *Variable(s).*

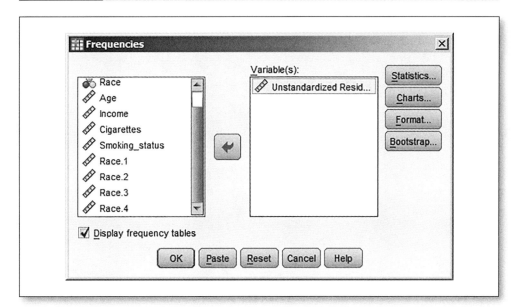

4. On the *Frequencies: Charts* menu, select *Histograms* with *Show normal curve on histogram* (Figure 12.18)

5. Click *Continue.*

6. On the *Frequencies* menu, click *OK.*

7. The residual distribution for the outcome variable (*Smoking_status*) shows a normal distribution (Figure 12.19); hence, this criterion is satisfied.

Figure 12.18   On the *Frequencies: Charts* menu, order a histogram with normal curve.

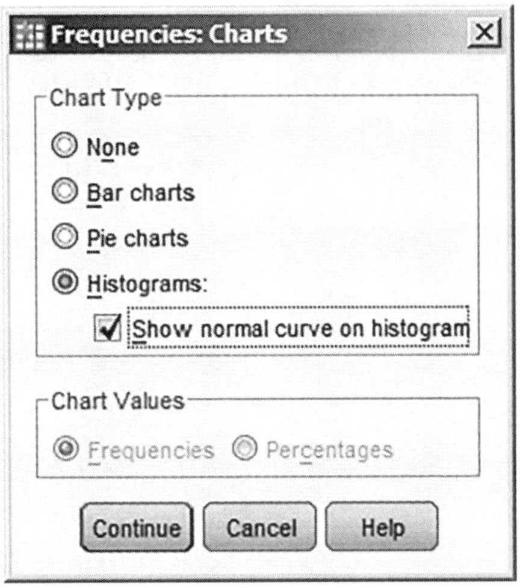

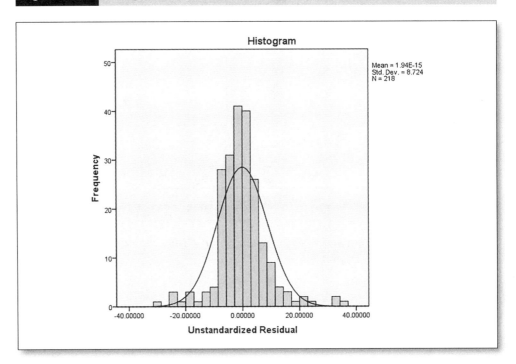

Figure 12.19   Histogram shows a normal distribution for *Smoking_status* residuals.

The primary results of the multiple regression are contained in the *Model Summary* table (Table 12.4). To better comprehend the key figures on this table, we will first briefly discuss how the multiple regression processor works: The multiple regression algorithm is an iterative process, meaning that it makes several passes through the data in order to construct the final model. We opted to use the ***Forward processing*** method for the first block of variables, which involved all of the predictor variables except for the dummy-coded polychotomous variable, *Race*. Dummy-coded variables need to be loaded into the model using a different method, which will be explained shortly.

The *Forward processing* method begins with an empty model, wherein the R^2 is initially set to 0. Next, it determines which predictor variable in that block (*Gender, Age, Income, Cigarettes*) has the strongest statistically significant correlation with the outcome variable (*Smoking_status*) and brings that variable into the model. On the *Model Summary* table (Figure 12.4), *Model 1*, we see that *Age* was brought in first. According to the *R Squared* (R^2) column, *Age* accounts for 53.1% of the variability in *Smoking_status*. Notice that the *R Squared Change* (R^2 *Change*) is .531 also, meaning that .531 has been added to the model since the last step, which makes sense because the R^2 begins at 0. The last column, *Sig. F Change*, indicates the *p* value for each model; because .000 < .05, this indicates that the *Age* predictor produced a statistically significant correlation to the outcome variable (*Smoking_status*).

This process will repeat itself until all of the predictor variables have been assessed. At this point, the processor evaluates the three remaining predictors (*Gender, Income, Cigarettes*) in this block and determined that among those, *Cigarettes* has the next strongest statistically significant correlation to the outcome variable (*Smoking_status*) (Figure 12.5). On the *Model 2* row, notice that with *Age* and *Cigarettes* included in the model, the overall R^2 is .576, indicating that *Age* and *Cigarettes*, together account for 57.6% of the variability observed in *Smoking_status*. The R^2 change is .045, meaning that the overall R^2 increased by .045 since the prior model (.576 – .531 = .045). The figures in the R^2 column will be particularly useful when documenting the results. Also,

Table 12.4 Multiple Regression Model Summary table—Model 1 (*Age*).

Model Summary

Model	R	R Square	Adjusted R Square	Std. Error of the Estimate	Change Statistics				
					R Square Change	F Change	df1	df2	Sig. F Change
1	.729[a]	.531	.529	9.488	.531	244.409	1	216	.000
2	.759[b]	.576	.572	9.044	.045	22.725	1	215	.000
3	.773[c]	.597	.591	8.834	.021	11.323	1	214	.001
4	.776[d]	.601	.588	8.868	.004	.589	4	210	.671

a. Predictors: (Constant), Age
b. Predictors: (Constant), Age, Cigarettes
c. Predictors: (Constant), Age, Cigarettes, Gender
d. Predictors: (Constant), Age, Cigarettes, Gender, Race.3, Race.1, Race.4, Race.2

Table 12.5 Multiple Regression Model Summary table—Model 2 (*Age, Cigarettes*).

Model Summary

Model	R	R Square	Adjusted R Square	Std. Error of the Estimate	Change Statistics				
					R Square Change	F Change	df1	df2	Sig. F Change
1	.729ᵃ	.531	.529	9.488	.531	244.409	1	216	.000
2	.759ᵇ	.576	.572	9.044	.045	22.725	1	215	.000
3	.773ᶜ	.597	.591	8.834	.021	11.323	1	214	.001
4	.776ᵈ	.601	.588	8.868	.004	.589	4	210	.671

a. Predictors: (Constant), Age
b. Predictors: (Constant), Age, Cigarettes
c. Predictors: (Constant), Age, Cigarettes, Gender
d. Predictors: (Constant), Age, Cigarettes, Gender, Race.3, Race.1, Race.4, Race.2

Table 12.6 Multiple Regression Model Summary table—Model 3 (*Age, Cigarettes, Gender*).

Model Summary

Model	R	R Square	Adjusted R Square	Std. Error of the Estimate	Change Statistics				
					R Square Change	F Change	df1	df2	Sig. F Change
1	.729ᵃ	.531	.529	9.488	.531	244.409	1	216	.000
2	.759ᵇ	.576	.572	9.044	.045	22.725	1	215	.000
3	.773ᶜ	.597	.591	8.834	.021	11.323	1	214	.001
4	.776ᵈ	.601	.588	8.868	.004	.589	4	210	.671

a. Predictors: (Constant), Age
b. Predictors: (Constant), Age, Cigarettes
c. Predictors: (Constant), Age, Cigarettes, Gender
d. Predictors: (Constant), Age, Cigarettes, Gender, Race.3, Race.1, Race.4, Race.2

notice that the *p* value (*Sig. F Change*) is .000; this is < .05 and thus explains why *Cigarettes* was brought into this model—it is statistically significant.

In the next iteration, this processor evaluates the two remaining predictors (*Gender, Income*) in this block and determined that among those, *Gender* has the next strongest statistically significant correlation to the outcome variable (*Smoking_status*) (Figure 12.6). On the *Model 3* row, notice that with *Age, Cigarettes,* and *Gender* included in the model, bringing the overall R^2 to .597, indicating that *Age, Cigarettes* and *Gender*, together account for 59.7% of the variability observed in *Smoking_status*. The R^2 change is .021, meaning that the overall R^2 increased by .021 because the prior model is as follows: (.597 − .576 = .021). Notice that the *p* value (*Sig. F Change*) is .001; this is < .05, and thus explains why *Gender* was brought into this model—it is statistically significant.

To conclude our discussion of the predictor variables in Block 1, notice that *Income* is not included in the model because *Income* does not have (statistically significant) predictive value with respect to *Smoking_status*.

Finally, notice that *Race* is included in the last row of the Model Summary table even though it is statistically insignificant ($p = .671$). This is because we used the **Enter processing** method to force *Race.1*, *Race.2*, *Race.3*, and *Race.4* into the model (together) regardless of the statistical significance. Notice that when multiple variables are loaded into the model together using the *enter* method, it bundles all of the variables together to produce a single set of results (Row 4). This produced a statistically insignificant correlation ($p = .671$), so we will not regard *Race* as a viable predictor in this model.

Hypothesis Resolution

Referring to the Model Summary table, Age, Cigarettes, and Gender produced statistically significant results ($p < .05$), so we would reject H_0 and accept H_1.

REJECT H_0: There is no correlation between age, income, baseline smoking, gender, or race and

postintervention smoking rates.

ACCEPT H_1: There is a correlation between age, income, baseline smoking, gender, or race and

postintervention smoking rates.

Abstract

As a public service, the Acme Health Center advertises and offers a free 90-day smoking cessation program, consisting of nurse-facilitated psychoeducational meetings, peer support from those who have been smoke free for more than 1 year, and multimedia resources designed to promote smoking cessation. This program attracted 218 voluntary participants. To better comprehend the variables associated with the postintervention smoking rate, at the conclusion of the intervention, we conducted an anonymous self-administered survey to gather each participant's age, gender, race, income, average number of cigarettes smoked per day prior to the intervention, and current daily smoking. Multiple regression analysis revealed an overall R^2 of .597, wherein age accounts for 53.1% of the variability observed in the current smoking rate, baseline smoking rate accounts for an additional 4.5%, and gender accounts for 2.1%. The remaining predictor variables were found to be statistically insignificant ($\alpha = .05$).

SUPPLEMENTAL PROCESSING METHODS

The multiple regression statistics demonstrated in this chapter were processed using the *Forward* method for the first block of data, which contained continuous and dichotomous predictors (*Gender*, *Age*, *Income*), and the *Enter* method was used in the second block to load the dummy predictor variables that represent *Race* (*Race.1*, *Race.2*, *Race.3*, *Race.4*) into the processor. These processing methods should be used to run the Practice Exercises in this chapter; however, in addition to *Forward* and *Enter*, it is worth mentioning the other processing *methods*: *Stepwise, Remove, Backward*.

Forward progressively identifies and loads statistically significant predictors into the model, starting with the predictor that has the highest correlation to the outcome variable.

Stepwise is similar to *Forward*, except that each time the processor accepts the next statistically significant predictor into the model, it checks to determine if there is an interaction effect between the new predictor and the predictors that have already been admitted into the model. If such an interaction causes a predictor to lose statistical significance, then that variable will be dropped from the model.

Enter forces a predictor into the model whether it is statistically significant or not. As with the other methods, you can include one or several predictors at a time. The *Enter* method produces one set of results for each block of predictors; hence if a block includes more than one predictor, it would be unclear which specific predictor(s) in that block were statistically significant and which were not. In the example in this chapter, *Race.1*, *Race.2*, *Race.3*, and *Race.4* were all loaded together into *Block 2* using the *Enter* method, which produced a single set of results.

Remove is the opposite of *Enter*. Whereas *Enter* loads predictors into the model regardless of its statistical significance, *Remove* deletes predictors from the model even if a predictor is statistically significant.

Backward is the opposite of *Forward*. Whereas *Forward* begins with an empty model and systematically loads statistically significant predictors into the model, *Backward* begins by loading all the predictors into the model and then systematically drops statistically insignificant predictors out of the model.

Upon completing each of the Practice Exercises in this chapter using the *Forward* method for the first block of data, you may want to rerun selected exercises using other processing methods and observe the effect that each method has on the results.

GOOD COMMON SENSE

If you are interested in gaining a more detailed understanding of the predictor variables, you can conduct further tests. For example, for a continuous predictor, you could run a (Pearson) bivariate correlation between *Age* and *Smoking_status* and refer to the scatterplot that you ran as part of the pretest checklist. Additionally, for categorical predictors, you could use a *t* test or ANOVA test (e.g., Group [Factor] = *Gender* and outcome variable [Dependent] = *Smoking_status*).

There may be times when it is plausible to recode the DV (outcome variable) to a dichotomous variable; this would enable you to (re)assess the data using logistic regression, which will be covered in the next chapter. For example, suppose the goal for the first month of a smoking cessation program is to get the participant's smoking rate down to 10 or fewer cigarettes per day. To represent the results of this first month (success or failure) in the data set, we could use the *Recode* function to create a new variable called *Month1_status*. This would be a dichotomous variable (0 = Fail, 1 = Success), that is derived from the contents of *Smoking_status*, which contains the mean number of cigarettes that the participants are currently smoking per day. The logic for the recoding would say *If Smoking_status > 10, then Month1_status = 0 (Fail), otherwise, Month1_status = 1 (Pass)*. As you will see in the next chapter, logistic regression produces a different system of results that may provide additional insights regarding the relationships among the variables.

Key Concepts

- Multiple regression
- Pretest checklist

    ○ *n* quota
    ○ Linearity
    ○ Homoscedasticity
    ○ Multicollinearity
    ○ Normality

- R^2 statistic
- Categorical variable labeling
- Dichotomous/polychotomous categorical variables
- Dummy coding polychotomous categorical variables
- *Forward processing*
- *Enter processing*
- Hypothesis resolution
- Documenting results
- Good common sense

Practice Exercises

Exercises 12.3, 12.4, 12.5, 12.6, 12.9, and 12.10 involve polychotomous predictor variables; these data sets contain the corresponding dummy-coded variables. Each of these exercises includes a Technical Tip to help guide you load the variables into the multiple regression processor.

Exercise 12.1

A public health nurse has conducted a survey of people in the community to better comprehend the effectiveness of the flu shot this season using the following survey instrument:

Flu Survey

1. Gender: ☐ Female   ☐ Male

2. How old are you? _____

3. Did you have a flu shot this season?   ☐ No   ☐ Yes

4. Do you have any chronic disease(s)?   ☐ No   ☐ Yes

5. How many days were you sick with the flu this season? _____

Data set: **Ch 12 – Exercise 01A.sav**

Codebook

Variable:	Flu_sick
Definition:	[Outcome] How many days were you sick with the flu this season?
Type:	Continuous

Variable:	Gender
Definition:	[Predictor] Gender
Type:	Categorical (0 = Female, 1 = Male)

Variable:	Flu_shot
Definition:	[Predictor] Did person have a flu shot this season?
Type:	Categorical (0 = Got a flu shot, 1 = Did not get a flu shot)

Variable:	Chronic_disease
Definition:	[Predictor] Does the person have chronic disease(s)?
Type:	Categorical (0 = Has chronic disease(s), 1 = No chronic disease(s))

Variable:	Age
Definition:	[Predictor] Age
Type:	Continuous

a. Write the hypotheses.

b. Run each criterion of the pretest checklist (sample size, normality, multicollinearity) and discuss your findings.

c. Run the multiple regression analysis and document your findings (overall R^2, R^2 change of statistically significant predictors, hypotheses resolution).

d. Write an abstract under 200 words detailing a summary of the study, the multiple regression analysis results, hypothesis resolution, and implications of your findings.

Repeat this exercise using data set: **Ch 12 – Exercise 01B.sav**.

NOTE: This data set (**Ch 12 – Exercise 01B.sav**) is the same as the first data set except the *Age* variable has been recoded from a continuous variable that contained the actual ages to a categorical variable, now coded as *Pediatric/Adult*, using the following recoding criteria:

- If Age < 18, then recode as 0 = Pediatric
- If Age ≥ 18, then recode as 1 = Adult

The corresponding modification has been made to the codebook:

Variable:	Age
Definition:	[Predictor] Age
Type:	Categorical (0 = Pediatric, 1 = Adult)

Exercise 12.2

Acme Solar Systems wants to discover the characteristics of those who intend to install solar energy systems in their homes.

Data set: **Ch 12 – Exercise 02A.sav**

Codebook

Variable:	Install
Definition:	[Outcome] Self-reported likelihood that the person would opt for solar energy within the next 12 months.
Type:	Continuous (1 = Absolutely will not . . . 10 = Absolutely will)
Variable:	Age
Definition:	[Predictor] Age
Type:	Continuous

Variable:	Gender
Definition:	[Predictor] Gender
Type:	Categorical (0 = Female, 1 = Male)

Variable:	Income
Definition:	[Predictor] Annual household income
Type:	Continuous

Variable:	Neighborhood
Definition:	[Predictor] Type of neighborhood
Type:	Categorical (0 = Urban, 1 = Rural)

Variable:	Family
Definition:	[Predictor] Number of people living in the household
Type:	Continuous

a. Write the hypotheses.

b. Run each criterion of the pretest checklist (sample size, normality, multicollinearity) and discuss your findings.

c. Run the multiple regression analysis and document your findings (overall R^2, R^2 change of statistically significant predictors, hypotheses resolution).

d. Write an abstract under 200 words detailing a summary of the study, the multiple regression analysis results, hypothesis resolution, and implications of your findings.

Repeat this exercise using data set: **Ch 12 – Exercise 02B.sav**.

Exercise 12.3

A public opinion consultant is interested in the demographics of those who are in favor of capital punishment (death penalty).

Data set: **Ch 12 – Exercise 03A.sav**

Codebook

Variable:	Death_penalty
Definition:	[Outcome] Are you in favor of the death penalty?
Type:	Continuous (1 = Anti-death penalty . . . 10 = Pro-death penalty)

Variable:	Age
Definition:	[Predictor] Age
Type:	Continuous

Variable:	Gender
Definition:	[Predictor] Gender
Type:	Categorical (0 = Female, 1 = Male)

Variable:	Race
Definition:	[Predictor] Race
Type:	Categorical (0 = African American, 1 = Asian, 2 = Caucasian, 3 = Latino, 4 = Other)

Variable:	Religion
Definition:	[Predictor] Religion
Type:	Categorical (0 = Atheist, 1 = Buddhist, 2 = Catholic, 3 = Hindu, 4 = Jewish, 5 = Other)

Variable:	Education
Definition:	[Predictor] Years of education (High school = 12, Associate's = 14, Bachelor's = 16, Master's = 18, Doctorate > 18)
Type:	Continuous

This data set contains two polychotomous predictor variables (*Race* and *Religion*), which are represented by the corresponding dummy-coded variables. Follow this load procedure:

1. Move *Death_penalty* into the *Dependent* box.

2. Move *Age*, *Gender*, and *Education* into the *Independent(s)* box.

3. Set *Method* to *Forward*.

4. Click *Next*.

5. Move *Race.1*, *Race.2*, *Race.3*, and *Race.4* into the *Independent(s)* box.

6. Click *Next*.

7. Move *Religion.1*, *Religion.2*, *Religion.3*, *Religion.4*, and *Religion.5* into the *Independent(s)* box.

a. Write the hypotheses.

b. Run each criterion of the pretest checklist (sample size, normality, multi-collinearity) and discuss your findings.

c. Run the multiple regression analysis and document your findings (overall R^2, R^2 change of statistically significant predictors, hypotheses resolution).

d. Write an abstract under 200 words detailing a summary of the study, the multiple regression analysis results, hypothesis resolution, and implications of your findings.

Repeat this exercise using data set: **Ch 12 – Exercise 03B.sav**.

NOTE: The B data set is the same as the A data set with the following modifications:

- The *Education* variable has been recoded from a continuous variable (total number of years of education) to a categorical variable (0 = No college degree, 1 = College degree)

Exercise 12.4

Acme Employment Services wants to evaluate the effectiveness of its "Get That Job" seminars, which consists of experts facilitating sessions designed to enhance resume writing, job search strategies, and interviewing techniques. After 90 days, participants are surveyed to assess their characteristics and outcomes.

Data set: **Ch 12 – Exercise 04A.sav**

Codebook

Variable:	Employment_status
Definition:	[Outcome] Number of days it took to find a job
Type:	Continuous (1 . . . 90; 90 = Still looking for work)

Variable:	Age
Definition:	[Predictor] Age
Type:	Continuous

Variable:	Gender
Definition:	[Predictor] Gender
Type:	Categorical (0 = Female, 1 = Male)

Variable: Race

Definition: [Predictor] Race

Type: Categorical (0 = African American, 1 = Asian, 2 = Caucasian, 3 = Latino, 4 = Other)

Variable: Experience

Definition: [Predictor] Years of experience working in their current field

Type: Continuous

Variable: Applications

Definition: [Predictor] Total number of job applications submitted

Type: Continuous

This data set contains a polychotomous predictor variable (*Race*), which is represented by the corresponding dummy-coded variables. Follow this load procedure:

1. Move *Employment_status* into the *Dependent* box.

2. Move *Gender, Experience*, and *Applications* into the *Independent(s)* box.

3. Set *Method* to *Forward*.

4. Click *Next*.

5. Move *Race.1, Race.2, Race.3*, and *Race.4* into the *Independent(s)* box.

   a. Write the hypotheses.

   b. Run each criterion of the pretest checklist (sample size, normality, multicollinearity) and discuss your findings.

   c. Run the multiple regression analysis and document your findings (overall R^2, R^2 change of statistically significant predictors, hypotheses resolution).

   d. Write an abstract under 200 words detailing a summary of the study, the multiple regression analysis results, hypothesis resolution, and implications of your findings.

Repeat this exercise using data set: **Ch 12 – Exercise 04B.sav**.

Exercise 12.5

A therapist at the Acme College Counseling Center noted a high prevalence of adjustment disorder among incoming freshmen, with depression being the predominate symptom. The clinicians want to determine the characteristics of those most amenable to therapy over a course of 10 sessions.

Data set: **Ch 12 – Exercise 05A.sav**

Codebook

> Variable: Treatment_effectiveness
>
> Definition: [Outcome] Score on the Acme Adjustment Scale
>
> Type: Continuous (5 = Poorly adjusted . . . 40 = Well adjusted)

> Variable: Gender
>
> Definition: [Predictor] Gender
>
> Type: Categorical (0 = Female, 1 = Male)

> Variable: Age
>
> Definition: [Predictor] Age
>
> Type: Continuous

> Variable: Units
>
> Definition: [Predictor] Number of units the student is enrolled in
>
> Type: Continuous

> Variable: Work
>
> Definition: [Predictor] Number of hours of (nonacademic) work per week
>
> Type: Continuous

> Variable: Treatment_modality
>
> Definition: [Predictor] Form of treatment
>
> Type: Categorical (0 = Individual, 1 = Group)

> Variable: Home
>
> Definition: [Predictor] Living conditions at home
>
> Type: Categorical (0 = Lives with family, 1 = Lives with roommate(s), 2 = Lives alone)

This data set contains a polychotomous predictor variable (*Home*), which is represented by the corresponding dummy-coded variables. Follow this load procedure:

1. Move *Treatment_effectiveness* into the *Dependent* box.

2. Move *Gender, Age, Units, Work,* and *Treatment_modality* into the *Independent(s)* box.

3. Set *Method* to *Forward*.

4. Click *Next*.

5. Move *Home.1* and *Home.2* into the *Independent(s)* box.

    a. Write the hypotheses.

    b. Run each criterion of the pretest checklist (sample size, normality, multicollinearity) and discuss your findings.

    c. Run the multiple regression analysis and document your findings (overall R^2, R^2 change of statistically significant predictors, hypotheses resolution).

    d. Write an abstract under 200 words detailing a summary of the study, the multiple regression analysis results, hypothesis resolution, and implications of your findings.

Repeat this exercise using data set: **Ch 12 – Exercise 05B.sav**.

Exercise 12.6

A technology firm wants to determine the characteristics of potential customers for a new voice-activated home entertainment system.

Data set: **Ch 12 – Exercise 06A.sav**

Codebook

    Variable: Purchase

    Definition: [Outcome] Will the person buy this within 6 months?

    Type: Continuous (0 = Will not buy it . . . 100 = Will buy it)

    Variable: Gender

    Definition: [Predictor] Gender

    Type: Categorical (0 = Female, 1 = Male)

    Variable: Race

    Definition: [Predictor] Race

    Type: Categorical (0 = African American, 1 = Asian, 2 = Caucasian, 3 = Latino, 4 = Other)

    Variable: Partner

    Definition: [Predictor] Relational status

    Type: Categorical (0 = Single, 1 = Partner)

Variable: Age

Definition: [Predictor] Age

Type: Continuous

Variable: Income

Definition: [Predictor] Annual income

Type: Continuous

Variable: Brand_ownership

Definition: [Predictor] Does the person already own any other product(s) of this brand

Type: Categorical (0 = Does not own this brand, 1 = Owns this brand)

This data set contains a polychotomous predictor variable (*Race*), which is represented by the corresponding dummy-coded variables. Follow this load procedure:

1. Move *Purchase* into the *Dependent* box.

2. Move *Gender, Partner, Age, Income,* and *Brand_ownership* into the *Independent(s)* box.

3. Set *Method* to *Forward*.

4. Click *Next*.

5. Move *Race.1, Race.2, Race.3,* and *Race.4* into the *Independent(s)* box.

   a. Write the hypotheses.

   b. Run each criterion of the pretest checklist (sample size, normality, multicollinearity) and discuss your findings.

   c. Run the multiple regression analysis and document your findings (overall R^2, R^2 change of statistically significant predictors, hypotheses resolution).

   d. Write an abstract under 200 words detailing a summary of the study, the multiple regression analysis results, hypothesis resolution, and implications of your findings.

Repeat this exercise using data set: **Ch 12 – Exercise 06B.sav**.

Exercise 12.7

Acme Coffee, which currently sells gourmet coffee blends, is now considering selling a single-serve coffee maker that brews a cup of coffee in 30 seconds. They conduct a survey to help identify the characteristics of potential customers for this high-tech coffee brewer.

Data set: **Ch 12 – Exercise 07A.sav**

Codebook

Variable:	Buy
Definition:	[Outcome] Would you consider buying this coffee brewer?
Type:	Continuous (1 = Will not buy it, 5 = Might buy it, 9 = Will buy it)

Variable:	Age
Definition:	[Predictor] Age
Type:	Continuous

Variable:	Gender
Definition:	[Predictor] Gender
Type:	Categorical (0 = Female, 1 = Male)

Variable:	Acme_Coffee
Definition:	[Predictor] Does the person currently drink Acme Coffee?
Type:	Categorical (0 = Not an Acme Coffee drinker, 1 = Drinks Acme Coffee)

Variable:	Income
Definition:	[Predictor] Annual household income
Type:	Continuous

a. Write the hypotheses.

b. Run each criterion of the pretest checklist (sample size, normality, multicollinearity) and discuss your findings.

c. Run the multiple regression analysis and document your findings (overall R^2, R^2 change of statistically significant predictors, hypotheses resolution).

d. Write an abstract under 200 words detailing a summary of the study, the multiple regression analysis results, hypothesis resolution, and implications of your findings.

Repeat this exercise using data set: **Ch 12 – Exercise 07B.sav**.

Exercise 12.8

In an effort to identify the characteristics of incoming high school students who are most vulnerable to dropping out, the research staff gathered data on the senior students at the end of the school year. Based on these data, freshmen who are identified as vulnerable to dropping out will be offered access to free comprehensive tutorial services.

Data set: **Ch 12 – Exercise 08A.sav**

Codebook

Variable:	HS_completion
Definition:	[Outcome] Overall academic performance (0 . . . 100)
Type:	Continuous

Variable:	Gender
Definition:	[Predictor] Gender
Type:	Categorical (0 = Female, 1 = Male)

Variable:	Adjusted_income
Definition:	[Predictor] Annual household income ÷ number of people in household
Type:	Continuous

Variable:	Education_parents
Definition:	[Predictor] Highest years of parent's education
Type:	Continuous (e.g., High school = 12, Associate's = 14, Bachelor's = 16, Master's = 18, Doctorate > 18)

Variable:	Language_skill
Definition: exam	[Predictor] Pre–high school reading and writing skills placement
Type:	Continuous

Variable:	Math_skill
Definition:	[Predictor] Pre–high school math skills placement exam
Type:	Continuous

a. Write the hypotheses.

b. Run each criterion of the pretest checklist (sample size, normality, multicollinearity) and discuss your findings.

c. Run the multiple regression analysis and document your findings (overall R^2, R^2 change of statistically significant predictors, hypotheses resolution).

d. Write an abstract under 200 words detailing a summary of the study, the multiple regression analysis results, hypothesis resolution, and implications of your findings.

Repeat this exercise using data set: **Ch 12 – Exercise 08B.sav**.

NOTE:

- The *Education_parents* variable has been recoded from a continuous variable (total number of years of education) to a categorical variable (0 = No college degree, 1 = College degree)

Exercise 12.9

The Transplant Committee wants to gain a better understanding of those who opt to be an organ donor upon their death.

Data set: **Ch 12 – Exercise 09A.sav**

Codebook

Variable:	Organ_donor
Definition:	[Outcome] Likelihood that the person will be an organ donor?
Type:	Continuous (0 = Would not be an organ donor . . . 100 = Would willingly be an organ donor)

Variable:	Gender
Definition:	[Predictor] Gender
Type:	Categorical (0 = Female, 1 = Male)

Variable:	Age
Definition:	[Predictor] Age
Type:	Continuous

Variable:	Religion
Definition:	[Predictor] Religion
Type:	Categorical (0 = Atheist, 1 = Buddhist, 2 = Catholic, 3 = Hindu, 4 = Jewish, 5 = Other)

Variable:	SES
Definition:	[Predictor] Socioeconomic status
Type:	Categorical (0 = Lower class, 1 = Middle class, 2 = Upper class)

This data set contains two polychotomous predictor variables (*Religion* and *SES*), which are represented by the corresponding dummy-coded variables. Follow this load procedure:

1. Move *Organ_donor* into the *Dependent* box.

2. Move *Gender* and *Age* into the *Independent(s)* box.

3. Set *Method* to *Forward*.

4. Click *Next*.

5. Move *Religion.1*, *Religion.2*, *Religion.3*, *Religion.4*, *Religion.5*, into the *Independent(s)* box.

6. Click *Next*.

7. Move *SES.1*, and *SES.2* into the *Independent(s)* box.

   a. Write the hypotheses.

   b. Run each criterion of the pretest checklist (sample size, normality, multicollinearity) and discuss your findings.

   c. Run the multiple regression analysis and document your findings (overall R^2, R^2 change of statistically significant predictors, hypotheses resolution).

   d. Write an abstract under 200 words detailing a summary of the study, the multiple regression analysis results, hypothesis resolution, and implications of your findings.

Repeat this exercise using data set: **Ch 12 – Exercise 09B.sav**.

Exercise 12.10

The Acme Industries Safety Supervisor wants to determine the factors that predict employees passing the annual required site safety competency training course.

Data set: **Ch 12 – Exercise 10A.sav**

Codebook

Variable:	Test_result
Definition:	[Outcome] Score (percentage) on annual safety exam?
Type:	Continuous (0 . . . 100)

Variable:	Training_type
Definition:	[Predictor] Training type
Type:	Categorical (0 = Workbook, 1 = Online course, 2 = Simulation lab)

Variable: Years

Definition: [Predictor] Years of professional experience

Type: Continuous

Variable: Employment_hours

Definition: [Predictor] Part-time or full-time

Type: Categorical (0 = Part-time, 1 = Full-time)

This data set contains a polychotomous predictor variables (*Training_type*), which is represented by the corresponding dummy-coded variables. Follow this load procedure:

1. Move *Test_result* into the *Dependent* box.

2. Move *Years* and *Employment_hours* into the *Independent(s)* box.

3. Set *Method* to *Forward*.

4. Click *Next*.

5. Move *Training_type.1* and *Training_type.2* into the *Independent(s)* box.

   a. Write the hypotheses.

   b. Run each criterion of the pretest checklist (sample size, normality, multicollinearity) and discuss your findings.

   c. Run the multiple regression analysis and document your findings (overall R^2, R^2 change of statistically significant predictors, hypotheses resolution).

   d. Write an abstract under 200 words detailing a summary of the study, the multiple regression analysis results, hypothesis resolution, and implications of your findings.

Repeat this exercise using data set: **Ch 12 – Exercise 10B.sav**.

CHAPTER 13

Logistic Regression

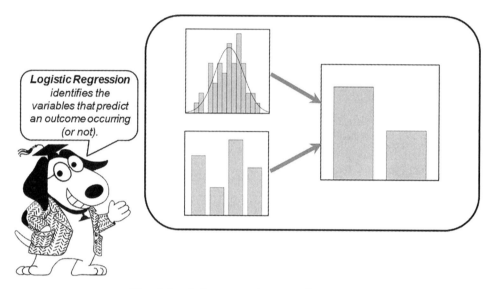

Logistic Regression identifies the variables that predict an outcome occurring (or not).

*The right choices over time greatly improve
your odds of a long and healthy life.*

—Tom Rath

Learning Objectives

Upon completing this chapter, you will be able to do the following:

- Determine when it is appropriate to run a logistic regression analysis.
- Verify that the data meet the criteria for logistic regression processing: sample size, normality, and multicollinearity.
- Order a logistic regression test.
- Comprehend the logistic regression R^2 statistic.
- Label and derive results from the *Variables in the Equation* table.
- Selectively process findings to respond to a variety of research questions.
- Understand the rationale for recoding categorical variables.
- Resolve the hypotheses.
- Write an appropriate abstract.

WHEN TO USE THIS STATISTIC

Guidelines for Selecting the Logistic Regression Test

Overview: This statistic indicates which variables predict a dichotomous (two-category) outcome.

Variables: This statistic can accommodate multiple continuous and categorical predictor variables with one dichotomous outcome variable for each record.

Results: After a group of smokers engaged in a smoking cessation program, we gathered data detailing their baseline daily smoking rates, age, gender, race, and income. Logistic regression analysis revealed that males had 22.223 times the odds of quitting smoking compared to females ($p < .001$; 95% CI 8.63, 57.24). Those who indicated that their race designation was "Other" had 8 times the odds of quitting smoking compared to African Americans ($p = .004$; 95% CI 1.95, 32.97). Older participants were more likely to quit than those who were younger; for every additional year of age, the odds of quitting smoking increased by 10.7% ($p < .001$; 95% CI 1.06, 1.16). For every additional cigarette smoked per day at baseline, the odds of quitting smoking decreased by 5.4% ($p = .015$; 95% CI .90, .99, $\alpha = .05$).

VIDEO

The tutorial video for this chapter is **Ch 13 – Logistic Regression.mp4**. This video provides an overview of the logistic regression statistic, followed by the SPSS procedures for processing the pretest checklist, ordering the statistical run, and interpreting the results of this test using the data set: **Ch 13 – Example 01 – Logistic Regression.sav.**

OVERVIEW—LOGISTIC REGRESSION

In health science, there are interventions, experiments, and general happenstances that produce dichotomous results, wherein one of two possible outcomes occurs. For example, resuscitation could be thought of as having one of two possible outcomes—the patient either does or does not survive. Other examples that could be considered as having dichotomous outcomes involve the following: did/did not pass an exam, did/did not get a job, did/did not achieve a goal, did/did not submit an assignment on time, and does/does not own a pet.

In addition to including the outcome variable (e.g., still smoking/quit smoking) in a **logistic regression** model, it also includes (predictor) variables (e.g., age, income, baseline daily smoking, gender, race); these are variables that are reasonably thought to be associated with the outcome variable. The logistic regression processor assesses the relationships among the variables to provide a model that describes the (predictive) factors associated with the observed outcome.

While the logistic regression model insists on a dichotomous (two-category) outcome variable, you may have surmised from this example that this statistic is liberal in terms of the types of predictor variables that can be included. Logistic regression accommodates continuous predictor variables (e.g., age, income, baseline daily smoking), categorical predictor variables (e.g., gender, race), or any combinations(s) thereof.

The findings from a logistic regression model can provide insights as to the outcome of a current investigation, or in some cases, the findings may serve as a viable predictive model, anticipating the outcome of a future similar circumstance.

Example

A nurse has conducted a smoking cessation workshop for a wide variety of patients who wish to quit smoking. At the conclusion of the series, instead of simply calculating the percentage of the participants who quit smoking, logistic regression is used to better comprehend the characteristics of those who succeeded.

Research Question

What influences do (predictive) variables such as age, income, baseline mean number of cigarettes smoked daily, gender, and race have when it comes to quitting (or not quitting) smoking?

Groups

In this example, all the members are included in a single group—everyone receives the same smoking cessation intervention.

Procedure

As a public service, the Acme Health Center advertises and offers a free 90-day smoking cessation program, consisting of nurse-facilitated psychoeducational meetings, peer support from those who have been smoke free for more than 1 year, and multimedia resources designed to promote smoking cessation.

At the conclusion of the intervention, each participant is requested to respond to a self-administered anonymous Smoking Cessation Survey card (Figure 13.1).

Hypotheses

Considering that this is the first run of this intervention, we have no plausible basis for presuming that any of the predictors will produce statistically significant findings (e.g., females will quit more frequently than males, those with higher income will have a better chance at quitting than those with lower income, etc.). Naturally, such hypotheses could be drafted; however, for this initial run, we will take a less specific exploratory approach:

H_0: Age, income, baseline smoking, gender, and race do not influence one's success in a smoking cessation intervention.

H_1: Age, income, baseline smoking, gender, or race influence one's success in a smoking cessation intervention.

Figure 13.1 Smoking Cessation Survey card, anonymously completed by each participant at the conclusion of the intervention.

Smoking Cessation Survey

1. What is your age? _____

2. What is your annual (gross) income? _____

3. Prior to this intervention, how many cigarettes did you smoke in an average day? _____

4. What is your gender?
   ☐ Female ☐ Male

5. What is your race?
   ☐ African American ☐ Asian ☐ Caucasian ☐ Latino ☐ Other

6. What is your current smoking status?
   ☐ Still smoking ☐ Quit smoking

Please drop this card into the survey box.

Thank you for your participation.

Data Set

Use the following data set: **Ch 13 – Example 01 – Logistic Regression.sav.**

Codebook

Variable: Smoking_status

Definition: [Outcome] Smoking status at conclusion of smoking cessation intervention

Type: Categorical

            0 = Still smoking

            1 = Quit smoking [←*BASIS FOR MODEL*]

Variable: Gender

Definition: [Predictor] Gender

Type: Categorical

            0 = Female [←*REFERENCE*]

            1 = Male

Variable: Race

Definition: [Predictor] Race

Type: Categorical

            0 = African American [←*REFERENCE*]

            1 = Asian

            2 = Caucasian

            3 = Latino

            4 = Other

Variable: Age

Definition: [Predictor] Age

Type: Continuous

Variable: Income

Definition: [Predictor] Annual gross income (in dollars)

Type: Continuous

Variable: Cigarettes

Definition: [Predictor] Baseline mean number of cigarettes smoked daily

Type: Continuous

This codebook includes six variables: The five predictor variables consist of two categorical variables (*Gender* and *Race*) and three continuous variables (*Age, Income,* and *Cigarettes*). The (one) outcome variable is a dichotomous categorical variable (*Smoking_status*).

For the most part, this codebook resembles the others presented throughout this text; in fact, there are no modifications to the way that the continuous variables (*Age, Income,* and *Cigarettes*) are presented, but in preparation for logistic regression processing, notice that some of the attributes for the categorical variables are different:

- The values for each categorical variable are arranged vertically to facilitate better visual clarity.
- The numbering of the categorical values begins with 0 instead of 1.
- For each of the categorical predictor variables (*Gender* and *Race*), the first category (0) is identified as the *REFERENCE* category; this will be explained in further detail in the Results section.
- For the outcome variable (*Smoking_status*), the last category (1 = *Quit smoking*) is identified as the *BASIS* for this logistic regression model; this will be explained in further detail in the Results section.

Pretest Checklist

Logistic Regression Pretest Checklist

☑ 1. *n* quota*

☑ 2. Normality*

☑ 3. Multicollinearity*

*Run prior to logistic regression test.

NOTE: If any of the pretest checklist criteria are not satisfied, proceed with the analysis, but concisely discuss such anomalies in the Results or Limitations sections of the documentation so the reader can more plausibly interpret the precision of the findings.

Three pretest criteria need to be assessed to better ensure the robustness of the findings: (1) n *quota*, (2) *normality*, and (3) *multicollinearity*.

Pretest Checklist Criterion 1—*n* Quota

Considering that the logistic regression statistic is unique in that it accommodates both continuous and categorical predictor variables, there are several steps involved in determining the minimum required sample size.

First, determine the minimum *n* (NOTE: This is the same procedure that is used to determine the minimum *n* for multiple regression):

1. Count the total number of continuous predictor variables (*Age, Income, Cigarettes*) = **3**.

2. Count the number of categories contained within each categorical variable (*Gender* and *Race*) and subtract 1 from each:

   - *Gender* has 2 categories (*Female, Male*): 2 – 1 = **1**.
   - *Race* has 5 categories (*African American, Asian, Caucasian, Latino, Other*): 5 – 1 = **4**.

3. Add the (**bold**) figures together: **3 + 1 + 4 = 8.**

4. Multiply that sum by 10: **8** × 10 = 80. The minimum *n* required to run this logistic regression is 80.

You may find it clearer to organize the variables in a table (Table 13.1).

- For each continuous variable, *n* = 10.
- For each categorical variable, *n* = (number of categories – 1) × 10.

Table 13.1 Assess the variables to determine the minimum *n* required to run a robust logistic regression (in this case, *n* = 80).

Variable	Type	Categorical (Categories – 1) × 10	Continuous 10
Age	Continuous		10
Income	Continuous		10
Cigarettes	Continuous		10
Gender	Categorical	10	
Race	Categorical	40	
Total *n* quota = 80		50	30

Proceed by verifying that the data set contains the minimum required *n* (80):

5. On the SPSS main menu, click on *Analyze, Descriptive Statistics, Frequency* (Figure 13.2).

6. Move the outcome variable (*Smoking_Status*) into the *Variable(s)* window (Figure 13.3).

7. Click on *OK*.

Figure 13.2 To determine the *n* of the data set, click on *Analyze, Descriptive Statistics, Frequencies.*

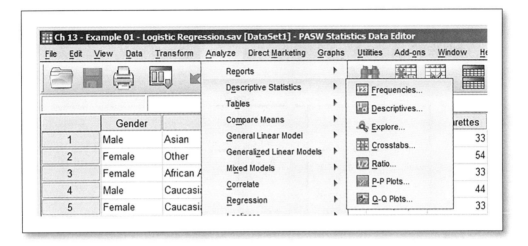

Figure 13.3 On the *Frequencies* menu, move the outcome variable (*Smoking_status*) into the *Variable(s)* window.

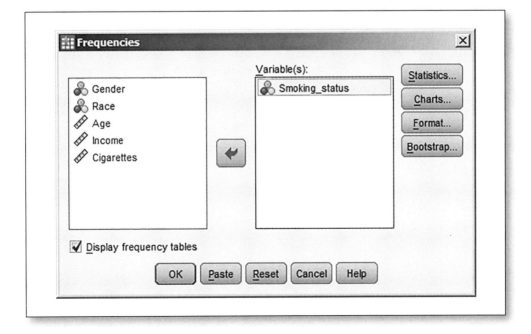

The *Smoking_status* table shows a *Total Frequency* (*n*) of 218, which is greater than the minimum required (*n* = 80); hence, this pretest criterion is satisfied (Table 13.2).

Table 13.2 Descriptive statistics for smoking status: total (*n*) = 218.

Smoking_status

		Frequency	Percent	Valid Percent	Cumulative Percent
Valid	Still smoking	111	50.9	50.9	50.9
	Quit smoking	107	49.1	49.1	100.0
	Total	218	100.0	100.0	

Figure 13.4 To order histograms with normal curves for the continuous variables, click on *Analyze, Descriptive Statistics, Frequencies.*

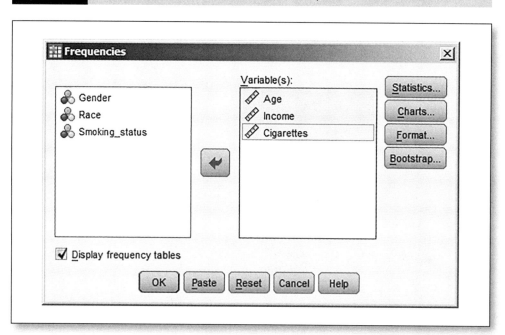

Figure 13.5   Histogram for *Age*.

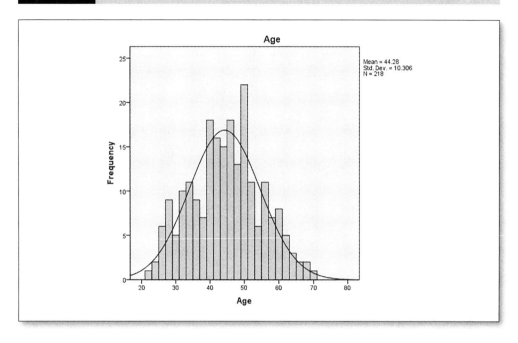

Figure 13.6   Histogram for *Income*.

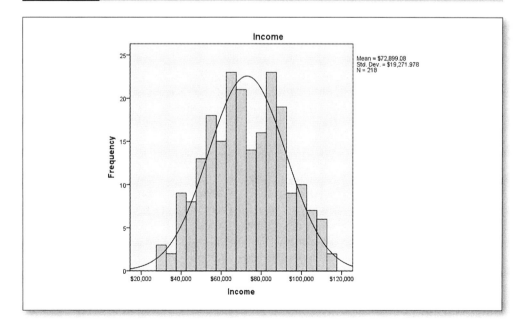

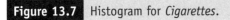

Figure 13.7 Histogram for *Cigarettes*.

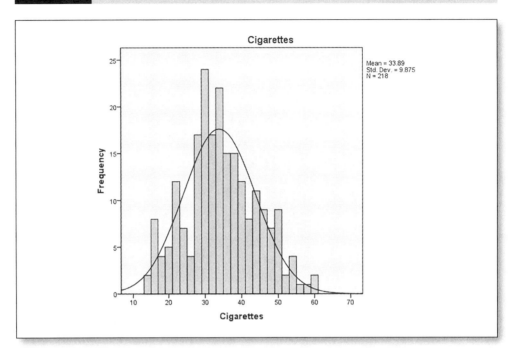

Pretest Checklist Criterion 2—Normality

Each of the (three) continuous variables should be normally distributed. This will involve ordering histograms with normal curves and inspecting each for normality. The procedure for ordering these charts is detailed on page 52; at the ★ icon; move *Age, Income, Cigarettes* into the *Variable(s)* window (Figure 13.4).

The histograms with normal curves for *Age, Income,* and *Cigarettes* (Figures 13.5, 13.6, and 13.7) are normally distributed; hence, this criterion is satisfied.

Pretest Checklist Criterion 3—Multicollinearity

As discussed in Chapter 12, *multicollinearity* describes continuous variables that are very highly correlated. Loading two such variables into a logistic regression model essentially constitutes double-loading the processor; *checking that we do not have multicollinearity* assures us that each continuous variable that we intend to load into the logistic regression model is (statistically) unique. As a rule, in logistic regression, variables that have a (Pearson) correlation that is either less than −.9 or greater than +.9 are considered too highly correlated, which would constitute multicollinearity. In such instances, one of the variables should be eliminated from the model—presumably the one that has less utility (e.g., conceptually less critical, more costly/inconvenient to gather). We will use the ±.9 cutoff to assess for multicollinearity, but this threshold is not set in stone; some statisticians set the cutoff at ±.7 or ±.8.

It is possible to construct a perfectly viable logistic regression model primarily consisting of categorical variables. If there are 0 or 1 continuous predictor variables in the logistic regression model, then you do not need to be concerned with multicollinearity—there would be no (other) continuous variable(s) to be too highly correlated with. In such cases, you can simply skip this step.

Considering that there are three continuous predictor variables in this model, we need to check for multicollinearity; we will run a correlational analysis involving all (three) continuous variables:

1. On the main screen, click on *Analyze, Correlate, Bivariate* (Figure 13.8).

2. On the *Bivariate Correlations* menu (Figure 13.9), move the continuous variables (*Age, Income, Cigarettes*) into the *Variables* window.

3. Click on *OK*.

Figure 13.8 Check for multicollinearity; click on *Analyze, Correlate, Bivariate.*

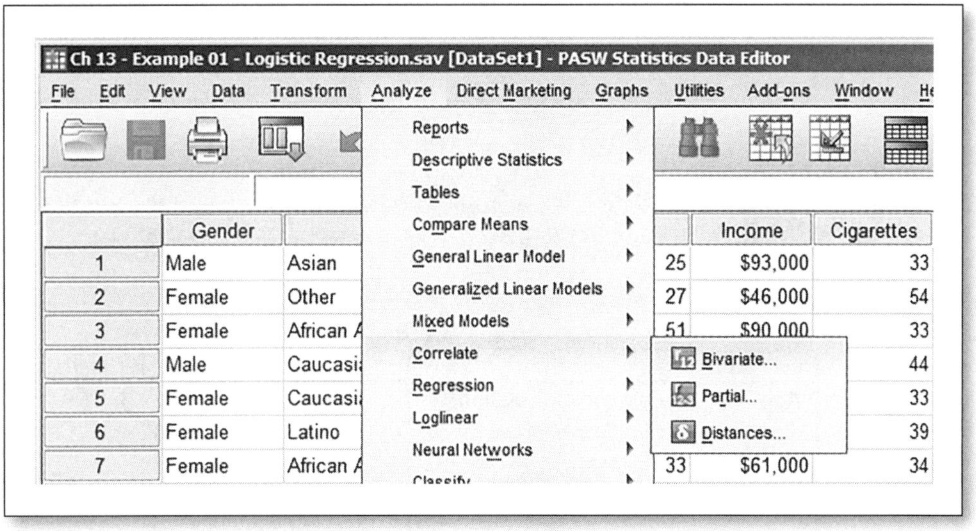

The *Correlations* table indicates the correlations between each pair of continuous variables (Table 13.3). For further clarity, these correlations are summarized in Table 13.4.

Each of the Pearson correlation scores are between –.9 and +.9; hence, this criterion is satisfied.

Figure 13.9	*Bivariate Correlation* menu—load *Age, Income,* and *Cigarettes* into *Variables* window.

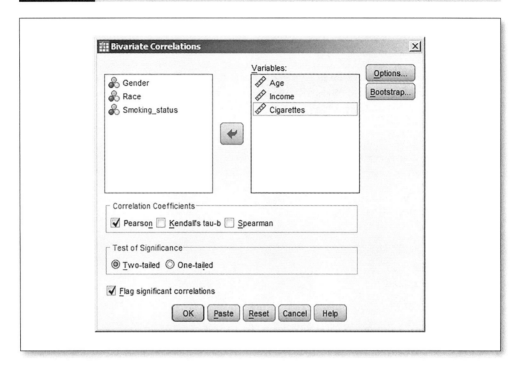

Table 13.3	*Correlations* table shows the Pearson correlations for each pair of continuous variables (*Age : Income, Age : Cigarettes, Income : Cigarettes*).

Correlations

		Age	Income	Cigarettes
Age	Pearson Correlation	1	.073	-.250**
	Sig. (2-tailed)		.284	.000
	N	218	218	218
Income	Pearson Correlation	.073	1	-.095
	Sig. (2-tailed)	.284		.161
	N	218	218	218
Cigarettes	Pearson Correlation	-.250**	-.095	1
	Sig. (2-tailed)	.000	.161	
	N	218	218	218

**. Correlation is significant at the 0.01 level (2-tailed).

Table 13.4	Summary Correlation table.

Pair	Pearson r
Age : Income	.073
Age : Cigarettes	−.250
Income : Cigarettes	−.095

Test Run

1. On the main SPSS menu, click on *Analyze, Regression, Binary Logistic* (Figure 13.10).

2. On the *Logistic Regression* menu (Figure 13.11), move the outcome variable *(Smoking_status)* into the *Dependent box.*

3. Move the predictor variables (*Gender, Race, Age, Income, Cigarettes*) into the *Covariates* window.

Figure 13.10	To run a logistic regression, click on *Analyze, Regression, Binary Logistic.*

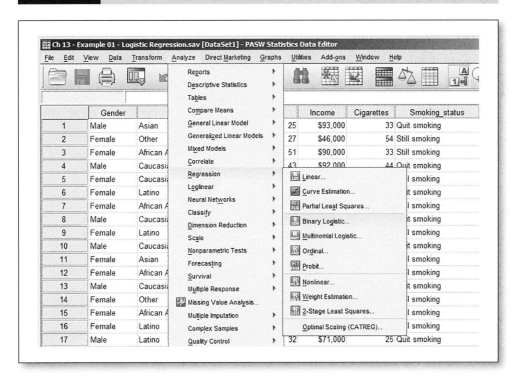

Figure 13.11   *Logistic Regression* menu—move outcome variable into the *Dependent* box and predictor variables into the *Covariates* window.

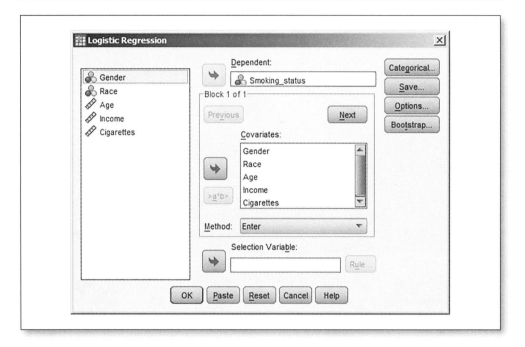

4. Next, identify the categorical variables: Click on *Categorical*.

5. On the *Logistic Regression: Define Categorical Variables* menu, move the two categorical variables (*Gender* and *Race*) into the *Categorical Covariates* window (Figure 13.12).

6. In this example, the first category within each categorical variable will be designated as the *Reference Category*; as such, select (highlight) the two variables in the *Categorical Covariates* window.

7. For the *Reference Category*, click on ⊙ *First*, and click on *Change*.

NOTE: The notion of the *Reference Category* will be discussed in the Results section.

8. Click on *Continue*—this will return you to the *Logistic Regression* menu.

9. Click on *Options*.

10. On the *Logistic Regression Options* menu, check ⊙ *CI for exp(B)*. Use the default value of 95% (Figure 13.13).

11. Click on *Continue*—this will return you to the *Logistic Regression* menu.

12. Click on *OK*.

Figure 13.12   *Logistic Regression: Define Categorical Variables* menu—move categorical predictor variables into the *Categorical Variables* window.

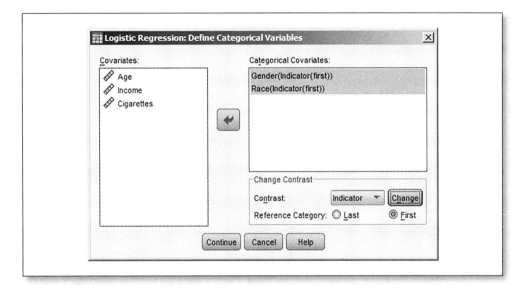

Figure 13.13   *Logistic Regression Options* menu—select the *CI for exp(B)* (confidence interval), using the default value of 95%.

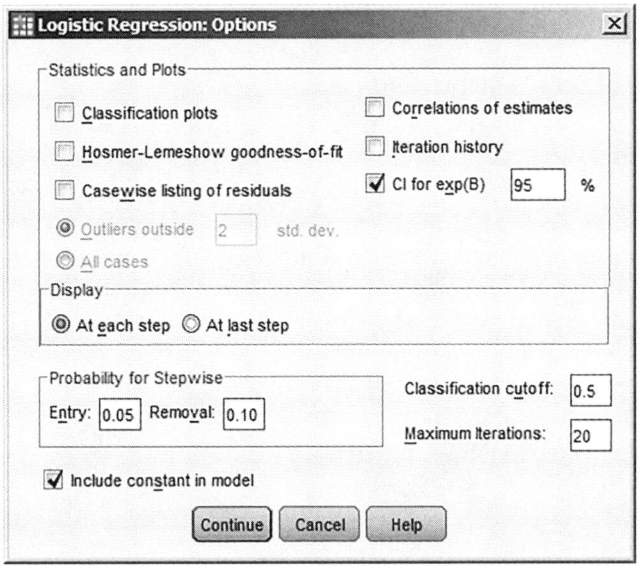

Results

Examine the first row of the *Omnibus Tests of Model Coefficients* table (Table 13.5). The Sig. (*p*) is .000, which is less than .05; this indicates that somewhere in the model, at least one of the predictor variables is statistically significant with respect to predicting the outcome variable (did/did not quit smoking). If this Sig. (*p*) is greater than .05, then this would indicate that the overall model is statistically insignificant, meaning that none of the predictors strongly predict the outcome variable. To discover *which* predictor variable(s) statistically significantly predict the outcome variable, we will look to the *Variables in the Equation* table and identify the rows where Sig. (*p*) is less than or equal to .05.

Table 13.5	*Omnibus Tests of Model Coefficients* table shows a Sig. (*p*) < .05—hence, at least one predictor in the model is statistically significant.

Omnibus Tests of Model Coefficients

		Chi-square	df	Sig.
Step 1	Step	129.192	8	.000
	Block	129.192	8	.000
	Model	129.192	8	.000

Comprehending Logistic Regression R^2

Prior to investigating the *Variables in the Equation* table, we will take a short diversion to discuss the R^2 statistic in the logistic regression context. In **Chapter 12: Multiple Regression**, we saw that the R^2 indicates the extent to which each predictor variable, and the overall set of predictors, correlate with the (continuous) outcome variable. Currently, there is no perfect R^2 equation for logistic regression; hence, this statistic is commonly referred to as a **pseudo-R^2**. In Table 13.6, notice that the Cox & Snell R^2 = .447, whereas the Nagelkerke R^2 = .596; clearly, these results are quite different. Typically, the Nagelkerke R^2 is considered the better option, but there remains some debate regarding the wisdom of reporting the R^2 for logistic regression. If this statistic were to be included in the documentation, it could be phrased as such: *The Nagelkerke R^2 indicates that this model accounts for 59.6% of the variability in smoking cessation.*

The essential findings of the logistic regression are found in the *Variables in the Equation* table (Table 13.7).

Table 13.6 *Model Summary* table shows Nagelkerke R² = .596.

Model Summary

Step	-2 Log likelihood	Cox & Snell R Square	Nagelkerke R Square
1	172.947ª	.447	.596

a. Estimation terminated at iteration number 6 because parameter estimates changed by less than .001.

Table 13.7 Unedited *Variables in the Equation* table.

Variables in the Equation

		B	S.E.	Wald	df	Sig.	Exp(B)	95% C.I.for EXP(B) Lower	Upper
Step 1ª	Gender(1)	3.101	.483	41.269	1	.000	22.223	8.628	57.241
	Race			9.873	4	.043			
	Race(1)	.913	.917	.990	1	.320	2.492	.413	15.043
	Race(2)	.218	.615	.125	1	.723	1.243	.372	4.150
	Race(3)	.504	.601	.704	1	.402	1.656	.510	5.376
	Race(4)	2.082	.721	8.335	1	.004	8.022	1.951	32.973
	Age	.101	.023	19.505	1	.000	1.107	1.058	1.158
	Income	.000	.000	1.138	1	.286	1.000	1.000	1.000
	Cigarettes	-.056	.023	5.904	1	.015	.946	.904	.989
	Constant	-3.720	1.528	5.926	1	.015	.024		

a. Variable(s) entered on step 1: Gender, Race, Age, Income, Cigarettes.

Notice that the numeric values are presented for the categorical variables but not the assigned text labels. In preparation for the documentation process, it is recommended that you manually include the text value labels for each categorical variable:

1. Copy the *Variables in the Equation* table from SPSS into the word processor.

2. Refer to the codebook (see the ★ icon on page 351), and manually type in the text value labels that correspond to each categorical variable (you will need to adjust the column sizes of the table).

3. If a separate codebook document is not provided, these categorical labels can be derived from viewing the *Values* assigned to each categorical variable on the *Variable View* screen.

4. The **[BRACKETED BOLD]** text in Table 13.8 was typed in manually.

Notice that the confidence interval [*95% C.I. for EXP(B)*] is included in Table 13.8. The first row (*Gender*) indicates a lower CI of 8.628 and an upper CI of 57.241, pertaining to the *Exp(B)* of 22.233. This is saying that for the odds ratio pertaining to *Gender,* 95% of the values are expected to be between 8.628 and 57.241. Confidence intervals are traditionally included in logistic regression documentation for statistically significant predictors.

Table 13.8 Edited *Variables in the Equation* table.

Variables in the Equation

| | | B | S.E. | Wald | df | Sig. | Exp(B) | 95% C.I.for EXP(B) | |
								Lower	Upper
Step 1[a]	Gender(1) [0 = Female, 1 = Male]	3.101	.483	41.269	1	.000	22.223	8.628	57.241
	Race [0 = African American]			9.873	4	.043			
	Race(1) [1 = Asian]	.913	.917	.990	1	.320	2.492	.413	15.043
	Race(2) [2 = Caucasian]	.218	.615	.125	1	.723	1.243	.372	4.150
	Race(3) [3 = Latino]	.504	.601	.704	1	.402	1.656	.510	5.376
	Race(4) [4 = Other]	2.082	.721	8.335	1	.004	8.022	1.951	32.973
	Age	.101	.023	19.505	1	.000	1.107	1.058	1.158
	Income	.000	.000	1.138	1	.286	1.000	1.000	1.000
	Cigarettes	-.056	.023	5.904	1	.015	.946	.904	.989
	Constant	-3.720	1.528	5.926	1	.015	.024		

a. Variable(s) entered on step 1: Gender, Race, Age, Income, Cigarettes.

NOTE: **[BRACKETED BOLD]** text manually typed in to clearly label categorical variables.

Hypothesis Resolution

The *Omnibus Tests of Model Coefficients* table indicates a Sig. (*p*) value of .000. Because this is less than the .05 α level, this indicates that at least one of the (predictor) variables is statistically significant; hence, we reject H_0 and accept H_1:

REJECT: H_0: Age, income, baseline smoking, gender, and race do not influence one's success in a smoking cessation intervention.

ACCEPT: H₁: Age, income, baseline smoking, gender, and race influence one's success in a smoking cessation intervention.

The next step is to identify and document the specific predictor variable(s) that produced statistically significant results.

Documentation Overview

Abstract

Considering that the logistic regression statistic accommodates an assortment of variables—(1) dichotomous outcome variable, (2) categorical predictor variables, and (3) continuous predictor variables—the documentation procedure will be presented in three parts:

- Part 1: Comprehending the outcome variable
- Part 2: Documenting categorical predictors
- Part 3: Documenting continuous predictors

Additionally, the logistic regression model is versatile in terms of its capacity to produce a variety of results. As such, this documentation section consists of three models:

- Model 1: Initial results
- Model 2: Selective results
- Model 3: Redefining a reference category

Model 1: Initial Results

Documenting Results Part 1: Outcome Variable

Consider this excerpt from the codebook detailing the dichotomous outcome variable:

Outcome variable: Smoking_status

0 = Still smoking (FAILED)

1 = Quit smoking (SUCCEEDED) [←*BASIS FOR MODEL*]

Although it may sound a bit redundant, because the intended goal of this intervention was to have patients successfully *Quit smoking,* we will want to discuss the results in terms of the characteristics of those who successfully *Quit smoking,* as opposed to those who are *Still smoking;* hence, the label *Quit smoking* is assigned a value of 1 in the outcome variable *Smoking_status.* This will serve as the (semantic) basis for this model. As you will see in Parts 2 and 3, the results in the *Variables in the Equation* table pertain to those who *Quit smoking.*

| Table 13.9 | Labeled *Variables in the Equation* table, focusing on categorical variables. |

Variables in the Equation

		B	S.E.	Wald	df	Sig.	Exp(B)	95% C.I.for EXP(B) Lower	Upper
Step 1[a]	Gender(1) [0 = Female, 1 = Male]	3.101	.483	41.269	1	.000	22.223	8.628	57.241
	Race [0 = African American]			9.873	4	.043			
	Race(1) [1 = Asian]	.913	.917	.990	1	.320	2.492	.413	15.043
	Race(2) [2 = Caucasian]	.218	.615	.125	1	.723	1.243	.372	4.150
	Race(3) [3 = Latino]	.504	.601	.704	1	.402	1.656	.510	5.376
	Race(4) [4 = Other]	2.082	.721	8.335	1	.004	8.022	1.951	32.973
	Age	.101	.023	19.505	1	.000	1.107	1.058	1.158
	Income	.000	.000	1.138	1	.286	1.000	1.000	1.000
	Cigarettes	-.056	.023	5.904	1	.015	.946	.904	.989
	Constant	-3.720	1.528	5.926	1	.015	.024		

a. Variable(s) entered on step 1: Gender, Race, Age, Income, Cigarettes.

Documenting Results Part 2: Categorical Predictors

We will begin by documenting the results from all the values in each categorical variable regardless of the Sig. (*p*) value to thoroughly demonstrate how to translate the data on this table into appropriately written results. After that process, as expected, we will narrow our discussion to only those variables that are statistically significant (where $p \leq .05$).

This model contains two categorical predictor variables: *Gender* and *Race*. We will begin by interpreting and documenting the *Gender* variable.

For *Gender, Female* is coded as 0, establishing it as the *reference category* for *Gender*. As such, all of the results for *Gender* will be expressed as comparisons to *Females*. Referring to the data in the first column (which contains the variable names) and the figures in the *Exp(B)* column, we document the results as such:

- *Males have 22.223 times the odds of quitting smoking compared to females (95% CI 8.63, 57.24) (meaning that the men in this study succeeded in quitting smoking significantly more frequently than women).*

Alternatively, this could be rephrased as follows:

- *The odds of quitting smoking are 22.223 times higher for males compared to females (95% CI 8.63, 57.24).*

For *Race,* the categories are arranged alphabetically; hence, *African American* is coded as 0, establishing it as the reference category for *Race.* As such, all of the results for *Race* will be expressed as comparisons to *African Americans.*

- *Asians have 2.492 times the odds of quitting smoking compared to African Americans (95% CI .41, 15.04).*
- *Caucasians have 1.243 times the odds of quitting smoking compared to African Americans (95% CI .37, 4.15).*
- *Latinos have 1.656 times the odds of quitting smoking compared to African Americans (95% CI .51, 5.38).*
- *Others have 8.022 times the odds of quitting smoking compared to African Americans (95% CI 1.95, 32.97).*

You may include the corresponding *p* (Sig.) values, flagging those where $p \le .05$. Alternatively, you may wish to provide detailed discussion of only those categories wherein $p \le .05$ (*Other*) and briefly mention the others as statistically insignificant (*Asians, Caucasians, Latinos*). These findings will be carried forward when we draft the abstract.

Categorical Documentation Option: Alternate Write-Up if Exp(B) Is Less Than 1

In the above table, *Gender* produced *Exp(B) = 22.223,* which is greater than 1. Suppose instead of *22.223,* it was *.456.* When *Exp(B)* is less than 1 for a categorical predictor, the semantics of the write-up may seem a bit awkward (see ORIGINAL documentation phrasing below). One option that may help to clarify the documentation is to "flip" the sentence. This involves calculating the reciprocal of *Exp(B),* which is simply **1 ÷ *Exp(B)***; this would be **1 ÷ .456 = 2.193**, and swapping the variable labels in the sentence.

- ORIGINAL: *Males have .456 times the odds of quitting smoking compared to females.*
- FLIPPED: *Females have 2.193 times the odds of quitting smoking compared to males.*

Documenting Results Part 3: Continuous Predictors

Next, we will document the results produced by the three continuous predictors (*Age, Income, Cigarettes*) in Table 13.10.

Continuous variables are best expressed in terms of odds percentages. There are two possible outcomes and documentation procedures for continuous predictors: Either *Exp(B)* is less than 1 or *Exp(B)* is greater than 1:

Table 13.10   Labeled *Variables in the Equation* table, focusing on continuous variables.

Variables in the Equation

		B	S.E.	Wald	df	Sig.	Exp(B)	95% C.I.for EXP(B) Lower	Upper
Step 1ᵃ	Gender(1) [0 = Female, 1 = Male]	3.101	.483	41.269	1	.000	22.223	8.628	57.241
	Race [0 = African American]			9.873	4	.043			
	Race(1) [1 = Asian]	.913	.917	.990	1	.320	2.492	.413	15.043
	Race(2) [2 = Caucasian]	.218	.615	.125	1	.723	1.243	.372	4.150
	Race(3) [3 = Latino]	.504	.601	.704	1	.402	1.656	.510	5.376
	Race(4) [4 = Other]	2.082	.721	8.335	1	.004	8.022	1.951	32.973
	Age	.101	.023	19.505	1	.000	1.107	1.058	1.158
	Income	.000	.000	1.138	1	.286	1.000	1.000	1.000
	Cigarettes	-.056	.023	5.904	1	.015	.946	.904	.989
	Constant	-3.720	1.528	5.926	1	.015	.024		

a. Variable(s) entered on step 1: Gender, Race, Age, Income, Cigarettes.

Documenting Continuous Variable Results if Exp(B) Is Less Than 1

If *Exp(B)* < 1, then the percentage = (1 – *Exp(B)*) × 100.

For *Cigarettes*, *Exp(B)* = .946; because this is less than 1, this indicates a *decrease*. We compute (1 – .946) × 100 = 5.4; hence, the write-up would be as follows:

- *For every additional cigarette smoked per day, the odds of quitting smoking decrease by 5.4% (95% CI .90, .99).*

Documenting Continuous Variable Results if Exp(B) Is Greater Than 1

If *Exp(B)* > 1, then the percentage = (*Exp(B)* – 1) × 100.

For *Age*, *Exp(B)* = 1.107; because this is greater than 1, this indicates an *increase*. We compute (1.107 – 1) × 100 = 10.7; hence, the write-up would be as follows:

- *For every additional year of age, the odds of quitting smoking increase by 10.7% (95% CI 1.06, 1.16).*

Documenting Continuous Variable Results if Exp(B) *Equals 1*

For *Income, Exp(B)* = 1.000, indicating that *Income* produced 1:1 odds in terms of income predicting the likelihood that a participant will quit smoking. In other words, about the same number of people with high income as low income quit smoking—the odds of quitting smoking are the same regardless of high/low income. As expected, the Sig. (*p*) value for *Income* is .286; this is greater than the .05 α level, so *Income* is considered statistically insignificant when it comes to predicting the likelihood that a participant will successfully quit smoking.

Logistic Regression Documentation Summary

Categorical Predictors

If *Exp(B)* > 1, then odds ratio = *Exp(B)*.

The comparison category is **more likely** than the reference category to predict the outcome variable (basis for model).

If *Exp(B)* < 1, then odds ratio can be expressed as 1 ÷ *Exp(B)* and flip the variables.

The comparison category is **less likely** than the reference category to predict the outcome variable (basis for model).

Continuous Predictors

If *Exp(B)* > 1, then percentage = (*Exp(B)* − 1) × 100.
The comparison category **increases** in relation to the outcome variable (basis for model).

If *Exp(B)* < 1, then percentage = (1 − *Exp(B)*) × 100.
The comparison category **decreases** in relation to the outcome variable (basis for model).

Abstract for Model 1: Initial Results

You may include the corresponding *p* (Sig.) values, flagging those where *p* ≤ .05. Alternatively, you may wish to provide detailed discussion of only those categories wherein *p* ≤ .05 and briefly mention the others as statistically insignificant:

As a public service, the Acme Health Center advertises and offers a free 90-day smoking cessation program, consisting of nurse-facilitated psychoeducational meetings, peer support from those who have been smoke free for more than 1 year, and multimedia resources designed to promote smoking cessation.

At the conclusion of the intervention, each participant (n = 218) responded to a self-administered anonymous Smoking Cessation Survey card, which gathered data on gender, race, age, income, baseline mean number of cigarettes smoked per day, and current smoking status (still smoking/quit smoking).

To better comprehend the factors associated with successfully quitting smoking, we conducted a logistic regression analysis. We discovered that males had 22.223 times the odds of quitting smoking compared to females (p < .001, 95% CI 8.63, 57.24). Those who indicated that their race designation was "Other" had 8.022 times the odds of quitting smoking compared to African Americans (p = .004, 95% CI 1.95, 32.97). Older participants were more likely to quit than those who were younger; for every additional year of age, the odds of quitting smoking increased by 10.7% (p < .001, 95% CI 1.06, 1.16). We also discovered that baseline smoking was an influential factor; for every additional cigarette smoked per day, the odds of quitting smoking decreased by 5.4% (p = .015, 95% CI .90, .99). Income was not found to be a viable predictor when it comes to predicting who successfully quit smoking (p = .286, 95% CI 1.00, 1.00).

Considering the volume of results produced by a logistic regression analysis in light of the relative brevity of an abstract (usually about 200 words), not every possible statistic was discussed. In a more comprehensive Results section, other statistical findings could be included (e.g., overall percentage of those who quit smoking, descriptive statistics for each categorical and continuous variable, discussion of statistically insignificant predictors).

Model 2: Selective Results

In the initial model, the results reflected the overall findings from both *Genders* (*Female* and *Male*); it was found that the men in this group were substantially more successful in quitting smoking than women. Such an observation may lead one to ponder: *Among the males (only), what were the significant predictors when it comes to successfully quitting smoking?* Statistically, this question is asking, *What would the results of this logistic regression look like if the females were removed from the picture?* This would be akin to recruiting only males to partake in this intervention.

Fortunately, we do not need to repeat this study as a *men-only* intervention to address this question; instead, we can access the existing database, using the *Select Cases* function to process only those records (rows of data) pertaining to males (*Gender* = 1).

1. On the main screen, click on the *Select Cases* icon.

2. On the *Select Cases* menu, click on ⊙ *If condition is satisfied*.

3. Click on *If.*

Figure 13.14 Selecting cases where *Gender* = 1 (Male).

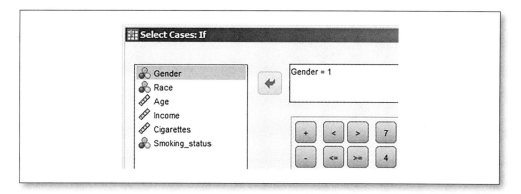

4. On the *Select Cases: If* menu, enter *Gender = 1* (Figure 13.14).

5. Click on *Continue* (this will return you to the *Select Cases* menu).

6. On the *Select Cases* menu, click on *OK*.

7. Now that only *Males* are selected, proceed to rerun the logistic regression analysis using each of the steps detailed in this chapter, as if all of the records were in play.

This analysis produces a table (Table 13.11) pertaining to the data gathered from the *Males* only. As expected, these findings are quite different compared to the initial run, which involved both genders.

Table 13.11 Labeled *Variables in the Equation* table, for *Males*.

Variables in the Equation

		B	S.E.	Wald	df	Sig.	Exp(B)	95% C.I.for EXP(B) Lower	Upper
Step 1ª	Race [0 = African American]			5.976	3	.113			
	Race(1) [1 = Asian]	2.395	13243.109	.000	1	1.000	10.967	.000	.
	Race(2) [2 = Caucasian]	-17.739	8095.370	.000	1	.998	.000	.000	.
	Race(3) [3 = Latino]	-20.050	8095.370	.000	1	.998	.000	.000	.
	Age	.163	.057	8.053	1	.005	1.176	1.052	1.316
	Income	.000	.000	.330	1	.566	1.000	1.000	1.000
	Cigarettes	-.151	.053	8.147	1	.004	.860	.775	.954
	Constant	18.863	8095.371	.000	1	.998	1.557E8		

a. Variable(s) entered on step 1: Race, Age, Income, Cigarettes.

First, notice that even if you attempted to load *Gender* as a variable, it was eliminated from the process because (now) *Gender* contains only one (selected) value: 1, signifying *Males* (only). Because all of the values for *Gender* = 1, technically, *Gender* ceases to be a *variable* because it does not vary; it is constantly 1, and hence, it is considered a constant. In this process, a constant has no predictive capacity because it is constantly 1 no matter what is happening among the other variables. As such, *Gender* is appropriately eliminated from the table.

Next, notice that *Race(4)* is missing. This is because there are no *Males* who specified their *Race* as category 4 (*Other*). For proof, run descriptive statistics (with a bar chart) for the *Race* variable, and notice that *Other* is absent.

As for documenting the results, although we may notice that *Asians* have 10.967 times the odds of quitting smoking compared to *African Americans,* we see that this finding is considered statistically insignificant (*p* = 1.000).

Abstract for Model 2: Selective Results

*Assessing only the male participants, we discovered that those who were older were more likely to quit than those who were younger; for every additional year of age, the odds of quitting smoking increased by 17.6% (*p = .005, 95% CI 1.05, 1.32*). We also discovered that baseline smoking was an influential factor; for every additional cigarette smoked per day, the odds of quitting smoking decreased by 14% (*p = .004, 95% CI .77, .95*).*

Model 3: Redefining a Reference Category

Data Set

Use the following data set: **Ch 13 – Example 02 – Logistic Regression.sav**.

In the prior two models, the reference category for *Race* has been *African American,* which produced statistics that compared all of the other racial categories to *African Americans* in terms of quitting smoking. This designation was merely due to the alphabetical arrangement of the categories—*African Americans* just happen to occupy the first position. There may be instances where you want to designate a different category as the reference category for a variable. For this example, we will change the original coding so that *Other* becomes the new reference category for *Race.* One way to do this involves changing the categorical coding of *Other* from 4 to 0 and recode *African American* from 0 to 4.

The current database (**Ch 13 – Example 02 – Logistic Regression.sav**) is the same as the original, except the variable *Race* (which was initially coded as 0 = *African American* and 4 = *Other*) has been recoded to create *Race_O,* wherein 0 = *Other* and 4 = *African American* (Table 13.12). With *Other* now serving as the reference category for *Race_O,* all racial results will be presented as comparisons to *Other.*

As a side note, the Recode process was used to create *Race_O,* wherein all the 0s were replaced with 4s, all the 4s were replaced with 0s, and all the other numbers (1, 2, 3) were kept as is. Finally, the value labels for *Race_O* were (manually) edited accordingly: 0 was changed to *Other,* and 4 was changed to *African American.*

Table 13.12	To set *Other* as the new reference category, recode *Other* from 4 to 0 and recode *African American* from 0 to 4.

Recoding Race Reference (Swap *African American* With *Other*)

Race	Race_0
0 = African American [← *REFERENCE*]	0 = Other [← *REFERENCE*]
1 = Asian	1 = Asian
2 = Caucasian	2 = Caucasian
3 = Latino	3 = Latino
4 = Other	4 = African American

The step-by-step instructions for this recoding procedure are detailed in **Chapter 14: Supplemental SPSS Operations**, on page 411 at the ★ icon.

Notice that the figures for *Race* are different from the initial results, because the reference category is now *Other* instead of *African American*. Additionally, notice that all of the other figures match the results in the initial run. The point is, recoding a variable only changes the presentation of the data contained within that variable.

As expected, a new write-up for *Race_O* is warranted:

Table 13.13	Labeled *Variables in the Equation* table, with *Other* set to reference category in *Race_O*.

Variables in the Equation

		B	S.E.	Wald	df	Sig.	Exp(B)	95% C.I.for EXP(B) Lower	Upper
Step 1ᵃ	Gender(1) [0 = Female, 1 = Male]	3.101	.483	41.269	1	.000	22.223	8.628	57.241
	Race_O [0 = Other]			9.873	4	.043			
	Race_O(1) [1 = Asian]	-1.169	.956	1.495	1	.221	.311	.048	2.024
	Race_O(2) [2 = Caucasian]	-1.864	.716	6.779	1	.009	.155	.038	.631
	Race_O(3) [3 = Latino]	-1.578	.624	6.399	1	.011	.206	.061	.701
	Race_O(4) [4 = African American]	-2.082	.721	8.335	1	.004	.125	.030	.512
	Age	.101	.023	19.505	1	.000	1.107	1.058	1.158
	Income	.000	.000	1.138	1	.286	1.000	1.000	1.000
	Cigarettes	-.056	.023	5.904	1	.015	.946	.904	.989
	Constant	-1.637	1.446	1.283	1	.257	.194		

a. Variable(s) entered on step 1: Gender, Race_O, Age, Income, Cigarettes.

Abstract for Model 3: Redefining a Reference Category

In terms of race, Caucasians have .155 times the odds of quitting smoking compared to those who identify their race as Other (p = .009, 95% CI .04, .63). Latinos were found to have .206 times the odds of quitting smoking compared to those who identify their race as Other (p = .011, 95% CI .06, .70), and African Americans have .125 times the odds of quitting compared to Other (p = .015, 95% CI .03, .51).

Alternatively, these odds ratios are less than 1, so the reading may be clearer if the semantics were flipped and the reciprocals **[1 ÷ Exp(B)]** were presented:

Those who identified their race as Other had 6.45 times the odds of quitting smoking compared to Caucasians (p = .009, 95% CI .04, .63), and Other (race category) had 4.85 times the odds of quitting smoking compared to Latinos (p = .011, 95% CI .06, .70). Additionally, Other had 8 times the odds of quitting smoking compared to African Americans (p = .015, 95% CI .03, .51).

GOOD COMMON SENSE

Logistic regression is a sophisticated type of analytic procedure that enables one to gain a deeper understanding of the relationships among the variables in terms of predicting a dichotomous outcome. In some cases, the findings from a logistic regression model can be used to predict/anticipate the likelihood of an outcome.

Despite the detailed findings produced by logistic regression, keep in mind that the model pertains to *a group of people*—it does not describe or predict the outcome of any one individual. In the same way that descriptive statistics can be used to compute the mean age of people in a sample, knowing that mean age (e.g., 25) does not empower you to point to any one person in the sample (or population) and confidently proclaim, "You are 25 years old." Keep in mind that this same principle also applies to more advanced processes, such as logistic regression.

Key Concepts

- Logistic regression
- Pretest checklist:

  - Sample size
  - Normality
  - Multicollinearity

- Logistic regression R^2 statistic
- Categorical variable labeling
- Selectively processing

- Categorical recoding principles
- Hypothesis resolution
- Documenting results
- Multiple regression overview
- Good common sense

Practice Exercises

Exercise 13.1

A public health nurse has conducted a survey of people in the community to better comprehend the effectiveness of the flu shot this season using the following survey instrument:

Flu Survey

1. Gender: ☐ Female   ☐ Male

2. How old are you? _____

3. Did you have a flu shot this season?   ☐ No   ☐ Yes

4. Do you have any chronic disease(s)?   ☐ No   ☐ Yes

5. Have you been sick with the flu this season?   ☐ No   ☐ Yes

---

Data set: **Ch 13 – Exercise 01A.sav**

Codebook

Variable:	Flu_sick
Definition:	Outcome: Did this person get sick with the flu this season?
Type:	Categorical
	0 = Got the flu
	1 = No flu [**←BASIS FOR MODEL**]
Variable:	Gender
Definition:	[Predictor] Gender

Type: Categorical

              0 = Female [**←REFERENCE**]

              1 = Male

Variable: Flu_shot

Definition: [Predictor] Did person have a flu shot this season?

Type: Categorical

              0 = Got a flu shot [**←REFERENCE**]

              1 = Did not get a flu shot

Variable: Chronic_disease

Definition: [Predictor] Does the person have chronic disease(s)?

Type: Categorical

              0 = Has chronic disease(s) [**←REFERENCE**]

              1 = No chronic disease(s)

Variable: Age

Definition: [Predictor] Age

Type: Continuous

a. Write the hypotheses.

b. Run each criterion of the pretest checklist (sample size, normality, multicollinearity) and discuss your findings.

c. Run the logistic regression analysis and document your findings (odds ratios and Sig. [*p* value], hypotheses resolution).

d. Write an abstract under 200 words detailing a summary of the study, the logistic regression analysis results, hypothesis resolution, and implications of your findings.

Repeat this exercise using data set: **Ch 13 – Exercise 01B.sav**.

NOTE: This data set (**Ch 13 – Exercise 01B.sav**) is the same as the first data set except the Age variable has been recoded from a continuous variable that contained the actual ages to a categorical variable, now coded as Pediatric/Adult, using the following recoding criteria:

- If Age < 18, then recode as 0 = Pediatric
- If Age ≥ 18, then recode as 1 = Adult

The corresponding modification has been made to the codebook:

Variable: Age

Definition: [Predictor] Age

Type: Categorical

                0 = Pediatric [←*REFERENCE*]

                1 = Adult

Exercise 13.2

Acme Solar Systems wants to discover the characteristics of those who intend to install solar energy systems in their homes.

Data set: **Ch 13 – Exercise 02A.sav**

Codebook

Variable: Install

Definition: [Outcome] Does this customer intend to install a solar energy system within the next 12 months?

Type: Categorical

                0 = Will not install solar energy

                1 = Will install solar energy [←*BASIS FOR MODEL*]

Variable: Age

Definition: [Predictor] Age

Type: Continuous

Variable: Gender

Definition: [Predictor] Gender

Type: Categorical

                0 = Female [←*REFERENCE*]

                1 = Male

Variable: Income

Definition: Annual household income

Type: Continuous

Variable: Neighborhood

Definition: [Predictor] Type of neighborhood

Type: Categorical

                 0 = Urban [←*REFERENCE*]

                 1 = Rural

Variable: Family

Definition: Number of people living in the household

Type: Continuous

a. Write the hypotheses.

b. Run each criterion of the pretest checklist (sample size, normality, multicollinearity) and discuss your findings.

c. Run the logistic regression analysis and document your findings (odds ratios and Sig. [*p* value], hypotheses resolution).

d. Write an abstract under 200 words detailing a summary of the study, the logistic regression analysis results, hypothesis resolution, and implications of your findings.

Repeat this exercise using data set: **Ch 13 – Exercise 02B.sav**.

Exercise 13.3

A public opinion consultant is interested in the demographics of those who are in favor of capital punishment (death penalty).

Data set: **Ch 13 – Exercise 03A.sav**

Codebook

Variable: Death_penalty

Definition: [Outcome] Are you in favor of the death penalty?

Type: Categorical

                 0 = Anti-death penalty

                 1 = Pro-death penalty [←*BASIS FOR MODEL*]

Variable: Age

Definition: [Predictor] Age

Type: Continuous

Variable:	Gender
Definition:	[Predictor] Gender
Type:	Categorical
	0 = Female [←*REFERENCE*]
	1 = Male

Variable:	Race
Definition:	[Predictor] Race
Type:	Categorical
	0 = African American [←*REFERENCE*]
	1 = Asian
	2 = Caucasian
	3 = Latino
	4 = Other

Variable:	Religion
Definition:	[Predictor] Religion
Type:	Categorical
	0 = Atheist [←*REFERENCE*]
	1 = Buddhist
	2 = Catholic
	3 = Hindu
	4 = Jewish
	5 = Other

Variable:	Education
Definition:	[Predictor] Years of education
Type:	Continuous (High school = 12, Associate's = 14, Bachelor's = 16, Master's = 18, Doctorate > 18)

a. Write the hypotheses.

b. Run each criterion of the pretest checklist (sample size, normality, multicollinearity) and discuss your findings.

c. Run the logistic regression analysis and document your findings (odds ratios and Sig. [p value], hypotheses resolution).

d. Write an abstract under 200 words detailing a summary of the study, the logistic regression analysis results, hypothesis resolution, and implications of your findings.

Repeat this exercise using data set: **Ch 13 – Exercise 03B.sav**.

NOTE: The B data set is the same as the A data set with the following modifications:

- The Race variable has been recoded so that Other is now the reference category:

Categorical

0 = Other [←*REFERENCE*]

1 = Asian

2 = Caucasian

3 = Latino

4 = African American

- The Religion variable has been recoded so that Other is now the reference category:

Categorical

0 = Other [←*REFERENCE*]

1 = Buddhist

2 = Catholic

3 = Hindu

4 = Jewish

5 = Atheist

Exercise 13.4

Acme Employment Services wants to evaluate the effectiveness of its "Get That Job" seminars, which consists of experts facilitating sessions designed to enhance resume writing, job search strategies, and interviewing techniques. After 90 days, participants are surveyed to assess their characteristics and outcomes.

Data set: **Ch 13 – Exercise 04A.sav**

Codebook

    Variable: Employment_status

    Definition: [Outcome] Are you currently employed?

Type: Categorical

               0 = Unemployed

               1 = Employed [←*BASIS FOR MODEL*]

Variable: Age

Definition: [Predictor] Age

Type: Continuous

Variable: Gender

Definition: [Predictor] Gender

Type: Categorical

               0 = Female [←*REFERENCE*]

               1 = Male

Variable: Race

Definition: Predictor: Race

Type: Categorical

               0 = African American [←*REFERENCE*]

               1 = Asian

               2 = Caucasian

               3 = Latino

               4 = Other

Variable: Experience

Definition: [Predictor] Years of experience working in their current field

Type: Continuous

Variable: Applications

Definition: [Predictor] Total number of job applications submitted

Type: Continuous

a. Write the hypotheses.

b. Run each criterion of the pretest checklist (sample size, normality, multicollinearity) and discuss your findings.

c. Run the logistic regression analysis and document your findings (odds ratios and Sig. [*p* value], hypotheses resolution).

d. Write an abstract under 200 words detailing a summary of the study, the logistic regression analysis results, hypothesis resolution, and implications of your findings.

Repeat this exercise using data set: **Ch 13 – Exercise 04B.sav**.

Exercise 13.5

A therapist at the Acme College Counseling Center noted a high prevalence of adjustment disorder among incoming freshmen, with depression being the predominate symptom. The clinicians want to determine the characteristics of those most amenable to therapy over a course of 10 sessions.

Data set: **Ch 13 – Exercise 05A.sav**

Codebook

Variable:	Treatment_effectiveness
Definition:	[Outcome] Did the treatment resolve the adjustment disorder?
Type:	Categorical
	0 = Treatment ineffective
	1 = Treatment effective [←*BASIS FOR MODEL*]

Variable:	Gender
Definition:	[Predictor] Gender
Type:	Categorical
	0 = Female [←*REFERENCE*]
	1 = Male

Variable:	Age
Definition:	[Predictor] Age
Type:	Continuous

Variable:	Units
Definition:	[Predictor] Number of units the student is enrolled in
Type:	Continuous

Variable:	Work
Definition:	[Predictor] Number of hours of (nonacademic) work per week
Type:	Continuous

Variable:	Treatment_modality
Definition:	[Predictor] Form of treatment
Type:	Categorical
	0 = Individual [←*REFERENCE*]
	1 = Group

Variable:	Home
Definition:	[Predictor] Living conditions at home
Type:	Categorical
	0 = Lives with family [←*REFERENCE*]
	1 = Lives with roommate(s)
	2 = Lives alone

a. Write the hypotheses.

b. Run each criterion of the pretest checklist (sample size, normality, multicollinearity) and discuss your findings.

c. Run the logistic regression analysis and document your findings (odds ratios and Sig. [*p* value], hypotheses resolution).

d. Write an abstract under 200 words detailing a summary of the study, the logistic regression analysis results, hypothesis resolution, and implications of your findings.

Repeat this exercise using data set: **Ch 13 – Exercise 05B.sav**.

Exercise 13.6

A technology firm wants to determine the characteristics of potential customers for a new voice-activated home entertainment system.

Data set: **Ch 13 – Exercise 06A.sav**

Codebook

Variable:	Purchase
Definition:	[Outcome] Will the person buy this within 6 months?

Type:	Categorical
	0 = Will not buy it
	1 = Will buy it [←*BASIS FOR MODEL*]
Variable:	Gender
Definition:	[Predictor] Gender
Type:	Categorical
	0 = Female [←*REFERENCE*]
	1 = Male
Variable:	Race
Definition:	[Predictor] Race
Type:	Categorical
	0 = African American [←*REFERENCE*]
	1 = Asian
	2 = Caucasian
	3 = Latino
	4 = Other
Variable:	Partner
Definition:	[Predictor] Relational status
Type:	Categorical
	0 = Single [←*REFERENCE*]
	1 = Partner
Variable:	Age
Definition:	[Predictor] Age
Type:	Continuous
Variable:	Income
Definition:	[Predictor] Annual income
Type:	Continuous
Variable:	Brand_ownership
Definition:	[Predictor] Does the person already own any other product(s) of this brand

Type: Categorical

               0 = Does not own this brand [←*REFERENCE*]

               1 = Owns this brand

a. Write the hypotheses.

b. Run each criterion of the pretest checklist (sample size, normality, multicollinearity) and discuss your findings.

c. Run the logistic regression analysis and document your findings (odds ratios and Sig. [*p* value], hypotheses resolution).

d. Write an abstract under 200 words detailing a summary of the study, the logistic regression analysis results, hypothesis resolution, and implications of your findings.

Repeat this exercise using data set: **Ch 13 – Exercise 06B.sav**.

Exercise 13.7

Acme Coffee, which currently sells gourmet coffee blends, is now considering selling a single-serve coffee maker that brews a cup of coffee in 30 seconds. They conduct a survey to help identify the characteristics of potential customers for this high-tech coffee brewer.

Data set: **Ch 13 – Exercise 07A.sav**

Codebook

Variable: Buy

Definition: [Outcome] Would you consider buying this coffee brewer?

Type: Categorical

               0 = No

               1 = Yes [←*BASIS FOR MODEL*]

Variable: Age

Definition: [Predictor] Age

Type: Continuous

Variable: Gender

Definition: [Predictor] Gender

Type: Categorical

               0 = Female [←*REFERENCE*]

               1 = Male

Variable: Acme_Coffee

Definition: [Predictor] Does the person currently drink Acme Coffee?

Type: Categorical

    0 = Doesn't drink Acme Coffee [**←REFERENCE**]

    1 = Drinks Acme Coffee

Variable: Income

Definition: [Predictor] Annual household income

Type: Continuous

a. Write the hypotheses.

b. Run each criterion of the pretest checklist (sample size, normality, multicollinearity) and discuss your findings.

c. Run the logistic regression analysis and document your findings (odds ratios and Sig. [p value], hypotheses resolution).

d. Write an abstract under 200 words detailing a summary of the study, the logistic regression analysis results, hypothesis resolution, and implications of your findings.

Repeat this exercise using data set: **Ch 13 – Exercise 07B.sav**.

Exercise 13.8

In an effort to identify the characteristics of incoming high school students who are most vulnerable to dropping out, the research staff gathered data on the senior students at the end of the school year. Based on this data, freshmen who are identified as vulnerable to dropping out will be offered access to free comprehensive tutorial services.

Data set: **Ch 13 – Exercise 08A.sav**

Codebook

Variable: HS_completion

Definition: [Outcome] Did the student drop out or graduate?

Type: Categorical

    0 = Graduated

    1 = Drop-out [**←BASIS FOR MODEL**]

Variable: Gender

Definition: [Predictor] Gender

Type:	Categorical
	0 = Female [←*REFERENCE*]
	1 = Male

Variable:	Adjusted_income
Definition:	[Predictor] Annual household income ÷ number of people in household
Type:	Continuous

Variable:	Education_parents
Definition:	[Predictor] Highest years of parent's education
Type:	Continuous (e.g., High school = 12, Associate's = 14, Bachelor's = 16, Master's = 18, Doctorate > 18)

Variable:	Language_skill
Definition:	[Predictor] Pre–high school reading and writing skills placement exam
Type:	Continuous (1 . . . 30)

Variable:	Math_skill
Definition:	[Predictor] Pre–high school math skills placement exam
Type:	Continuous (1 . . . 30)

a. Write the hypotheses.

b. Run each criterion of the pretest checklist (sample size, normality, multicollinearity) and discuss your findings.

c. Run the logistic regression analysis and document your findings (odds ratios and Sig. [*p* value], hypotheses resolution).

d. Write an abstract under 200 words detailing a summary of the study, the logistic regression analysis results, hypothesis resolution, and implications of your findings.

Repeat this exercise using data set: **Ch 13 – Exercise 08B.sav**.

Exercise 13.9

The Transplant Committee wants to gain a better understanding of those who opt to be an organ donor upon their death.

Data set: **Ch 13 – Exercise 09A.sav**

Codebook

Variable:	Organ_donor
Definition:	[Outcome] Is the person an organ donor?
Type:	Categorical
	0 = Not organ donor
	1 = Organ donor [←*BASIS FOR MODEL*]

Variable:	Gender
Definition:	[Predictor] Gender
Type:	Categorical
	0 = Female [←*REFERENCE*]
	1 = Male

Variable:	Age
Definition:	[Predictor] Age
Type:	Continuous

Variable:	Religion
Definition:	[Predictor] Religion
Type:	Categorical
	0 = Atheist [←*REFERENCE*]
	1 = Buddhist
	2 = Catholic
	3 = Hindu
	4 = Jewish
	5 = Other

Variable:	SES
Definition:	[Predictor] Socioeconomic status
Type:	Categorical
	0 = Lower class [←*REFERENCE*]
	1 = Middle class
	2 = Upper class

a. Write the hypotheses.

b. Run each criterion of the pretest checklist (sample size, normality, multicollinearity) and discuss your findings.

c. Run the logistic regression analysis and document your findings (odds ratios and Sig. [*p* value], hypotheses resolution).

d. Write an abstract under 200 words detailing a summary of the study, the logistic regression analysis results, hypothesis resolution, and implications of your findings.

Repeat this exercise using data set: **Ch 13 – Exercise 09B.sav**.

Exercise 13.10

The Acme Industries Safety Supervisor wants to determine the factors that predict employees passing the annual required site safety competency training course.

Data set: **Ch 13 – Exercise 10A.sav**

Codebook

Variable:	Test_result
Definition:	[Outcome] Did the employee pass the annual safety exam?
Type:	Categorical
	0 = Fail
	1 = Pass [**←BASIS FOR MODEL**]

Variable:	Training_type
Definition:	[Predictor] Training type
Type:	Categorical
	0 = Workbook [**←REFERENCE**]
	1 = Online course
	2 = Simulation lab

Variable:	Years
Definition:	[Predictor] Years of professional experience
Type:	Continuous

Variable:	Employment_hours
Definition:	[Predictor] Part-time or full-time

Type: Categorical

               0 = Part-time [←*REFERENCE*]

               1 = Full-time

a. Write the hypotheses.

b. Run each criterion of the pretest checklist (sample size, normality, multicollinearity) and discuss your findings.

c. Run the logistic regression analysis and document your findings (odds ratios and Sig. [*p* value], hypotheses resolution).

d. Write an abstract under 200 words detailing a summary of the study, the logistic regression analysis results, hypothesis resolution, and implications of your findings.

Repeat this exercise using data set: **Ch 13 – Exercise 10B.sav**.

PART VI

Data Handling

This chapter demonstrates supplemental techniques in SPSS to enhance your capabilities, versatility, and data-processing efficiency.

Chapter 14: Supplemental SPSS Operations explains how to generate random numbers, sort and select cases, recode variables, import non-SPSS data, and practice appropriate data storage protocols.

C H A P T E R   1 4

Supplemental SPSS Operations

We can get **SPSS** to do all the hard work for us.

- Generate Random Numbers
- Sort Cases
- Select Cases
- Recode Variables
- Import Data
- SPSS Syntax

Never trust a computer you can't throw out a window.

—Steve Wozniak

Learning Objectives

Upon completing this chapter, you will be able to do the following:

- Perform extended SPSS operations to enhance your capabilities, versatility, and data-processing efficiency.
- Generate a list of random numbers to your specifications.
- Perform single and multilevel sorting.
- Select cases using multiple criteria.
- Recode variables.
- Import data from external sources: Excel and ASCII (text) files.
- Practice safe data storage protocols.
- Comprehend the basics of the SPSS Syntax language.

OVERVIEW—SUPPLEMENTAL SPSS OPERATIONS

The data sets that have been provided thus far have been crafted to work as is in the SPSS environment, but as you become more statistically proficient, your research curiosity and scientific creative thinking are likely to further develop. You may want to analyze data of your own, examine data from other non-SPSS sources, or run more elaborate statistical analyses. This chapter explains some of the most useful supplemental SPSS features and functions to help you work more productively.

 ## Data Sets

This chapter includes examples involving the following files:

- Ch 14 – Example 01 – Sort, Select, Recode.sav
- Ch 14 – Example 02 – Recode.sav
- Ch 14 – Example 03 – Excel Data.xls
- Ch 14 – Example 04 – Comma Delimited Data.txt
- Ch 14 - Example 04 – Syntax.sav
- Ch 14 - Example 04 – Syntax.sps
- Ch 14 - Example 05 – Dummy Coding.sav
- Ch 14 - Example 05 – Dummy Coding.sps

The codebook for each data set will be presented with each demonstration.

Generating Random Numbers

Many of the statistics contained in this text involve randomly assigning participants to groups. **Random assignment** is a powerful technique that helps to create balanced, unbiased groups. Suppose you want to test the effectiveness of a new method of teaching math and you have two groups: a control group and a treatment group; random assignment enhances the likelihood that the groups will be sufficiently balanced, meaning that the groups will contain about the same proportions of those with high, medium, and low math skills in each group. Random assignment will also help to balance the groups with respect to other variables endemic within the participants (e.g., age, gender, ethnicity, academic performance, etc.). Because this is a two-group design, it is possible to use a simple coin-flip to assign participants to the groups (e.g., heads = control group, tails = treatment group); however, the coin-flip technique falls short when it comes to multigroup designs, or larger sample sizes. In such circumstances, it is useful to have the computer generate random numbers to make such group assignments. Specifically, if you had an experiment that involved three groups, and you recruited 70 participants, you could order the computer to provide 70 numbers that will each have a random value between 1 and 3 and use that list to randomly assign the participants to their corresponding groups.

Computer generated **random numbers** are also useful when it comes to selecting the sample (those who will actually participate in a study) from the (larger) sample frame (the list of potentially accessible individuals). For example, suppose you have a sample frame consisting of 500 names, and you want to gather a 6% sample. You would calculate the sample size: $500 \times .06 = 30$. Based on this, you would tell the computer to generate 30 random numbers between 1 and 500:

1. On the *Variable View* screen, create a numeric variable to contain the 30 random numbers that we will have SPSS generate; we will call it *RandNum*. Notice that the *Decimals* property is set to 0; this is optional (Figure 14.1).

Figure 14.1   Create a numeric variable (*RandNum*) to contain the random numbers.

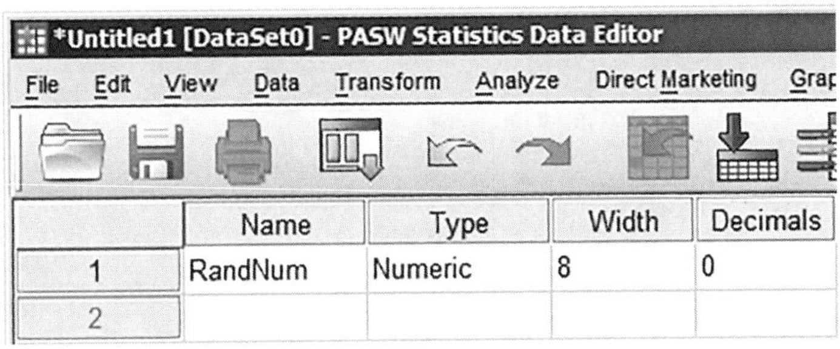

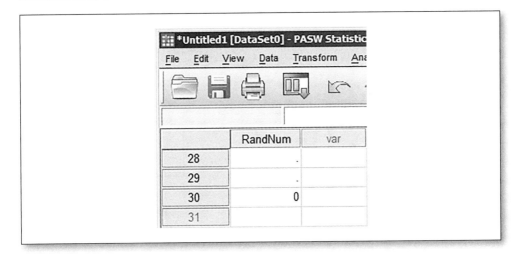

2. Switch to the *Data View* screen and put a 0 (or any number) in the *RandNum* column at record 30 (Figure 14.2).

Figure 14.2   Enter any number at record 30 for *RandNum* so SPSS will know how long the list should be. NOTE: The 0 will be overwritten with a random number.

3. Click on *Transform, Compute Variable* (Figure 14.3). This will take you to the *Compute Variable* menu.

Figure 14.3 Click on *Transform, Compute Variables*.

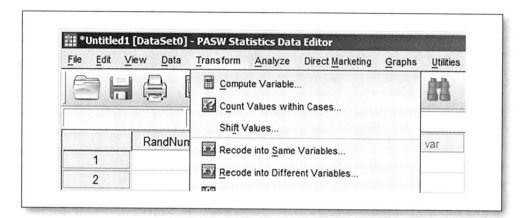

4. On the *Compute Variable* menu, in the *Target Variable* window, enter *RandNum*; in the *Numeric Expression* window, enter *rnd(rv.uniform(1,500))* (Figure 14.4).

Figure 14.4 On the *Compute Variable* menu, in the *Target Variable* window, enter *RandNum*; in the *Numeric Expression* window, enter *rnd(rv.uniform(1,500))*.

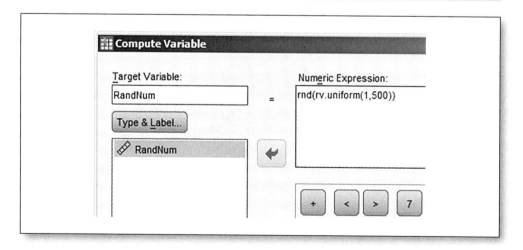

This tells SPSS to place the random values in the *RandNum* variable. Now to demystify the *rnd(rv.uniform(1,500))* expression:

- *rnd* means round the result to the nearest integer; if you wanted the random numbers to include decimal digits, you could enter *rv.uniform(1,500)*.
- *rv.uniform* means "random values, uniform," wherein each number has an equal chance of being selected.
- *(1,500)* specifies the minimum (1) and maximum (500) values.

5. Click on the *OK* button. If you are then asked if you wish to *Change existing variable?* click on the *OK* button.

6. The *Data View* screen should now show 30 random numbers in the *RandNum* column (Figure 14.5).

The random-number generator does not keep track of repeats among these numbers; hence, you may want to order more random numbers than you actually need so that you can discard duplicates.

Figure 14.5 *Data View* screen with resulting random numbers for *RandNum*.

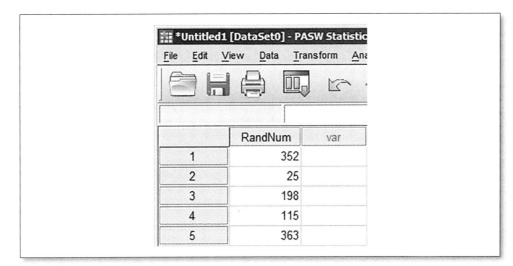

NOTE: Naturally, your results will produce a different set of random numbers.

Sort Cases

As you have probably noticed, the order of the data on the *Data View* screen has no effect on the statistical outcomes, but at times you may find it useful to inflict some order on the data. In data processing, the term *sort* is akin to alphabetizing; **sorting** the data to help you make sense of them. You might be interested in those who scored highest or lowest on a particular variable to better conceptualize the data set; inflicting such order may help you identify patterns or trends within the data set that may not have been evident otherwise—you can then follow your curiosity with additional statistical tests.

SPSS supports multilevel sorting. This means that you could specify the first level to sort by *Name* and the second level to sort by *Age* (you can specify as many levels as you need). In this case, if two or more people have the same *Name*, the system would then look to *age* to finalize the sorting sequence (Table 14.1).

Table 14.1	Data sorted by *Name* (Level 1), then by *Age* (Level 2).

Name	Age
Adrian	15
Blake	12
Blake	27
Blake	38
Cary	19

The default is to sort the variable at each level in *ascending* order (from lowest to highest); alternatively, you can specify that you want to sort in *descending* order (from highest to lowest). For example, if you specify that Level 1 is *Name* ascending and Level 2 is *Age* descending, the system will sort the data with the names arranged from A to Z, but if there is a tie at Level 1 (*Name*), it will subsort those records by *Age,* from highest to lowest (Table 14.2).

Table 14.2	Data sorted ascending by *Name* (Level 1), then descending by *Age* (Level 2).

Name	Age
Adrian	15
Blake	38
Blake	27
Blake	12
Cary	19

Data Set

Load the following data file: **Ch 14 – Example 01 – Sort, Select, Recode.sav**. This data set contains bowling league information. Notice that initially, the records are in no particular order.

Codebook

Variable:	Name
Definition:	Bowler's name
Type:	Alphanumeric

Variable:	Gender
Definition:	Bowler's gender
Type:	Categorical (1 = Female, 2 = Male)

Variable:	Age
Definition:	Bowler's age
Type:	Continuous

Variable:	BowlAvg
Definition:	Bowler's current league average
Type:	Continuous

Variable:	Team
Definition:	Bowler's team
Type:	Categorical (1 = Strike Force, 2 = Lane Surfers, 3 = 7-10 Squad, 4 = Pinbots, 5 = Bowled Over, 6 = The Pin Boys)

1. Suppose you want to identify the top bowler on each team; this would involve a two-level sort:

   Level 1: *Team* (ascending) First, the data will be sequenced by team number with the lowest team number (Team 1: Strike Force) at the top.

   Level 2: *BowlAvg* (descending) Second, within each team, the bowlers will be sequenced with the best bowler (*BowlAvg*) at the top.

2. Click on *Data, Sort Cases* (Figure 14.6). This will take you to the *Sort Cases* menu (Figure 14.7).

Figure 14.6   To sort data, click on *Data, Sort Cases.*

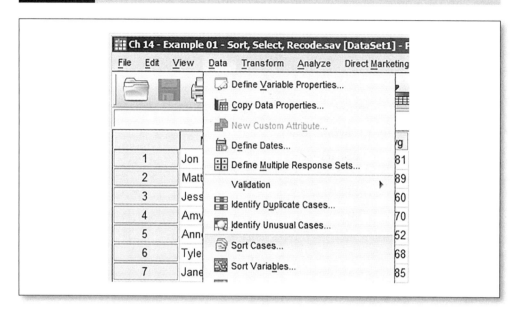

3. On the *Sort Cases* menu (Figure 14.7), move *Team* from the left window to the *Sort by* window, and click on ⊙ *Ascending.*

Figure 14.7   *Sort Cases* menu indicates a two-level sort: first by *Team* (in ascending order), and then by *BowlAvg* (in descending order).

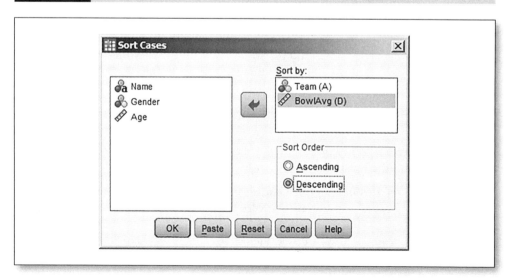

4. Move *BowlAvg* from the left window to the *Sort by* window and click on ⊙ *Descending*.
5. Notice that once a variable is in the *Sort by* window, you can click on a variable to drag it up and down the list, thereby altering the sorting levels. You can also change the *Sort Order* for a variable by clicking on the variable and then selecting *Ascending* or *Descending*.
6. Click on *OK*, and the system will sort the cases (rows).

Observe the order of the data on the *Data View* screen (Figure 14.8).

Figure 14.8 *Data View* screen showing labels (not values).

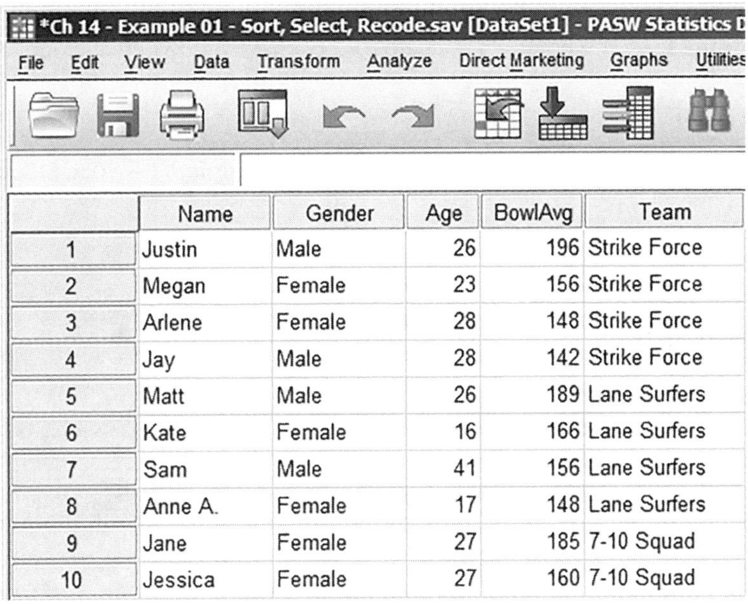

	Name	Gender	Age	BowlAvg	Team
1	Justin	Male	26	196	Strike Force
2	Megan	Female	23	156	Strike Force
3	Arlene	Female	28	148	Strike Force
4	Jay	Male	28	142	Strike Force
5	Matt	Male	26	189	Lane Surfers
6	Kate	Female	16	166	Lane Surfers
7	Sam	Male	41	156	Lane Surfers
8	Anne A.	Female	17	148	Lane Surfers
9	Jane	Female	27	185	7-10 Squad
10	Jessica	Female	27	160	7-10 Squad

Notice that the data are now grouped by *Team* (Figure 14.8) and then by highest to lowest bowling average (*BowlAvg*), but the teams are not arranged alphabetically. This is because *Team* is not really a string (alphanumeric) variable like *Name; Team* is actually a numeric (categorical) variable, with labels assigned. If you click on the *Value Labels* icon, you will see *team* switch to the numeric values for that variable (Figure 14.9), which will show that the sort actually did work as ordered—per the codebook, the label *Strike Force* is coded as 1, *Lane Surfers* is coded as 2, *7-10 Squad* is coded as 3, and so on.

Feel free to sort the data other ways and observe the resulting sequences:

- Within each team, alphabetize the bowlers by their names.
- Identify the highest bowlers in the league.
- Identify the highest female bowlers and the highest male bowlers.

Sorting will affect all of the records in the database, even if some have been unselected (slashed out) using the *Select Cases* function.

Select Cases

In prior chapters, we have used the *Select Cases* (icon) to run the pretest checklist for various statistical tests, which has enabled us to process statistics for one group at a time. The *Select Cases* function is also capable of isolating data using more complex selection criteria.

For example, you may wish to perform statistical analyses only on members of the bowling league who are (1) female *and* (2) have a bowling average of 120 or higher.

Data Set

1. Load the following data file: **Ch 14 – Example 01 – Sort, Select, Recode.sav**.

NOTE: If that file is already loaded from the prior example, you do not need to reload it.

Figure 14.9 *Data View* screen showing values (not labels).

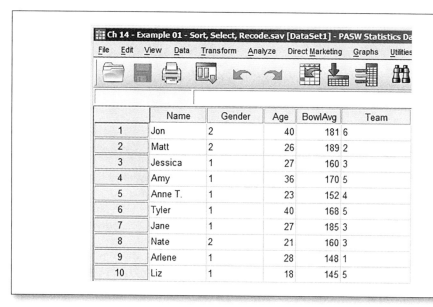

2. Click on the *Select Cases* icon.

3. In the Select group, click on the If condition is satisfied button.

4. Click on the *If* button. This will take you to the *Select Cases: If* menu; in the large box at the top, enter the following selection criteria: *Gender = 1 and BowlAvg >= 120* (Figure 14.10). Note: These criteria include *Gender = 1* because the *Gender* variable has the following labels assigned to it: 1 = Female, 2 = Male (Figure 14.10).

Figure 14.10 *Select Cases: If* menu, specifying two selection criteria.

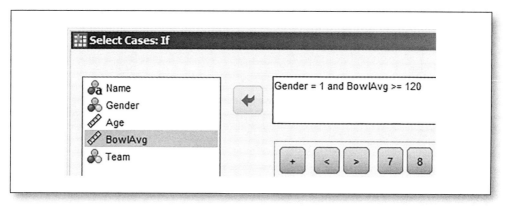

NOTE: These criteria include *Gender* = 1 because the *Gender* variable has the following labels assigned to it: 1 = *Female*, 2 = *Male*. The >= symbol means "greater than or equal to."

5. Click on the *Continue* button; this will take you back to the *Select Cases* menu.

6. Click on *OK*.

7. Go to the *Data View* screen.

8. Notice that all records are slashed out except for the *females with bowling averages that are at least 120*. Now you can proceed with whatever statistical analysis you wish to perform on the selected (non-slashed-out) records.

Try some other case selection criteria and observe which records are affected on the *Data View* screen:

- Team > 2 and Team <= 5 and BowlAvg > 150
- Team = 3 or Team = 5
- Name < "G"
- Name > "A" and Name < "F"
- Age >= 17 and Age < 31 and BowlAvg < 170

You have probably surmised some of the coding syntax from the preceding examples—just to clarify a few things:

- Single and compound *and/or* logic is supported.
- Commonly used logical relationships are symbolized as follows:

=	Equal to
<>	Not equal to
<	Less than
>	Greater than
<=	Less than or equal to
>=	Greater than or equal to

Although the system supports *not* logic, negative logic can be confusing; try to build your selection criteria using *and/or* parameters.

When your selection criteria involve alphanumeric (string) variables, be sure to wrap quotation marks around your parameter(s) (e.g., *Name* < "G"); otherwise, the processor will think you are referring to a variable named *G*.

Recoding—Example 1

Occasionally, you may wish to change the way a variable is presented in a data set. For example, in the current database, *Age* is a continuous variable that ranges from 16 to 41, but suppose you wanted to use a *t* test to compare bowling averages of minors versus adults. You would need a categorical variable to designate which group (minor vs. adult) each record belonged to based on *Age*. This is accomplished via *recoding*. We will leave *Age* (a continuous variable) intact, but we can use the *recode* function to create the new variable, *Age2* (a categorical variable), which will be based on *Age* using the following (two) criteria:

- If Age < 18, then Age2 = 1.
- If Age >= 18, then Age2 = 2.

Remember: >=notation is computer language for "greater than or equal to." After the *recode* function generates the values for *Age2*, we will make the following addition to the codebook:

Variable:	Age2
Definition:	Age designation
Type:	Categorical (1 = Minor, 2 = Adult)

Data Set

1. Load the following data file: **Ch 14 – Example 01 – Sort, Select, Recode.sav**.

NOTE: If that file is already loaded from the prior example, you do not need to reload it.

2. Click on *Transform*, *Recode into Different Variables* (Figure 14.11).

Figure 14.11 To begin recoding, click on *Transform, Recode into Different Variables.*

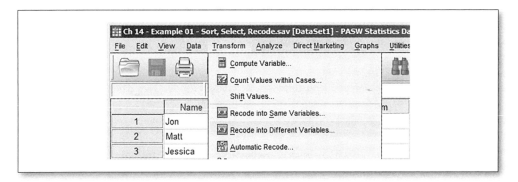

3. On the *Recode into Different Variables* menu, move *Age* from the left window to the *Numeric Variable* → *Output Variable* window (Figure 14.12)

Figure 14.12 *Recode into Different Variables* menu.

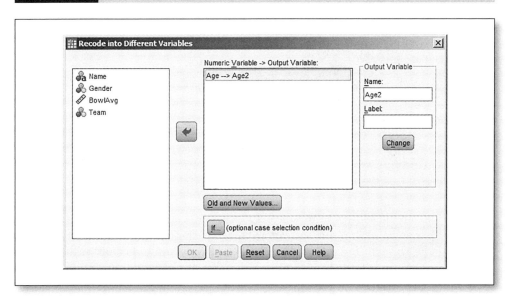

4. Enter *Age2* in the *Output Variable, Name* box.

5. Click on the *Change* button.

6. So far, you have indicated that the (continuous) variable *Age* will be recoded into the new (categorical) variable *Age2*. Now you need to indicate how *Age* will be recoded into *Age2*. Click on the *Old and New Values* button.

7. Notice that there is a variety of recoding options; we will use a simple method. In the *Old Value* area, select *Range*, and enter *1 through 17* (Figure 14.13). In the *New Value* area, select *Value* and enter *1*. Then click on the *Add* button. This tells the processor to look at *Age*, and for any record with an *Age* between 1 and 17 (inclusive), write a *1* in that record in the *Age2* variable (and do not change the contents of the *Age* variable).

Figure 14.13	*Recode into Different Variables*: *Old and New Values* menu, recoding ages *1 through 17* to *Age2* as *1*.

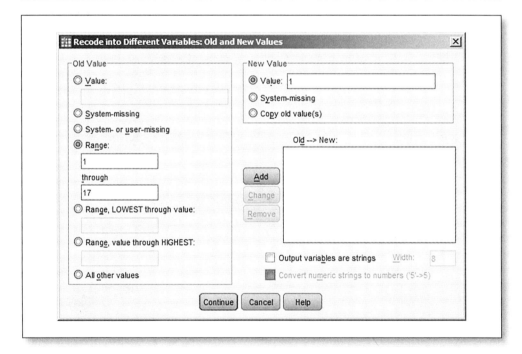

8. In the *Old Value* area, select *Range,* and enter *18 through 99*. In the *New Value* area, select *Value* and enter *2*. Then click on the *Add* button (Figure 14.14). This tells the processor to look at *Age,* and for any record with an *Age* between 18 and 99 (inclusive), write a *2* in that record in the *Age2* variable (and do not change the contents of the *Age* variable).

Figure 14.14   *Recode into Different Variables*: *Old and New Values* menu, recoding ages *18 through 99* to *Age2* as 2.

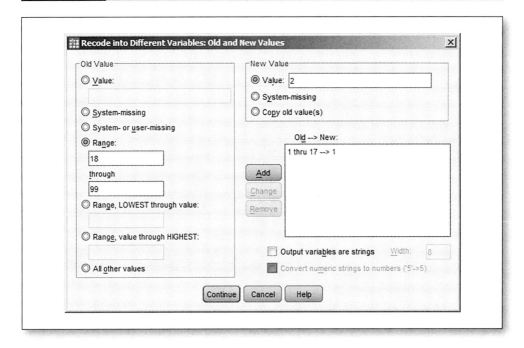

9. At this point, the *Old* → *New* window shows the recoding criteria (Figure 14.15).

Figure 14.15   Excerpt from *Recode into Different Variables*: *Old and New Values* menu: criteria used to recode *Age* to *Age2*.

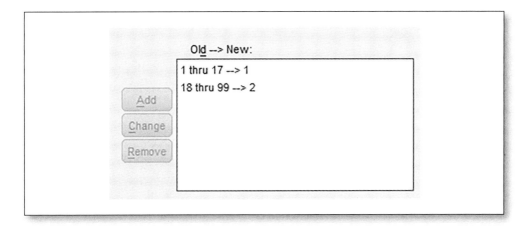

10. Click on the *Continue* button; this will return you to the *Recode into Different Variables* menu.

11. Click on the *OK* button, and the recoding will process.

12. Go to the *Data View* screen, and notice that the new variable *Age2* now contains 1s and 2s based on the *Age* for each record.

13. To finalize the process, go to the *Variable View* screen and specify the corresponding *Value Labels* for *Age2* (1 = Minor, 2 = Adult) (Figure 14.16).

Figure 14.16   Assign *Value Labels* to *Age2* (1 = Minor, 2 = Adult).

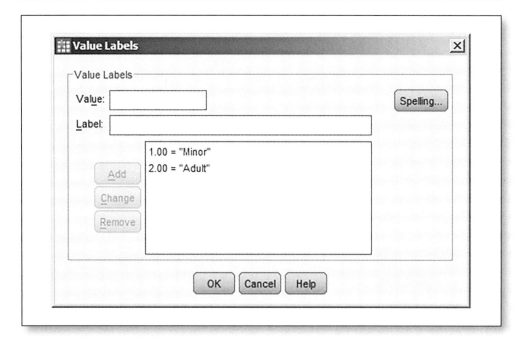

 In this example, notice that we opted to *Recode into Different Variables* as opposed to *Recode into Same Variables*. This deliberate choice preserved the original (continuous) *age* variable so that we could perform further analyses on it. Had we used *Recode into Same Variables,* each original *Age* would have been overwritten with 1s and 2s as we specified (signifying minors and adults). As such, you would not be able to get back to the original *Age*(s), and hence, it would no longer be possible to compute a mean *Age*.

Recoding—Example 2

Data Set

Load the file: **Ch 14 – Example 02 – Recode.sav** (this is a copy of **Ch 13 – Example 01 – Logistic Regression.sav**).

Codebook

Variable:	Gender
Definition:	Gender
Type:	Categorical (1 = Female, 2 = Male)
Variable:	Race
Definition:	Race
Type:	Categorical (0 = African American, 1 = Asian, 2 = Caucasian, 3 = Latino, 4 = Other)
Variable:	Age
Definition:	Age
Type:	Continuous
Variable:	Income
Definition:	Income (in dollars)
Type:	Continuous
Variable:	Cigarettes
Definition:	Average number of cigarettes participant smokes per day
Type:	Continuous
Variable:	Smoking_status
Definition:	Current smoking status
Type:	Categorical (0 = Still smoking, 1 = Quit smoking)

As mentioned briefly in **Chapter 13: Logistic Regression**, recoding enables you to examine variables in a variety of ways. In this data set, the *Race* variable is initially coded alphabetically, as such:

Race

0 = African American

1 = Asian

2 = Caucasian

3 = Latino

4 = Other

This coding scheme means that when the *Race* variable is included in a logistic regression model, *African American* will constitute the reference category because it is coded as 0 (per the alphabetical arrangement of the categories within the *Race* variable). As such, all of the resulting odds ratios for *Race* will be computed in terms of comparisons to *African Americans*. Recoding enables you to designate a different *Race* (e.g., *Other*) as the reference category (category 0).

To summarize, the goal is to use the *Recode into Different Variables* function to

- recode *Race* (wherein *African American* = 0 and *Other* = 4) into a new variable (*Race_O*) wherein *Other = 0* and *African American = 4*.
- copy all the other category codes within *Race* (1 = Asian, 2 = Caucasian, 3 = Latino) as is to *Race_O*.
- leave the original *Race* variable intact (Figure 14.17).

Figure 14.17   Recoding *Race* (without altering *Race*) to create *Race_O*.

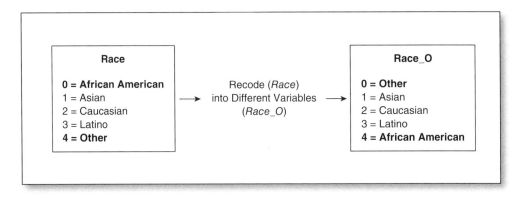

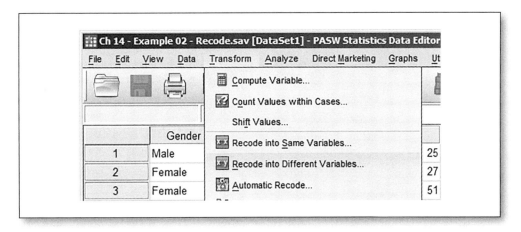

Figure 14.18 Click on *Transform, Recode into Different Variables*.

1. Click on *Transform, Recode into Different Variables* (Figure 14.18).

2. On the *Recode into Different Variables* menu, move *Race* into the *Numeric Variable → Output Variable*: box.

3. In the *Output Variable, Name* box, type in *Race_O* (which stands for *Race* with *Other* as 0—the reference category).

4. Click on *Change*.

5. Click on *Old and New Values*.

6. In the *Old Value, Value* box, enter 0, and in the *New Value, Value* box, enter 4 (this will recode *African Americans* to 4 in the *Race_O* variable) (Figure 4.19).

7. Click on *Add*.

8. In the *Old Value, Value* box, enter 4, and in the *New Value, Value* box, enter 0 (this will recode *Other* to 0 in the *Race_O* variable) (Figure 4.20).

9. Click on *Add*.

10. To copy the other values from *Race* to *Race_O* as is, click on *Old Value, All other values*.

11. Click on *New Value, Copy old value(s)* (Figure 14.21).

12. Click *Add*. The menu should resemble Figure 14.22, indicating that 0 will be recoded as 4, 4 will be recoded as 0, and everything else will be copied as is: 1 will be recoded as 1, 2 will be recoded as 2, and 3 will be recoded as 3.

13. Click *Continue;* this will return you to the *Recode into Different Variable* menu.

Figure 14.19 Define recoding: Change *Old Value* (*Race* = 0) to *New Value* (*Race_0* = 4).

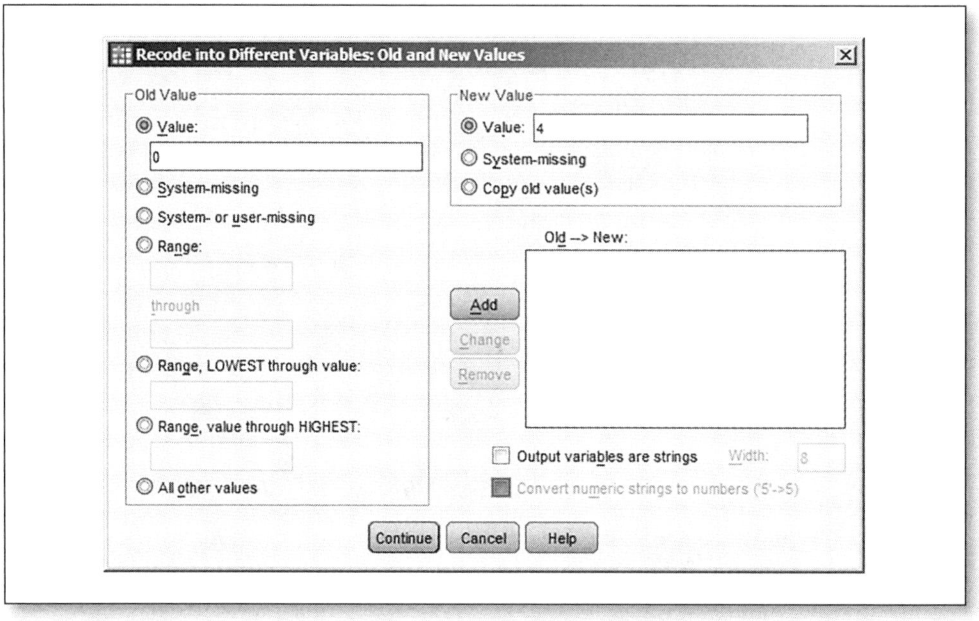

Figure 14.20 Define recoding: Change *Old Value* (*Race* = 4) to *New Value* (*Race_0* = 0).

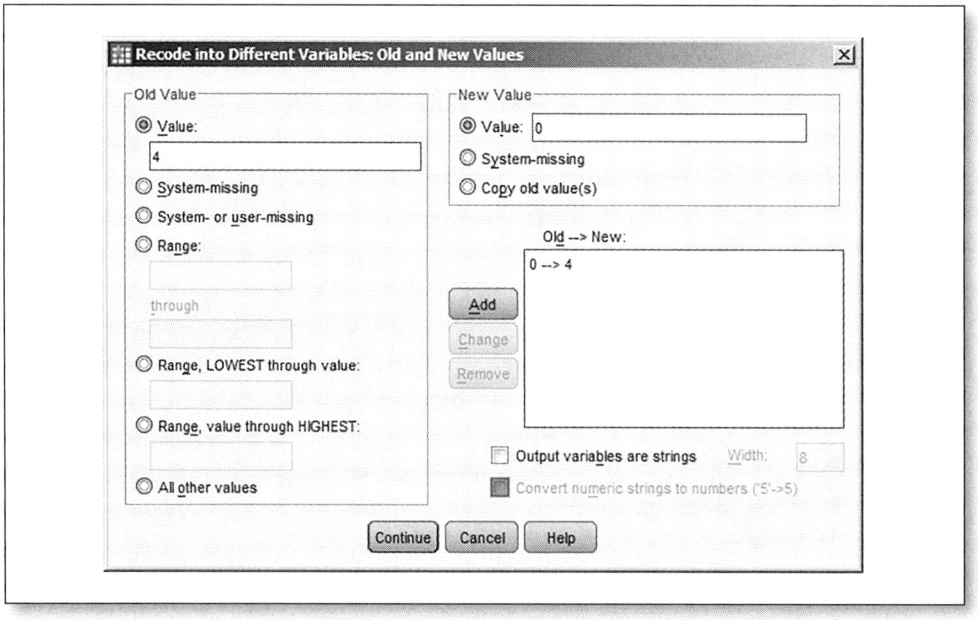

Figure 14.21 Define recoding: Change *Old Value* (*Race* = 0) to *New Value* (*Race_0* = 4).

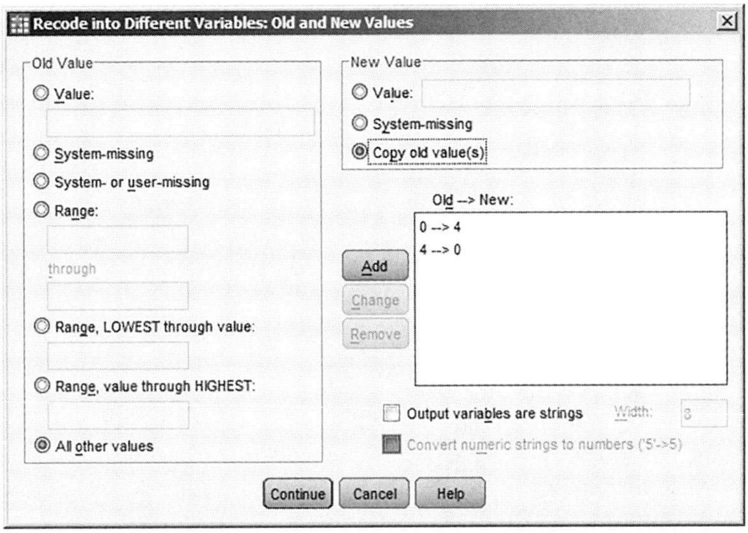

Figure 14.22 Final recoding definitions.

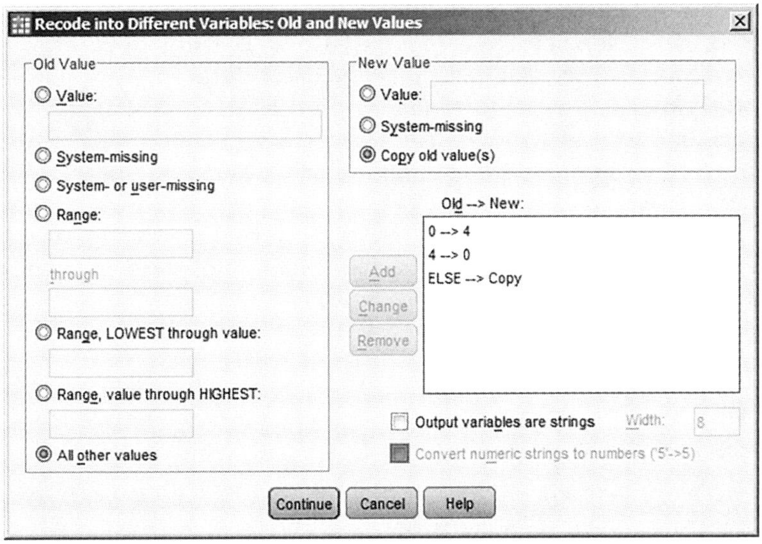

14. On the *Recode into Different Variable* menu, click *OK*.

15. To finalize the process, go to the *Variable View* menu and make the following modifications to configure the properties of the (new) *Race_O* variable:

   a. Set *Width* to *20*

   b. Set *Decimals* to *0*

   c. Set *Align* to *Right*

   d. Set *Measure* to *Nominal*

   e. Set *Values* to *0 = Other, 1 = Asian, 2 = Caucasian, 3 = Latino, 4 = African American*

Notice that in both of the *Recoding* examples, we opted to *Recode into Different Variables* as opposed to *Recode into Same Variables*. This choice preserved the original variables, which enables us to perform further analyses on them. Had we used *Recode into Same Variables*, the original values would have been overwritten; hence, the source data would be compromised. In addition, if an error had occurred during the recoding process, the (source) variable would have been corrupted, and hence, it would not be possible to reattempt the recoding procedure. A reasonable rule of thumb is this: *Recode all you want (to other variables), but always keep your source data intact*.

Importing Data

So far, all data we have used have been prepared to operate properly in SPSS, but as you might expect, there is a world of worthy data out there, not necessarily in SPSS format. When the data are only available on paper, naturally you will have to enter the data manually. Fortunately, more and more data are available in a digital form; even if the data are not in SPSS format, SPSS is equipped with some fairly versatile features for **importing data**, designed to promptly load non-SPSS data into the SPSS environment for processing.

The two most common forms of non-SPSS data are Microsoft Excel and ASCII (pronounced *ask-key*) files, also known as *text* files. Once you see how to import data from these two sources, you should be able to reason your way through importing other data formats.

The import data feature in SPSS tends to vary somewhat from version to version. If there is a discrepancy between the instructions in this section and how your version of SPSS operates, then consult the Help menu in your software and search for *import* or *import data*.

Importing Excel Data

Data Set

The data set that will be imported into SPSS is **Ch 14 – Example 03 – Excel Data.xls**. SPSS contains an import utility that enables you to load data from multiple (non-SPSS) sources, including Excel. The Excel file that we will be importing contains 101 rows;

the first row contains the variable name for each column (*ID, Age, Score*), followed by 100 records, each with three variables (columns):

Codebook

Variable:	ID
Definition:	Identification code
Type:	Alphanumeric

Variable:	Age
Definition:	Age
Type:	Continuous

Variable:	Score
Definition:	Exam score
Type:	Continuous

The first row of the Excel file that you will be importing has the variable names at the top of each column; this will be useful when it comes to the import process. If these names were not present, you could still proceed with the import, but you would need a codebook to know how to label the variables after the file has been imported.

1. Click on *File, Open, Data* (Figure 14.23). This will take you to the *Open File* menu (Figure 14.24).

Figure 14.23 To begin import process, click on *File, Open, Data.*

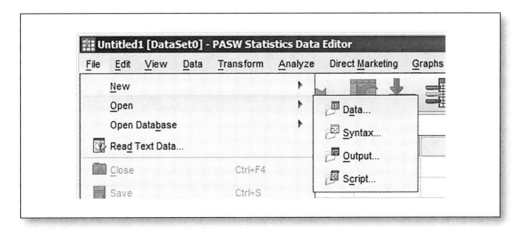

Figure 14.24 *Open Data* menu; for *Files of type,* select *Excel,* and for *File name,* select **Ch 14 – Example 03 – Excel Data.xls.**

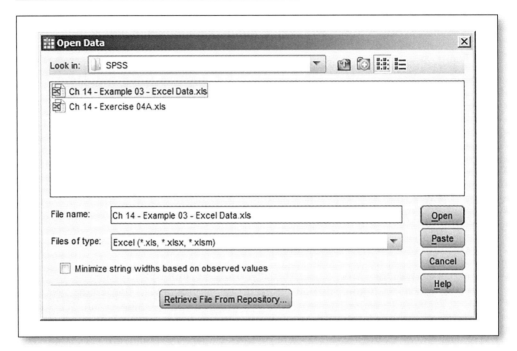

2. On the *Open Data* menu (Figure 14.23) for *Files of type,* select *Excel;* this will narrow the file list to Excel worksheets only.

3. In the large file list window, select **Chapter 14 – Example 03 – Excel Data.xls** and click on the *Open* button. This will take you to the *Opening Excel Data Source* menu (Figure 14.25).

4. In this case, in the *Opening Excel Data Source* menu (Figure 14.25), the defaults are correct: Because the Excel worksheet has the variable names at the top of each column, the corresponding checkbox (☑ *Read variable names from the first row of data*) is checked. If the variable names are not included as the first row in the Excel sheet, then uncheck that box.

5. The input utility also identified the worksheet and cells involved correctly: *Sheet1 [A1:C101].* Click on the *OK* button.

6. SPSS will process the import; notice that the system loaded the Excel file, and the variable names have been assigned accordingly (Figure 14.26).

7. To further verify that the import worked properly, switch to the *Variable View* screen (Figure 14.27). Notice that *ID* has been brought in as a string variable

because it contains alphanumeric characters, and *Age* and *Score* have been correctly configured as numeric variables.

8. You can now proceed with statistical analyses. When you are ready to save the file, the system will write it out as an SPSS file unless you specify otherwise.

Figure 14.25 Opening *Excel Data Source* menu.

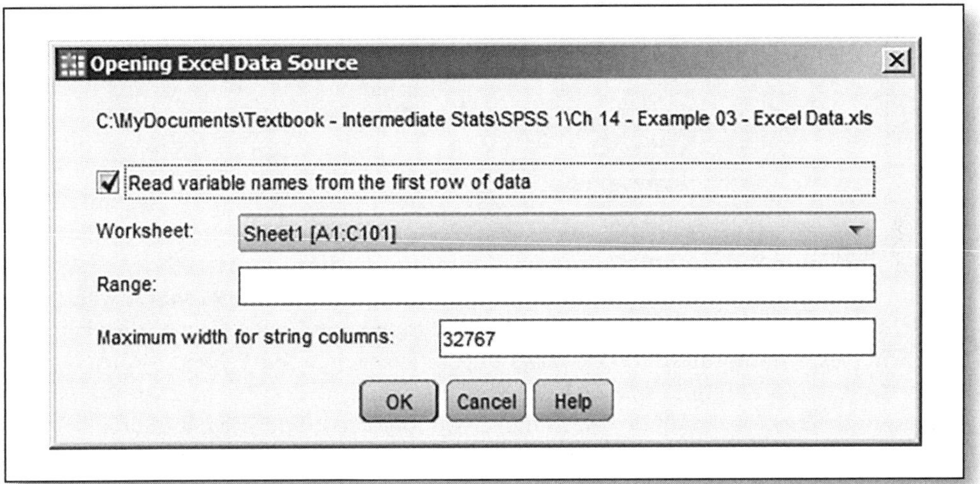

Figure 14.26 *Data View* screen after Excel file import.

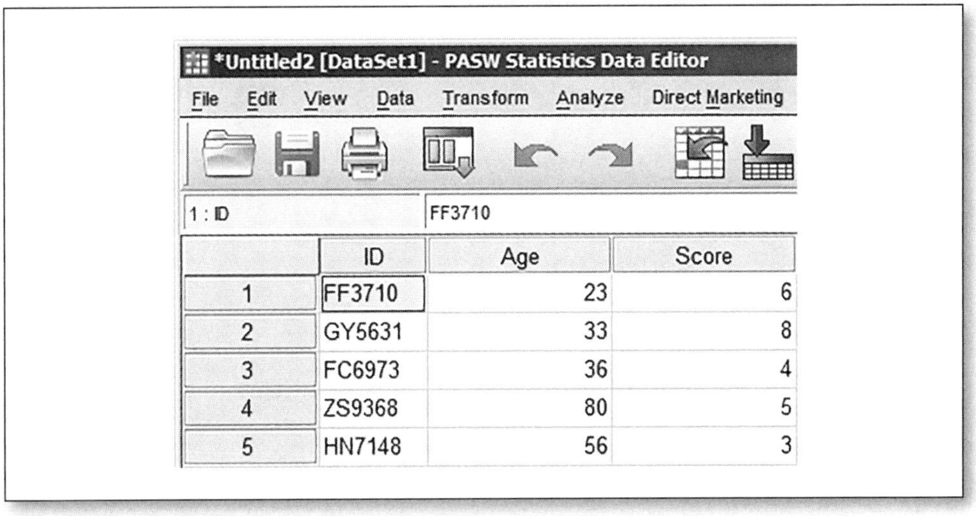

Figure 14.27 *Variable View* screen after Excel file import.

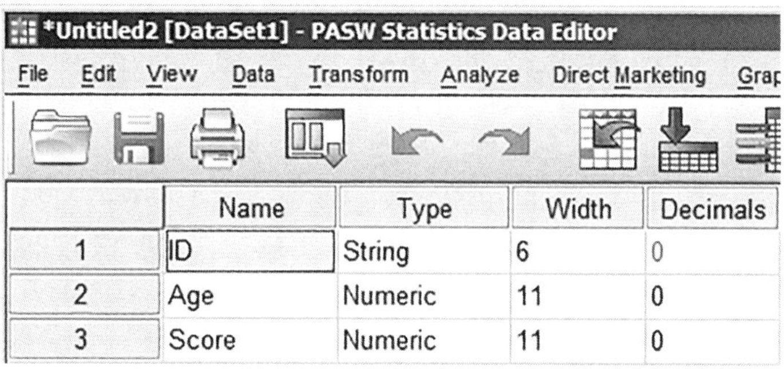

	Name	Type	Width	Decimals
1	ID	String	6	0
2	Age	Numeric	11	0
3	Score	Numeric	11	0

Importing ASCII Data

ASCII stands for *American Standard Code for Information Interchange;* it is basically a generic, plain text file, not associated with any particular software package. ASCII file names typically have a.*txt* (text),.*csv* (Comma Separated Values), or, less often, an *asc* (ASCII) suffix (e.g., *Experiment18.txt, Test_Scores_Cycle_23.csv, DistrictA.asc*). The data in such files are traditionally arranged with one record per row; the variables within each row are usually separated by a delimiter character, such as a comma or other symbol (Figure 14.28). Alternatively, some files do not use delimiters to separate variables; instead, they use a fixed number of characters per variable, producing columns of data padded with spaces (Figure 14.29).

Delimited files are more common, so this example will involve a comma-delimited ASCII file, although by specifying the right options in the import process, SPSS can accurately import fixed-column ASCII data as well.

Figure 14.28 Comma-delimited ASCII data.

```
ID,Age,Score
DE7015,72,5
LP4964,35,6
PF9120,51,6
HC4109,49,10
EH8610,66,3
RV3966,31,3
JZ4866,61,8
```

Figure 14.29 Fixed-column ASCII data.

ID	Age	Score
DE7015	72	5
LP4964	35	6
PF9120	51	6
HC4109	49	10
EH8610	66	3
RV3966	31	3
JZ4866	61	8

Data Set

The data set that will be imported into SPSS is **Ch 14 – Example 04 – Comma Delimited Data.txt.**

1. Click on *File, Open, Data* (Figure 14.30). This will take you to the *Open File* menu (Figure 14.31).

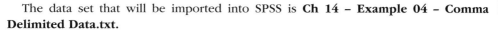

Figure 14.30 To begin import process, click on *File, Open, Data.*

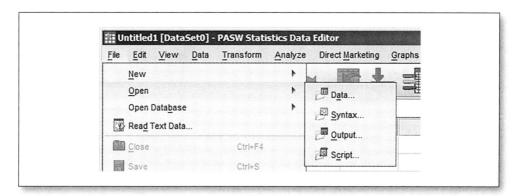

Figure 14.31 *Open Data* menu; for *Files of type,* select *Text (*.txt, *.dat),* and for *File name,* select **Ch 14 – Example 04 – Comma Delimited Data.txt.**

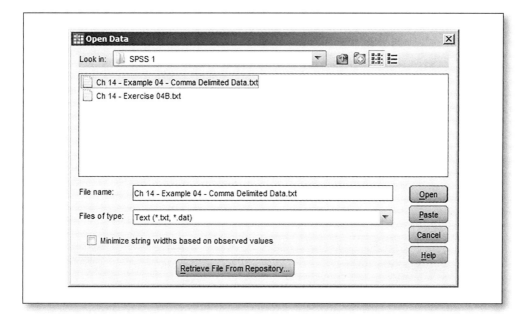

2. On the *Open Data* menu (Figure 14.31) for *Files of type,* select *Text*; this will narrow the file list. If the file name has a suffix other than.*txt,* then at the *Files of type* option, select *All Files.*

3. On the large file list window, select **Ch 14 – Example 04 – Comma Delimited Data.txt** and click on the *Open* button. This will take you to the *Text Import Wizard—Step 1 of 6* menu (Figure 14.32).

Figure 14.32 *Text Import Wizard—Step 1 of 6* menu.

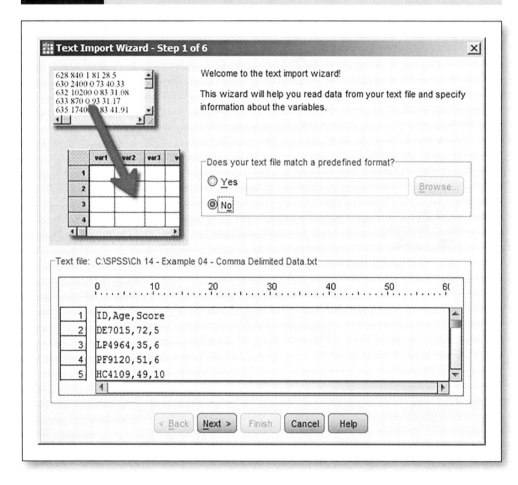

4. On the *Text Import Wizard—Step 1 of 6* menu, click on the *Next >* button. This will take you to the *Text Import Wizard—Step 2 of 6* menu (Figure 14.33).

5. On the *Text Import Wizard—Step 2 of 6* menu, because this is a comma-delimited data set, for the *How are your variables arranged?* question, select *Delimited.*

Figure 14.33   *Text Import Wizard—Step 2 of 6* menu.

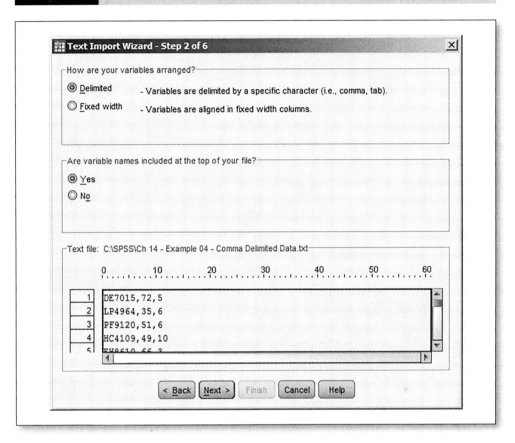

6. For the *Are variable names included at the top of your file?* question, select *Yes*. Then, click on the *Next >* button; this will take you to the *Text Import Wizard—Step 3 of 6* menu.

7. On the *Text Import Wizard—Steps 3–5* menus, the defaults are all appropriate. Click on the *Next >* button for each of these menus until you reach the *Text Import Wizard—Step 6 of 6* menu.

8. On the *Text Import Wizard—Step 6 of 6* menu, click on the *Finish* button.

9. SPSS will process the import; notice that the system loaded the ASCII comma-delimited text file, with the variable names assigned accordingly (Figure 14.34).

10. To further verify that the import worked properly, switch to the *Variable View* screen (Figure 14.35). Notice that *ID* has been brought in as a string variable because it contains alphanumeric characters, and *Age* and *Score* have been correctly configured as numeric variables.

Figure 14.34 *Data View* screen after text file import.

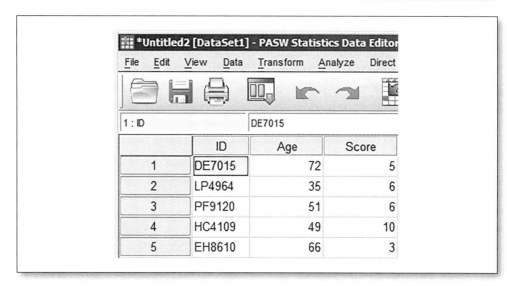

Figure 14.35 *Variable View* screen after text file import.

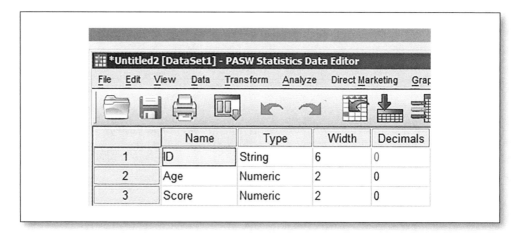

11. You can now proceed with statistical analyses. When you are ready to save the file, the system will write it out as an SPSS file unless you specify otherwise.

If the data that you are importing contain categorical variables coded as numbers (e.g., 1 = *Yes*, 2 = *No*), it would be to your advantage to gather as much codebook information as you can so that you can assign the appropriate data labels for each such variable.

SPSS Syntax

The convenient point-and-click menu system that we have used to operate SPSS is ideal for the kind of statistical processing that we have performed in this book, wherein each data set is processed just once.

In instances involving complex analyses that will be run repeatedly (e.g., weekly/monthly reports on an evolving database), there is an alternative to clicking through multiple menus, hoping to specify each parameter perfectly every time. In such instances, it would be more efficient to store the statistical processing commands in a program that could be reliably run on demand.

Historically speaking, SPSS was initially implemented before the advent of menu-driven software—as such, the **SPSS Syntax** language was developed, wherein statistical processing commands were typed in, one line at a time. The SPSS Syntax language is still a part of the SPSS system, but you do not necessarily need to learn an entire programming language to use it.

You may have noticed that on most of the menus, there is a *Paste* button next to the *OK* button. Whereas *OK* executes the instructions that you specified on the menu(s) immediately, *Paste* does not; instead, *Paste* assesses the parameters that you specified on the associated menu(s) and automatically produces the equivalent SPSS Syntax code.

Data Set

The data set that will be imported into SPSS is **Ch 14 – Example 04 – Syntax.sav**.

Codebook

Variable:	Age
Definition:	Age
Type:	Continuous

For example, suppose you wanted to produce descriptive statistics and a histogram with a normal curve for the variable *Age*. You would begin at the *Analyze, Descriptive, Statistics, Frequencies* menu (Figure 14.36).

Next, on the *Statistics* (sub)menu, you would specify the descriptive statistics that you want processed (Figure 14.37), and on the *Charts* (sub)menu, you would order the corresponding histogram with normal curve (Figure 14.38).

At this point, we would usually click on *OK* (Figure 14.36) to run the analysis, but instead, click on *Paste*. Instead of running the analysis (now), *Paste* tells the system to assess the parameters specified in the menu(s) and then generate the equivalent block of SPSS Syntax code (Figure 14.39).

Each time you click on the *Paste* button, SPSS makes this menu-to-Syntax conversion and adds the lines of Syntax programming code to the bottom of the accumulating Syntax file—essentially, you are building a Syntax program, one block of code at a time.

Figure 14.36 *Frequencies* menu (for descriptive statistics).

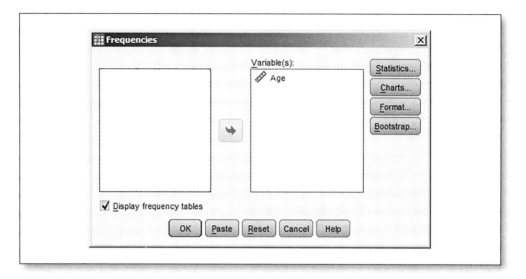

Figure 14.37 *Frequencies Statistics* menu.

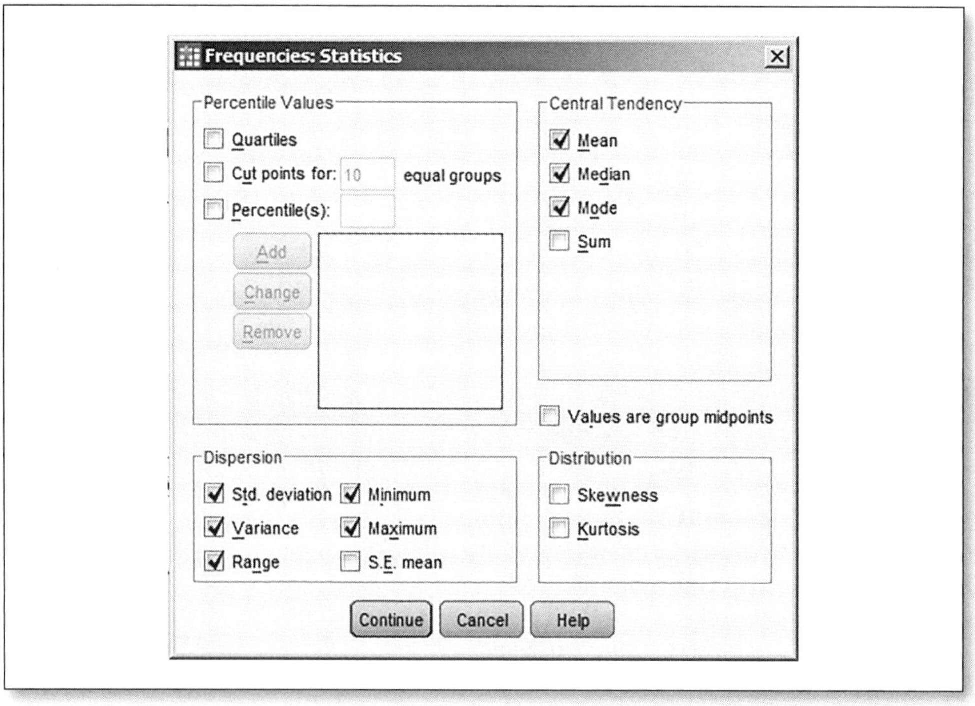

Figure 14.38   *Frequencies Charts* menu.

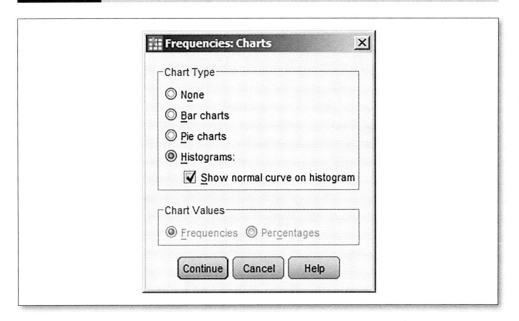

Figure 14.39   SPSS *Syntax Editor* window.

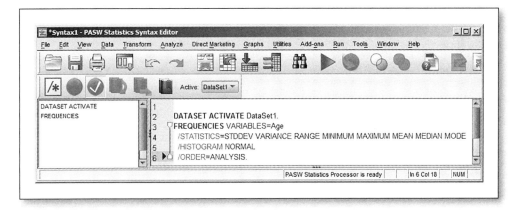

When you save the Syntax code, it will be assigned the **sps** suffix to the file name (e.g., *Monthly_Sales.sps*). You have probably already noticed that SPSS data files have the *sav* file name suffix.

Using a Syntax file to run analyses spares you from having to visit multiple menus and correctly specifying the variables and processing parameters each time. To run this code, highlight the lines that you want processed (in this case, all of the lines), and then click on the *Run* (▶) icon.

Most but not all menus in SPSS contain the *Paste* button; hence, if you opt for the SPSS Syntax language to run your analyses, occasionally you may need to do some manual editing or coding. The SPSS Syntax language is a fully developed programming language that extends well beyond the blocks of code that you can generate by clicking on the *Paste* button.

As you might expect, as more blocks of SPSS Syntax code are included, the programs become more sophisticated. Considering how abstract any programming language can appear, it is useful to include comments in the code. Clearly written comments help to make such programs more maintainable over time, as modifications are often required over the life of a project.

Comments are manually typed in, and the rules are simple: Start the new line with the word **Comment** or an asterisk (*). The *Comment* command is not case sensitive, so you can enter it as *COMMENT*, *comment*, *Comment*, or even *coMmENt*. The system will ignore everything that follows until it encounters a period (.). For example, notice the two comments that have been entered at the top of the Syntax code as follows:

```
Comment Programmed by H. Knapp.

* This produces the descriptive statistics and histogram with normal curve for Age.

FREQUENCIES VARIABLES=Age

/STATISTICS=STDDEV VARIANCE RANGE MINIMUM MAXIMUM MEAN MEDIAN
MODE SUM

/HISTOGRAM NORMAL

/ORDER=ANALYSIS.
```

In addition to writing meaningful comments, you can also include blank lines to separate blocks of code.

CREATING DUMMY VARIABLES USING SYNTAX

In **Chapter 12: Multiple Regression**, all of the data sets that involved polychotomous categorical predictor variables included the dummy-coded corresponding variables using the binary matrix coding scheme. Typically, data sets do not contain these dummy-coded supplemental variables. As such, when it comes to creating these variables, there are two choices: (1) Manually type in all of the 0s and 1s, which considering the large number of records involved in multiple regression data sets would be time consuming and vulnerable to typographical errors, or (2) use a brief SPSS Syntax program to generate these dummy-coded variables quickly and accurately.

DATA SETS

This example involves two files:

1. First, open **Ch 14 - Example 05 - Dummy Coding.sav**. To simplify this example, this data set contains only one polychotomous variable and seven records.

Codebook

>   Variable: EyeColor
>
>   Definition: The participant's eye color
>
>   Type: Categorical (0 = Amber, 1 = Blue, 2 = Brown, 3 = Gray, 4 = Green, 5 = Hazel, 6 = Violet)

2. Next, open **Ch 14 - Example 05 - Dummy Coding.sps**. This Syntax file will automatically generate the dummy-coded variables (*EyeColor.1*...*EyeColor.6*) for *EyeColor*. To open this Syntax file, click on *File, Open, Syntax* (Figure 14.40).

Figure 14.40   To open a Syntax file, click on *File, Open, Syntax*.

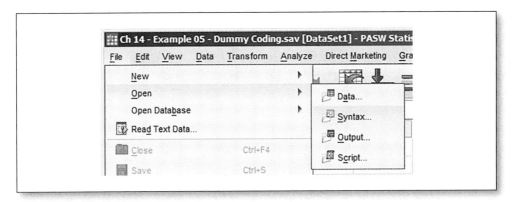

3. Select **Ch 14 - Example 05 - Dummy Coding.sps** (Figure 14.41).
4. To run the Syntax file, highlight all of the lines and click on the ▶ icon.

Figure 14.41 Open *Example 05 - Dummy Coding.sps*.

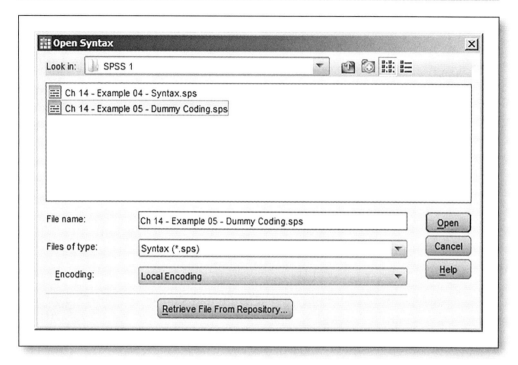

Notice that it promptly and accurately created the variables *EyeColor.1*, *EyeColor.2*, *EyeColor.3*, *EyeColor.4*, *EyeColor.5*, *and EyeColor.6* with all of the 0s and 1s properly placed. As detailed in the comments, the program begins by putting all 0s into the dummy variables. Next, the program refers to *EyeColor* and puts the 1s in the proper places in each of the dummy variables (*EyeColor.1*. . . *EyeColor.6*). After that, the program performs some (optional) formatting strictly for esthetics; if these formatting instructions are deleted, it will not affect the statistical results. (NOTE: Remember, the * means "comment.")

```
* SPSS Syntax file: Ch14 - Example 05 – Dummy Coding.sps.

* SPSS table: Ch14 - Example 05 – Dummy Coding.sav.

* Programmed by H. Knapp.

* This program creates dummy variables for EyeColor.
```

(Continued)

(Continued)

```
* Put 0s in all of the dummy variables.

compute EyeColor.1 = 0.

compute EyeColor.2 = 0.

compute EyeColor.3 = 0.

compute EyeColor.4 = 0.

compute EyeColor.5 = 0.

compute EyeColor.6 = 0.

* Put 1s in the dummy variables based on EyeColor.

if EyeColor = 1 EyeColor.1 = 1.

if EyeColor = 2 EyeColor.2 = 1.

if EyeColor = 3 EyeColor.3 = 1.

if EyeColor = 4 EyeColor.4 = 1.

if EyeColor = 5 EyeColor.5 = 1.

if EyeColor = 6 EyeColor.6 = 1.

* This optional code sets the decimals = 0 and the column width to 8.

format EyeColor.1 EyeColor.2 EyeColor.3 EyeColor.4 EyeColor.5 EyeColor.6 (f).

var width EyeColor.1 EyeColor.2 EyeColor.3 EyeColor.4 EyeColor.5 EyeColor.6 (8).

* Run the above code.

execute.
```

You can edit this Syntax code to efficiently generate dummy variables for other polychotomous variables. The procedure is fairly simple: Count the number of categories contained within the polychotomous variable and subtract 1; this will tell you how many dummy variables to create. In this example, *EyeColor* contains seven categories (0 = Amber, 1 = Blue, 2 = Brown, 3 = Gray, 4 = Green, 5 = Hazel, 6 = Violet); hence, six dummy variables (*EyeColor.1*, *EyeColor.2*, *EyeColor.3*, *EyeColor.4*, *EyeColor.5* and *EyeColor.6*) are used to represent *EyeColor*.

After running the Syntax program, notice how the numbers in the dummy variables form a binary matrix to represent the values in *EyeColor* (Figure 14.42).

Figure 14.42	Polychotomous variable *EyeColor* with dummy-coded variables (*EyeColor.1. . . EyeColor.6*).

Figure 14.42 — Polychotomous variable *EyeColor* with dummy-coded variables (*EyeColor.1. . . EyeColor.6*).

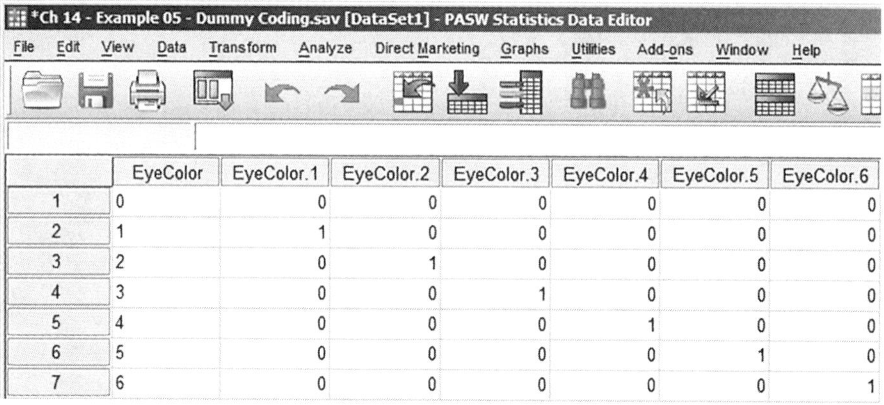

	EyeColor	EyeColor.1	EyeColor.2	EyeColor.3	EyeColor.4	EyeColor.5	EyeColor.6
1	0	0	0	0	0	0	0
2	1	1	0	0	0	0	0
3	2	0	1	0	0	0	0
4	3	0	0	1	0	0	0
5	4	0	0	0	1	0	0
6	5	0	0	0	0	1	0
7	6	0	0	0	0	0	1

For a more comprehensive guide detailing the commands and functions available in the SPSS Syntax language, a useful introductory manual is *How to Use SPSS Syntax: An Overview of Common Commands* by Manfred te Grotenhuis and Chris Visscher.

GOOD COMMON SENSE

It is good practice to save an unedited **master file** of your source data sets (e.g., *File_Name[MASTER].sav*) and only perform your analysis on a **work file**—a copy of the file (e.g., *File_Name[WORK].sav*).

Even for the most careful person, data loss or data corruption is just an accidental keystroke away. Try to avoid deleting records; a better practice is to use *Select Cases* to rule such data out of the analyses.

If you have source data (e.g., survey cards, written records, recordings, etc.), keep them intact and stored in a secured fashion. It is generally considered good practice not to destroy or discard source media just because the information has been entered into a database. You may need to refer to such materials over the course of your investigation (e.g., to resolve discrepancies, verify that some anomalous data are coded properly, etc.). Occasionally, such references to source materials take place during the analytic process as outliers, and other reasonably questionable data begin to emerge in reports or in visual inspection of the coded data.

All hardware fails at some point; as such, **data storage** should involve more than simply clicking *Save*. It is good practice to keep secured/encrypted up-to-date backups of data files in at least two safe locations (e.g., a copy at home and another copy at work), unless your research protocol prohibits this. The rationale for two sites is to offer additional protection against unforeseen adverse events at a site (e.g., fire, water damage, natural disaster, theft, electrical problems, etc.).

Some research protocols specify how long the research team is required to retain the source data (e.g., surveys, field notes, recordings, etc.). The time frame may range from days to years. The research protocol may also indicate a specific method for **data disposal** on the specified expiration date (e.g., shredding, purging media, transfer to a secured storage site, etc.) so as to facilitate participant confidentiality. As a responsible researcher, be sure you fully understand and adhere to these protocols.

Key Concepts

- Generating random numbers
- Sorting cases
  - Ascending
  - Descending
- Selecting cases
- Recoding
- Importing data
- SPSS Syntax
- Data management
  - Master file
  - Work file
  - Data handling
  - Data storage
  - Data disposal

Practice Exercises

Exercise 14.1

You have been given a data set reflecting the baseline test results of a group of people administered a pretest prior to a training.

Data set: **Ch 14 - Exercise 01.sav**

Codebook

Variable:	Name
Definition:	The participant's name
Type:	Alphanumeric

Variable: Score

Definition: The participant's pretest score

Type: Continuous

Variable: Skill

Definition: The participant's skill level, based on score

Type: Categorical (1 = Novice, 2 = Intermediate, 3 = Expert)

a. Sort the data alphabetically by name.

b. Sort the data from highest to lowest score; in cases where the score is a tie, subsort alphabetically by name.

Exercise 14.2

You have been given a sample frame with record numbers ranging from 852 through 5723; the research team wants to gather a 2% sample ($n = 97$). Use SPSS to generate this list of random numbers.

Exercise 14.3

You have been requested to compute statistics using only certain records within a data set.

Data set: **Ch 14 - Exercise 03.sav** (this is the same data set as **Ch 14 - Exercise 01.sav**)

Codebook

Variable: Name

Definition: The participant's name

Type: Alphanumeric

Variable: Score

Definition: The participant's pretest score

Type: Continuous

Variable: Skill

Definition: The participant's skill level, based on score

Type: Categorical (1 = Novice, 2 = Intermediate, 3 = Expert)

a. Compute descriptive statistics and histograms with a normal curve for *Score* for participants with a skill level that is Intermediate.

b. Compute descriptive statistics and histograms with a normal curve for *Score* for participants with a score between 20 and 65.

Exercise 14.4

You have been given two non-SPSS data sets to import into SPSS and process:

a. Data set: Import the Excel file **Ch 14 - Exercise 04A.xls** into SPSS (NOTE: This Excel file has the variable names Group and Score on the top row.)

Codebook

Variable:	Group
Definition:	Group assignment
Type:	Categorical (1 = Control, 2 = Treatment)
Variable:	Score
Definition:	Participant's pretest score
Type:	Continuous

NOTE: The import utility does not know what value labels are involved in the (categorical) group variable; it will just bring in the 1s and 2s. You will need to assign the corresponding value labels per the earlier codebook.

Compute a *t* test on Score using Group as the grouping variable.

b. Data set: Import the ASCII (text) file **Ch 14 - Exercise 04B.txt** into SPSS (NOTE: This text file has the variable names ID, Pretest and Posttest on the top row.)

Codebook

Variable:	ID
Definition:	Participant's ID
Type:	Continuous
Variable:	Pretest
Definition:	Pretest score
Type:	Continuous

Variable:	Posttest
Definition:	Posttest score
Type:	Continuous

Compute a paired *t* test using pretest and posttest.

Exercise 14.5

Prior to a training, those who enrolled were given a pretest to determine their baseline knowledge of the subject. Those who scored 70 or higher on a pretest will be issued a pass and will be excused from the training session.

Data set: **Ch 14 - Exercise 05.sav** (this is the same data set as **Ch 14 – Exercise 01.sav**)

Codebook

Variable:	Name
Definition:	The participant's name
Type:	Alphanumeric

Variable:	Score
Definition:	The participant's pretest score
Type:	Continuous

Variable:	Skill
Definition:	The participant's skill level, based on score
Type:	Categorical (1 = Novice, 2 = Intermediate, 3 = Expert)

a. Use the Recode function to create a new variable *Result* (based on *Score*) that identifies those who passed and those who failed; use the following codebook to assign the categorical value labels for result:

Codebook

Variable:	Result
Definition:	The participant's result on their score
Type:	Categorical (1 = Fail [under 70], 2 = Pass [70 or over])

b. Run descriptive statistics on score with a histogram and normal curve for those who failed. HINT: Use *Result* to guide the Select Cases process.

c. Run descriptive statistics on score with a histogram and normal curve for those who passed. HINT: Use *Result* to guide the Select Cases process.

Exercise 14.6

Acme Research Labs gathers data on an ongoing basis; you have been asked to automate the analytic process for a data set that is updated each week.

Data set: **Ch 14 - Exercise 06.sav**

Codebook

Variable:	ID
Definition:	The participant's ID
Type:	Alphanumeric
Variable:	Reading
Definition:	The participant's reading score
Type:	Continuous
Variable:	Writing
Definition:	The participant's writing score
Type:	Continuous
Variable:	Math
Definition:	The participant's math score
Type:	Continuous

a. Use the *Paste* function to create an SPSS Syntax file that performs the following operations:

Perform a multilevel sort:

1. Reading (ascending)

2. Writing (descending)

3. Math (ascending)

b. Run descriptive statistics with histograms and normal curves for Reading and *Math*, but instead of clicking the OK button to run the analysis, click the *Paste* button to append the Syntax commands to the existing Syntax file. Finally, save the SPSS Syntax file as *Report1.sps* (NOTE: This SPSS Syntax file will be used in Exercise 14.7).

Exercise 14.7

Open the SPSS Syntax file created in Exercise 14.6 (*Report1.sps*) and (manually) add comments detailing the following:

- Appropriate header information (your name, the version number, and summary of what this SPSS Syntax program does)
- Notes explaining what each block of code does

Exercise 14.8

Describe what a master file is and the rationale for safely preserving it.

Exercise 14.9

Describe what a work file is and the rationale for performing analyses on it.

Exercise 14.10

Data safety and confidentiality are essential in the realm of responsible and ethical research and analysis. Such data can exist on a variety of media (e.g., hard copy [paper], handwritten notes, images, audio recordings, video recordings, electronic data). Discuss the rationale and protocol for appropriate data handling, data storage, and data disposal.

Glossary

!: See *Factorial.*

*: See *Comment.*

% formula: See *Percent.*

.sps file extension: .sps files contain SPSS syntax code (programs).

.sav file extension: .sav files contain SPSS data sets.

α error: See *Type I error level.*

α value: See *Alpha value.*

β error: See *Type II error.*

Δ%: *See Delta %.*

Alpha value: The cutoff score for the p value; alpha is typically set to .05, wherein p values $\leq .05$ suggest statistically significant finding(s).

Alternate hypothesis (H₁): The hypothesis that states that the treatment effect will be significant; the score for the control group will be different from the score for the treatment group.

ANCOVA: Analysis of covariance similar to ANOVA, except results are adjusted per the identified confounding variable (covariate).

ANOVA: Analysis of variance similar to the t test, except it compares all pairs of groups ($G_1 : G_2, G_1 : G_3, G_2 : G_3$).

ANOVA repeated measures: Similar to the paired t test, except it compares scores from all pairs of time points ($T_1 : T_2, T_2 : T_3, T_1 : T_3$).

Area sampling: A probability sampling technique typically used to draw proportional random samples from multiple domains (e.g., blocks spanning a community).

ASCII: Acronym for American Standard Code for Information Interchange (a generic/alphanumeric data file).

Backward processing: Specifies the processing order of predictors in a multiple regression model, wherein all of the predictor variables are initially loaded into the model regardless of their statistical significance, then statistically insignificant predictor(s) are dropped.

Bar chart: A graphical representation of the numbers contained within a categorical variable, consisting of a bar chart.

Bimodal: Descriptor for two numbers tied for the most common number contained within a continuous variable (both numbers are equally frequent within the variable).

Box's *M* test: See *Homogeneity of variance-covariance (Box's M test)*.

Categorical variable: A variable that contains a discrete value (e.g., Gender = Female/Male).

Causation: Correlation demonstrating that one variable influenced the outcome of another by meeting three criteria: (1) association/correlation, (2) temporality, and (3) nonspurious relationship.

Chi-square: Indicates if there is a statistically significant difference between two categorical variables.

Comma delimited data: A data set wherein a comma (,) separates the variables.

Comment: Comments manually entered into SPSS Syntax code to internally document the program. (e.g., Comment This section computes the descriptive statistics.) NOTE: * can be substituted for Comment.

Confounding variable: A variable or factor, other than the independent variable (IV), that influences the dependent (outcome) variable (DV).

Continuous variable: A variable that contains a number along a continuum (e.g., Age = 0 . . . 100).

Control group: The group that receives either no treatment or treatment as usual (TAU) to serve as a comparison against the group(s) that receive the (experimental) treatment.

Correlation: Indicates the strength of the relationship between two continuous variables gathered from each participant/data record.

Correlation strength: Indicator for correlations nearer to -1 or $+1$, suggesting stronger correlations than correlations nearer to 0.

Covariate: See *Confounding variable*.

Crosstabs: A statistical table that contains results based on column : row.

Crosstabulation: See *Crosstabs*.

Data disposal: Pertains to when and how data (electronic and other) are to be disposed of (e.g., secure reformat/erasure of electronic media, shredding paper, relocating media to secured facility).

Data set: A table of alphanumeric information prepared for statistical processing.

Data storage: Pertains to where and how data (electronic and other) are securely kept.

Data View: SPSS screen wherein the actual information contained in the SPSS data set is viewed/edited.

Delta %: Also represented as $\Delta\%$, expressing the change percentage in a variable: $\Delta\% = (\text{New} - \text{Old}) \div \text{Old} \times 100$.

Descriptive statistics: A summary of a variable using figures and graphs that can characterize continuous or categorical variables.

Dichotomous: A categorical variable that contains two values (e.g., Gender: Female/Male).

Dummy coding: A method of representing a polychotomous using a binary matrix in multiple regression processing

Dummy variables: A binary variable representing the value of a categorical variable in multiple regression processing.

Enter processing: Specifies the processing order of predictors in a multiple regression model, wherein the predictor variable(s) are loaded into the model regardless of their statistical or R^2 value.

Experimental group: The group(s) that receives the (experimental) treatment, which will be compared to the control group.

Factorial: Also represented as !, a probability calculation wherein a number is multiplied by all of the integers between 1 and the specified number (e.g., 3! = 1 × 2 × 3, which equals 6).

Forward processing: Specifies the processing order of predictors in a multiple regression model, wherein statistically significant predictor variables are loaded into descending based on their R^2 value.

GIGO: Acronym for *Garbage In, Garbage Out* pertaining to the necessity of entering and processing quality data to produce quality results

H_0: See *Null hypothesis.*

H_1: See *Alternate hypothesis.*

Histogram with normal curve: A graphical representation of the numbers contained within a continuous variable, consisting of a bar chart with a bell-shaped curve superimposed on it.

Historical threat to internal validity: Most relevant to longitudinal designs (e.g., *t* test, ANOVA repeated measures), wherein events outside the experimental procedure may act as confounding variables.

Homogeneity of regression slopes: A pretest criterion for ANCOVA that evaluates the similarity of the regression slopes among the independent variables (IVs).

Homogeneity of variance: Similarity of variance (SD^2) among two or more variables.

Homogeneity of variance-covariance (Box's *M* test): A pretest criterion for MANOVA that evaluates the similarity of the covariances among the independent variables (IVs).

Homoscedastic: See *Homoscedasticity.*

Homoscedasticity: The arrangement of points on a scatterplot wherein most of the points are in the middle of the distribution.

Hypothesis resolution: Using the statistical results to determine which hypothesis came true.

Importing data: Transforming data that were initially coded in a foreign format to accurately load into an application.

Incremental monitoring (O X O X O): A research design that can be used with ANOVA repeated measures to assess the effectiveness of a treatment on an ongoing basis.

Interval variable: A continuous variable wherein the values are equally spaced and can be negative (e.g., bank account balance).

Kruskal-Wallis test: Similar to ANOVA but used when data distribution does not meet normality criteria.

Levene statistic: See *Homogeneity of variance.*

Linearity: Points on a scatterplot align in a (fairly) straight line.

Logistic regression: Indicates the odds that a variable predicts one of two possible outcomes.

M: See *Mean.*

Mann-Whitney *U* test: Similar to the *t* test but used when data distribution does not meet normality criteria.

MANOVA: Multiple analysis of variance similar to ANOVA, except instead of results revealing between-group differences for one (outcome) variable, the results reflect differences between groups for a combined (blended) set of variables.

Master file: The source data set that is typically not edited or worked on.

Mauchly's test of sphericity: A pretest criterion for ANOVA repeated measures that evaluates the similarity of the variances of the independent variables (IVs) across the specified time points.

Maximum: The highest number contained within a continuous variable.

Mean (M): The average of the numbers contained within a continuous variable.

Median: The center number contained within the sorted list (lowest to highest) of a variable.

Minimum: The lowest number contained within a continuous variable.

Mode: The most common number contained within a continuous variable.

Moderate correlation: A pretest criterion for MANOVA, wherein the (bivariate) correlation among the independent variables (IVs) should be between $-.9$ and $-.3$ or between $.3$ and $.9$.

Multicollinearity: A strong correlation among the predictor variables, wherein $r < -.7$ or $r > +.7$ (some statisticians use $\pm.8$ or $\pm.9$ as the cutoff).

Multimodal: Descriptor for more than two numbers tied for the most common number contained within a continuous variable (the numbers are equally frequent within the variable).

Multiple regression: A statistical process that determines the percentage that continuous and/or categorical predictor variables have in terms of predicting the value of a (single) continuous outcome variable.

***N*:** The total number (count) of elements contained within a variable for a population.

***n*:** The total number (count) of elements contained with a variable for a sample.

***n* quota:** The minimum number of elements required in a data set to produce robust results.

Negative correlation: Among the specified pair of scores, occurs when one variable increases as the other decreases.

Nominal variable: A categorical variable wherein the values have no sequence (e.g., Color = Red, Green, Blue).

Nonprobability sample: A sample wherein each item/participant does not have an equal chance of being selected to partake in the research procedure.

Normal curve: See *Histogram with normal curve.*

Normality: See *Histogram with normal curve.*

Null hypothesis (H_0): The hypothesis that states that the treatment effect will be null; the score for the control group will be the same as the score for the treatment group.

O O X O (design): See *Stable baseline and treatment effect (O O X O).*

O X O design: See *Pretest/treatment/posttest.*

O X O O (design): See *Treatment effect and sustainability (O X O O).*

O X O X O (design): See *Incremental monitoring (O X O X O).*

Ordinal variable: A categorical variable wherein the values have a sequence (e.g., Meal = Breakfast, Lunch, Dinner).

p: See *p value.*

p value: A score generated by inferential statistical tests to indicate the likelihood that the differences detected would emerge by chance alone.

Paired *t* test: Indicates if there is a statistically significant difference between the pretest and posttest (T1 : T2), for continuous variables.

Paste: The button that assesses the parameters specified on the associated menu(s) and produces the equivalent block of SPSS Syntax code.

Pearson correlation: See *Regression.*

Pie chart: A graphical representation of the numbers contained within a categorical variable, consisting of a circle wherein each "pie slice" represents the proportion of each category.

Polychotomous: A categorical variable that contains more than two values (e.g., Meal: Breakfast/Lunch/Dinner).

Positive correlation: Occurs when the specified pair of scores tends to increase or decrease concurrently.

Pretest/posttest design: See *Pretest/treatment/posttest.*

Pretest/treatment/posttest: Longitudinal design model, typically using a single group, wherein a pretest is administered, followed by the treatment, followed by the posttest, which involves (re)administering the same instrument/metric used at the pretest to detect the effectiveness of the treatment.

Pretest checklist: Assumptions regarding the characteristics of the data that must be assessed prior to running a statistical test.

Pseudo-R²: Typically refers to Cox and Snell or Nagelkerke statistics, which are an estimate of the total variability accounted for in a logistic regression model.

r: See *Regression*.

R²: The total predictive value of a multiple regression or logistic regression model.

Random assignment: Randomly assigning members to (control/experimental) groups to reduce the likelihood of creating biased/unbalanced groups.

Random numbers: Figures that have no predictable sequence.

Range: The maximum–minimum.

Ratio variable: A continuous variable wherein the values are equally spaced and cannot be negative (e.g., Age).

Recoding: Systematically altering the way a variable is represented in a data set.

Regression: Indicates the direction of the relationship between two continuous variables gathered from each participant/data record.

Regression line: The line drawn through a scatterplot that shows the average pathway through those points.

Remove processing: Specifies the processing order of predictors in a multiple regression model, wherein the predictor variable(s) are removed from the model regardless of their statistical significance.

Representative sample: A sample that is proportionally equivalent to the population.

Research question: The inquiry that forms the basis for the hypotheses construction, analyses, and documentation of results.

Sample: A sublist of the sample frame or population specifying those who will actually partake in the research procedure.

Sample frame: A sublist of the population that could be accessed to comprise the sample.

Scatterplot: A graphical representation of a bivariate correlation.

SD: See *Standard deviation*.

Sidak test: A test used to detect pairwise score differences wherein the groups have unequal *n*s; typically used as an ANOVA post hoc test.

Simple time-series design: See *Pretest/treatment/posttest*.

Skewed distribution: A nonnormal (asymmetrical) distribution within a continuous variable wherein most of the numbers are either high or low.

Sort cases: See *Sorting*.

Sorting: Arranging items in ascending or descending sequence.

Spearman correlation: Assesses the similarly two sequenced lists.

Spearman's rho: See *Spearman correlation.*

SPSS Syntax: A language used to code and run SPSS statistical programs.

Stable baseline and treatment effect (O O X O): A research design that can be used with ANOVA repeated measures to assess the stability of the baseline and treatment effectiveness.

Standard deviation (SD): A statistic that indicates the amount of similarity/diversity among the numbers contained within a variable.

Stepwise processing: Specifies the processing order of predictors in a multiple regression model, wherein statistically significant predictor variables are loaded into the model. Variables may be dropped from the model if they lose statistical significance due to an interaction effect with other variable(s).

Syntax: See *SPSS Syntax.*

Systemic sampling: A probability sampling technique wherein periodic selections of items/participants are made.

***t* test:** Indicates if there is a statistically significant difference between the two groups $(G_1 : G_2)$ containing continuous variables.

Treatment effect and sustainability (O X O O): A research design that can be used with ANOVA repeated measures to assess the sustainability of a treatment.

Treatment group: See *Experimental group.*

Tukey test: A test used to detect pairwise score differences wherein the groups have equal *ns*; typically used as an ANOVA post hoc test.

Type I error: Occurs when the findings indicate that there is a statistically significant difference between two variables (or groups) $(p \leq .05)$ when, in fact, on the whole, there actually is not, meaning that you would erroneously reject the null hypothesis.

Type II error: Occurs when the findings indicate that there is no statistically significant difference between two variables (or groups) $(p > .05)$ when, in fact, on the whole, there actually is, meaning that you would erroneously accept the null hypothesis.

Unique pairs formula: Computes the total number of comparisons that can be made when groups are gathered two at a time (G = total number of groups); unique pairs = G! ÷ (2 × (G − 2)!).

Variable View: SPSS screen wherein the attributes (properties) for each variable are defined.

Variance: The standard deviation squared (variance = SD^2).

Wilcoxon test: Similar to the paired *t* test but used when data distribution (posttest–pretest) does not meet normality criteria.

Work file: Typically a copy of the Master file that statistical analyses/recoding is carried out on.

Index